Voting at the Politi

Voting at the Political Fault Line

California's Experiment with the Blanket Primary

EDITED BY

Bruce E. Cain and Elisabeth R. Gerber

Published in association with
the U.C. Berkeley Institute of Governmental Studies

UNIVERSITY OF CALIFORNIA PRESS
Berkeley   Los Angeles   London

University of California Press
Berkeley and Los Angeles, California

University of California Press, Ltd.
London, England

© 2002 by the Regents of the University of California

Library of Congress Cataloging-in-Publication Data

Voting at the political fault line : California's experiment with the blanket primary /
edited by Bruce E. Cain and Elisabeth R. Gerber.
    p.   cm.
    "Published in association with the U.C. Berkeley Institute of Governmental Studies."
Includes bibliographical references and index.
    ISBN 0-520-22833-2 (cloth : alk. paper)—ISBN 0-520-22834-0 (pbk. : alk. paper)
        1. Primaries—California.   I. Cain, Bruce E.   II. Gerber, Elisabeth R.   III.
University of California, Berkeley. Institute of Governmental Studies.

JK2075.C2 V68 2002
324.2794'0154'09049—dc21

                                                                    2001027817

Manufactured in the United States of America
11   10   09   08   07   06   05   04   03   02
     10   9   8   7   6   5   4   3   2   1

CONTENTS

LIST OF TABLES / *vii*

LIST OF FIGURES / *xi*

PART ONE • INTRODUCTION AND BACKGROUND

1. California's Blanket Primary Experiment
   Bruce E. Cain and Elisabeth R. Gerber / *3*

2. Crossover Voting before the Blanket: Primaries versus
   Parties in California History
   Brian J. Gaines and Wendy K. Tam Cho / *12*

3. Political Reform via the Initiative Process: What Voters Think about
   When They Change the Rules
   Shaun Bowler and Todd Donovan / *36*

4. Context and Setting: The Mood of the California Electorate
   Mark Baldassare / *59*

PART TWO • CROSSOVER VOTING

5. The Causes and Consequences of Crossover Voting
   in the 1998 California Elections
   John Sides, Jonathan Cohen, and Jack Citrin / *77*

6. Should I Stay or Should I Go? Sincere and Strategic Crossover
   Voting in California Assembly Races
   R. Michael Alvarez and Jonathan Nagler / *107*

7. Peeking Under the Blanket: A Direct Look at Crossover Voting
in the 1998 Primary
Anthony M. Salvanto and Martin P. Wattenberg / *124*

PART THREE • EFFECTS OF THE BLANKET PRIMARY

8. Crossing Over When It Counts: How the Motives of Voters in Blanket Primaries
Are Revealed by Their Actions in General Elections
Thad Kousser / *143*

9. Candidates, Donors, and Voters in California's Blanket Primary Elections
Wendy K. Tam Cho and Brian J. Gaines / *171*

10. Strategic Voting and Candidate Policy Positions
Elisabeth R. Gerber / *192*

11. Openness Begets Opportunity: Minor Parties and
California's Blanket Primary
Christian Collet / *214*

12. Thinner Ranks: Women as Candidates and California's Blanket Primary
Miki Caul and Katherine Tate / *234*

13. Targets of Opportunity: California's Blanket Primary and the
Political Representation of Latinos
Gary M. Segura and Nathan D. Woods / *248*

14. Candidate Strategy, Voter Response, and Party Cohesion
John R. Petrocik / *270*

PART FOUR • CONCLUSIONS AND IMPLICATIONS

15. The Blanket Primary in the Courts: The Precedent and
Implications of *California Democratic Party v. Jones*
Nathaniel Persily / *303*

16. Strategies and Rules: Lessons from the 2000 Presidential Primary
Bruce E. Cain and Megan Mullin / *324*

17. Conclusion
Bruce E. Cain and Elisabeth R. Gerber / *344*

LIST OF CONTRIBUTORS / *355*
INDEX / *361*

TABLES

2.1. Primary election regimes in California's history / *21*

2.2. Crossover vote proportions in California Senate and U.S. House, 1910–64 / *28*

3.1. Institutional reform proposals as share of all California initiatives, 1912–98 / *39*

3.2. Frequency of pre- and post-1980 institutional reform initiatives / *40*

3.3. Logit models of decision to support Proposition 198 / *48*

3.4. Predicted probabilities of voting yes on Proposition 198 (from full model estimated in table 3.3) / *50*

3.5. Logit model of decision to support Proposition 198, by level of education / *51*

3.6. Predicted probabilities of voting yes on Proposition 198 (from models estimated in table 3.5) / *52*

4.1. State conditions / *61*

4.2. State policy issues / *63*

4.3. Political apathy / *65*

4.4. Sources of political information / *67*

4.5. Political distrust / *68*

4.6. Candidate qualifications / *71*

5.1. Preference for Governor, by party identification / *82*

5.2.   Preference for Senator, by party identification   /   *84*

5.3.   Primary vote choice, by party registration   /   *87*

5.4.   Logit models of crossover voting for Governor   /   *92*

5.5.   Logit models of crossover voting for Senator   /   *94*

5.6.   Characteristics of consistent and inconsistent crossover voters   /   *97*

5.7.   General election preferences   /   *99*

6.1.   Crossover voting, by Assembly district   /   *112*

6.2.   Voting results in five Assembly districts   /   *114*

6.3.   Classification of sincere and strategic intent among crossover voters   /   *117*

6.4.   Multinominal logit estimates for Assembly District 61 voting   /   *120*

7.1.   Patterns of party voting for eleven major offices, by party registration   /   *128*

7.2.   Patterns of party voting for eleven offices in 1998 California primary and 1994 general election   /   *129*

7.3.   Major partisan defections and the nonpartisan vote for eight statewide elections   /   *130*

7.4.   Comparison of a Democratic nonminority district (HR 29) to a Republican district (HR 28)   /   *131*

7.5.   Drawing power of incumbents: conditions under which partisans crossed   /   *133*

7.6.   Drawing power of a competitive race: conditions under which partisans followed the action   /   *134*

7.7.   Votes of potential partisan raiders in districts where an incumbent faced opposition   /   *135*

7.8.   Voting for Fong versus Issa (U.S. Senate), by party registration   /   *136*

7.9.   Where the minor-party vote came from   /   *137*

7.10. Absentee sample percentages compared to overall percentages for eight statewide offices, major partisan candidates   /   *140*

8.1.   Mean crossover rates under different primary conditions   /   *149*

8.2.   Explaining November crossover rates of Republican voters   /   *152*

8.3.   Explaining November crossover rates of Democratic voters   /   *153*

8.4. Behavior of Republican crossover voters / *154*

8.5. Behavior of Democratic crossover voters / *154*

8.6. Estimates of crossover vote, with 95 percent confidence interval / *158*

8.7. Estimates of crossover rates in each California 1998 election / *160*

8.8. Behavior of Republican crossover voters (March 2000) / *164*

8.9. Behavior of Democratic crossover voters (March 2000) / *164*

8.10. Estimates of crossover rates in 2000 California elections / *165*

9.1. Competitiveness of primary elections to U.S. House in California, 1992–98 / *178*

9.2. Competitiveness of general elections to U.S. House in California, 1992–98 / *179*

9.3. Timing of individual campaign donations, 1992–98, U.S. House, California delegation / *186*

10.1. Primary and general election candidates, U.S. House elections, California delegation, 1998 / *201*

10.2. Characteristics of winning candidates, California State Assembly races, 1998 / *205*

10.3. Characteristics of winning candidates, California State Assembly races, 1996 / *207*

10.4. Percentage of contested California Assembly primaries won by moderates / *208*

10.5. Moderates nominated in contested Assembly primaries, logit estimates / *208*

10.6. Predicted probabilities of nominating moderates, based on model 1 logit estimates / *210*

11.1. Average number of votes in contested minor-party primaries, 1968–96 versus 1998 / *220*

11.2. Mean minor-party candidate percentages of the total vote in California primaries, by party, 1994 and 1998 / *220*

11.3. Mean minor-party candidate vote in 1998 U.S. House, State Senate, and State Assembly primaries / *221*

11.4. Candidate attitudes toward the blanket primary, by party / *228*

12.1. Differences in percentage of candidates who brought "personal political capital" to nonpartisan and partisan primaries / *242*

12.2. Women in partisan and nonpartisan primaries: Senate and gubernatorial races, 1994–98 / *244*

13.1. Turnout and registration in Assembly districts with Latino GOP primary candidates, June 1998 / *255*

13.2. Key characteristics of districts with Latino GOP primary candidates, June 1998 / *257*

14.1. Policy preferences of primary and nonprimary voters, 1980 / *274*

14.2. A crossover strategy to win a primary / *281*

14.3. Crossover voting as a function of ideological cues / *284*

14.4. Demographic contours of moderate crossover voting / *285*

14.5. Political preferences of moderates / *289*

14.6. The partisan meaning of moderation / *290*

16.1. Voting systems over time / *327*

16.2. Correspondence of 2000 Republican and Democratic presidential nominating events / *328*

16.3. 2000 Republican nominating season / *331*

16.4. Early and mid-season Republican primary vote choice, by party self-identification / *333*

FIGURES

2.1. Competition in California general elections, district averages, 1910–64 / *19*

2.2. Crossover voting in California primaries, 1910–64 / *23*

2.3. Average rates for types of crossover votes, 1910–64 / *25*

8.1. Estimated Republican crossover rate in the Democratic primary / *150*

8.2. Estimated Republican crossover rate in the general election / *150*

9.1. Turnout and registration in primary and general elections in California, 1944–98 / *175*

9.2. Total receipts and expenditures in U.S. House races, 1992–98 / *183*

9.3. Total PAC funding of U.S. House races in California, 1978–98 / *184*

10.1. Example of crossover voting / *195*

11.1. Contested minor-party primaries in California, 1968–98 / *218*

11.2. Comparison of mean minor-party candidate vote for primary and general election, 1998 / *222*

14.1. Crossovers to moderate challengers as a function of ideological commitment / *287*

14.2. Projected issue positions of electorates in closed and blanket primaries / *291*

PART ONE

Introduction and Background

California's Blanket Primary Experiment

Bruce E. Cain and Elisabeth R. Gerber

There are some who tout physics as the model field for the social sciences, admiring its deductive rigor and explanatory power. But, plausibly, the more appropriate analogy is geology, in which unpredictable events such as earthquakes sometimes create opportunities to study more basic underlying processes and laws. The earthquake metaphor is particularly applicable to California, which has been the site of several dramatic political as well as geological ruptures in recent years. One of the most significant was the passage of Proposition 198, the Blanket Primary Initiative, in 1996. The blanket primary itself is not new (Washington has used it since 1938), but it is unusual (only three states including California have adopted it). Moreover, the rule changes that Prop 198 introduced reconfigured the electoral landscape in distinctive ways. Thrust upon the political parties and incumbent policy makers by an initiative that received little press attention until it passed, the move to blanket rules forced political actors to alter their strategies and tactics for the 1998 election; it rewarded some candidates and hurt others. But then, almost as abruptly, the blanket primary era in California was brought to a close when the U.S. Supreme Court ruled in June 2000 that it violated the political parties' associational rights.

The transition from a pure, closed primary system (i.e., in which only voters who are registered with a party can participate in its primary) to a blanket primary (i.e., in which voters are free to participate in any party primary), and then back again, creates a fortuitous natural experiment that allows us to compare behavior and outcomes before and after an electoral rule change. Political scientists contend that rules and institutional structures matter because they determine the incentives and opportunities that voters and candidates face. Change the rules, and the incentives and opportunities should change as well. At least, that is the empirical expectation that the introduction of the blanket primary allows us to test.

The California blanket primary experiment raises two different kinds of questions. One type, which is dealt with only briefly in this volume, is legal and normative. These issues were central in the lawsuits directed against Prop 198 (*California Democratic Party v. Jones* U.S. District Court, 9th Circuit, Eastern Division of California, CIV-S-96–2038 DFL PAN), culminating in the Supreme Court's decision (530 U.S. 567 2000). They were also raised in the earlier Washington and Alaska blanket primary cases (*Heavey et al. v. Chapman* [1980] 93 Wash. 2d 700; *O'Callaghan et al. v. Alaska* 914 P. 2d 1250 [Alaska 1996]) and concern such questions as whether parties have the exclusive right to determine their rules for choosing nominees, whether primaries are public elections or private party affairs, whether the legislature or the initiative process can impose these rules over the opposition of the official party apparatus, what standard of constitutional scrutiny the Court should apply, and so forth. Even more basically, legal scholars are divided over whether political parties are private associations or instruments of state action and whether the courts should be deciding issues of such a political nature. Political science has much to contribute to a discussion about these issues, and they are discussed ably in Nate Persily's chapter. However, they are not the primary focus of this study.

Rather, our orientation is toward the empirical and analytic tasks of (1) describing and relating the behavior of political actors to the changes in electoral rules (the micro considerations) and (2) discussing the aggregate features of systems that use different types of rules (the macro considerations). Understanding the micro behavior of political actors—voters, candidates, and party elites—is critical to understanding the causes behind the macro differences that rules produce. Rules condition strategic and rational choices, leading to certain behaviors. As the burgeoning political science literature on strategic voting demonstrates, voter choices are not completely independent of rules and expected outcomes (Cain 1978; Black 1978; Cox 1994, 1997; Niemi, Whitten, and Franklin 1992; Gerber and Morton 1998, 2001). For example, political scientists have come to appreciate how particular forms of strategic behavior (i.e., the desire not to waste a vote) underlie the two-party equilibrium in single-member, district-based systems. When rules change, choices that produced favorable outcomes may no longer make sense, and actors adapt their behaviors in response. The aggregate consequence of those new behaviors is a system with different features than the previous one: higher or lower turnout, more or less moderate candidates, increased or diminished costs, and the like.

In order to take advantage of this unique opportunity to study a natural political science experiment, we assembled a distinguished group of political scientists with expertise in various aspects of elections. In the chapters that follow, they employ a wide range of data, methods, and approaches to evaluate the micro and macro changes induced by the change in electoral systems.

MICRO QUESTIONS

With only a few exceptions, most states use the direct primary as their predominant mechanism for selecting the state and national candidates who will run in general elections.[1] The forms of direct primary include the closed primary, in which voters must register some specified period of time before the election with the party whose primary they intend to participate in, and several types of open primaries, in which some or all voters are free to select the primary ballot or race they wish to participate in on election day. One of the most "open" primary systems, in the sense of placing the fewest restrictions on participation, is the blanket primary (see Gerber and Morton 1998). Under the blanket primary rules, voters receive one ballot with all of the various party nominees on it. They can then cast up to one vote for any of the nominees for each office, regardless of the partisanship of either the voters or the candidates. Hence, voters are free to vote in different party primaries for different offices: the Democratic primary for Governor, the Republican primary for U.S. Senator, and the like.

The lack of restrictions on participation in blanket primaries creates incentives and opportunities for voters to engage in different patterns of behavior than under closed primaries. Specifically, we expect the blanket primary to increase incentives for voters to engage in crossover voting, where crossover voting is defined as voting in a party primary other than the one the voter identifies or is registered with. This expectation follows from a general opportunity-cost argument. For instance, if a voter is registered as a Democrat, a closed primary system requires the voter to re-register with another party if she wants to participate in that party's primary. A hypothetical Democrat who wants to vote in the Republican primary must register in advance as a Republican. If this person is primarily interested in just one Republican race, she forfeits the opportunity to vote in the other Democratic primary races in order to participate in the one Republican Party primary of interest. This is a high opportunity cost. In addition, if the voter wants her Democratic affiliation back, she must pay the cost of re-registration at a later time. Under a blanket primary, this same Democratic voter would not have to re-register to participate in the Republican race of interest, nor would she lose the opportunity to vote in the other Democratic races. In short, lowering the opportunity costs of participating in another party's primary should increase the probability that voters will engage in crossover voting, *ceteris paribus*. Therefore, the first micro questions addressed in the chapters by Sides, Cohen, and Citrin (chapter 5), Alvarez and Nagler (chapter 6), and Salvanto and Wattenberg (chapter 7) are whether crossover voting increased with the adoption of the blanket primary, by how much, and under what circumstances.

Beyond the question of the extent of crossover voting is the more difficult problem of motivation. Several of the studies in this volume address the question of why people cross over. To better understand this discussion, it is useful to make certain definitional distinctions about the various forms of voting behavior. The first form we consider is *sincere voting*. A person who votes sincerely votes for his most preferred candidate, regardless of how this choice may affect strategic opportunities later in the electoral process. In other words, if a voter were to rank order the candidates for a given office and then cast a ballot for the one with the highest ranking, the voter would be voting sincerely. Sincere crossover voting, then, occurs when a voter votes for his first-choice candidate who happens to be running in another party's primary; hence, a Democrat who most prefers a Republican candidate for Governor and who crosses over to vote for that candidate in the primary is voting sincerely. We should note that not all voters who vote in their own party's primary are voting sincerely. A Democrat who most prefers a Republican candidate but who chooses, for whatever reason, to vote in the Democratic party's primary is not voting sincerely.

In addition, there are several forms of *strategic voting*. Strategic voting involves voting for a candidate who is not the voter's most preferred candidate—that is, voting for any candidate who is ranked lower than number one. Strategic voting can be divided into several types based on the voter's motivation. When voters choose a candidate who is the most preferred of the candidates in another party, but is not their highest ranked candidate overall, they are engaging in a form of strategic behavior known as *hedging*. One situation in which hedging might arise is when voters believe their own party's nomination is virtually certain and the general election outcome is competitive, and they hedge their chances by voting for the most palatable of the other party nominees, just in case their most preferred candidate were to lose. A second reason for hedging is that voters may expect their most preferred candidate to lose in November and so want to make sure that at least their second choice is nominated and elected. From a normative perspective, we term this *benign* strategic voting because the voters' intentions are not mischievous.

Other forms of strategic voting are less benign, particularly when the motive is to saddle the other party with a weak candidate. This form of strategic behavior is sometimes called *raiding* or *sabotage*. The following is an example of raiding. Suppose, as before, a voter knows that the outcome in her own party's primary is a foregone conclusion, and rather than waste a vote in that contest, the voter decides to cross over to participate in the other party's primary. If the voter crosses over to support the weakest candidate in the opposition party's primary in the hopes of enhancing the prospects of her preferred candidate in the general election, this would be raiding. In other words, a raider votes for a candidate in the primary that she neither hopes nor expects will win in the general election.

The second micro question thus centers on whether the blanket primary encourages sincere voting, hedging, raiding, or some combination of the three. The relative frequency of each behavior has important implications for how we assess the manipulability of the electoral system. A finding that all or nearly all voters are sincere suggests that there is little need to worry about manipulated outcomes. However, if raiding is prevalent, then it raises serious questions about how robust elections are against attempts by elites or groups in the electorate to produce outcomes that are not majority-preferred. For example, imagine a situation in which a candidate defeated by raiders in the primary could have been the eventual winner in November. In such a case, the majority will is frustrated by the strategic behavior of a voting bloc.

Another possibility is that hedging rather than raiding may be prevalent. Widespread hedging raises questions about the power of voters and elites in uncontested primary races to influence the outcomes of contested races in other parties. Is a voter's influence a function of competitive circumstance? Does this in turn discourage competition in party primaries so as to make the party less vulnerable to crossover voters? The chapters by Sides, Cohen, and Citrin; Alvarez and Nagler; Salvanto and Wattenberg; and Kousser (chapter 8) all take up the question of who crosses over and why. In addition, Bowler and Donovan (chapter 3) consider the explicit motives of those who voted for Prop 198, asking whether those who would benefit from the rule changes voted for them.

The impact of crossover voting is most obvious in the primary since it may affect which candidates are nominated. Crossover voting may also have important consequences for the general election, either directly, in terms of deciding the candidates that ultimately face each other in November, or indirectly, in terms of the propensity of voters to cross party lines a second time. If crossover voters remain loyal to the candidates they support in the primary, then candidates who attract crossovers in the primary may gain a lasting advantage in terms of increased general election support. Chapters 5 and 8 specifically consider some of these long-term effects.

A third micro question deals with turnout. If, as rational voting models suggest, the probability of voting is a function of expected vote impact (i.e., closeness of the race) and enthusiasm for the candidate (i.e., proximity of the candidate to the voter's ideal point), then the blanket primary might affect the likelihood of participation on the margin. For instance, if a voter is stuck in an uncompetitive primary under closed rules, the incentive to participate might be low; but if the voter is given the opportunity to cast a

potentially decisive vote in another party's primary, he might be more willing to participate. On the other hand, if the blanket primary creates confusion and effectively increases the costs of voting, it might depress voters'
incentives to participate. These issues are considered in greater detail in
the chapter by Cho and Gaines (chapter 9) on participation and competitiveness.

The micro level effects of the blanket primary are not limited to voters.
Candidates, their supporters, and their consultants are also affected by rule
changes. Previous research has shown how contribution patterns are
shaped by expectations of a candidate's prospects and resources (see
McCarty and Rothenberg 2000 for a recent discussion of contributor motivations). Since the blanket primary changes campaign dynamics and potentially the electoral fortunes of different kinds of candidates, we would
expect contributors to anticipate and perhaps amplify these changes. Chapter 9 also considers whether individual contributors adapt their behavior
to the expanded potential voter base created by the blanket primary.

Under closed primary rules, the universe of voters is defined as the subset of the electorate that is registered with the candidate's party and is
eligible to participate. Under blanket primary rules, the universe of voters
is larger and includes all registered voters, regardless of their party.
Therefore, different campaign strategies might make sense. Furthermore,
whatever method of campaigning the candidate and consultants choose
(e.g., mail, voter contact, registration, get-out-the-vote, etc.), the blanket
system increases the set of voters that candidates must appeal to. Increasing
the pool of potential supporters may affect both the cost and the content
of campaigns. It potentially affects campaign costs in the sense that the
larger set of voters might, on average, require greater overall expense, or
it could mean that campaigns are able to spend less per capita while appealing to a larger set of voters. It affects campaign content in that the
blanket primary widens the potential ideological space by adding to the
primary electorate voters from parts of the spectrum that are not well represented in a given party. Many of these questions are taken up in the
chapters on campaign dynamics and strategies by Gerber and Petrocik
(chapters 10 and 14, respectively).

MACRO CONSIDERATIONS

Rule changes affect the behavior of individual political actors, and these
behaviors, in turn, alter aggregate patterns of behavior and outcomes.
Much of the popular debate over Prop 198 focused on these macro questions: in essence, whether the electoral system would be improved as a
result of adopting a blanket primary. As a means of understanding what
people thought the macro consequences of the blanket primary would be,

chapter 3 by Bowler and Donovan examines the reasons voters gave for supporting Prop 198. In many ways, its passage was an extraordinary event; registered Democratic and Republican primary voters (presumably the most attentive and partisan voters) decided to replace a system that empowered party loyalists with a system that allowed other party identifiers and independents to participate in selecting their parties' nominees. Whatever the actual effects of this decision, it is important to try to understand what voters, and especially major party identifiers, thought the effects of adopting the blanket primary would be.

People's expectations aside, what have been the actual macro-level consequences of adopting the blanket primary? We first consider whether changes in voter behavior under the blanket primary altered the outcomes of any primary and / or general election races. Did the blanket primary lead to outcomes that would not have been produced under closed primary rules? Specifically, is there compelling evidence that crossover voting was decisive in any races, particularly the most competitive ones? Several of the chapters on crossover voting suggest that, in at least a handful of races, the extent and direction of crossover voting was, in fact, sufficient to alter election outcomes.

Second, we examine whether the blanket primary reinforces the moderating features of California's electoral system. A common criticism of the closed primary is that it produces candidates who deviate from the median voter because they must appeal to a primary electorate with extreme preferences. This may result in the nomination of either candidates who themselves hold extreme preferences or more pragmatic candidates who are nevertheless constrained to maintain positions that are consistent with the ones that got them nominated. In either case, the closed primary may result in candidates whose positions diverge from the vote-maximizing median position in the general election. In theory, the blanket primary forces candidates to take more moderate positions in the primary, because they must appeal to a wider range of the ideological spectrum. To the extent that candidates respond in this way, the blanket primary should produce more ideologically moderate candidates. This moderation hypothesis is taken up in detail in chapter 10 by Gerber on candidate positions.

The other side of the moderation hypothesis, however, is that groups with interests that diverge from those of the median voter may be less well represented under the blanket primary. This could have the important result that women and minorities, who often hold minority positions within the general electorate but have been able to gain access to political positions by cultivating constituencies within their parties (especially the Democratic party) may be less able to compete for their parties' nominations. On the other hand, to the extent that women and minorities can appeal to voters across party lines, the blanket primary might have the opposite impact. To assess these representational consequences, Caul and Tate (chapter 12) analyze the ability of women candidates to compete for their parties' nominations under the blanket primary; Segura and Woods analyze the fates of Latina/o candidates in chapter 13.

Third, we consider the system-level effects of campaign dynamics under the blanket primary. We noted in our discussion of micro considerations that by expanding the universe of voters, the blanket primary might have altered the strategic decisions of candidates and consultants. Under the changed strategic environment of the blanket primary, candidates may have made different decisions about when to enter elections and in what capacity. As a consequence, we may observe different patterns of electoral competition. Chapters 7 and 9 (by Salvanto and Wattenberg, and Cho and Gaines) both consider patterns of candidate entry and the consequences of these decisions for electoral competition. Candidates may also allocate resources in different ways, further affecting campaign competition and costs. Cho and Gaines consider whether micro-level changes in campaign tactics, strategies, and dynamics contribute to a macro effect of higher over-all costs in the primary and general elections.

Finally, we consider the implications of the blanket primary for the health of the party system as a whole. Minor parties have been a persistent, if understudied, feature of California politics. The main purpose of minor parties and minor-party candidates is not to win office per se, but rather to provide voters with an important outlet for voicing alternative political views. How did the minor parties fare in the blanket primary? Did the crossover vote draw primary voters away from the minor parties, or did it increase the minor-party vote by allowing major-party voters to shop in minor-party elections? In his chapter on minor parties (chapter 11), Collet considers these possibilities.

The purpose of the chapters that follow is to analyze in greater depth political behavior and outcomes in California's first blanket primary. For several reasons, however, we caution the reader to interpret these results with some care. First, since California held only two primaries (and one corresponding general election) under its blanket rules, and since we ex-pect that voters, contributors, candidates, and other political actors would continue to adapt their behavior as they learned more about the strategic opportunities created by these rules, the dynamics observed in the 1998 elections reflect perhaps only a small part of the maximum changes that the blanket primary would eventually have brought if California had em-ployed the system for a number of years. Second, as Baldassare shows in chapter 4, the economic, political, and social context in which this election took place was unique in several respects and may mask important effects of the blanket primary. These caveats aside, however, we do feel that these chapters provide a valuable first cut in exploring California's important po-

litical experiment with the blanket primary. In addition, as chapter 16 by
Cain and Mullin points out, the issues raised by the blanket primary experiment are related to issues that arise in other types of open primary
systems, particularly when the Democratic and Republican primaries are
not held concurrently. This is well illustrated by the controversy surrounding the John McCain candidacy for the 2000 Republican presidential
nomination.

NOTES

1. To nominate major-party candidates for statewide, state legislative, and congressional offices, nearly all states use some form of direct primaries. Thirty-eight
states require major parties to use direct primaries exclusively, three allow primaries
or conventions, three require preprimary conventions, and the rest allow preprimary conventions under certain circumstances (Bott 1990, 173–5). To select delegates to the 2000 national party conventions (which nominate presidential candidates), forty-three states used presidential primaries to select some or all of the
delegates for at least one party, while the others used party caucuses. Rules regarding
ballot access for minor parties and the nomination of minor-party candidates vary
a great deal from state to state.

REFERENCES

Black, Jerome H. 1978. "The Multicandidate Calculus of Voting: Application to
Canadian Federal Elections." *American Journal of Political Science* 22, no. 3: 609–
38.
Bott, Alexander J. 1990. *Handbook of United States Election Laws and Practices: Political
Rights.* New York: Greenwood Press.
Cain, Bruce E. 1978. "Strategic Voting in Britain." *American Journal of Political Science*
22, no. 3: 639–55.
Cox, Gary W. 1994. "Strategic Voting Equilibria under the Single, Non-Transferable
Vote." *American Political Science Review* 88, no. 3: 608–21.
———. 1997. *Making Votes Count: Strategic Coordination in the World's Electoral Systems.*
Cambridge: Cambridge University Press.
Gerber, Elisabeth R., and Rebecca B. Morton. 1998. "Primary Election Systems and
Representation." *Journal of Law, Economics, and Organization* 14, no. 2: 304–24.
———. 2001. "Electoral Institutions and Party Competition: The Effects of Nomi-
nation Procedures on Electoral Coalition Formation." Unpublished working pa-
per, University of California, San Diego.
McCarty, Nolan, and Lawrence S. Rothenberg. 2000. "The Time to Give: PAC Mo-
tivations and Electoral Timing." *Political Analysis* 8, no. 3: 239–60.
Niemi, Richard; Guy Whitten; and Mark Franklin. 1992. "Constituency Characteristics, Individual Characteristics, and Tactical Voting in the 1987 British General
Election." *British Journal of Political Science* 23, no. 1: 131–37.
Wolfinger, Raymond E., and Steven J. Rosenstone. 1980. *Who Votes?* New Haven,
CT: Yale University Press.

CHAPTER TWO

Crossover Voting before the Blanket

Primaries versus Parties
in California History

Brian J. Gaines and Wendy K. Tam Cho

The passage of Proposition 198 was in plain defiance of the preferences and advice of most elites, including, notably, both of the major political parties. In this chapter, we briefly trace the chronology of primary elections in the Golden State, with an emphasis on how they have been intertwined, from the beginning, with an anti-party spirit. We thus orient the blanket primary, as delivered by direct democracy, in a distinctive state political culture of independence from, and ambivalence or even hostility toward, political parties. We then focus on the parallels between voting options under the blanket primary law and those presented in the mid-twentieth century during the multi- (or "cross-") filing era. This comparison provides a historical baseline against which to place California's experience with the blanket primary.

The easy passage of Proposition 198 can be understood as yet another instance of defiant populism, wherein a healthy majority of California voters thumb their noses at elite advice and embrace a measure whose appeal is simple and whose alleged flaws evidently do not trouble many. As such, Proposition 198 followed in the wake of numerous other initiatives, the most famous of which is probably still 1978's Proposition 13, a property-tax-freezing measure that is sometimes said to have set off a nation-wide "tax revolt" (see, e.g., Kettl 1992, 58, 152). But the change from a closed to a fully open primary originated in something more specific than populism: it was clearly an act of *anti-party* populism, which tapped a sentiment that dates from the founding of the country and has been especially strong in California.

The blanket primary was a novelty in California's electoral history, but it was closely related to a prior innovation in primary electoral law, cross-filing (aka multifiling). Among American states, only California and New

York have had long and plentiful experience with allowing candidates to enter multiple party primaries, and thereby possibly to secure several party nominations for the general election. California's multifiling history and New York's ongoing experiment with this practice have produced rather different outcomes in the two states. In New York, a right-wing Conservative party, a left-wing Liberal party, and the occasional very small special-interest party have all become interesting supporting players, whose presence acts as a centrifugal force on candidates from the major parties. Most often, the identifiable blocs of votes cast for fusion candidates under the Conservative and / or Liberal lines simply inflate or deflate existing Republican-Democratic margins of victory or defeat. On occasion, though, they provide the critical difference.[1] It has, in any case, always been rare in New York for any candidate to seek, let alone secure, nominations from more than one of the *major* parties (i.e., Democrats and Republicans).[2]

Initially, multiple filing in California followed this same general pattern, with some Republicans and Democrats seeking to bolster their appeal by adding Progressive, Socialist, or Prohibition nominations to their principal party designation. After all of these minor parties receded to the fringe in the 1920s, multifiling took a new shape: "double-filing" in the two major-party primaries became the modal practice for incumbents and an occasional tactic for challengers and open-seat contestants. The direct impact was that, even though the primaries were closed, in many seats, registered Democrats and Republicans were able to vote for candidates from their own party *or* for candidates from the other major party who had cross-filed. This is, more or less, what opening the primary under the blanket system achieves as well. The cross-filing period, then, is a natural era to examine for insight and clues into what we might expect in the situation of a blanket primary.

This chapter explores the comparison between these two distinct but obviously related electoral systems. We first provide a brief background discussion of primary elections in American political history and the original passage of a primary election law in California. No sooner had California inaugurated a system of party-controlled nominations than candidates and voters invented a means of bypassing party control via cross-filing. We discuss the significance of this practice, and present evidence on its incidence and on how it affected voting. Our goal, at this stage, is to explore the similarities and dissimilarities between multifiling primaries and blanket primaries, in an effort to extract the history most relevant to those whose interest lies in how the blanket can be expected to settle once it has been draped over a state. Finally, we review the multiple stages by which the blanket primary became law and then, immediately, was modified, yet again uncovering a tale of partisan elites versus the party-wary masses.

ORIGINS AND IMPLICATIONS OF PRIMARY ELECTIONS

The primary election is an early-twentieth-century "progressive" invention. Primaries were adopted in many American states as a substitute for conventions, in an effort to pry power away from strong party bosses and machines and relocate it with candidates and the mass electorate. In California, as in some other states, much of the controversy surrounding the adoption of direct primaries concerned provisions for electing U.S. Senators. The first attempt to establish mandatory primaries in California occurred in 1897. That act fell to court challenges without actually being implemented, as did similar legislation passed in 1899 and 1900 (Young 1943, 117–18). Since all of these legislative efforts preceded the advent of popular election of U.S. Senators (i.e., the Seventeenth Amendment), they were regarded as being partly—or even principally—back-door means of transferring the power to elect Senators from state legislators to the general public, and were applauded or abhorred accordingly. Oregon had set an early example of how a direct primary could achieve this exact purpose of tying the state legislature's hands, and so there was growing popular support in California for some form of primary. By 1908, a constitutionally satisfactory approach was found: ACA 3, which directed the legislature to "enact laws providing for the direct nomination of candidates for public office," thereby amending section 2½ of Article II of the Constitution, passed both houses by more than the two-thirds required for constitutional amendments (State of California 1920, 74). At the general election of 1908, the public approved ACA 3 by 76.6 percent to 23.4 percent, with every county favoring the amendment by a lopsided margin.

The 1909 session of the California legislature then opened with a three-month-long battle between a bipartisan reform (pro-primary) coalition and a bipartisan pro-machine (anti-primary) coalition. Some type of primary seemed inevitable, but opponents strove to craft either an innocuous law that would change nothing or an unconstitutional one that would be struck down by the courts before it could take effect. Following a tortuous chronology of amendments and reconsiderations, several near-tie roll calls, a week of deadlock in the Senate (maintained by hourly postponements!), plus various reversals of position by individual legislators, the law that was ultimately passed did not allow for de facto election of U.S. Senators, but did establish closed, partisan primaries for other offices (see Hichborn 1909, 68–120, for a detailed, if clearly biased, account of the bill's passage). This legislation emerged from a populist movement that spanned the major parties, uniting the members who were most likely to vote against entrenched interests (particularly big business) and to vote for major social reforms and institutional innovations that promoted more transparent government.

Since 1910, then, California's state and national elective offices have been filled by elections occurring in two rounds. In the spring or summer, the major (and minor) parties hold primary elections to select nominees for the state's elective offices. Primary winners then compete in November for elevation to the office in question. While the advent of the primary weakened central party organizations by admitting the mass electorate into the nomination process, the closed nature of the primary strengthened parties *in the electorate*. That is, only those registered with a given party were permitted to vote in that party's primary, and so party membership (by way of registration) became important. Moreover, part of the compromise by which the primary was passed was the inclusion of rules intended to ensure that *candidates* were authentic partisans. A candidate was required "to make affidavit 'that he affiliated with [the party whose nomination he sought] at the last preceding general election, and either that he did not vote there at, or voted for a majority of the candidates of said party at said preceding general election, and intends to so vote at the ensuing election'" (California Statutes 1909, 694, quoted in Hichborn 1909, 72).

The closedness of the primary and the affiliation pledge required of candidates were plainly at odds with the nonpartisan, or (perhaps more accurately) anti-party, spirit that was sweeping the state at that time. Enough Progressives were carried into office on Hiram Johnson's coattails in 1910 that the legislature was able, after the passage of only two election campaigns, to do away with the affiliation pledge requirement and to make explicit the right of candidates to seek multiple party nominations without regard to their own registration or voting history. "Cross-filing," whereby candidates ran in two (or more) primaries, quickly became normal, first for state races, then for congressional races. Indeed, the first election in which candidates could file for multiple party nominations was 1914, and nearly half the members of the 1915 Assembly won their seats holding the nominations of more than one party.[3]

By 1915, the state had made local elective offices nonpartisan, and Governor Johnson was urging the legislature to follow suit by making its own elections nonpartisan as well (see Hichborn 1922, 221–22, for the text of Johnson's biennial message to the legislature in 1915). In 1910, Johnson had won a five-way Republican primary before besting Democratic, Socialist, and Prohibition candidates in the general election. In 1914, however, he opted to run only as a Progressive, eschewing major-party designation despite the fact that Progressives accounted for less than 20 percent of all registered voters. His personal popularity was so great that he nearly won a majority of the vote all the same. In yet another five-way race, he took 49.7 percent of the vote, with the Republican and Democrat finishing 20 percent and 37 percent behind, respectively. Johnson was much less successful in his efforts to persuade the legislature to rid itself of parties, perhaps in part because of a mistake in tactics.

The primary remained inextricably linked to nonpartisanship, and both were subjected to popular approval in a 1915 special election, wherein the key item was a measure that would make the primary, and hence the operation of the legislature, nonpartisan. By Hichborn's account, this election "more than anything else seemed in its results to voice a protest at calling special elections for the consideration of such matters" (1922, 222). Turnout was low, and all eleven measures submitted were defeated, even the ones against which no opposition campaign at all had been waged. As a consequence, the legislature did not establish a nonpartisan primary to do away with its partisan organization.

In the 1917 session, moreover, the legislature amended the Direct Primary Law in the opposite direction. On the justification that the special election had revealed little support for ridding the state houses of parties, state legislators added a new requirement that a candidate could not win the nomination of a party other than the one with which he was registered without also winning his own party's nomination. In the August 1918 primaries, this precise scenario played out at the top of the ticket, as James Rolph Jr., a registered Republican, took 45.6 percent of the Democratic vote, compared to 36.9 percent and 17.6 percent for two rivals, but finished second in the Republican race, with 39.2 percent against 45.1 percent (the balance being distributed among four others). Rolph was thus defeated as the Republican nominee for Governor and disqualified as the Democratic nominee, and so no one was permitted to run under the Democrat banner in the general. Before the 1920 elections, still further amendments empowered county party committees to fill vacancies created in this manner by appointment, just as they could fill vacancies created by death or by an absence of any filers for the primary. So it was that, under special circumstances, party organizations again took control of nominations, in stark violation of the spirit of the primary.[4]

Over the next decades, scarcely a legislative session passed without some proposal to amend the direct primary. Efforts to extend the anti-party elements by making the primaries (and, hence, the legislature) nonpartisan were about as common as counterproposals to forbid cross-filing altogether and revert to basic closed primaries in which registered Republicans select Republican nominees, registered Democrats select Democratic nominees, and never the twain do meet.

Neither side triumphed in extending or defeating cross-filing principles until 1952, when two propositions on the general election ballot competed to change the status quo. Proposition 13, an initiative, would have prohibited cross-filing by specifying that "no person shall be a candidate or nominee of a political party for any office unless he has been registered as affiliated with such party for at least three months prior to filing nomination papers." The campaign for signatures to qualify this initiative was, in a strictly literal sense, bipartisan, as the League of Women Voters joined a former Republican state senator and a Democratic oil millionaire in its support (Davies 1951). The support for Proposition 13, however, was much more Democratic than Republican. Not too surprisingly, then, the Republican-controlled legislature drafted an alternative to Proposition 13. Proposition 7 merely required that "the ballot shall show political party affiliation of each candidate for partisan office, as shown by candidate's registration affidavit." Proposition 7 passed easily, 72.8 percent to 27.2 percent, with majority support in every county (most counties closely matching the statewide breakdown). Proposition 13 fared less well: it barely failed to achieve majority support with 49.96 percent approval statewide (majorities approved in only 19 of 58 counties). Fittingly, where Proposition 7 did well, Proposition 13 did poorly (compared to its statewide performance), and vice versa: the correlation between county percentage approval rates for the two measures is $-.42$. By contrast, the correlation between the Democratic registration percentages and Proposition 13 was $+.21$, reinforcing the suspicion that opinions on the primary were becoming bound up in normal party politics, notwithstanding the fact that some Republicans had taken part in the campaign for Proposition 13.

The other shoe dropped in April of 1959. The 1958 elections delivered the first unified Democratic control of California of the twentieth century, and Governor Pat Brown and the legislature wasted little time in abolishing cross-filing. Media coverage of the bill at the time emphasized that cross-filing was widely thought to favor Republicans. The *New York Times* opined, "California's Republicans, outnumbered [in registration] for the last twenty-seven years, capitalized on cross-filing to maintain a half century's domination of state politics" (Hill 1959a). Closer to the action, a report in the *Los Angeles Times* on passage of the repeal by the State Senate emphasized that "abolition of cross-filing has been a Democratic Party objective for years" ("Legislature Repeals Cross-Filing in State," 1959). The roll calls reflected that same partisan story. The Assembly passed AB 118 on February 24, 1959, with forty-five Democrats and four Republicans voting in favor against one Democrat and twenty-eight Republicans (one Democrat and one Republican abstained). In the Senate, the bill passed twenty-two to fifteen, twenty-one Democrats and one Republican defeating four Democrats and eleven Republicans (two Democrats and one Republican abstained).[5]

The interpretation that the Democrats of 1959 were finally in a position to close a pro-Republican loophole is complicated just slightly by the fact that some prominent Republicans expressed support for the change in primary law, and some Democrats lamented the end of the cross-filing era.

Only one member of California's congressional delegation spoke out against the repeal, Senator Thomas Kuchel (R), who struck a very Progressive tone: "The people of California are not extremely partisan—they want clean, strong, and honest government. In my judgment, cross-filing has helped them get it" (Shannon 1959). Moreover, the contention that cross-filing was somehow inevitably favorable to Republicans was rarely backed with any explicit logic. From the advent of party labels in 1954 to 1958, there were eleven instances of Democrats winning the Republican nomination for U.S. House seats, against no Republican victories in Democratic primaries. It seems plausible that cross-filing might have favored incumbents, insofar as simple name recognition ensured them an advantage over challengers among the less intensely partisan registered voters. If this were so, it would mean that the ability to cross-file worked to the advantage of the Republicans when they were the stronger state party, but started to help Democrats, on balance, after the state began to lean their way in the late 1930s. We shall return to this question in the next section.

Figure 2.1 shows three indirect indicators of the prevalence of multiple filing for U.S. House and California Senate contests between 1910 and 1964.[6] Before and after the period in which cross-filing was permitted (1914–1958), general election winners almost invariably held only one party's nomination, the exceptions being candidates who won extra nominations by write-in campaigns. By contrast, the dashed line shows that, on average, winners held about 1.5 nominations in this era, and in 1918 actually averaged more than 2 party nominations each. The average number of candidates in competition for California's U.S. House seats was high at the outset of the era, when the Progressive, Socialist, and Prohibition parties were still active. However, it quickly fell, as fewer and fewer individuals secured more and more nominations. Accordingly, the average value for a size-weighted count of candidates (the so-called "effective number") fell nearly to one, indicating that most districts were dominated by one individual standing as the candidate for more than one party.[7] Not until the late 1950s did California's U.S. House elections take the familiar modern American shape of competition between two candidates, each of whom represents one of the two major parties.

The significance of the foregoing is that primary elections in which a voter may cross over to support candidates from a party other than one's own are not new to California. Whereas the modern practice has been to "open" primaries by permitting some party-crossing behavior on the part of voters, in California's past, parties' influence was bypassed on the supply side, by allowing candidates to straddle party organizations for electoral purposes.[8] We turn now to an analysis of the actual voting patterns under these rules.

A. U.S. House seats

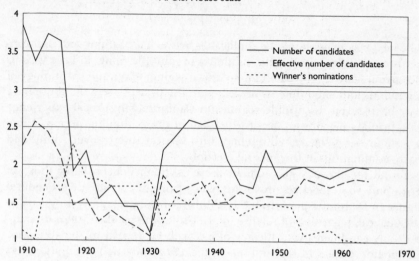

B. California State Senate seats
20 seats per election, 40 total

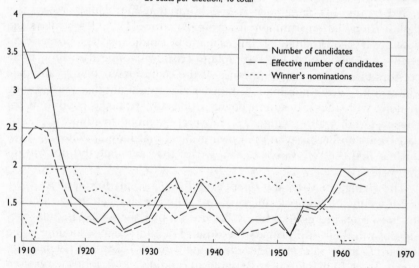

Figure 2.1. Competition in California general elections, district averages, 1910–64.

WHO WERE THE X-FILERS? CONTEXTS, CANDIDATES, AND CROSSOVER VOTING

The next task in assessing the similarities between cross-filing and the blanket primary is to consider the subtleties of multiple filing and the various possible incentives it created for crossover voting. Given the chronology of alterations and amendments described in the previous section, there have now been seven discernible regimes in California's historical experience with primary elections, four of which fall in the multifiling period. Table 2.1 summarizes the key differences with respect to crossover voting and party nominations at the general election.

Of all the primary elections in the cross-filing era, probably those of 1914 and 1916 most resemble the blanket primary in strictly procedural terms. In both time periods, the top finisher from each party moves on to the general, regardless of relative totals. Under the blanket, voters can support any candidates who file for office, without regard to the voters' or candidates' parties of registration. In the 1914 and 1916 elections, voters could support any candidates who filed in their parties' primaries or even candidates who did not do so, if they (the voters) took the extraordinary step of casting write-in votes. Since write-in votes are important only in races which are already aberrant, typically because the seat has been deserted by one major party, it is safe to say that the blanket system is a slightly friendlier environment for crossover voting. Or, at least, voters' options are less constrained by choices made by candidates. The primaries of 1920–52 were, in turn, less favorable to crossover voting than their predecessors of 1914 and 1916 because of the requirement that a candidate win his own party's nomination in order also to win another party's nomination. With this procedural change, objective strategic conditions for crossover voting also changed. Some voters inclined to support a candidate from another party in their own primary may have hesitated to do so for fear that the vote would be "wasted" if the candidate did not win his own primary.

The change in 1918 also opened up the possibility for "spoilers," candidates who could knock others out of the general election by receiving the most votes in a given primary, but not advance themselves because they did not win their own primary. Because of domino effects, spoiling could be hard to anticipate. Consider the primary in the Thirty-Sixth Senate District in 1922. In that election, Republican candidate A. B. Johnson received 7,571 votes in the Republican primary. Republican F. D. Mather won 6,961 Republican votes, 531 Prohibition votes, and 14 Socialist (write-in) votes. Prohibition candidate C. R. Burger received 1,809 Democratic votes and 414 Prohibition votes. Had 60 Prohibition voters switched from Mather to Burger, the general election would have pitted a Republican against a Pro-

TABLE 2.1   Primary Election Regimes in California's History

Election Years	Primary Type	Crossover Voting?	Multiply Nominated Candidates?
1910–12	Closed	By write-in vote only	Only in districts in which one party is *very* weak
1914–16	Closed with cross-filing	Yes, provided candidates cross-file (or by write-in)	Yes
1918	As in 1916, plus win-own-party requirement	Yes, provided candidates cross-file (or by write-in)	Only for candidates who win nomination of party with which they register
1920–52	As in 1918, plus party commit-tee substitutes	Yes, provided candidates cross-file (or by write-in)	Only for candidates who win nomination of party with which they register
1954–58	As in 1952, plus candidates' parties identified on ballots	Yes, provided candidates cross-file (or by write-in)	Only for candidates who win nomination of party with which they register
1960–96	Closed	By write-in vote only	Only in districts in which one party is *very* weak
1998–2000	Fully open "blanket"	Yes (but not di-rectly observ-able, except in presidential voting)	Only in districts in which one party is *very* weak

hibition-Democrat, rather than having a Republican waltz to victory uncontested.

There are, in short, both institutional and non-institutional distinctions to be drawn between the different types of primary systems and their receptivity to crossover voting. A fairly common scenario is for the primary to pit one Republican against one Democrat. Under the blanket primary, both candidates are assured of advancing to the general election, and the primary simply provides a preview of how the general might unfold by giving a preliminary reading of the candidates' relative appeals. In the cross-filing years, by contrast, these races could predetermine the general election result, since a candidate who won both nominations was guaranteed to face no major party opponent in the general. So, in symmetric races that lack real intraparty competition, the stakes were somewhat higher under cross-filing than under the blanket. Note, though, that this does not necessarily mean that crossover voting should have been more or less likely, on average, since the amount of crossover voting is ultimately dependent on candidates' strategies.

Figure 2.2 shows how much crossover voting occurred in U.S. House and state Senate races between 1910 and 1964. The dashed lines are party-specific: they show what proportion of votes cast in the Democratic primary went to candidates who were registered Republicans (and who were running in the Republican primary simultaneously) and what proportion of votes cast in the Republican primary were won by registered Democrats (who were also competing in the Democratic primary). The solid line marked "Total" is the proportion of primary votes that were cast for other party candidates. It includes Republican and Democratic crossover votes as well as votes cast for Progressives, Socialists, or Prohibitionists running in the Republican or Democratic primaries.[9]

The two panels tell similar stories. In 1910 and 1912, before cross-filing was permitted, a tiny amount of crossover voting occurred by way of write-in votes. In a few cases (e.g., the Third U.S. House District in 1910), a candidate won Democratic and Republican nominations simply because no opponent from the other major party ran, and so a campaign to generate a small number of write-in votes was sufficient for victory. When multiple filing became legal in 1914, crossover voting increased markedly. In 1914 and 1916, crossover voting accounted for about 10 percent of the primary vote. From 1918 to the mid-1930s, it was more common still, constituting about 20 percent of the primary vote. This was an era of Republican strength, and crossover voting was, accordingly, very asymmetric: Republican candidates dominated the Democratic primaries, while only a handful of Democrats captured any votes on the Republican side. With the New Deal realignment, the picture changed again. From the mid-1930s to the mid-1950s, crossover voting accounted for about 30 percent of the U.S. House vote and about 40 percent of the State Senate vote, and it was nearly evenly balanced between Democrats drawing support from Republican voters and Republicans drawing support from Democratic voters (the minor parties having all but vanished). Finally, the explicit labeling of candidates' own registration status on primary ballots in 1954, 1956, and 1958 seems to have been consequential: crossover rates fell back to the 20 percent range over these elections. Once multiple filing was abolished, crossover voting dropped to negligible rates as it was, again, possible only through write-in campaigns. In the early 1960s, these were symbolic (and futile) protests against the abolition of multiple filing. Thereafter, they disappeared altogether.

Another point about figure 2.2 is that it is especially sensitive to malapportionment. Because U.S. House districts varied considerably in population

A. U.S. House primaries

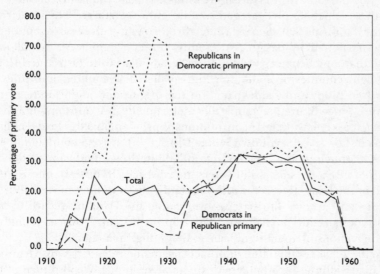

B. California State Senate primaries

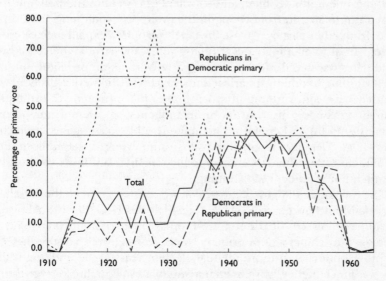

Figure 2.2. Crossover voting in California primaries, 1910–64.

over this era, some districts are more influential than others in computations like these, which simply aggregate over the entire electorate. This is truer still for the California State Senate, which, from 1932 to 1964, was exceptionally malapportioned by design. No county, however populous, was allotted more than one Senator, and the forty Senate seats were distributed to the fifty-eight counties by combining the smallest few counties into duos or trios (see Brady and Gaines 1995 on the origins and implications of this system). Since figure 2.2 counts all voters equally, it is appropriate for analyzing mass behavior, taking institutions as prior and fixed. The 2.8 million voters in Los Angeles county (Senate District 38) in 1958 count about 350 times as much as the 8,000 voters in Alpine, Inyo, and Mono counties (District 28) in an analysis of voters, not districts. If, instead, one is interested in the joint effects of institutions and behavior, one can treat districts as units and average district crossover voting rates without regard to how many voters reside in each one. This approach treats Districts 38 and 28 as observations of equal significance, weighting them equally.

Figure 2.3 takes this latter approach, averaging rates across districts without any weighting for numbers of voters or residents. We also turn to the issue of distinguishing different reasons to cross over in primary elections by plotting time series for the four categories of crossover vote. Some crossover voting occurred for the simplest of reasons: no candidate registered with the relevant party filed, and so voters who went to the polls and preferred not to abstain from voting in the given race could only back candidates from other parties. We use the label "no option" for all such crossover voting. In all remaining cases, primary voters did have a choice between candidates registered with their own party (who might or might not have been running in other primaries) and cross-filers who were registered with another party and running in at least one other primary. We distinguish between crossover votes cast for an incumbent (e.g., Democratic primary voters supporting a Republican incumbent), those cast against an incumbent (e.g., Democratic primary voters supporting a Republican non-incumbent rather than a Democratic incumbent), and those cast in races in which no incumbent was running.

The two panels of figure 2.3 reveal more contrast between the two chambers than did figure 2.2. Panel 2.3A, which describes the U.S. House, is broadly reminiscent of panel 2.2A. From 1914 to 1940, districts saw, on average, 5 to 10 percent of primary voters crossing over because they had no other option. In two presidential election years (1924 and 1928), this rate was much higher, as 15 to 20 percent of all votes in the average district were forced crossovers. After 1940, there was very little voting of this kind. Open-seat and anti-incumbent crossover voting, by contrast, were unimportant until the 1940s. Thereafter, from 1940 to 1950, the district averages for each chamber were about 5 to 10 percent. These rates fell sharply

A. U.S. House

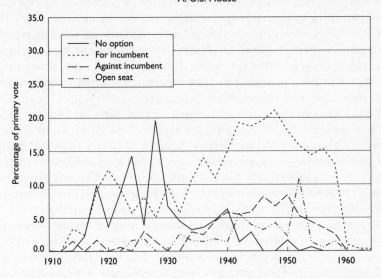

B. California State Senate

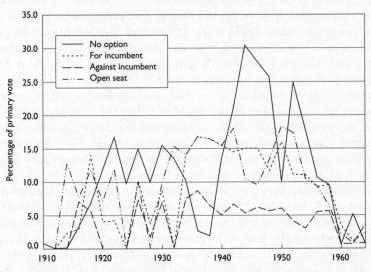

Figure 2.3. Average rates for types of crossover votes, 1910–64.

in the 1950s, even before the final abolition of cross-filing in 1960. The dominant form of crossover voting, then, was pro-incumbent. From 1914 to 1932, the average rate of crossover voting in favor of incumbents was 5 to 10 percent. From 1932 to 1948, this share rose steadily, peaking at over 20 percent. Even after the candidate-labeling rules of 1954, about 15 percent of the primary vote was cast against party registration, for incumbents, until the changes of 1960 ended the practice.

No patterns in the California Senate are as clear. In most years, the districts averaged higher rates of all varieties of crossover voting than did their U.S. House counterparts. In stark contrast to the patterns found in U.S. House elections, forced crossover voting was somewhat more common late in the series than early. On the other hand, as in the U.S. House case, there were declines in the average district rates of all kinds of crossover voting after the 1954 candidate-labeling rules came into play.

The implication of this drop in crossover voting after candidates' party registrations were printed on the ballots is that some voters must have been crossing over unintentionally, not realizing that the candidates they were supporting were in fact registered members of another party. A plausible conjecture about such voting is that much of it originated in incumbency status. Indeed, it is a staple of research on the incumbency advantage in congressional *general* elections that incumbents are able disproportionately to attract support from voters who do not identify with the incumbent's party. Case studies bolster the impression that crossover voting extended this incumbency advantage in reaching across parties into the primary stage as well. For instance, years after he lost the 1948 Democratic primary in California's Twelfth District to Richard Nixon, Democrat Stephen Zetterberg cited cross-filing as the culprit, complaining that "Nixon, concealing his Republican Party affiliation, used to advantage that his name came first on the ballot due to his incumbency and that his campaign committee promoted the 'Dear Fellow Democrat' advertising format, enticing enough unsophisticated Democratic voters, who did not understand the crossfiling procedure, into casting their ballots for him." Indeed, it appears that crafting a separate appeal aimed directly at Democrats was "the media strategy in the local newspapers" for the Nixon campaign (Gellman 1999, 179–80).

Zetterberg's description conflates a few different points. Incumbents may have profited from the simple advantage of appearing first on ballots, but they undoubtedly had an edge in name recognition to boot. The post-1952 drop-off in pro-incumbent crossover voting that occurred in both the U.S. House and State Senate is indirect evidence that "unsophisticated" voters may well have been mistaking the better-known candidates for their own partisan brethren. On the other hand, pro-incumbent crossover voting continued to make up about 10 percent of the vote in districts after candidates' parties were explicitly noted on the ballot, so some of the cross-party appeal seems to have been genuine. Nixon's strategy was not so much to "conceal" his identity as a Republican, as to advertise the support of prominent Democrats for his candidacy. And, of course, Nixon had earned his incumbency status by beating then-incumbent Democrat Jerry Voorhis in 1946, not only in the general election, but in the Republican primary as well. In short, the ability to cross-file and cultivate crossover support rendered primary elections more like general elections, where incumbents could successfully transcend partisan ties and were vulnerable only to concerted efforts by high-quality opponents.

This general climate is precisely what the blanket system is supposed to deliver as well. Candidates able to craft appeals to all voters, not only those who share their party registration, can broaden their bases, encourage cross-party coalitions of moderates, take advantage of nonpartisan appeal and superior recognition, and so on. There is little reason to believe that Nixon was alone in taking advantage of the institutional environment by developing a two-track strategy to win Democratic and Republican votes.

Table 2.2 presents one more analysis of crossover voting rates and the effects of institutional context (the different combinations of rules in place) and political context (incumbency status). Our observations include both U.S. House and State Senate districts. We regress the proportion of the primary vote that consists of crossover votes on indicator variables for each period, an indicator for whether there was a cross-filing incumbent in the race, another indicator for races having incumbents who did not cross-file, a simple count of how many non-incumbents had cross-filed, and a variable identifying a district as competitive.[10] Finally, because the district populations vary widely, we added the natural logarithm of the total number of primary votes cast as a further control variable.

Models 1 and 3 include, respectively, all districts and all U.S. House districts. Models 2 and 4 investigate the robustness of the findings by omitting all cases in which there was no crossover vote at all. The results reemphasize the points illustrated in figure 2.3. First, the presence of a cross-filing incumbent greatly increased the amount of crossover voting in all models, by a substantial 15 to 25 percent. In models 1 and 2, races in which an incumbent ran but did not cross-file saw 3 to 8 percentage point declines in crossover voting, presumably because the incumbent drew support in his or her own primary that might otherwise have gone to cross-filers from other parties. Since the coefficient on this variable was not significant in models 3 and 4, it appears that this dampening effect was stronger in the State Senate than in the U.S. House, and / or that it was mostly when seats were competitive that incumbents ran without cross-filing in the House. The direct effect of the competitive-district variable, was, in any case, not significant, so crossover voting does not seem to have been sensitive to the prospects of a close race ensuing in the general for the U.S.

TABLE 2.2   Crossover Vote Proportions in California Senate and
U.S. House, 1910–64

	U.S. House and State Senate	Crossover Vote > 0	U.S. House Only	U.S. House, Crossover Vote > 0
	Model 1	Model 2	Model 3	Model 4
Intercept	0.32*	0.40*	−0.16	−0.40*
	(0.04)	(0.05)	(0.12)	(0.17)
1914–16	−0.04*	0.00	−0.02	0.06
	(0.02)	(0.03)	(0.03)	(0.04)
1918–52	0.16*	0.25*	0.14*	0.26*
	(0.01)	(0.02)	(0.01)	(0.02)
1954–58	0.10*	0.19*	0.05*	0.15*
	(0.02)	(0.02)	(0.02)	(0.02)
Cross-filing incumbent	0.14*	0.09*	0.14*	0.09*
	(0.01)	(0.01)	(0.01)	(0.02)
Non-cross-filing incumbent	−0.03*	−0.08*	−0.01	−0.04
	(0.01)	(0.03)	(0.02)	(0.04)
Number of other cross-filers	0.03*	0.01*	0.03*	0.01*
	(0.004)	(0.005)	(0.005)	(0.006)
ln (total votes cast)	−0.03*	−0.04*	0.01	0.03*
	(0.004)	(0.005)	(0.01)	(0.02)
Competitive district			0.002	0.002
			(0.009)	(0.01)
N	1,119	877	559	425
Adjusted R^2	0.50	0.35	0.56	0.37

*$p < .05$

House, *ceteris paribus*. As expected, the number of cross-filing non-incumbents mattered: the greater the number of such candidates, the higher the crossover vote. Finally, the period-indicator variables verify that the 1918–52 period saw the highest levels of crossing over; the 1954–58 period saw the second highest levels; and 1914–16 was, all else equal, barely distinguishable from 1910–12 and 1960–64, when crossover voting happened only by write-in.

We take this finding to signify that voters and candidates require time to learn how institutions shape their incentives. Some cross-filing and, in turn, crossover voting, quickly followed the introduction of the new primary rules in 1914, but several elections had passed before the phenomenon peaked in importance. Most, but not all, of the party-defying votes were cast for incumbents, suggesting that cross-filing institutions, by weakening parties in the primaries, assisted those already in power. Differences between the U.S. House and California Senate alert us to the need to qualify this claim, however. Whether incumbents sought to exploit cross-filing and how voters then responded seem also to be connected to the context of the race in ways we cannot precisely delineate. Finally, the continuation of crossover voting even after ballots were altered to alert voters to candidates' true partisanship implies that some voters were consciously supporting candidates from other parties, presumably because the candidates appealed to them in some nonpartisan manner.

A few implications for how the blanket primary would have developed had the blanket rules remained in place follow. First, and most obviously, it is not wise to draw strong conclusions about how the blanket rules affect candidate and voter behavior after only one election. It may take a few elections before any kind of equilibrium is reached. Crossover voting in a blanket primary is something like crossover voting in the 1954–58 elections, since the candidates' party identities are known. Some of the strategic decisions of the past, though, such as whether or not to cross-file, no longer apply. Voter strategy is thus slightly less intertwined with candidate strategy under blanket rules than under cross-filing. Probably, all else equal, incumbents were favored by the blanket's removal of party registration walls, as they were in the past. Some of the variation in voting behavior between the U.S. House and the California State Senate may have followed from other institutional differences, such as the vastly dissimilar methods of apportionment used for each from 1930 to 1964. The fact that Senate districts were, with very few exceptions, not altered over this period had implications for district competitiveness. Although we have not presented evidence that crossover voting levels having been responsive to districts' general election competitiveness, we continue to suspect that the expectation of a competitive race may be an important determinant of *how* crossover votes are cast. The effects of blanket primary rules would have been filtered through other contextual factors, such as how competitive are any new districts drawn for 2002 and beyond, how campaign finance laws vary across venues, and so forth.

WEAVING (AND UNWEAVING) THE BLANKET

Passed in 1996 and overturned in June 2000, California's blanket primary had a short but eventful life: (1) it became law when Proposition 198 was approved in the primary election of March 1996; (2) it survived a court challenge mounted by the major and minor parties in decisions handed down by the U.S. District Court in 1997 and the Ninth Circuit Court of Appeals in March of 1999; (3) its application to presidential elections was threatened in July 1998 when Governor Wilson signed SB 1505 into law, thereby placing Proposition 3 on the November 1998 ballot; (4) however, it then remained unaltered as Proposition 3 was soundly defeated at the polls; (5) in a further reversal, it was subsequently altered, all the same, in May of 1999 by the passage into law of SB 100, a bill making the "openness" of presidential primaries merely cosmetic and requiring a simultaneous closed vote to occur and to be controlling with respect to actual convention delegate selection; (6) in April 2000, the U.S. Supreme Court reviewed the Appeals Court decision; and (7) in June 2000, the Supreme Court over-turned the blanket primary, thereby ending California's latest experiment in primary law.

Perhaps surprisingly, the electoral battle over Proposition 198 was not waged in dollars. The initiative was opposed by both major parties, but they allowed themselves to be outspent, possibly having been lulled into inac-tivity because the measure enjoyed endorsements from only three big-name-value politicians: Republicans Tom Campbell and Becky Morgan, and Independent Lucy Killea. State Senator Killea, significantly, was not only a former Democrat, but was already associated with quixotic reform efforts because of her prior campaign to promote unicameralism for the state legislature. The reasons underlying the support by the two major-party figures for the open primary measure, meanwhile, can be discerned from their intertwined career paths.

Campbell was a moderate who believed he (and other moderates) would benefit by being able to appeal to moderate voters and independents. Mor-gan, meanwhile, was drawn to the cause by her disgruntlement with the state Republican organization. Each made substantial contributions ($100,000 and $150,000, respectively) from their political war chests.

Another $150,000 was supplied to the pro–Proposition 198 forces in small donations (i.e., under $10,000 each), with most of the balance com-ing from Hewlett-Packard ($45,000 directly; $300,000 from David Packard; and $120,000 from William Hewlett). In all, the pro–Proposition 198 cam-paign raised about a million dollars, while the opponents raised only $100,000: $50,000 given by Rupert Murdoch and $50,000 from the state Republican party.[11] Elite opposition, then, was not expressed financially, but in public statements and endorsements. The official "Argument Against Proposition 198" in the *1996 Primary Voters' Handbook* was, after all, signed by the chairmen of the California Republican and Democratic parties.

Despite official party opposition and strong elite antagonism at the rhe-torical level, most of those who made their way to the polls in March of 1996 endorsed the measure. Not only did Prop 198 pass easily, it was one of six propositions (out of twelve) that won majority support in every county of the state.[12] Roughly 92.3 percent of all ballots featured a vote on Prop198, which was just slightly below the average participation rate (92.7 percent) for that batch of propositions.

Even before a blanket primary had been held under the new law, the state legislature was attempting to modify its key features. SB 1505, passed with little opposition in either chamber and signed into law in July of 1998, placed Proposition 3 on the general election ballot for the following November.[13] That proposition would have reversed Proposition 198 with respect to presidential primaries by making voting for presidential convention delegates closed by party registration. The justification was that, under standing rules, both major national parties could exclude California delegations elected in a blanket primary in 2000 and thereafter.

The *Voters' Handbook* debate on Proposition 3 was even less balanced, in terms of prestige of the participants, than had been its Proposition 198 counterpart. United in favor of the modification were the senior State Senators from each party, the Assembly leaders of each party, and Proposition 198's old nemesis Bruce Herschensohn. Only first-term Assemblyman Jack Scott (D–44) opposed the proposition. And yet, perhaps because they were unconvinced that either major party would dare freeze the largest state out of its convention, whatever the formal rules specified, voters rejected Proposition 3 almost as unambiguously as their counterparts had supported Proposition 198 just twenty-nine months earlier. Proposition 3 lost by a margin of 46 percent to 54 percent, and won majority support in only one county (Los Angeles). The proposition was also ignored by an unusually large number of voters: only 86.1 percent of all ballots included votes (pro or con) on the measure, giving it the fifth lowest participation rate of the forty-seven propositions considered by California voters in the 1996 and 1998 primary and general elections.

The new legislature, however, was not willing to follow the voters' advice to play chicken with the national parties. Within months, both chambers had passed a substitute for Proposition 3, again by overwhelming margins. When Governor Davis signed SB 100 into law in May of 1999, the state government had effectively negated the impact of Proposition 198 with respect to presidential primaries.

Under the revised law used in the 2000 presidential primary, the presidential election appeared to the voter to be open, since one could select delegates (in the minds of most voters, presidential candidates) without regard to one's own registration status. However, not all votes counted equally. It was required of local election officials that they identify presidential ballots by the voters' party affiliation so that they could perform a double tabulation. California's presidential convention delegates in 2000 were thus selected not according to the overall vote, but according to "the number of votes each delegate candidate receives from voters affiliated with the same political party as the delegate candidate." Whether one regards this revised law as a betrayal of the spirit of the blanket primary or a necessary corrective, a nice feature for political scientists is that the dual counting system allows recovery of directly observable evidence on cross-party voting. For most races, however, the study of voting behavior under the blanket rules remains more complicated than the study of crossover voting in the past, because the important vote totals must be estimated rather than simply read off of official returns. In the 2000 presidential election, though, the "faux-blanket" may have introduced useful objective data. Depending on how well voters understood the complicated law, it could be that levels of crossover voting in the presidential race will provide future analysts with useful information about voter strategy.

CONCLUSION

Analysts eager to understand California's blanket primary system have typically looked to Washington and Alaska, the other two states that have used this type of primary. They have entirely missed the clues buried in California's own electoral history and the natural link between the blanket primary and its ancestor, the multiple-filing primary. The parallels are clearly numerous, and we have only begun to mine the wealth of data on how Californians behaved in past primaries, given the opportunity to vote outside of party registration lines.

There is clear evidence that the strategies behind cross-filing and crossover voting were not immediately obvious to Californians in the 1910s and 1920s. Though the Assembly saw a proliferation of "hyphenated," multiply-nominated members immediately (see note 4), rates of crossover voting did not rise dramatically until after a few elections had passed. We see no reason to expect modern-day voters and candidates to determine their optimal strategies under a blanket primary system any more quickly. Hence, a subtheme for this entire book is that all conclusions should be qualified with an understanding that the full potential impact of the blanket primary may not have been realized in the short period it was in place. We counsel continued attention to historical precedent as analysts struggle to understand Californians, their parties, and their primaries.

NOTES

Our thanks to Bruce Cain, Michael Caldwell, Christophe Crombez, and Elisabeth Gerber for helpful suggestions, and to Lloyd Gruber for extraordinary assistance with locating primary sources.

1. An example of the minor parties being decisive is New York's Sixth Congressional District in 1980. John LeBoutillier received 71,838 votes as the Republican candidate, while Lester Wolff won 74,319 votes as the Democrat. It was LeBoutillier who went to Washington, though, since he also won 11,299 votes as the Conservative candidate, while Wolff won only 5,890 Liberal votes. A more typical result is that of the Ninth District in 1984: Tom Manton won the seat with 71,420 votes as a Dem-

ocrat over an opponent who combined 54,089 Republican, 7,458 Conservative, and 2,363 Right-to-Life votes.

2. In modern elections, this is possible only if the candidate wins one nomination as a write-in. The only U.S. Representative from New York to hold Republican and Democratic nominations in a general election in the 1990s was Charlie Rangel in 1990, running in what was then the Sixteenth District (Harlem), a very safe Democratic seat routinely abandoned by the Republican party.

3. Joining twenty-four Republicans, ten Democrats, seven Progressives, and two Socialists were ten members with both Republican and Progressive nominations (or "Republican-Progressives"), eight Republican-Democrats, seven Democratic-Progressives, six Republican-Democratic-Progressives, one Republican-Democratic-Prohibitionist, one Republican-Progressive-Prohibitionist, one Democratic-Progressive-Prohibitionist, one Republican-Democratic-Progressive-Prohibitionist, and even one member nominated by all five parties, a Republican-Democratic-Progressive-Prohibitionist-Socialist (Calif. Secretary of State, *Statement of the Vote at the General Election of November 3, 1914*, 4–5).

4. It might seem that this power to appoint nominees was unlikely to have mattered, given that committees could act only if all the candidates registered with their own party had lost to outsiders, an outcome that would seem to signal that the seat was a lost cause. In general, primary races with many candidates and/or many cross-filers seem not to have been very good predictors of subsequent general election results, and committee-appointed stand-ins who actually won were not unheard of.

5. Voting against cross-filing in the Senate were seven of ten Democrats who had won Republican nominations in the 1958 primaries, and one of four Republicans who had won Democratic nominations. In the Assembly, twelve of the thirteen Democrats who had also carried the Republican nomination in 1958 voted to abolish cross-filing, while both of the Republicans who had won the Democratic nomination voted against abolition.

6. The data analyzed in this chapter were obtained from the relevant official primary and general *Statement of Vote* reports released by the California Secretary of State. The electronic dataset was created from these sources by the authors.

7. The "effective" number of candidates is an index that weights the actual number of candidates according to their vote shares, so that strong candidates count far more than weak ones. We used the most common such measure in the voting literature, the Laakso-Taagepera index (1979), computed for each district. The values in figure 2.1 are averages, computed as follows:

$$\bar{N}_e = 1/n \, \Sigma_i \, [(\Sigma_j V_{ij})^2 / (\Sigma_j V_{ij}^2)]$$

where V_{ij} is the number of votes won by candidate j in district i, and there are a total of n districts in the state (or, as applicable, n districts in which there is some competition).

8. Candidates elected with both Democratic and Republican nominations were *not*, of course, in any legislative sense representatives of both parties. Richard Nixon and Cecil Young were both elected with both major-party nominations in 1948, but there was no doubt that the former was a partisan Republican and the latter a partisan Democrat once they arrived in D.C. to sit in the Eighty-First Congress.

9. The figure very slightly undercounts crossover voting because, as a conse-

quence of the way we collected the data, we do not include in our crossover totals those votes won by other-party candidates in minor-party primaries (e.g., Prohibition primary votes cast for a registered Socialist or registered Democrat who cross-filed).

10. This competitive-district dummy variable was developed by computing normal votes for districts, using general election returns, and then adjusting these according to whether or not there was any partisan turnover observed in the relevant reapportionment period. We used a simple dichotomy: safe (Democratic or Republican) seat (i.e., high or low normal Democratic vote, little turnover) versus competitive (middle-sized normal vote plus some turnover.) A paucity of contested general elections made the estimation difficult for the State Senate, so we computed this measure for the U.S. House districts only.

11. All data on contribution amounts are taken from Jones (1996).

12. Unusually, all twelve propositions on the March 1996 ballot passed.

13. It passed the Senate 35–0 on April 2 and passed in the Assembly 52–12 on July 10, 1998. Three days later the Senate concurred with Assembly amendments, 28–0, and on July 13, 1998, the law was signed by the Governor and chaptered by the Secretary of State.

REFERENCES

Birtel, Marc. 1996. "Ballot: 'Jungle Primaries' Adopted . . . Reclassifying Lions Rejected." *Congressional Quarterly Weekly Report* 54, no. 13 (March 30): 902–3.

Block, A. G., and Claudia Buck, eds. 1997. *California Political Almanac, 1997–1998.* 5th ed. Sacramento, CA: California Journal / State Net.

Brady, David W., and Brian J. Gaines. 1995. "A House Discarded? Evaluating the Case for a Unicameral California Legislature." In Bruce E. Cain and Roger G. Noll, eds., *Constitutional Reform in California: Making State Government More Effective and Responsive.* Berkeley, CA: Institute of Governmental Studies Press, 195–238.

California Secretary of State (various). 1904–1964. *Statement of the Vote at General Election.* Various volumes. Sacramento.

California Secretary of State (various). 1904–1964. *Statement of the Vote at Primary Election.* Various volumes. Sacramento.

"Coast Rivals Agree." 1959. *New York Times,* Saturday February 28, 7.

Davies, Lawrence E. 1951. "New Warren Term Starts Tomorrow." *New York Times,* Sunday, January 7, 57.

———. 1952. "Knowland Seeks California Sweep." *New York Times,* Sunday, May 4, 49.

Dubin, Michael J. 1998. *United States Congressional Elections, 1788–1997.* Jefferson, NC: McFarland.

Gellman, Irwin F. 1999. *The Contender: Richard Nixon, the Congress Years, 1946–1952.* New York: Free Press.

Green, Stephen, et al. 1995. *California Political Almanac, 1995–1996.* 4th ed. Sacramento, CA: California Journal Press.

Hichborn, Franklin. 1909. *Story of the Session of the California Legislature of 1909.* San Francisco: Press of the James H. Barry Company.

————. 1922. *Story of the Session of the California Legislature of 1921.* San Francisco: Press of the James H. Barry Company.

Hill, Gladwin. 1959a. "California Bills Rushed by Brown." *New York Times,* Sunday, January 18, 64.

————. 1959b. "Cross-Filing Ban in Peril on Coast." *New York Times,* Monday, March 16, 15.

————. 1959c. "California Shift Will Help Voter." *New York Times,* Sunday, April 26, 67.

Jones, Bill (Secretary of State of California). 1996. *Financing California's Statewide Ballot Measures: 1996 Primary and General Elections Campaign Receipts and Expenditures through June 30, 1996.* Sacramento, CA: Secretary of State, Political Reform Division.

Kettl, Donald F. 1992. *Deficit Politics: Public Budgeting in Its Institutional and Historical Context.* New York: Macmillan.

Laakso, Markku, and Rein Taagepera. 1979. "'Effective' Number of Parties: A Measure with Application to Western Europe." *Comparative Political Studies* 12, no. 1 (April): 3–27.

Lee, Eugene C. 1960. *The Politics of Nonpartisanship: A Study of California City Elections.* Berkeley, CA: University of California Press.

"Legislature Repeals Cross-Filing in State: Signature of Governor Assured." 1959. *Los Angeles Times,* Friday, April 24, 1.

Shannon, Don. 1959. "Repeal of Cross-Filing Hailed by Congressmen." *Los Angeles Times,* Saturday, April 25, 4.

State of California. 1920. *State of California Direct Primary Law with the Official Forms Prepared by the Secretary of State and the Attorney General.* Sacramento.

Young, C. C., ed. 1943. *The Legislature of California: Its Membership, Procedure, and Work.* San Francisco: Press of the Parker Printing Company.

CHAPTER THREE

Political Reform via the Initiative Process

What Voters Think about
When They Change the Rules

Shaun Bowler and Todd Donovan

INTRODUCTION

This chapter examines support for Proposition 198, California's 1996 blanket primary initiative. Proposition 198 is considered to be part of a long series of initiatives that have presented California voters with choices about how their political institutions should be structured. We use public opinion data to test hypotheses about the nature of mass support for such political reform initiatives. We test if support is associated with voters' self-interest and with general dissatisfaction with politics. Our findings support the idea that voting for Proposition 198 was structured by reasoning about the consequences of the proposed reform. Strong partisans were opposed to the measure, yet partisans dissatisfied with their party's candidates were more supportive. We also find evidence consistent with the idea that some voting was structured by generalized dissatisfaction that had no specific relation to election rules, particularly among less-educated voters. Less-educated voters with personal economic worries were more supportive.

VOTER CHOICE OVER INSTITUTIONS

Ballot measures often generate a great deal of controversy. Recent examples from California include initiatives on state services for immigrants (Proposition 187), affirmative action (Proposition 209), the legalization of marijuana (Proposition 215), and Indian gaming (Proposition 5). A quick glance through old textbooks on California politics readily provides a similar list from previous decades. Heated debates were seen in the 1960s, for example, over the repeal of the legislature's fair housing Rumford Act via Proposition 14 (Wolfinger and Greenstein 1968), while the 1970s saw controversies over the anti-obscenity Proposition 18 and anti-nuclear Proposition 15 (Hensler and Hensler 1979). In the 1980s, controversial initiatives targeted AIDS patients (Donovan and Bowler 1997) and declared English the state's official language (Citrin, Reingold, and Waters 1990). Despite the controversies generated at the time, these initiatives and the issues related to them often faded. Either the proposition failed on election day, or was nullified in court, or was passed and was largely forgotten. In general, it seems, attention to the initiative process is directed toward the hot button issue of the moment. Once the moment passes, so, too, does interest in the issue.

Less noticed, but of potentially long-term influence, are those propositions that regulate the political and institutional structure of the state. Initiatives that change the way elected officials do their business or contest elections, "governance policies" (Tolbert 1998), have effects that endure over a long period of time. Term-limit measures (Donovan and Snipp 1994), tax and expenditure proposals such as Proposition 13 of 1978 (Sears and Citrin 1982; Tolbert 1998), Proposition 4 of 1979, and campaign finance reforms are examples of citizen-enacted institutional changes that have had major effects on state politics (for discussion of the effects of some of these policies see Mondak 1995; Moncrief and Thompson 1991; Clingermayer and Wood 1995; Donovan and Bowler 1998; Schrag 1998; Gerber et al. 2000). Proposition 198 is another example of an initiative that proposed an institutional change and which therefore had far-reaching consequences for the conduct of politics in the state.

The broad potential importance of political reform initiatives can perhaps be made clearer by reference to a simple spatial analogy. In spatial terms, policy proposals move the status quo to a particular point in an issue space, but institutional reforms change the very space available to policy makers. Consequently any future flow of policy may then be restricted to, or restricted from, a particular region in the space. The cumulative impact of an institutional change can therefore be much greater than the move from a single point to another point within a given space.

All of this raises a familiar criticism of the initiative process yet more pointedly: if voters have a hard time figuring out how to vote on individual policies (Magleby 1984), how can they possibly understand issues of institutional change? Initiatives like Prop 198 present additional, fundamental concerns about democracy: should voters have a free hand in shaping institutions? When they can, do they make changes in institutional rules that reflect some manner of deliberation about the consequences of change? The answers to these questions are of broad relevance. Theories of political legitimacy have long depended on the idea that voters like—or at least have modest regard for—the institutions which govern them. Political legitimacy may also rest on the permanence of these institutions (March and

Olson 1984). As Hibbing and Theiss-Morse (1998) state, "Whatever the overall talents of the rank and file, political change in the realm of process should *not* be as sensitive to the public's wishes as political change in the realm of policy" (28; emphasis in original). We should be "glad," they continue, "that ordinary people are not in a position to leave their every mark on questions of political process and institutional design" (29). The "stickiness" of institutions identified by Riker (1982) thus has a positive value in contributing to legitimacy. While one implication of this argument skirts uncomfortably close to tautology (legitimacy grows as institutions endure and we know institutions are legitimate because they endure), another implication has clear relevance for the initiative process: procedural change introduced without consideration of the consequences, or by mere whim or fad, threatens legitimacy and is to be avoided.

Luckily, at least so far as institutional legitimacy is concerned, it is typically very difficult to introduce such changes. It is often especially difficult to translate popular discontent into proposals and then into actual reform. In addition to procedural hurdles, simple delaying actions (Commissions of Inquiry or blue-ribbon panels of experts) can be relied on to leave reform proposals to die a peaceful and unimplemented death. The initiative process, however, allows voters to introduce and enact institutional reform proposals fairly readily, and with it, California voters have been given, and have taken, several chances to introduce real procedural change.

Proposition 198 is far from unique as an example of institutional reform via the initiative process. Tables 3.1 and 3.2 show that California voters have been presented with dozens of choices over their political institutions since 1912. The data and subject categorizations are taken from the California Secretary of State's office,[1] which considers proposals to change the rules that structure state revenues and expenditures (e.g., Proposition 13, Proposition 98) as a different category. If anything, then, these data underestimate the frequency with which Californians can vote to change (or retain) their political institutions.

The first two columns of table 3.1 show that between 1912 and 1998, 169 of California's 1,043 initiative proposals fell into the category of "institutional reform." Of these 169, 45 eventually qualified for the ballot, representing 16 percent (45 of 272) of all California initiatives qualified from 1912 to 1998. Eighteen of these passed, or 40 percent, which is slightly higher than the 32 percent pass rate for all California initiatives during this period.

Columns 3–7 of table 3.1 show the variety of topics covered by the institutional reform initiatives. The range of proposals varies from the major to the relatively minor. Examples of the former are term limits, campaign finance reform, and changes in the structure of primaries. Examples of the latter include nineteen of the fifty-two proposals concerning "Elected

TABLE 3.1 Institutional Reform Proposals as Share of All California Initiatives, 1912–98

	All Initiatives	All Reform Initiatives	Campaigns	Elected Officials and Civil Service	Term Limits	Elections	Reapportionment
Number titled on this subject	1,043	169	27	52	16	63	27
Number qualified for ballot	272	45	11	10	3	15	9
Percentage of initiatives qualified for ballot[a]	26%	26%	24%	22%	6%	33%	20%
Number approved by voters	87	18	5	4	3	8	1
Percentage approved by voters	32%	40%	45%	40%	100%	53%	11%

SOURCE: Bill Jones, "A History of the California Initiative Process" (Sacramento, August 1998).
[a]Some initiatives were placed in two categories, so these do not sum to 100 percent.

TABLE 3.2   Frequency of Pre- and Post-1980
Institutional Reform Initiatives

	Titled N	Qualified N	Approved N
All initiatives			
Total 1912–98	1,043	272	87
Total 1980–98	593	103	41
Institutional reform initiatives			
Total 1912–98	169	45	18
Total 1980–98	120	25	11

SOURCE: Bill Jones, "A History of the California Initiative Process" (Sacramento, August 1998).

Officials and Civil Service" that involved public salaries. Proposition 198 was counted under the "Elections" category, the most common category of institutional reform initiatives and, apart from three recent term-limit measures, institutional reforms affecting the conduct of elections are the ones most likely to be approved by voters.[2]

Table 3.2 illustrates that a majority of these reform efforts occurred after 1980. While over a third (103 of 272) of California's initiatives on all subjects have qualified for ballots since 1980, well over half of all institutional reform initiatives (25 of 45) have qualified since then. Prior to 1980, voters faced an institutional reform proposal on the ballot once every four years, on average. After 1980, the figure becomes six every four years. Table 3.1 demonstrates that voters are more sympathetic to these initiatives than they are to initiatives generally. This presents several questions. Why do voters support institutional reform? Do they change institutions on the basis of mere whim or discontent, or does support reflect a deeper understanding of the consequences of change?

WHAT DETERMINES VOTER CHOICES
ABOUT INSTITUTIONAL REFORM?

We advance two related but distinct arguments about how voters assess institutions. One argument is grounded in an understanding of voter behavior as relatively self-interested and rational. According to the self-interest view, we hypothesize that voters will support the current institutions if they do well under them, and support change if they believe the alternative will make them better off. By contrast, a second series of explanations stresses more general orientations toward, and disaffection from, institutions. Here we may think of voter opinions toward institutions being guided by a sense of discontent, driven perhaps by economic factors (unemployment), demographic factors (race, ethnicity) or simple disillusionment brought about by scandal and corruption.

The argument which emphasizes winners and losers implies that voters understand institutional changes. Voters have sufficient information to vote sensibly on institutional change initiatives or at least receive effective cues that allow them to vote in response to how an institutional change might affect them (Lupia 1994; Bowler and Donovan 1998). If it is possible to show that decisions are consistent with patterns of who wins and loses under different rules, then we may infer that voters are reasoning in a quite sophisticated way about how institutions work. In terms of recent term-limit initiatives, for example, this means that many voters make decisions consistent with the (political) gains and losses that might result from the proposals. Voters supporting the party out of power will thus support term limits as a way of opening new opportunities (competitive, open seats) for access to the legislature. As evidence, Donovan and Snipp (1994) found with California's Prop 140, and Magleby and Patterson (1996) found with a term-limit initiative in Utah, that voters aligned with the majority party in a legislature were more likely to oppose term limits, while partisans of the minority were more likely to be in favor.

It is also possible to view voters as thinking about institutions instrumentally but not necessarily on narrowly self-interested grounds. In place of a concern for who wins and who loses under various institutional reforms, some voters may have ideological predispositions in favor of certain institutional arrangements that we may distinguish—at least in principle—from self-interested concerns. The overlap between self-interest and ideology is, of course, a strong one. Differentiating between the two effects can be enormously difficult. Nevertheless, if voters make decisions on taxes, vouchers, environmental regulations, Prohibition, bonds, and term limits based on assessments of how the measure affects their group, party, community, or themselves (Bowler and Donovan 1998), we may reasonably expect that they would use similar criteria when assessing proposals such as Proposition 198.

If the link between understanding and vote choice is at issue when discussing specific targeted policies such as environmental or educational reforms, it is even more critical in considering votes on institutional reforms such as Prop 198. If voters have a hard time understanding individual issues, they may have an even harder time understanding the impact of changing institutions. The link between voter understanding of institutions and vote choice is thus of substantive importance in developing an understanding of vote choice anchored in a self-interested model.

An alternative to the self-interested hypothesis is that votes to change institutions may reflect discontent and alienation with politics and society in general, rather than with the actual role of the institution targeted by the proposed reform. Here we may find regularities which have a demographic component: younger people (Abramson 1979), racial or ethnic minorities (Bobo and Gilliam 1990), and political minorities (Banducci, Donovan, and Karp 1999) may well feel more alienated than the rest of society due to lack of descriptive representation and / or socialization processes that fail to build attachments to institutions. This could cause them to be more likely to vote against the status quo. Such voters may favor institutional reform not as a result of evaluating the gains and losses resulting from change, but as an extension of some general lack of attachment to the institution.[3]

As a variant on the alienation argument, we note that demands for institutional change could be driven by short-term factors, most notably anger about politics and politicians, economic uncertainty, or short-term reactions to scandal (Karp 1995; Bowler and Donovan 1998, 69–70). Although these opinions may be systematic, they may not necessarily involve choice based on the consequences of the proposed change in political institutions. For example, voter dissatisfaction with parties and legislatures could be merely an episodic, media-driven response to corruption or adverse coverage of "wasteful" government (Tolchin 1996) which spills over into votes in favor of changing institutional arrangements. Correlations between measures of these sentiments and support for reform may simply reflect an "across the board" distaste for the status quo, rather than instrumental voting with regard to particular institutions. Likewise, economic uncertainty might cause some voters to lash out at institutions, regardless of the institution's relationship to economic conditions.

Proposition 198, then, presented voters with a chance to introduce specific institutional reforms. Thus, it provides an example of institutional reform which we may use to examine some of these more general arguments concerning voter responses to political reform efforts.

PROPOSITION 198:
CHANGING THE RULES FOR PRIMARY ELECTIONS

Relative to some of the other items on the March 1996 ballot, Proposition 198 was a low-visibility issue with very little surrounding campaign. For the average voter, information about the blanket primary proposal would have been buried under about $80 million in commercials for several tort reform initiatives,[4] and by media coverage of the Republican presidential primary. Of the $1 million spent on Prop 198, $950,000 was spent by the yes side, most of which went to covering the costs of acquiring signatures.

This does not mean that most voters lacked information that would allow for low-level instrumental voting. California's publicly provided ballot pamphlet includes a series of explicit arguments about who would win and who would lose under each proposed measure, and lists the names of elites who support and oppose the measures. Over half of California's voters use information from these pamphlets, relying upon them more than any other source of information when voting on ballot measures (Bowler and Donovan 1998, 57). This information is particularly useful when arguments allow voters to identify proponents and opponents of a measure, since elite cues provide valuable information for reasoning about the consequences of a proposal (Lupia 1994; Bowler and Donovan 1998). One study found that 94 percent of voters who use the pamphlets look to arguments for and against the measure when making their decisions (Dubois, Feeney, and Constantini 1991). With these minimal bits of information, many voters can make decisions based on the consequences of proposed initiatives (Bowler and Donovan 1998, 37–39).

In the case of Proposition 198, the ballot arguments targeted specific groups of voters who would win and lose from the proposed reform. Arguments in favor were signed by a former chair of the state's political watchdog agency (the Fair Political Practices Commission), a U.C. Berkeley professor (former IGS Director Eugene Lee), and two well-regarded state senators, Bay Area Republican Becky Morgan and San Diego Independent Lucy Killea. Proponents of the reform submitted arguments that contained specific information about consequences, stressing the inherent virtue of broadening the choices available to voters: "California's closed primary election system limits voters' choices to candidates within their own party, and excludes 1.5 million independent voters from voting in primary elections at all. It favors the election of party hard-liners, contributes to legislative gridlock, and stacks the deck against more moderate problem-solvers" (California Secretary of State 1996).

Proponents also sought to portray the initiative as an attempt to take power from Democratic and Republican party leaders. Their theme of "party hard-liners" was repeated at several points: for example, "Hard-liners in both major political parties oppose the Open Primary because it will weaken their power and the power of special-interest groups which support them. . . . The party chairmen don't want you to have a choice unless it matches theirs. If all voters are allowed to participate, they fear they will lose their power, as will the hard-liners and special-interest groups who support them" (California Secretary of State 1996).

To some extent, these arguments constitute a call for greater freedom for independents and moderates to split their tickets and cast votes across party lines. Since specific proponents named in the ballot pamphlet were identifiably nonpartisan (at least symbolically) and independent, their arguments for open primaries could be credible with such voters. Lacking institutional constraints, independents, weak partisans, and minor-party voters may be more likely than partisans to divide their choices across party lines. Studies from Australia (Bowler and Denemark 1993), Germany (Jesse 1988), New Zealand (Banducci et al. 1998) and the United States (Campbell et al. 1960; Stanley and Niemi 1991) demonstrate that strong partisans are more immune to ticket splitting, and by extension, would be less supportive of institutional changes that facilitate this in primaries.

Similarly, California's minor-party identifiers, who comprise about 5 percent of registered voters, may also evaluate the initiative in a positive light. The argument that closed primaries limit participation might appeal to registered minor-party voters who realize the constraint of voting only for their own party's candidates in all races. In general elections California's minor-party voters may opt for a minor-party candidate in some races, and major-party candidates in others.[5] Blanket primaries would allow them to engage in similar ticket splitting in primary contests and so should lead them to favor the reform.[6] We test hypotheses about how the blanket primary appealed to independents, weak partisans, and minor-party voters below.

Proponent arguments also suggested that closed primaries produced candidates that many voters were dissatisfied with and suggested that reform would produce more satisfactory candidates as in the following example: "Party registration in most California legislative districts heavily favors one party or the other. In these so-called 'safe' districts, the winner of the majority party's primary election is virtually guaranteed victory in the general election, regardless of how extreme the candidate's views. In these districts, voters in the minority party have no real voice in the selection of their representative" (California Secretary of State 1996).

One implication of this argument is that voters who did not like the candidates produced by a closed primary system would support the opportunity to vote for candidates from other parties in the future. This hypothesis can be evaluated by testing whether partisans who disliked their own party's candidates in a closed nomination process favored change to an open primary. In the context of the March 1996 elections, we expect this group to include Republicans dissatisfied with their party's presidential candidates (Buchanan and Dole). Since the Democratic primary was not contested, it is not possible to test the effects of Democratic voter dissatisfaction with the nomination choices within their party.

Intentionally or not, opponents of Proposition 198 clearly signaled their partisan credentials with the elites selected to sign their ballot arguments. These included the state chairmen of the Democratic and Republican parties, and prominent partisan figures, including conservative Republican commentator Bruce Hershensohn and former Democratic candidate for Governor John Van de Kamp. The name of former Democratic Assembly boss Jesse "Big Daddy" Unruh was even linked to one of the opponents (as director of the Unruh Institute at USC).

Opponents largely portrayed the blanket primary as a bad thing in and of itself, likening the reform to "letting UCLA's football team choose USC's head coach!" (California Secretary of State 1996). Compared to proponents' claims, arguments against the initiative were less clear about the likely consequences of the proposal, beyond claiming (as did the proponents) that "special interests" were somehow involved. Consider the following claims:

> Proposition 198 is an invitation to political mischief. This would be a dream come true for the politicians, political consultants and special interests who will use specialized targeting to manipulate the political system to the benefit of their hand-picked candidates.
>
> WHO SUPPORTS PROPOSITION 198?
> Proposition 198 is a cynical attempt by a few ambitious politicians who cannot win the support of their own political party. So now they want to change the rules to serve their own self-interest. (California Secretary of State 1996)

Both proponents and opponents claimed that special interests would somehow benefit: For proponents, special interests would benefit by the defeat of Prop 198, while opponents argued that special interests would gain if it passed. One difference was that proponents identified the "special interests" as party leaders and those who backed the political parties. All of this should have sent signals to strong partisans that the initiative would be bad for their party's interests. For others, the arguments and elites listed both for and against the measure may have signaled that the initiative was supported by partisans whom they opposed. In the analysis below, we examine evidence about how voters responded to these signals.

HYPOTHESES AND DATA

Our hypotheses may be grouped into two broad categories corresponding to the two arguments about voter motivation advanced above. One group of hypotheses tests the degree of self-interest—and hence understanding of institutional effects—that underpins vote choice. The other group tests whether opinion toward institutions is driven not so much by self-interest as by general affect and disaffection.

If voters are acting out of self-interest, we expect those with strong partisan attachments to dislike the idea of reform which would allow voters with weak or even rival party attachments to help decide who their nominees should be. We also expect political activists—those who make contributions to parties and attend political functions—to be resistant to a reform that opens their party's nomination process up to rank-and-file voters from any party.

Conversely, we expect supporters of minor parties and voters who identify themselves as independents to be supportive of a measure which gives them a wider choice in primary elections. Furthermore, some major-party supporters may remain dissatisfied with their party's nominees and so may favor a reform which widens the choices open to them. Indeed, the individuals who proposed the reform in the first place fall into this latter category.

We have mixed expectations, however, concerning the impact of the proposal upon minority groups. On the one hand we might expect minorities to support the proposal. Opening up the nomination process would give candidates more incentive to cultivate ethnic voting blocs—especially in attempts to encourage voting across party lines and along ethnic lines. On the other hand, we might expect minorities to regard political parties as appropriate vehicles for bringing minority candidates into the political system and, hence, to be wary of attempts to change that process.

These instrumental motivations are readily operationalized with standard survey responses. It is much more difficult, however, to find measures which tap into non-self-interested motivations. Nevertheless, some survey questions allow us to test how some general and less narrowly self-interested forms of voter discontent might also affect support for the Proposition 198 reform. General disaffection from the political parties may generate support for reform proposals. So, too, may economic hardship. Voters who are generally fed up—either with the political establishment or with their current lot in life—may vote for reform proposals not necessarily out of any deep understanding of the reform proposal itself, but simply out of frustration with the status quo.

Age effects, too, may represent something of a less-than-instrumental response to institutional change, since older voters may simply be more resistant to change of any kind.[7] Education is also included in our models, since we expect that voters with different cognitive abilities reason differently about politics (Sniderman, Brody, and Tetlock 1991). Voters with more education may well be more supportive of reforms that increase choices in elections, since they will have an easier time processing information in a more demanding decision setting like a blanket primary.[8]

If the variables in this second group (age, economic hard times, and general disaffection from the parties) are the only significant predictors of vote choice, this would suggest a more affect-driven, and consequently less rational, understanding of institutions by voters. On the other hand, if our measures of self-interest are the only significant predictors, then the evidence would tend to support the view that citizens reason instrumentally about reforming institutions.

Our tests are conducted with data from a *Los Angeles Times* poll (*Los*

Angeles Times 1996). The *Times* poll included attitudinal questions that allow us to develop refined tests of the basis of support for the blanket primary.

RESULTS

Table 3.3 presents results from a basic model of partisan-based instrumental voting on the open primary proposal. Two additional models build on the basic model by accounting for attitudes toward the parties in general (using a question that measures whether a respondent thinks neither party has good ideas), and for concerns about personal economic well-being (specifically, the respondents' concerns over being laid off). The full models also include a measure of political activism. Each model includes several dummy variables reflecting party status and / or strength of attachments to party, as well as controls that account for potential attachments to status quo institutions (age and race). Republicans who were dissatisfied with their choices in the GOP presidential primary are represented by a separate dummy term (see the appendix for coding details).

As expected, strong partisans of both major parties opposed the initiative. Voters registered with minor parties were also significantly more likely to support the proposal, as were Republicans dissatisfied with the range of choices provided to them in their own presidential primary. The effects of strong party status, for both Democrats and Republicans, and for Republican voters who were unimpressed by their party's nominees, were consistent in each estimation. Overall, these results demonstrate that voters who would probably be least likely to make use of an open primary (by crossing party lines) were less supportive of Prop 198. In each estimation, Anglo voters were not any more supportive of the measure than minority voters, other factors held constant. Younger voters, whom we assumed to be less attached to established institutions, were found to be more supportive of the change to blanket primaries.

More interesting are independent voters, who probably had the most to gain under an open primary in terms of increased access to election decisions. Contrary to the instrumental voting thesis, they were not especially supportive of the measure relative to everyone else. Since this ran so counter to our expectations, we estimated a model that used an interactive term to distinguish between the "thoughtful independent" as opposed to the "disinterested independent." The third model in table 3.3 builds on the basic model by including a term representing the interaction between independence and interest in order to test if the most politically interested independents are more supportive of the open primaries. As with the other specifications, the effect of independent identification is insignificant.

Even when a wide range of variables are included in the second and

TABLE 3.3 Logit Models of Decision to Support Proposition 198:
Attitudes, Views on Parties' Issue Positions, and
Thoughtful Independents

	Base Model	Plus General Attitudes	Plus "Thoughtful Independents"
Constant	0.38	0.16	0.19
	(0.33)	(0.35)	(0.35)
Anglo	0.22	0.23	0.23
	(0.16)	(0.16)	(0.16)
Minor-party registered	0.35*	0.33*	0.34*
	(0.19)	(0.19)	(0.20)
Education	0.02	0.04	0.04
	(0.03)	(0.03)	(0.03)
Age	−0.009**	−0.009**	−0.009**
	(0.003)	(0.003)	(0.004)
Strong Democrat	−0.60**	−0.63**	−0.62**
	(0.17)	(0.18)	(0.18)
Strong Republican	−0.72**	−0.70**	−0.69**
	(0.17)	(0.17)	(0.17)
Republican dissatisfied with GOP nominees	0.40**	0.41**	0.40**
	(0.18)	(0.18)	(0.18)
Independent	−0.12	−0.12	−0.24
	(0.18)	(0.19)	(0.23)
Independent*Interest			0.30
			(0.36)
Interest in politics			−0.07
			(0.14)
Activist		−0.22*	−0.22*
		(0.13)	(0.14)
Neither major party has best ideas		−0.09	−0.09
		(0.22)	(0.22)
Fear of layoff		0.08*	0.08*
		(0.04)	(0.04)
N	1,039	1,039	1,039
Percentage correct	59	59	59
−2LL Model	1,391	1,385	1,384
Improvement (X^2)	48**	54**	55**

SOURCE: "California Pre-Primary Survey," *Los Angeles Times* Poll 372 (March 1996).
NOTE: Sample is limited to registered voters.
*Significant at $p < .05$
**Significant at $p < .01$

third models estimated in table 3.3, the instrumental-partisan effects evident in the basic model remain significant. In each specification, strong
partisans remain less supportive than other voters, and minor-party voters
remain more supportive. The same is true with Republicans dissatisfied with
their presidential choices as provided by status quo institutions. Political
activists, whom we expect to be most closely linked with the interests of
party leaders, were less supportive than nonactivists. The results in table
3.3, however, also demonstrate that support for Proposition 198 extended
beyond instrumental voting. Most notably, voters who feared layoffs were
more supportive of the open primary reform than other voters.[9] General
discontent with parties (the attitude that no party has good ideas) is not
associated with support.

Table 3.4 reports the effects of some key variables on the probability
that a respondent would vote yes on Prop 198. When all variables from the
full logit model (column 3) in table 3.3 are held at their mean values, a
voter would have a .51 baseline probability of voting yes on Prop 198. With
these things held constant, respondents who most feared layoffs had a .59
probability of voting yes, while those fearing layoffs the least had only a .47
probability of voting yes.

The significant impact of personal economic uncertainty does raise the
possibility that some voters, generally fed up with "something," would vote
for any proposed reform that would change the institutional status quo,
regardless of the real relationship between the reform and the voter's dis-
enchantment. Even though voters who feared layoffs were more likely to
support Prop 198, there is no clear relationship between rules about primaries and an individuals' job prospects.

Having said that, we move on to note indications that many voters were
behaving in a manner consistent with thoughtfulness and an understanding
of the consequences of changing institutions. This is most obvious in the
opposition of strong partisans to the change. As shown in table 3.4, coefficients from table 3.3 predict that strongly identifying Democrats had only
a .36 probability of voting yes on Prop 198, which is substantially lower
than the .51 baseline probability of support. Republicans present a slightly
more complex picture in that their regard for their party's nominee had a
significant impact on their vote on the measure. Republicans satisfied with
their nominee had only a .38 probability of supporting the measure, while
those who were dissatisfied had a .48 probability of voting yes. Clearly, party
stalwarts really did not like this proposal to change the primary system.
Although this pattern of findings is in line with the self-interest thesis, we
should note that, overall, our results illustrate that a mix of motivations
underlay the desire to support Proposition 198.

We have proposed elsewhere (Bowler and Donovan 1998, 62–64) that
different types of voters reason differently about ballot measures, with a

TABLE 3.4   Predicted Probabilities of Voting Yes on
Proposition 198 (from Full Model Estimated
in Column 3 of Table 3.3)

All respondents	
Baseline probability[a]	.51
Minor-party registration	.63
Strong Democratic identification	.39
Activist	.48
Strong Democratic activist	.36
Strong GOP dissatisfied with GOP candidates	.48
Strong GOP satisfied with GOP candidates	.38
Fearing layoffs	.59
Not fearing layoffs	.47

NOTE: Probabilities of voting yes given highest score on relevant independent variable when all other variables set at their mode or mean value.

[a]Probability of a yes vote with all variables in table 3.3, column 3, set at mode or mean values.

critical distinguishing factor being the voter's cognitive resources. Voters with greater resources—higher levels of education—are able to make use of a more sophisticated set of cues, heuristics, and ideology. We expect that the better educated are thus more likely to use party and elite cues (and ballot pamphlet arguments) to reason about the consequences involved in changing political institutions. If this is the case, the better educated should be more likely to demonstrate patterns of support for Proposition 198 that are consistent with assumptions about partisan-instrumental voting.

Conversely, if less-educated voters have fewer of the cognitive resources which facilitate processing elite cues and ballot pamphlet information into conclusions about the open primary, support for Prop 198 among those voters could be structured less by partisan-instrumental reasoning and more by factors requiring less detailed information about the specific policy choice. Narrow economic self-interest (Bowler and Donovan 1998, 103), general economic concerns, and general concerns about the state's economy (Bowler and Donovan 1998, 74) have all been found to play a larger role among less-educated voters in decisions about initiatives.

Following this logic, in table 3.5 we report reestimations of the second model from table 3.3 (which includes partisan variables and measures of general dissatisfaction), with the sample divided into two sets of voters: the highly educated and those not highly educated. It is important to note that the direction of the effects of education displayed in table 3.3 might reflect that well-educated voters were simply more supportive of Prop 198. This effect could hold at the same time that education also caused differences

TABLE 3.5   Logit Model of Decision to Support Proposition 198
(Sample Divided by Level of Education)

	Not Highly Educated	Highly Educated
Constant	−0.20	1.52**
	(0.32)	(0.42)
Anglo	0.40**	−0.03
	(0.20)	(0.27)
Minor-party registered	0.59**	−0.04
	(0.26)	(0.31)
Age	−0.004	−0.02**
	(0.004)	(0.006)
Strong Democrat	−0.38*	−1.04**
	(0.23)	(0.29)
Strong Republican	−0.67**	−0.69**
	(0.24)	(0.26)
Republican dissatisfied with GOP nominees	0.54**	0.23
	(0.24)	(0.28)
Independent	−0.14	−0.10
	(0.24)	(0.30)
Neither major party has best ideas	−0.12	−0.03
	(0.30)	(0.34)
Fear of layoff	0.12**	0.03
	(0.05)	(0.07)
Activist	−0.27	−0.15
	(0.18)	(0.20)
N	606	435
Percentage correct	58	63
−2LL Model	805	569
Improvement (X^2)	34**	31*

SOURCE: "California Pre-Primary Survey," *Los Angeles Times* Poll 372 (March 1996).
NOTE: Sample is limited to registered voters.
*Significant at $p < .05$
**Significant at $p < .01$

in reasoning between the less-educated and the more-educated subgroups. These effects are clarified in table 3.6. The fact that educated voters may have been more supportive of Prop 198, other things held equal, is reflected in the baseline level of support for the less educated of .50, compared to .55 among the more educated.

Table 3.5 also demonstrates variation in support within each education group that is consistent with the idea that variation in cognitive resources (education) causes citizens to reason differently about ballot initiatives. Well-educated voters reflect instrumental reasoning, while less-educated

TABLE 3.6   Predicted Probabilities of
Voting Yes on Proposition 198
(from Models Estimated in Table 3.5)

Voters with low education levels	Probability
Baseline probability[a]	.50
Strong Democrat	.42
Strong Republican satisfied with GOP candidates	.35
Strong GOP dissatisfied with GOP candidates	.48
Fearing layoffs	.61
Not fearing layoffs	.43
Voters with high education levels	*Probability*
Baseline probability[a]	.55
Strong Democrat	.36
Strong Republican	.45
Strong GOP dissatisfied with GOP candidates	.50
Fearing layoffs	Not significant

NOTE: Probabilities of voting yes given highest score on relevant independent variable when all other variables set at their mode or mean value.
[a]Probability of a yes vote with all variables in table 3.5 set at mode or mean values.

voters cast ballots for instrumental and noninstrumental reasons. Table 3.5 also demonstrates that younger, well-educated voters were particularly supportive of the initiative, but that young voters in the other education group were not. This finding is consistent with Dalton's (1984, 265) suggestion that younger, well-educated voters have greater "cognitive mobilization," which is associated with making "their own political decisions" independently of external party cues.

Strong partisans in the more-educated group, for example, were more likely to decide on the initiative on the basis of partisan-based reasoning than were strong partisans in the less-educated group. The effect of strong party identification is substantially larger for Democrats among the better educated. This is illustrated in the predicted probabilities reported in table 3.6. Among the well educated, the probability of a strong Democrat voting yes was only .36, far lower than the .55 baseline probability of support among other well-educated voters. The effect is significant among the less educated, yet much smaller. In this group, strong Democrats had a .42 probability of supporting Prop 198, compared to the .50 baseline for all less-educated voters. Conversely, our indicator of generalized dissatisfaction that has no specific grounding in election rules—a fear of layoffs—structured support only among the less educated. Less-educated voters fearing layoffs had a .61 probability of supporting Prop 198, compared to a .43 probability for other less-educated voters who did not fear layoffs.

DISCUSSION

In California and other direct democracy states, voters have opportunities to constantly mold and shape their institutions. The initiative device ensures that institutional rules governing political processes are anything but sticky and permanent. Since institutional reform initiatives allow change in the very manner in which politics can be conducted, they have consequences well beyond their adoption. This chapter demonstrates that voting on the blanket primary initiative appears to have been structured by a significant component of instrumental reasoning about the consequences of changing the rules regarding voting in primary elections. Those whom we expect to be least likely to take advantage of a more open process, and thus to be motivated to oppose changing the rules, were in fact more opposed to Prop 198.

It is, of course, difficult to generalize about popular motives for changing institutions from the single case of the blanket primary initiative. We cannot say with certainty that the constituency approving the blanket primary is the same as that approving other institutional reforms such as term limits, campaign finance regulations, or new electoral systems. Nevertheless, our main findings are consistent with studies of mass support for such governance proposals. Term-limit initiatives that were largely opposed by major-party elites and partisans of the majority party were supported by independents, weak identifiers, and minority partisans (Donovan and Snipp 1994; Bowler and Donovan 1998). Referendums proposing change from plurality elections to proportional representation, while opposed by governing-party elites and their strong identifiers, have also been passed with support from weak partisans and minor-party voters (Banducci and Karp 1999). If a common thread exists in these patterns, it is that proposals striking at the power of established parties receive support from citizens who might be (or perceive themselves to be) disadvantaged by rules that give power to such parties.

We began our chapter with a discussion of normative issues surrounding institutional change. Although a standard theme in this literature emphasizes longevity as a source of legitimacy, results from this and other studies of popular support for institutional change might cause us to reconsider this assumption if change can be said to bring new legitimacy to the political process. Institutions are practices that stand the tests of time and endure, yet endurance can threaten legitimacy if practices come to be at odds with the experiences and preferences of a majority of citizens. In an era when parties have diminishing contact with citizens and when (major) parties claim a declining share of registration and popular votes, it is not surprising that the legitimacy of rules that maintain "strong" parties are occasionally challenged. As an example, consider the likelihood of the contemporary public accepting as legitimate those "traditional" rules used to nominate presidential candidates prior to the McGovern-Fraiser reforms enacted after 1968. When such institutionalized practices grow inconsistent with the preferences of a majority of voters, direct participation in reforming institutions might be a way to maintain some legitimacy for the process.

APPENDIX: CODING OF THE VARIABLES FOR TABLES 3.3–3.6

Anglo	1 = Anglo; 0 = not
Minor-party registered	1 = registered voter of minor party (including those who decline to state); 0 = not
Education	9-point scale, low to high
Age	in years
Strong Democrat	1 = Strong Democratic identifier; 0 = not
Strong Republican	1 = Strong Republican identifier; 0 = not
Republican dissatisfied with GOP nominees	Question: "Are you planning to vote for your candidate mostly because you like him and his policies, or mostly because he is the best of a bad lot, or mostly because you feel like sending a protest message?" Coding: 1 = if a Republican and answer was "best of a bad lot" or "a protest message"; 0 = other response or not a Republican
Independent	1 = self-identified independent; 0 = not
Activist	1 = respondent gave money to a political campaign, volunteered, or attended political meeting; 0 = did not do so
Neither major party has best ideas	Summary value = sum of "Neither" responses to the following question: "Regardless of which candidate for President you happen to prefer right now, which candidate, if any, do you think has the best ideas for handling the following issues: Bill Clinton or Bob Dole?" The seven issues were taxes, economic problems, affirmative action, balancing the budget, illegal immigrants, environmental issues, and foreign affairs.
Fear of layoff	Question: "Thinking about the next twelve months, how likely do you think it is that you or someone in your household will lose a job or be laid off—very likely, fairly likely, fairly unlikely, or very unlikely?"

NOTES

1. Subject matter categorization is always fraught with difficulties and involves a certain amount of double counting. Since our concern here is to arrive at some general overview of the number of institutional reform proposals, we accept that the Secretary of State categorizations will provide a rough but reasonable estimate for our current purposes.

2. Recent campaign finance reform measures such as Prop 208 and Prop 212 were counted under "Campaign Reform."

3. This logic is not to be confused with the assumption that alienation is reflected in "negative voting," or voting no on elite proposals.

4. The Secretary of State cannot determine the amount spent on the three March tort initiatives (200, 201, 202) since all spending was done by committees contesting multiple initiatives placed on the March and November ballots. Over $83 million was spent by multiple proposition committees that reported supporting or opposing 200, 201, 202 and other November 1996 initiatives. The committees must report contributions but are not required to report how funds were allocated to specific initiative contests.

5. Minor-party adherents are especially loyal to "their" candidates in the relatively less important races like Secretary of State. They are more likely to support major party candidates in the more prominent gubernatorial and senate races (Donovan, Bowler, and Terrio 1999).

6. For example, a loyal Green could support most Green Party candidates while still having the ability to support a far more credible leftist or environmental Democratic candidate for the Senate or for Governor in an open primary.

7. Alternatively, younger voters may simply be more receptive to any change, regardless of content.

8. It has been shown, for example, that the well educated are more supportive of proportional representation (Banducci and Karp 1999) and more likely to engage in strategic voting in complex settings like Mixed Member Proportional election systems (Banducci et al. 1998).

9. Alternative specifications that looked at the effect of having a general concern that the state's situation was poor (sociotropic evaluations) had no significant impact on support.

REFERENCES

Abramson, Paul. 1979. "Developing Party Identification: A Further Examination of Life-Cycle, Generational, and Period Effects." *American Journal of Political Science* 76: 502–21.

Banducci, Susan; Todd Donovan; and Jeffrey Karp. 1999. "Proportional Representation and Attitudes about Politics: Results from New Zealand." *Electoral Studies* 18, no. 4: 533–55.

Banducci, Susan, and Jeffrey Karp. 1999. "Perceptions of Fairness and Support for Proportional Representation." *Political Behavior* 21, no. 3: 217–38.

Banducci, Susan; Jeffrey Karp; Jack Vowels; and Todd Donovan. 1998. "Strategic

Voting in the 1996 New Zealand Election: Implications for a Mixed System." Paper presented at the American Political Science Association meeting, Boston, MA.

Bobo, Lawrence, and Frank Gilliam. 1990. "Race, Sociopolitical Participation, and Black Empowerment." *American Political Science Review* 84 : 377–97.

Bowler, Shaun, and David Denemark. 1993. "Split Ticket Voting in Australia: Dealignment and Inconsistent Votes Reconsidered." *Australian Journal of Political Science* 28: 19–37.

Bowler, Shaun, and Todd Donovan. 1998. *Demanding Choices: Opinion, Voting, and Direct Democracy.* Ann Arbor: University of Michigan Press.

Bowler, Shaun; Todd Donovan; Max Neiman; and Johnny Peel. 1999. "Elite Attitudes about Direct Democracy." Paper presented at the Western Political Science Association meeting, Seattle, WA.

Bridges, Amy. 1997. *Morning Glories: Municipal Reform in the Southwest.* Princeton, NJ: Princeton University Press.

"California Pre-Primary Survey." 1996. *Los Angeles Times* Poll 372 (March).

California Secretary of State. 1996. *Official Ballot Pamphlet: Primary Election.* Sacramento.

———. 1998. *A History of the California Initiative Process.* Sacramento.

Campbell, Angus; Philip Converse; Warren Miller; and Donald Stokes. 1960. *The American Voter.* Chicago: University of Chicago Press.

Citrin, Jack; Beth Reingold; and Evelyn Walters. 1990. "The 'Official English' Movement and the Symbolic Politics of Language in the United States." *Western Political Quarterly* 43: 553–60.

Clingermayer, James, and B. Dan Wood. 1995. "Disentangling Patterns of State Indebtedness." *American Political Science Review* 89: 108–20.

Dalton, Russell. 1984. "Cognitive Mobilization and Partisan Dealignment in Advanced Industrial Democracies." *Journal of Politics* 46: 264–84.

Donovan, Todd, and Shaun Bowler. 1997. "Direct Democracy and Minority Rights: Opinions on Anti-Gay and Lesbian Ballot Initiatives." In S. Witt and S. McCorkle, eds., *Anti-Gay Rights: Assessing Voter Initiatives.* Westport, CT: Praeger.

———. 1998. "Responsive or Responsible Government?" In S. Bowler, T. Donovan, and C. Tolbert, eds., *Citizens as Legislators: Direct Democracy in the American States.* Columbus: Ohio State University Press.

Donovan, Todd; Shaun Bowler; and Tammy Terrio. 2000. "Support for Third Parties in California." *American Politics Quarterly* 28, no. 1 (October): 50–71.

Donovan, Todd, and Joseph Snipp. 1994. "Support for Legislative Term Limits in California: Group Representation, Partisanship, and Campaign Information." *Journal of Politics* 56: 492–501.

Donovan, Todd; Tammy Terrio; and Shaun Bowler. 1997. "Loyal Attachments and Protest Voting for Third Parties in State Elections." Paper presented at the Western Political Science Association meeting, Tucson, AZ.

Dubois, P.; Floyd Feeney; and E. Constantini. 1991. *The California Ballot Pamphlet: A Survey of Voters.* Report prepared for the Secretary of State of California. Sacramento.

Gerber, E.; A. Lupia; M. McCubbins; and D. R. Kiewiet. 2000. *Stealing the Initiative.* Upper Saddle River, NJ: Prentice Hall.

Gibson, James, and Gregory Caldeira. 1998. "Changes in the Legitimacy of the European Court of Justice: A Post-Maastricht Analysis." *British Journal of Political Science* 28: 63–91.

Hensler, D., and C. Hensler. 1979. *Evaluating Nuclear Power: Voter Choice on the California Nuclear Initiative.* Santa Monica, CA: Rand Corp.

Hibbing, John, and Elizabeth Theiss-Morse. 1995. *Congress as Public Enemy.* Cambridge: Cambridge University Press.

———. 1998. "Too Much of a Good Thing: More Representative Is Not Necessarily Better." *PS: Political Science and Politics* 31: 28–31.

Jesse, Eckhard. 1988. "Split-Voting in the Federal Republic of Germany: An Analysis of the Federal Elections from 1953 to1987." *Electoral Studies* 7: 109–24.

Karp, Jeffrey. 1995. "Explaining Public Support for Legislative Term Limits." *Public Opinion Quarterly* 59: 373–91.

Lupia, Arthur. 1994. "Short Cuts versus Encyclopaedias: Information and Voting Behavior in California Insurance Reform Elections." *American Political Science Review* 88: 63–76.

Lupia, Arthur, and Mathew McCubbins. 1998. *The Democratic Dilemma: How Citizens Learn What They Need to Know.* New York: Cambridge University Press.

Magleby, David. 1984. *Direct Legislation: Voting on Ballot Propositions in the United States.* Baltimore, MD: Johns Hopkins University Press.

Magleby, David, and Kelly Patterson. 1996. "Political Knowledge and Term Limits: Can Angry Citizens Be Educated?" Paper presented at Western Political Science Association meeting, San Francisco, CA.

March, James, and Johan Olson. 1984. "The New Institutionalism: Organizational Factors in Political Life." *American Political Science Review* 78: 734–49.

Moncrief, Gary, and Joel Thompson. 1991. "The Term Limitation Movements: Assessing the Consequences for Female (and Other) State Legislators." Paper presented at Western Political Science Association meeting, Seattle, WA.

Mondak, Jeffrey. 1995. "Elections as Filters: Term Limits and the Composition of the U.S. House." *Political Research Quarterly* 48: 701–27.

Polsby, Nelson. 1983. *Consequences of Party Reform.* New York: Oxford University Press.

Riker, William. 1982. *Liberalism against Populism.* San Francisco CA: W. H. Freeman.

Schrag, Peter. 1998. *Paradise Lost: California's Experience, America's Future.* New York: The New Press.

Sears, David O., and Jack Citrin. 1982. *Tax Revolt: Something for Nothing in California.* Cambridge, MA: Harvard University Press.

Sniderman, Paul; Richard Brody; and Philip Tetlock. 1991. *Reasoning and Choice: Explorations in Political Psychology.* New York: Cambridge University Press.

Stanley, Harold, and Richard Niemi. 1991. "Partisanship and Group Support, 1952–1988." *American Politics Quarterly* 19: 189–210.

Tolbert, Caroline. 1998. "Changing the Rules for State Legislatures: Direct Democracy and Governance Policies." In Shaun Bowler, Todd Donovan, and C. Tolbert, eds., *Citizens as Legislators: Direct Democracy in the American States.* Columbus: Ohio State University Press.

Tolchin, Susan. 1996. *The Angry American: How Voter Rage Is Changing the Nation.* Boulder, CO: Westview Press.

Wolfinger, Raymond, and Fred Greenstein. 1968. "The Repeal of Fair Housing in California: An Analysis of Referendum Voting." *American Political Science Review* 2: 753–69.

CHAPTER FOUR

Context and Setting

The Mood of the California Electorate

Mark Baldassare

In this chapter, we analyze the mood of California voters during the 1998 primary. We use the Public Policy Institute of California (PPIC) Statewide Surveys conducted in April and May 1998, each with a total of two thousand adults, to gauge the political, social, and economic attitudes that provide the backdrop to voters' ballot choices (Baldassare 1998a, 1998b).

Voters nominated high-profile political insiders in both parties' gubernatorial races. The winners, Attorney General Dan Lungren and Lieutenant Governor Gray Davis, were conventional candidates, seemingly the kind who would have won in a closed primary. With the two-term Governor, Pete Wilson, termed out of office, voters chose the next-highest-ranking Republican and the highest-ranking Democrat in statewide elected office to run against each other in November. The losers in the governor's race, businessman Al Checchi and U.S. Representative Jane Harman, were the wealthy political outsiders who promised to shake up the Sacramento political establishment. In the U.S. Senate primary, the outcome was similarly predictable. Republican millionaire businessman Darell Issa lost to State Treasurer Matt Fong. The next-highest-ranking Republican in state office would face Democratic incumbent Barbara Boxer in the November election.

Why did voters make these choices? Why were Californians suddenly enamored with partisan favorites and the people who were holding high state offices? It was hard to imagine it was because they were feeling a great deal of trust and confidence in elected officials and state government. Instead, our survey evidence suggests that it was because the voters did not want to risk making changes. Some have argued that the rules of the blanket primary may have also helped incumbents (see chapter 7 by Salvanto and Wattenberg in this book), and they apparently did, as it was the current officeholders who succeeded. The voters' mood proved to be a powerful, reinforcing factor in maintaining the political status quo in 1998. This trend is evident for both the general public and for crossover voters before the June primary.

CONFIDENCE RETURNS

California had gone from among the worst of economic times to some of the best in the brief time span of four years. State residents were in a very upbeat mood while they were pondering their ballot choices in the spring of 1998.

When asked what direction the state was headed, about six in ten said California was moving in the right direction, and only a third said California was going in the wrong direction. Residents in the three major regions accounting for most of the state's voters (that is, the Los Angeles metro area, the San Francisco Bay area and the Central Valley) all had a positive outlook. Latinos, whites, and other racial and ethnic groups were all equally positive. Four years earlier, opinions were almost the reverse of what we found in the spring of 1998. In a California voter survey that I conducted for KCAL-TV News in the spring of 1994, only 32 percent thought the state was headed in the right direction, while 56 percent believed it was going the wrong way (see table 4.1).

The good feelings about the state of the state were rooted in very positive perceptions of the California economy. Six out of ten said the state's economy was in excellent or good shape today, while a third said it was in fair shape, and only one in ten said it was poor. Positive ratings were highest in the San Francisco Bay area at 70 percent, but about half in the Los Angeles and Central Valley regions also thought the California economy was in excellent or good shape. About half of Latinos felt the state's economy was in excellent or good shape, compared with six in ten whites and other races. Most important, few in any region or demographic group thought the economy was in trouble.

Ratings of the highly coveted "quality of life" in the state had also turned positive. When asked to think about the quality of life in California, seven in ten residents said the quality of life in California was going either very well or somewhat well, while only three in ten thought that things were going somewhat badly or very badly. There were no differences in ratings of the quality of life across the major regions or racial and ethnic groups. This was a remarkable change from the public's position only four years earlier. At that time, 37 percent of KCAL-TV News survey respondents thought that things were going well, while 63 percent thought they were going badly.

The biggest economic threat on the state's horizon in 1998 was the Asian

TABLE 4.1   State Conditions

	All	Crossover Voters
"Is California going in the right or wrong direction?"		
Right direction	55%	58%
Wrong direction	36	35
Don't know	9	7
"The economy in California today is . . ."		
Excellent	11%	13%
Good	46	48
Fair	33	33
Poor	10	6
"The quality of life in California today is going . . ."		
Very well	13%	15%
Somewhat well	57	62
Somewhat badly	21	20
Very badly	9	3

SOURCE: Baldassare 1998a and 1998b.
NOTE: Crossover voters are the Republicans who say they will vote for a Democrat in the gubernatorial primary.

financial crisis. While the economy was looking good to most Californians, many were concerned about the possibly contagious effects of a meltdown in the Asian economies. Fifty percent said that the Asian crisis would hurt the California economy in the next year or so, while 31 percent said it would not, and 19 percent were unsure (Baldassare 1998a). Of the 50 percent who believed the Asian crisis would have a negative effect, however, only 14 percent expected it to hurt the California economy "a great deal." Thus the economic impacts of this threat were seen as limited.

Californians were generally upbeat about their own finances, and they were much more optimistic about improving their economic fortunes than they had been four years earlier. Almost 40 percent said they were better off financially now than they were in 1997, while half said their financial conditions were the same, and only 12 percent said their financial state had become worse. More than 40 percent expected to be better off financially a year from now, half expected their conditions to be the same, and only one in sixteen expected to be worse off in 1999. Four years earlier, only 20 percent said they were better off than last year, and only one-third expected to be better off in the next year. In the 1998 survey, 87 percent described their current standard of living as "comfortable" or "more than comfortable." A similar number described themselves as having "just enough" or "more than enough" of a household income to meet their bills and financial obligations. Moreover, most thought there was a good chance that the period of economic stability would continue for some time. Only one in seven had deep concerns about being affected by unemployment.

The same attitudinal trends were evident among crossover voters, that is, Republicans who said they would vote for a candidate in the competitive Democratic gubernatorial primary.[1] Most crossover voters said that California was going in the right direction (58 percent), that the California economy was in excellent or good shape (61 percent), and that the quality of life was going very well or somewhat well (77 percent). Forty percent said their own finances were improving and would get better in the next year, while few had serious concerns about job loss.

The "angry voter" in the 1994 election had been replaced by the "status quo voter" in the 1998 election. This mood swing was a major factor in determining voter choices, as it took the appeal out of calls for economic change and political reform. Candidates with a track record became more attractive to voters, while those who were espousing a shift in government were viewed as a potential threat to the economic good times.

ISSUES CHANGE

Californians were focused on different policy issues now that the economy had improved. Education had become one of the biggest concerns of the public. While the fear of crime continued to be a worry, immigration was no longer a pressing issue.

In an open-ended question, we asked residents to name the most serious problem facing California today. Crime and education topped the list of public policy concerns, with these two issues named by nearly half of all respondents (see table 4.2). No other policy issue was named by more than 10 percent of respondents, including immigration and the economy. By contrast, the economy and crime (29 percent each) were named as the biggest state problems in the 1994 KCAL-TV News survey. Just before the November election in 1994, as a result of the attention generated by Proposition 187, immigration had joined these two issues as a big concern. Few had thought of education as a top issue in the turbulent social and economic times of the 1994 elections.

Follow-up questions in the 1998 PPIC Statewide Survey indicate that many Californians were concerned about the quality of public schools. Forty-six percent said that the quality of public schools was a "big problem" in the state today. One in three described the issue as somewhat of a problem. Only one in seven said it was not a problem at all. Public school parents were only slightly less likely to rate education as a big problem. Residents of Los Angeles and the San Francisco Bay area were most likely to rank

TABLE 4.2   State Policy Issues

	All	Crossover Voters
"Most serious state problem is . . ." (open-ended)		
Crime	28%	26%
Education	20	25
Immigration	7	10
Economy	5	2
"How much of a problem is . . . in California today?"		
Rated crime a "big problem"	66%	71%
Rated public schools a "big problem"	46	44

SOURCE: Baldassare 1998a and 1998b.

education as a big problem. Latinos were less likely than others to see the quality of public schools as a serious problem. Yet few in any region, political party, or racial and ethnic group said education was not a problem.

Californians' estimates of spending per pupil and student achievement were consistent with their deep concerns about the quality of public schools. Almost half were aware that their state spent less per pupil than other states on public schools. A quarter thought that California spending was on par with the national average, while only one in seven thought the state spent more on public schools than other states. A little more than half were aware that the state's student test scores were below the national average. A third thought that student performance was on par with the national average, while only one in ten believed that the state's test scores were above average.

Surprisingly, two in three Californians ranked crime as a big problem in the state, despite published reports that crime was decreasing. This is because nearly half of Californians believed that the crime rate had increased in recent years, another one in four thought it had stayed about the same, and only one in four thought it had decreased, as it actually had. Still, two in three Californians said they felt safe walking alone in their neighborhood at night, and only one in six described their area as "very unsafe." Perceptions of safety from local crime had actually improved somewhat from 1994.

While few Californians ranked immigration as the most pressing problem, people in all regions believed that the immigrant population of the state was still growing. Seventy-three percent said that the overall immigrant population had risen over the past few years, with nearly half maintaining that it had grown "a lot." Californians were deeply divided, however, about the impacts of immigration. Nearly as many said they perceived immigrants as a benefit to California because of their contributions to the economy as said they were a burden to California because of their use of public services. These perceptions differed sharply along racial and ethnic lines, with most non-Hispanic whites seeing immigrants as a burden and most Latinos and Asians seeing immigrants as a benefit.

The opinions of crossover voters on state policy issues were similar to those of the general public. Most mentioned crime and education as the top issues, while few named immigration and the economy. There was considerable awareness that the state was below average in student test scores and per pupil spending. Most thought that crime was increasing in the state, but most also felt that their own neighborhoods were safe. Eighty percent recognized that the immigrant population was increasing, though they were evenly divided in describing this trend as positive or negative.

With the economy in high gear, candidates from both parties focused their messages on improving the schools and controlling crime. The state budget was in a surplus, and thus voters were not moved as much by issues such as tax and spending cuts, limiting funds for immigrants, or efforts to create more jobs and rekindle the economy. Again, this mood seemed to favor candidates in the center of the political spectrum who represented the political status quo.

POLITICAL APATHY

Most Californians did not find the June 1998 primary to be very inspiring. In fact, elections today represent non-events in the lives of many state residents.[2] Keeping this public apathy in perspective helps us to understand the importance of the political and economic climate in determining the choices voters make in state elections.

In both of the PPIC Statewide Surveys before the primary, fewer than one in five of respondents expressed a great deal of interest in politics, about half said they had a fair amount of interest, and one in three expressed little or no interest in politics (see table 4.3). Similarly, 75 percent of Americans interviewed by the Pew Research Center in 1996 reported a great deal (25 percent) or fair amount (50 percent) of interest in politics. Consider the fact that the low political interest scores found in both of the 1998 PPIC Statewide Surveys were gathered with the backdrop of the Lewinsky-Clinton sex scandal in the spring, an event one would have expected to heighten interest in political news.

Political interest was not much higher among registered voters. About two in ten voters said they had a great deal of interest in politics, half had a fair amount of interest, and three in ten had little or no interest. Democrats and Republicans were alike in their low level of political interest, and both were more likely than independent voters to have a great deal or fair amount of interest in politics. Still, fewer than one in four voters in any of the political groups were highly interested in politics.

Only about a third of Californians said they followed what was going on

TABLE 4.3   Political Apathy

	All	Crossover Voters
"How much interest would you say you have in politics?"		
A great deal	16%	15%
Fair amount	47	50
Little or none	37	35
"Would you say you follow what's going on in government . . . ?"		
Most of the time	35%	39%
Some of the time	38	38
Only now and then	19	19
Hardly ever; never	8	4

SOURCE: Baldassare 1998a and 1998b.

in government and public affairs most of the time. Responses to this question changed very little over the course of the 1998 election year. On average, four in ten adults said they followed government and political news some of the time, while a quarter tuned in only now and then, hardly ever, or never. In the Pew Research Center Survey of June 1998, a similar 37 percent of Americans said they followed government and public affairs most of the time.

Registered voters were twice as likely as those who were not registered to say they regularly follow government and public affairs. About four in ten registered voters said they follow government issues most of the time. There were no large differences across party lines. In all, fewer than half of the state's voters said they were closely attuned to the world of government and public affairs.

What is impressive is the consistency in the responses to this question over the election cycle. The level of interest did not change very much as the primary grew closer, even among those defined as most likely to participate based on past voting. In April 1998, 9 percent of likely voters were following news stories about the upcoming elections "very closely," 43 percent said "fairly" closely, and 48 percent said "not too" or "not at all" closely. In May 1998, 13 percent were "very" closely following the election news, 48 percent said "fairly" closely, and 39 percent said "not too" or "not at all" closely.

There was also a high level of political apathy among the crossover voters. A third reported little or no interest in politics, and almost a quarter said they infrequently followed government and public affairs. About half said they followed news about the election "not too closely" or "not at all closely" in both April 1998 and May 1998.

The public's lack of interest in politics and election news has taken its toll on knowledge of even the most basic facts about state politics. In a December 1998 PPIC Statewide Survey, I asked an open-ended question, "California voters elected a new Governor on November 3. Could you give me the name of the new Governor of the State of California?" Fifty-three percent named Governor-elect Gray Davis, 5 percent gave other names and 42 percent said they were not sure about the name of the new Governor.

TELEVISION RULES

How does a mostly disinterested public learn about upcoming elections? Largely from television, which Californians ranked as their top source of information in response to the question "Where do you get most of your information about what's going on in politics today?" (see table 4.4). When we asked this survey question in both April and May 1998, 41 percent named television as the source of most of their political information, and 34 percent named newspapers. The remaining one in four residents said they got most of their political news from the radio (10 percent), talking to people (7 percent), magazines and the Internet (3 percent each), and other sources (2 percent). Even among registered voters, television had a slim lead over newspapers as the major source of political information. There were no differences in the sources of political information across party lines. Of those not registered to vote, more than half named television as their major source of political information, while only one in four named newspapers.

These results were similar for the crossover voters. Thirty-nine percent relied mostly on television, and 36 percent depended mostly on newspapers for political news. More than eight in ten said they recalled the television commercials for the gubernatorial candidates. When asked whose ads they had seen the most, most of those who had seen ads mentioned the Checchi ads.

There is little doubt that Californians are hooked on television news. State residents were much more likely to say they watched television news every day than to say they read a daily newspaper (59 percent to 45 percent). Even the registered voters were more likely to watch local television news every day than to read a daily newspaper, by a wide margin. Californians are less likely than adults nationwide to be reading a newspaper every day (45 percent to 51 percent), and they are also slightly less likely to watch local television news on a daily basis (62 percent to 59 percent), as reported elsewhere (Baldassare 2000). Overall, it appears that relatively few Californians make an active effort to gather election news and political information.

In addition to television news, Californians gathered much of their in-

TABLE 4.4   Sources of Political Information

	All	Crossover Voters
"Where do you get most of your information about what's going on in politics today?"		
Television	41%	39%
Newspapers	34	36
Radio	10	12
Talking to people	7	6
Magazines	3	3
Internet, online services	3	3
Other	2	1

SOURCE: Baldassare 1998a and 1998b.

formation about the candidates in the 1998 primary by watching paid television commercials. A record total of almost $70 million was spent in the gubernatorial race, with most of the money going to television commercials. Al Checchi spent $39 million; millionaire Rep. Jane Harman spent $16 million; Gray Davis spent $8 million; and Dan Lungren spent over $6 million (Gissinger 1998). It is not surprising, then, that many Californians could recall their paid advertisements before the June primary. Eight in ten likely voters recalled the television advertisements by the candidates for Governor in both April and May 1998, with more than half saying they recalled Al Checchi's commercials the most. Two in ten remembered the television advertisements in the U.S. Senate race, with most saying they recalled primarily the commercials by Darrell Issa. These results were similar for the crossover voters. More than eight in ten recalled the television commercials for the gubernatorial candidates, with most mentioning Al Checchi's advertisements.

In the end, the candidates who spent more money for their campaigns lost the major state races. The recall of political advertising is a testament to the power of television in reaching a broad audience with a political message. But the fact is that the record-setting spending on television commercials proved insufficient to propel the self-financed outsider candidates to victory.

DEEP DISTRUST

How did Californians regard their government and elected officials when they went to the polls in the spring of 1998? The survey evidence here is very consistent. Despite their rosier outlooks on the state economy and their personal finances, many continued to feel disillusioned with govern-

TABLE 4.5   Political Distrust

	All	*Crossover Voters*
"How much of the time can you trust the government in Washington to do what is right?"		
Always or most of the time	26%	26%
Only sometimes	62	61
Never	12	13
"When something is run by the government, it is usually wasteful and inefficient."		
Agree	62%	64%
Disagree	38	36
"Most elected officials care what people like me think."		
Agree	51%	52%
Disagree	49	48
"Most elected officials are trustworthy."		
Agree	56%	61%
Disagree	44	39

SOURCE: Baldassare 1998a.

ment and politicians. The public seemed to give their state's elected officials little credit for the economic upturn.

In response to a question repeated from the National Election Studies (1996), only a quarter of Californians said the federal government could be trusted to do what is right either all of the time or most of the time (see table 4.5). Six in ten trusted the federal government "only sometimes," while 12 percent said they never trusted the federal government. The Pew Research Center in 1998 reported that 34 percent of Americans had a high level of trust in the federal government. So, Californians were expressing less confidence than the nation as a whole. Twenty-six percent of the state's voters trusted the federal government "always" or "most of the time." By comparison, a similar 26 percent of the crossover voters were also very trusting. Few in any voter group said they always or mostly trust the federal government.

Californians were not very trusting of government when it came to its efficiency and fiscal performance. Two in three residents believed that "when something is run by the government, it is usually wasteful and inefficient." A similar number of crossover voters held this view. In the Pew Research Survey in 1997, a similar 64 percent of Americans agreed that there was a lot of waste in government.

Nor do state residents see their elected leaders as particularly responsive to their needs. Only half of Californians agreed that "most elected officials care what people like me think." The results are nearly identical when we consider the responses of only the crossover voters. However, their responses were higher than for Americans as a whole. In a survey by the Pew Research Center in 1998, only 41 percent of Americans agreed with this perspective on elected officials.

The lack of trust in elected officials was very closely replicated in another PPIC Statewide Survey question. Fifty-six percent of Californians agreed that "most elected officials are trustworthy," while 44 percent did not. The findings for crossover voters were, again, fairly similar. And, in a Pew Research Center Survey in 1997, 51 percent of Americans thought that most elected officials were trustworthy.

Californians' distrust in government is not limited to the federal level; they also showed little confidence in their state government. In a PPIC Statewide Survey conducted in the fall of 1998, only one in three Californians said they could trust the state government in Sacramento to do what was right either always or most of the time. About half of Californians thought that the state government wasted a lot of the money that was paid in taxes. Two in three residents saw the state government as pretty much run by a few big interests looking out for themselves. Californians are, in general, only a little less cynical about their state government than their national government.

Few Californians report a lot of confidence in their elected leaders. In the April 1998 PPIC Statewide Survey, only 11 percent said they had a great deal of trust and confidence in Governor Pete Wilson when it came to solving state problems. As for the California Legislature, only 4 percent had a great deal of trust and confidence in legislators to solve state problems. Their mayors and city councils (16 percent) were more trusted in solving city problems, though the number of Californians having a great deal of confidence in their Board of Supervisors (8 percent) to solve county problems was about the same as for the California Legislature. More Californians expressed a great deal of confidence in President Clinton (30 percent) than in the U.S. Congress (9 percent) in terms of handling national problems. For crossover voters, the results were very similar and the findings indicate a lack of confidence in all levels of government.

Californians gave mixed reviews to political leaders and legislative bodies. Most gave high ratings to President Clinton's overall job performance, despite ongoing investigations into his actions. Six in ten said he was doing an excellent or good job as President, though those ratings varied widely by party affiliation. Californians were much less generous towards Congress, the California Legislature and Governor Wilson, with one in three giving excellent or good ratings to each of them. The patterns in job ratings were, once again, very similar among the crossover voters. However, job performance ratings were somewhat higher than they were during the 1994 election. With the exception of the President, however, these approval ratings were not very impressive.[3]

MAKING CHOICES

Voters were in a cynical mood about politicians and government in the spring of 1998. Yet they liked the way things were going in the state. As a result, their preferences for candidates in the June primary were in the direction of making "safe" status quo choices, as is evident in their preferences for candidate qualifications and their ballot choices.

In the April 1998 PPIC Statewide Survey, California voters surprised us when 44 percent said they preferred statewide candidates with a track record in elected office. Forty percent said they wanted candidates who were political newcomers. A month later, in the May 1998 PPIC Statewide Survey, there was an eight-point margin in favor of seasoned politicians over political outsiders (46 percent to 38 percent) when voters were asked about the candidate qualifications they preferred (see table 4.6). Democrats were more likely to prefer experienced politicians than were Republicans and independents. In contrast to most other questions in the PPIC Statewide Surveys, the responses of crossover voters differed substantially, with only 38 percent saying experience in elected office was the most important qualification for candidates, and 48 percent saying experience in running a business was most important. Still, across all groups of respondents, the degree of emphasis placed on experience in office is in stark contrast to their deep distrust of elected officials.

In another rebuke of outsider politicians, a third of the voters in the April 1998 PPIC Statewide Survey said they would be less inclined to vote for candidates who spent millions of their own dollars for political campaigning, while only 11 percent said they would be more inclined to vote for such candidates. About half said this would make no difference in their ballot choices. In the May survey, 53 percent said they favored the candidates who raised money from their supporters to pay for their political campaigns, while only 35 percent said they preferred candidates who can spend their own money. There were no differences across parties. These findings were consistent with the success of the candidates in the primary. Those who had gone the conventional route of collecting contributions to finance their campaigns won, while the self-funded outsiders lost.

Voters thus went into the June primary in a risk-adverse mood. They wanted choices that would maintain the status quo of good economic times and avoid slipping back into the deep recession of the not-so-distant past. With this in mind, there would be no one like Jesse "The Body" Ventura emerging as the candidate for Governor of California or U.S. Senator in the state's first-ever blanket primary.

TABLE 4.6   Candidate Qualifications

	All	Crossover Voters
"People have different ideas about the qualifications they want when they vote for candidates for state-wide office, such as Governor or U.S. Senator. Which of these is most important to you?"		
Experience in elected office	46%	38%
Experience running a business	38	48
Other	10	10
Don't know	6	4

SOURCE: Baldassare 1998b.

The voters' wish list for candidates' qualities gave Lungren and Davis for Governor and Boxer and Fong for the U.S. Senate big advantages in June. Voters were unwilling to take a chance with politicians untested in statewide offices, such as Al Checchi, Jane Harman, and Darrell Issa, who each greatly outspent their rivals. Most Republicans stayed with Lungren and Fong, while most Democrats voted for Davis and Boxer. The voters had spoken. They didn't want a radical change in their state's elected officials to get in the way of the good times that were underway.[4]

CONCLUSION

California voters participated in their first-ever blanket primary in June 1998. In this election, voters were faced with a wide array of ballot choices. The blanket primary is an opportunity for political scientists to analyze voting trends for signs of strategic voting and other specific efforts to change the outcome of elections where party candidates are chosen. This was an unusual election for many reasons besides the change in primary rules. There were record amounts of money spent because of the entry of three millionaire candidates for Governor and U.S. Senator. The President faced a sex scandal and impending impeachment that had captured much of the attention that the media devotes to politics. The economy was booming in California after one of the darkest periods since the Great Depression.

Because of several unique features of the 1998 primary, we should not draw too many firm conclusions from this election. More observations would be needed to assess the fullest possible impact of crossover voting by party members and participation among independents. Still, it is worth speculating about the results of the 1998 election. The rules of the blanket primary are seen as reinforcing incumbency advantages and, thus, the political status quo (see chapter 7 by Salvanto and Wattenberg in this book).

Voters showed a strong preference for current state elected officeholders rather than political outsiders. In terms of candidate choices, then, the experience in 1998 may be typical of what we would expect from elections held under a blanket primary system.

This chapter focused on the impacts of political context and economic setting on California's blanket primary. I considered the two major state races, that is, the races for the Governor's office and the U.S. Senate. The outcome was highly conventional and one that would have been expected in a closed primary. The victorious Democrats were the highest-ranking Democratic state elected officeholder for Governor and an incumbent for U.S. Senator. The victorious Republicans were the two highest-ranking Republican state elected officeholders, since the Governor had been termed out of office. It appears that the good economy, in combination with the blanket rules that might have worked to reinforce incumbency advantages, produced an outcome that was dominated by experienced candidates who were already holding statewide offices. In contrast, the wealthy outsider candidates were defeated in the primary, and then the Democratic candidates won in the general election.

In sum, the voters' mood is an important key to understanding the ballot choices made in the June 1998 primary. Most Californians thought that things were going well in the state. There was a dramatic rebound from four years earlier in public attitudes towards the economy, quality of life, and personal finances. As a result, the state issues people cared most about changed from the economy and immigration to crime and the quality of education. Most Californians remained politically apathetic and cynical about government. They preferred the career politicians who were closely aligned with the major parties because these were the candidates providing the least risk that government would interfere with prosperity. In another context, the blanket primary rules may have had a different impact on the election. We would have to observe other elections under a blanket primary system in bad economic times to make that judgment. The 1998 primary was not one in which voters were looking for political tools that would provide them with significant electoral change.

NOTES

I wish to thank Jonathan Cohen and Ana Maria Arumi for research assistance. Bruce Cain and Elisabeth Gerber provided helpful comments on an earlier draft.

1. For the purposes of this analysis, crossover voters are defined as Republicans who said they would vote for Democratic candidates in the gubernatorial primary. In all, there were 333 crossover voters in our two preelection surveys, including 175 Republicans in April 1998 and 158 Republicans in May 1998. We did not include Democrats who voted for Republicans, since there were too few for separate analysis,

and the Republican gubernatorial primary was not a competitive race. We also did not include independents who voted for either the Democratic or Republican candidates, although their attitudinal profile is generally similar to what is reported in this chapter for the crossover voters.

2. As another indication of low public interest in state elections, about three in ten adults eligible to vote went to the polls in June 1998, and about four in ten adults eligible to vote went to the polls in November 1998 (California Secretary of State 1998a, 1998b).

3. The theme of voter distrust is also evident in policy preferences. Californians tend to be liberal on social issues and conservative on fiscal issues (i.e., "New Fiscal Populists"); in other words, they prefer that the government play a limited role in their lives (see also Baldassare 2000; Clark and Inglehart 1998; Schrag 1998).

4. In the statewide surveys before the November 1998 election, more than half of the voters said that the candidate's stands on the issues mattered the most to them, while only two in ten said character was most important when they go to vote for Governor. After the election, Lungren's pollster said that the focus on character over issues in the gubernatorial campaign was a "strategic fatal error" (Skelton 1999).

REFERENCES

Baldassare, Mark. 1998a. *PPIC Statewide Survey: April 1998*. San Francisco: Public Policy Institute of California.

———. 1998b. *PPIC Statewide Survey: May 1998*. San Francisco: Public Policy Institute of California.

———. 2000. *California in the New Millennium: The Changing Social and Political Landscape*. Berkeley: University of California Press.

California Secretary of State. 1998a. *Statement of the Vote: June 1998*. Sacramento.

———. 1998b. *Statement of the Vote: November 1998*. Sacramento.

Clark, Terry, and Vincent Hoffman-Martinot, eds. 1998. *The New Political Culture*. Boulder, CO: Westview Press.

Clark, Terry, and Ronald Inglehart. 1998. "The New Political Culture." Pp. 9–72 in Clark and Hoffman-Martinot 1998.

Gissinger, Steve. 1998. "Top Gubernatorial Vote-Getters Spend the Least, Records Show." *Orange County Register*, August 4.

National Election Studies. 1996. *National Election Studies*. Ann Arbor: University of Michigan.

Schrag, Peter. 1998. *Paradise Lost: California's Experience, America's Future*. New York: New Press.

Skelton, George. 1999. "Election Autopsy Shows Lungren Was DOA." *Los Angeles Times*, January 25.

PART TWO

Crossover Voting

CHAPTER FIVE

The Causes and Consequences of Crossover Voting in the 1998 California Elections

John Sides, Jonathan Cohen, and Jack Citrin

INTRODUCTION

Both advocates and opponents of the blanket primary believed that the change in rules could affect voting behavior, candidate attributes, campaign strategies, and ultimately election outcomes. In this chapter, we explore voting behavior, in particular the much-discussed, much-anticipated, and, in some quarters, much-maligned phenomenon of crossover voting—the act of voting for a candidate outside one's own party. Drawing upon a series of pre- and post-primary surveys conducted by the Field Institute as well as the *Los Angeles Times* primary election exit poll, we examine California's 1998 gubernatorial and U.S. Senate races.[1] Of course, with only one blanket primary having taken place in California, its full impact is impossible to determine. However, our analysis of the 1998 elections suggests that the blanket primary leads to neither the millennium envisaged by its advocates nor the apocalypse predicted by its detractors.

We first discuss crossover voting in relation to two manifestations of partisanship: party registration and party identification. Our analysis then addresses the following empirical questions: How much crossover voting occurred in the primary election? For whom did crossover voters vote? Did crossover voting affect the election outcome? Finally, what motivates crossover voting?

CONCEPTUALIZING CROSSOVER VOTING

Crossover voting is, on its face, a simple notion: voting for a candidate outside of one's political party. However, this basic definition masks several more complicated issues (see Wekkin 1988). First, how should the political party to which a person belongs be defined? One possibility is *party registration*. Under this definition, voters cross over when they vote for a candidate from a party other than the one in which they are registered. The blanket primary, in doing away with the party primary, makes party registration electorally superfluous. There is effectively only one primary, and any registered voter can participate fully.[2] The virtue of defining crossover voting based on party registration is that one can estimate what would likely have happened had the California primary still been closed. That is, one can "separate" the winning candidate's vote share received from minor-party, nonpartisan, and crossover voters, and then, given certain assumptions, gauge the chances of his or her winning this simulated primary. Defining crossover voting in terms of party registration therefore provides useful counterfactual comparisons across electoral regimes.

Another alternative is to define crossover voting based on *party identification*. Whereas party registration is a legal formality, party identification is a psychological construct, an enduring tie between a citizen and a particular political party. Party identification does not entirely determine one's vote, and therefore affiliating with a party is conceptually distinct from voting for that party's candidate (Miller and Shanks 1996). Nevertheless, if party identification constitutes, in V. O. Key's phrase, a "standing decision," then voting against one's normal affiliation in the absence of any strategic consideration implies a weakening of loyalty, either temporary or permanent. Because voters vary in the intensity of their party identification, defining crossover voting with this as the reference point allows for a deeper analysis of its underlying psychology, since one can compare strong and weak partisans.

Another definitional issue concerns the self-styled political independent. In the case of party registration, "independents" include both members of minor parties and those who do not register with any party ("nonpartisans").[3] In the case of party identification, "independents" profess no attachment to any party. Strictly speaking, any independent (however defined) who votes for a Democrat or Republican engages in crossover voting (Adamany 1976). Under California's closed primary system, major-party primaries were restricted to voters registered in those parties, and minor-party members, nonpartisans, and members of the opposing major party could not participate. A blanket primary system effectively enfranchises these groups and thus creates a population of nonparty members who can vote for a major party's candidates.[4] However, because Democratic and Republican party officials worry mostly about potential mischief by the major opposition party, not about the votes of minor-party members and nonpartisans, we focus primarily on crossover voting among Democrats and Republicans.

In California, party registration and party identification are closely interrelated. When the respondents from the four Field polls conducted before the primary are pooled ($N = 4,060$), 91 percent of both *registered* Republicans and *registered* Democrats had a consonant party *identification*.[5] A similarly strong relationship emerges when we construct measures of crossover voting.[6] These variables are simply dichotomous, coded 1 if a respondent crossed over (i.e., a registered Republican or a Republican party identifier voted for a Democratic candidate, and vice versa) and 0 if not. In the case of crossover voting for Governor, the correlation between these two measures was .75. In the U.S. Senate race, the correlation was .71. Crosstabulating the two measures demonstrates that 93 percent of party *identifiers* who intended to cross over in their vote for Governor also intended to cross over vis-à-vis their party *registration* (the comparable figure for the Senate race was 91 percent).

THE MAGNITUDE OF CROSSOVER VOTING

We calculated overall estimates of crossover voting in the 1998 primary election for both the Governor's and Senate races, again analyzing the pooled Field poll dataset. In light of the measurement issues raised in the previous section, we calculated these measures using both party registration and identification, and then both including and excluding independents.[7] In the gubernatorial race, 15.5 percent of respondents who identified with a major party planned to cross over by the identification measure, compared to 16.6 percent by the registration measure. The magnitude of crossover voting was similar in the Senate race: 13.7 percent as defined by identification and 14.8 percent as defined by registration. When independents were counted as crossover voters, the magnitude of crossover voting naturally increased (to the 20 to 30 percent range).[8]

However measured, the extent of crossover voting is quite substantial: in both the gubernatorial and senatorial races, about one in six voters said they would choose a candidate outside their own party. Whether crossover voting changed electoral outcomes obviously depended on the circumstances of individual races. Nevertheless, the observed level of crossover voting can be put in some perspective by comparing it with the level of crossover voting in past general elections. Blanket primaries and general elections possess similar structural constraints (or lack thereof) in that all registered voters can select any candidate for any office. It is therefore reasonable to expect primary elections to resemble general elections in some respects. This claim is born out in the aggregate level of crossover voting. The number of partisan crossover voters in the 1998 primary was quite similar to the traditional level of defection in general elections (DiCamillo 1998). In the twelve presidential, gubernatorial, and senatorial races from 1984 to 1996, 20.8 percent of registered Democrats voted for

Republican candidates and 14.3 percent of registered Republicans voted for Democratic candidates.[9]

The comparability of crossover voting in the blanket primary and past general elections suggests something about the motivation for crossover voting. In general elections, raiding or hedging are not relevant strategies because the election determines who governs and thus most voters sincerely select the candidate they prefer to hold office.[10] Because a segment of each party's registered voters regularly prefers candidates from the other party, the blanket primary, instead of creating partisan mischief, may simply allow these voters to express their true preferences earlier in the election season.[11]

CROSSOVER VOTING IN THE PRIMARY CAMPAIGN

How did crossover voters cast their ballots in the 1998 California primary? Tables 5.1 and 5.2 present the distribution of votes for Governor and U.S. Senator, broken down by a three-point party identification scale.[12] To portray the dynamics of voter preferences as the campaign unfolded, we present a separate distribution for each of the four pre-primary Field polls, beginning in February and ending in May.

The Gubernatorial Nomination Campaign

One dynamic of the campaign, as in most campaigns, was the winnowing of potential candidates. The earlier Field polls presented respondents with a broader array of candidates than did the later polls, when the candidate pool had narrowed. A second dynamic is the electoral fortunes of the candidates over time, as presented in the "Total within Party" column of table 5.1. Here, the major story was the come-from-behind victory of Lieutenant Governor Gray Davis in the Democratic primary. In the March poll, he lagged significantly behind both airline millionaire Al Checchi and Congresswoman Jane Harman, but by May he garnered more than half (51.3 percent) of the votes for Democratic candidates.

Tables 5.1 and 5.2 also track crossover intentions over time and by party identification. Though the large majority of partisan voters did not cross over, a notable fraction did, even in the earliest Field poll. In February 1998, 19.8 percent of Republicans and 7.6 percent of Democrats preferred a gubernatorial candidate in the other party. In the Governor's race, crossover voting was primarily a Republican phenomenon. This is not unexpected, since one might anticipate more crossover voters where there is electoral "action," that is, in races with several serious candidates. In the gubernatorial election, the Democratic race was contested, while the Republican, State Attorney General Dan Lungren, ran essentially unopposed.

This arguably created an incentive for Republicans to cross over, since the outcome of the Republican primary was predetermined. Whether this incentive stimulated raiding, hedging, or sincere voting is explored below.

The magnitude of intended crossover voting in the gubernatorial race was quite stable during the four months before the primary, hovering around 20 percent among Republicans and 5 percent among Democrats. This stability suggests that crossover voting was not much affected by campaign events, by the shifting electoral fortunes of various candidates, or by the reduction in undecided voters over time. There seemed to be some fraction of voters in each party who were ready and willing to cross over, even as the likely winner in each race changed.

In comparing the vote choice of crossover voters and noncrossover voters, two findings emerge. First, and most important, similar trends affected vote intention within each group. In the Democratic race, Davis gained support over time among Democrats, independents, and Republicans alike. By May 1998, he won pluralities of all three groups. While both Republican crossovers and independents demonstrated a greater and more durable preference for Checchi than did Democrats, the similarity of the trends across parties suggests that most crossover voting was a genuine response to the perceived qualities of the competing candidates.

The Senatorial Nomination Campaign

As table 5.2 shows, the U.S. Senate race mirrored the Governor's race in that it featured one competitive and one uncompetitive primary. In this case, the Democratic nomination was a foregone conclusion: the incumbent Barbara Boxer was the only serious candidate. All of the action was on the Republican side, where the race became a duel between State Treasurer Matt Fong and car alarm magnate Darrel Issa, which Fong ultimately won.[13]

Just as in the gubernatorial race, this disparity in competition resulted in asymmetric levels of crossover voting. As expected, there were fewer Republicans than Democrats crossing over. By May the fraction of crossover voters had shrunk to 8.6 percent among Republicans but had grown to 15.8 percent among Democrats. As in the Governor's race, trends in candidate preference appeared in all partisan groups. At first, the vote choice of Republicans, independents, and Democrats was somewhat different, but as the campaign unfolded Fong gradually became the preferred Republican among each group.

In sum, the locus of crossover voting varies with the competitiveness of the contest both *between parties* and *within each party*. Crossover voting tends to increase in primaries with asymmetric competition, as voters desert their own party's uncompetitive race to participate in a competitive race in the

TABLE 5.1 Preference for Governor, by Party Identification

	February 1998				March 1998			
	Republican (N = 318)	Independent (N = 56)	Democrat (N = 355)	Total within Party	Republican (N = 496)	Independent (N = 117)	Democrat (N = 565)	Total within Party
Republican	57.9	19.6	7.6	100.0	47.4	7.7	4.6	100.0
Lungren	36.5	7.1	1.7	56.8	45.0	6.8	3.4	92.6
Riordan	21.4	12.5	5.9	43.2	—	—	—	—
Peron	—	—	—	—	2.4	0.9	1.2	7.4
Democrat	19.8	32.2	65.6	100.0	20.1	28.1	65.0	100.0
Checchi	10.4	12.5	16.3	31.2	10.9	17.9	20.0	37.6
Davis	4.7	7.1	22.5	31.5	3.4	3.4	17.9	24.4
Harman	0.3	1.8	4.5	5.7	5.8	6.8	27.1	38.0
Panetta	3.8	5.4	18.6	25.8	—	—	—	
Vasconcellos	0.6	5.4	3.7	5.7	—	—	—	
Other	—	—	—		3.4	6.8	3.5	
Undecided	22.3	48.2	26.8		29.0	57.3	26.9	
	TOTAL CROSSOVER: 9.0%				TOTAL CROSSOVER: 8.9%			

	April 1998				May 1998			
	Republican (N = 353)	Independent (N = 99)	Democrat (N = 478)	Total within Party	Republican (N = 279)	Independent (N = 62)	Democrat (N = 373)	Total within Party
Republican	51.6	6.1	5.0	100.0	65.9	14.5	5.1	100.0
Lungren	51.6	6.1	5.0	100.0	65.9	14.5	5.1	100.0
Riordan	—	—	—		—	—	—	
Peron	—	—	—		—	—	—	
Democrat	21.5	48.4	68.7	100.0	22.6	48.4	80.1	100.0
Checchi	11.9	23.2	24.7	40.5	7.5	16.1	15.0	22.2
Davis	6.8	14.1	26.2	36.0	9.7	19.4	43.4	51.3
Harman	2.8	11.1	17.8	23.5	5.4	12.9	21.7	26.5
Panetta	—	—	—		—	—	—	
Vasconcellos	—	—	—		—	—	—	
Other	3.1	7.1	2.7		3.6	11.3	4.0	
Undecided	23.8	38.4	23.6		7.9	25.8	10.7	
	TOTAL CROSSOVER: 10.8%				TOTAL CROSSOVER: 11.5%			

SOURCE: Field Institute, Field Polls (San Francisco: The Field Institute, 1998).

NOTE: The total crossover rates differ from those presented earlier in the text because here they are expressed as a percentage of all voters, including those without a preference (undecideds).

TABLE 5.2 Preference for Senator, by Party Identification

	February 1998				March 1998			
	Republican (N = 318)	Independent (N = 56)	Democrat (N = 355)	Total within Party	Republican (N = 496)	Independent (N = 117)	Democrat (N = 565)	Total within Party
Democrat	9.4	35.7	67.6	100.0	10.3	30.8	72.2	100.0
Boxer	9.4	35.7	67.6	100.0	10.3	30.8	72.2	100.0
Republican	73.8	32.1	17.4	100.0	51.7	14.5	8.8	100.0
Fong	11.6	7.1	3.7	17.1	19.2	3.4	4.2	38.1
Issa	13.8	7.1	2.8	18.4	25.8	9.4	3.4	48.9
Riggs	2.5	0.0	0.8	3.5	6.7	1.7	1.2	13.0
Wilson	45.9	17.9	10.1	61.0	—	—	—	
Other	—	—	—		5.4	7.7	3.4	
Undecided	16.7	32.1	14.9		32.7	47.0	15.6	
	TOTAL CROSSOVER: 9.2%				TOTAL CROSSOVER: 7.2%			

	April 1998				May 1998			
	Republican (N = 353)	Independent (N = 99)	Democrat (N = 478)	Total within Party	Republican (N = 279)	Independent (N = 62)	Democrat (N = 373)	Total within Party
Democrat	11.6	30.3	69.7	100.0	8.6	38.7	73.7	100.0
Boxer	11.6	30.3	69.7	100.0	8.6	38.7	73.7	100.0
Republican	53.9	23.2	10.9	100.0	73.8	33.9	15.8	100.0
Fong	24.4	12.1	6.1	47.7	38.0	21.0	9.4	53.8
Issa	29.5	11.1	4.8	52.3	35.8	12.9	6.4	46.2
Riggs	—	—	—		—	—	—	
Wilson	—	—	—		—	—	—	
Other	4.2	6.1	5.0		2.9	8.1	2.9	
Undecided	30.3	40.4	14.4		14.7	19.4	7.5	
	TOTAL CROSSOVER: 10.0%				TOTAL CROSSOVER: 11.6%			

SOURCE: Field Institute, Field Polls (San Francisco: The Field Institute, 1998).

NOTE: The total crossover rates differ from those presented earlier in the text because here they are expressed as a percentage of all voters, including those without a preference (undecideds).

opposite party. Furthermore, within a given party's primary, the candidate preferences of crossover voters ebb and flow with candidate fortunes much as do party members' preferences. Since the trends in the preferences of loyal, presumably sincere partisans and crossover voters were very similar, it seems unlikely that many crossover voters were raiding the other party's primary in 1998.

THE IMPACT OF CROSSOVER VOTING
ON THE PRIMARY ELECTION'S OUTCOME

Several studies of crossover voting (e.g., Hedlund, Watts, and Hedge 1982; Hedlund and Watts 1986) conclude that crossover voting rarely changes the outcome of a primary election. Others (Adamany 1976; Wekkin 1988) argue that since crossover voters' preferences usually differ significantly from those of same-party voters, they may have an indirect impact on electoral outcomes by influencing factors such as a candidate's momentum and fund-raising capacity. The present analysis examines the election tally itself. It draws upon the *Los Angeles Times* primary election exit poll to address the counterfactual question of whether Gray Davis and Matt Fong would have won under a closed primary, where crossover voting is by definition impossible.

The Governor's Race

The top panel of table 5.3 shows that Davis won among exit poll respondents with 57.4 percent of the votes for Democratic candidates, a result quite close to the final tabulation (57.6 percent). If the old closed primary rules had been in effect, all Democratic candidates would have lost the votes of registered Republicans, decline-to-states, and members of minor parties. It appears that Davis would have won even with this restriction, other things equal. First, looking only at Democratic voters, Davis beat out his opponents with 59.3 percent of the vote. Second, even if all of the registered Democrats who crossed over and voted for Lungren had voted for either Checchi or Harman, Davis still would have won. Among Democrats in the exit poll, Davis's margin of victory over Checchi, his nearest challenger, was 994 respondents. There were only 224 Democratic crossovers in this sample, so even if every one of them had voted for Checchi rather than Lungren, Davis would have won handily.

Another indication that the new rules did not affect the outcome is the pattern of preferences among voters who were not registered Democrats. Davis won a majority or near-majority of the votes of Republican crossovers, decline-to-states, and minor-party members, so it seems quite certain that these voters did not help elect a different candidate than the one Democrats themselves preferred.

TABLE 5.3   Primary Vote Choice, by Party Registration

Vote for Democratic Gubernatorial Candidates

Party Registration	Vote Choice				
	Checchi	Davis	Harman	Other Democrat	Total
Democrat	18.5%	59.3%	20.8%	1.4%	100%
Decline-to-state	18.0	59.3	21.7	1.0	100
Republican	29.5	49.7	19.1	1.7	100
Other party	29.7	51.7	16.0	2.5	100
TOTAL	20.8	57.4	20.4	1.4	100

Vote for Republican Senate Candidates

Party Registration	Vote Choice			
	Fong	Issa	Other Republican	Total
Democrat	56.0%	31.5%	12.5%	100%
Decline-to-state	59.8	35.0	5.2	100
Republican	45.0	42.0	13.0	100
Other party	39.8	44.1	16.1	100
TOTAL	47.3	40.0	12.7	100

SOURCE: *Los Angeles Times* Primary Election Exit Poll, June 1998 (Los Angeles: Los Angeles Times Poll).

The U.S. Senate Race

According to the *Los Angeles Times* poll, Fong beat Issa in the Republican primary 47 percent to 40 percent, a result that overestimated Fong's actual margin of victory by about 2 percent. The lower panel of table 5.3 shows that Fong probably would have won under California's previous closed primary regime as well. First, Fong won among Republicans (i.e., the electorate in the hypothetical closed primary). At the same time, Fong's margin of victory among Republican voters (45 percent vs. 42 percent for Issa) was markedly smaller than it was among Democrats or decline-to-states. In this case, Republican crossovers, had they been limited to voting in the Republican race as a closed primary dictates, theoretically could have changed the outcome. In the exit poll sample, Fong beat Issa by only 156 votes among Republican voters; Republican crossovers numbered 219.

However, the interplay of two factors reduces the likelihood that these Republican crossovers would have changed the outcome: these voters were quite liberal (38 percent classified themselves as such), and Fong appeared more attractive than Issa to liberals. Among Fong voters, 17 percent classified themselves as liberals, 12 percent as conservatives, and the vast majority as moderates. The comparable percentages among Issa voters were 12 percent liberal and 40 percent conservative, with many fewer moderates. Thus, it appears that Republicans who voted for Boxer would have been more likely to vote for Fong than Issa in a closed primary (assuming constant turnout). Similarly, the 378 Democrats who voted for a Republican candidate could have changed the outcome of the Republican primary if they had favored Issa over Fong by a significant amount. However, Democrats, like Republicans, favored Fong and did so by even larger margins than Republicans did.[14]

In sum, while crossover voting was substantial, it does not appear to have altered the outcome of either the gubernatorial or the senatorial race in California in 1998. The distribution of candidate preferences among crossover voters in each primary was similar to the distribution among all voters. Moreover, because both Davis and Fong garnered the support of their respective party faithful, they probably would have won in a closed primary as well.

THE MOTIVATIONS BEHIND CROSSOVER VOTING

We now analyze the motivational basis of crossover voting, using the tripartite typology introduced in chapter 1. One motivation is *sincerity*, which means that voters select the candidate they like best. A second motivation is *hedging*. In this case, voters actually prefer a candidate in their own party, but cross over to select their favorite candidate in the other party, thereby hedging their bets in the general election. If their preferred candidate in each party wins the nomination, then no matter who wins the general election, hedgers will find the outcome acceptable. A third motivation is *raiding*. Raiders vote for the putatively weakest candidate in the opposing party in hopes of helping their own party's candidate win the general election. The incentive for organized raiding—by which outsiders could determine the nominee—is what political party organizations fear most about the blanket primary.

Previous studies have found little evidence of hedging and raiding in American primary elections (Hedlund, Watts, and Hedge 1982; Hedlund and Watts 1986; Abramowitz, McGlennon, and Rapoport 1981; Southwell 1991; Wekkin 1991). One hypothesized reason is that most voters lack the political sophistication to vote strategically, particularly in a state like California, where the length and complexity of the ballot challenges the interest and capacity of most citizens. Knowing how to hedge or raid is thus not always obvious, and organized efforts to mobilize voters to act in these ways are likely to be difficult and costly. If so, then crossover voting should be mostly sincere.

A *Los Angeles Times* Poll conducted in October 1997 provides initial support for this conclusion. Among the respondents, 90 percent of registered Democrats and 82 percent of registered Republicans said the most likely reason that they might vote for a candidate of another party was simply that they favored that person. Only 7 percent of Democrats and 5 percent of Republicans said they would be likely to raid. Eighty-seven percent of the decline-to-state respondents also said they would choose their most preferred candidate.

Theoretical Expectations

The analysis undertaken here assumes that most crossover voting is sincere or possibly hedging. Essentially, we propose that crossover voting will be more likely among respondents with attitudinal or demographic attributes that deviate from the core constituencies of their party—for example, a conservative Democrat or a female Republican. However, it is important to point out that crossover voting under these circumstances could reflect either sincere voting or hedging. A conservative Democrat could cross over because he or she genuinely prefers the views of the Republican candidate. Likewise, because this conservative Democrat sits somewhere "in between" the two parties, he or she could also hedge to ensure that if the Democrat lost the general election, the Republican victor would be entirely palatable. Given these preliminaries, we can then ask, What are the likely characteristics of crossover voters?

One obvious hypothesis is that the *strength of party identification* should influence the likelihood of crossover voting. Strong partisans should be less likely to cross over than weak partisans. Similarly, crossover voting should be more likely among those whose *ideology* is out-of-step with the dominant outlook of their party. Thus, conservative Democrats should cross over to the Republican party at a higher rate than do liberal Democrats. In the same vein, crossover voting might also have some specific issue content. For example, pro-choice Republicans might have an incentive to vote for a Democratic candidate if the Republican candidates are explicitly pro-life (as Dan Lungren was in the gubernatorial primary).[15]

It is quite likely that ideology, partisanship, and policy preferences do not exhaust the reasons for crossover voting. Because demographic variables may function as proxies for political values and interests, they may affect crossover voting as well. In the 1998 California elections, *gender* may have played a role, as numerous pundits speculated about the attractiveness of Democrats like Jane Harman and Barbara Boxer to female Republicans. The presence of female candidates thus may cue gender considerations otherwise absent in an all-male race.[16] However, the effects of gender might vary across party, "pushing" Republican women to cross over more than men without exerting a comparable "pull" on Democratic women to keep them in the party. Gender issues might also push Democratic men to defect.

Race and ethnicity could also have impacts on crossover voting. Blacks and, to a lesser extent, Latinos are predominantly Democratic constituencies. Black or Latino Democrats should be less likely to cross over than their white counterparts, especially because the California Republican party is often identified with conservative stances on affirmative action and immigration that tend to alienate racial minorities. The ethnic background of candidates themselves might make voters' ethnic ties even more salient. However, in June 1998, only one nonwhite, Matt Fong, was a major candidate. It is nevertheless possible that Asian voters in particular were attracted to Fong.

Similarly, given that high *income* is generally associated with a Republican vote, rich Democrats may be more likely to cross over to the Republican party, and rich Republicans less likely to cross over to the Democratic party. In the current electoral climate, *religiosity* may also benefit Republican candidates. *Union membership* could function the same way for Democrats, especially in an election featuring the anti-union Proposition 26.

Two variables, *age* and *education,* do not generate clear directional hypotheses. Age could have a consistently negative impact on the propensity to cross over regardless of party, if one assumes that partisan loyalties, whether Democratic or Republican, ossify with age. However, to the extent that age is associated with increasing conservatism, as is the conventional wisdom, it should associate negatively with crossover voting among Republicans, but positively with crossover voting among Democrats. As for the influence of formal education, one hypothesis is that it will have a consistently negative impact on crossover voting, since educated voters could be more dedicated partisans. However, it is probably also true that educated voters more diligently consume political information, and thus are likely to learn about and perhaps support candidates in the opposing party. Furthermore, educated voters' greater cognitive capacities may provide the wherewithal to vote strategically. Education could also have a varying impact on crossover voting among Democrats and Republicans if it is generally associated with a loyalty to one party or another—e.g., if more education leads to a stronger Democratic party identification.

Data and Measures

To test the hypotheses spelled out above, we estimate multivariate models of crossover voting. To ensure an adequate number of cases for analysis, we rely on the pooled Field poll dataset. The choice of dependent variable again depends on whether we define crossover voting as voting against one's party identification or party registration. Since an analysis of motivations is in essence an examination of the psychology of voters, crossover voting is measured as defecting from one's party identification. Thus, the dependent variable is coded one if the respondent intends to vote for a candidate in a party other than the one with which he or she identifies, and zero otherwise. Among our predictors, gender; ethnic identification as black, Latino, or Asian; and union membership are dichotomous variables.[17] Religiosity is measured with two dummy variables, one for Protestants and one for Catholics. Age is the number of years, education a ten-point scale, and income a five-point scale. (Detailed descriptions of variable coding are provided in the appendix to this chapter.)

Ideology is measured by a seven-point self-identification scale, with a score of one representing a strong conservative and seven a strong liberal (thus we refer to the measure as "liberalism"). Strength of partisanship is measured by "folding" the standard seven-point party identification scale at the mid-point to create a four-category measure, where one indicates independents, and four indicates strong partisans.[18] The only consistently available indicators of issue positions in our dataset are questions about two highly contested ballot propositions on the June ballot, Propositions 226 and 227. Proposition 226 would have mandated that unions obtain the permission of all members before spending their dues for political purposes. Proposition 227 radically limited bilingual education programs in California public schools. Proposition 226 failed by a narrow margin, while Proposition 227 passed easily. Although this interpretation is somewhat crude, we construe a vote for either of these propositions as conservative, and thus more congruent with a vote for a Republican candidate.[19]

Multivariate Results: The Governor's Race

The multivariate analysis is comprised of a series of logit models, one for each party-contest combination.[20] Table 5.4 presents the results for the gubernatorial race. The logit model for Republican crossover voting in the first column confirms several of our expectations. For one, the coefficient for liberalism is statistically significant and positive. As Republicans became more liberal, the probability of a crossover vote increased. Furthermore, the coefficient for strength of partisanship is negative and statistically significant, indicating that increased partisanship was associated with a declining probability of crossing over. The coefficient for gender is also significant and positive; other things equal, Republican women were more likely than their male counterparts to cross over in the gubernatorial race. By contrast, income is negatively associated with a crossover vote. The wealthier the Republican voter, the less likely he or she was to vote for a Democrat in the primary. Votes for both Prop 226 and Prop 227 are

TABLE 5.4 Logit Models of Crossover Voting for Governor

	Republicans		Democrats	
	Coefficient	Change in Probability	Coefficient	Change in Probability
Liberalism	0.18*	.27	−0.27**	−.07
	(0.07)		(0.11)	
Strength of partisanship	−0.63***	−.30	−0.14	
	(0.14)		(0.20)	
Prop 226 vote	−0.32		1.03**	.05
	(0.22)		(0.34)	
Prop 227 vote	−0.12		0.14	
	(0.25)		(0.34)	
Gender	0.41*	.10	−0.34	
	(0.20)		(0.31)	
Protestant	−0.19		−0.44	
	(0.23)		(0.38)	
Catholic	−0.06		−0.24	
	(0.27)		(0.39)	
Income	−0.22**	−.18	0.23*	.04
	(0.08)		(0.12)	
Age	−0.005		0.008	
	(0.006)		(0.01)	
Education	−0.04		−0.16*	−.07
	(0.05)		(0.08)	
Black	—		−0.59	
			(0.56)	
Latino	—		−0.79	
			(0.54)	
Union member	—		0.66*	.03
			(0.31)	
Constant	1.98**		−1.55	
	(0.73)		(1.11)	
−2 × log-likelihood	664.3		339.6	
Percentage correctly predicted	74.6		92.9	
No crossover	94.9		100.0	
Crossover	21.8		0.0	
Pseudo-R^2	.11		.11	
N	627		743	

SOURCE: Field Institute, Field Polls (San Francisco: The Field Institute, 1998).

NOTE: Table entries are logit coefficients, with standard errors in parentheses. The dependent variable is coded 1 for a crossover vote and 0 otherwise. The rate of Republican crossover was 27.8 percent, and the rate of Democratic crossover was 7.1 percent. Change in probability is the change in the probability of crossover voting associated with a shift from the minimum to the maximum value of the independent variable, holding all other variables at their mean values.

*$p < .05$
**$p < .01$
***$p < .0001$

insignificant: opinions about these two initiatives were not related to the probability of a crossover vote, net of the other variables in the model. The rest of the variables in the model are also insignificant at the .05 level, though the coefficients for Protestantism and Catholicism are in the expected direction.

Table 5.4 also presents the change in the predicted probability of crossing over associated with a shift from the minimum to the maximum value of the statistically significant variables. The results for Republican crossover voting demonstrate the power of partisanship and ideology. With all other variables held at their means, the probability that a strong liberal Republican crossed over was .27 greater than that of a strong conservative Republican. A comparable probability obtains for strength of partisanship. Income also had a strong effect: the highest income group is predicted to have a probability of crossing over .18 lower than that of the poorest group. Gender has a weaker effect.[21]

Comparable models of Democratic crossover for Governor, presented in column two of table 5.4, produce generally similar results. While liberalism has the hypothesized effect—the probability of crossing over declines with increasing liberalism—the strength of partisanship variable is insignificant. However, the Prop 226 vote is statistically significant. Support for Prop 226, which is in essence an anti-union vote, is associated with a higher probability of crossover voting among Democrats.

That gender is not significant in this or any model of Democratic crossover demonstrates that the "pull" effect of gender—its ability to keep Democrats within the party—is not as strong as its "push" effect—its ability to drive Republicans toward Democratic candidates. In other words, Democratic men are less likely to defect than Republican women are. Of the remaining demographic variables in this model, income, education, and union membership have significant effects. As income increases, the propensity to cross over among Democrats increases. Education has the opposite effect. As Democratic respondents become more educated, *ceteris paribus,* their propensity to cross over in the gubernatorial primary decreases. Curiously, the effect of union membership is in the opposite direction than expected: being a union member (or having one in the family) was associated with a greater likelihood to cross over and vote for Lungren. However, the associated change in predicted probability shows that this unanticipated effect was relatively weak.[22]

Multivariate Results: The U.S. Senate Race

Table 5.5 presents two comparable models of crossover voting for Senator. By and large the results for Republican crossover generally conform to those for the gubernatorial election, despite the differences in the size of

TABLE 5.5   Logit Models of Crossover Voting for Senator

	Republicans		Democrats	
	Coefficient	Change in Probability	Coefficient	Change in Probability
Liberalism	0.45***	0.34	−0.40***	−.30
	(0.10)		(0.08)	
Strength of partisanship	−0.40*	−.06	−0.76***	−.16
	(0.18)		(0.14)	
Prop 226 vote	−0.74**	−.06	0.40*	.04
	(0.28)		(0.21)	
Prop 227 vote	0.13		0.31	
	(0.33)		(0.23)	
Gender	0.44*	.03	−0.33	
	(0.26)		(0.21)	
Protestant	−0.14		0.35	
	(0.30)		(0.25)	
Catholic	0.08		−0.37	
	(0.35)		(0.30)	
Income	−0.07		−0.04	
	(0.11)		(0.09)	
Age	−0.002		0.005	
	(0.008)		(0.007)	
Education	0.02		−0.16**	−.14
	(0.06)		(0.05)	
Asian	0.55		—	
	(0.52)			
Black	—		−0.18	
			(0.32)	
Latino	—		0.07	
			(0.32)	
Union member	—		0.11	
			(0.22)	
Constant	−1.50		2.94***	
	(0.98)		(0.77)	
−2 × log-likelihood	414.2		621.0	
Percentage correctly predicted	86.7		82.9	
No crossover	99.4		98.0	
Crossover	6.1		12.2	
Pseudo-R^2	.13		.16	
N	600		791	

SOURCE: Field Institute, Field Polls (San Francisco: The Field Institute, 1998).

NOTE: Table entries are logit coefficients, with standard errors in parentheses. The dependent variable is coded 1 for a crossover vote and 0 otherwise. The rate of Republican crossover was 13.7 percent, and the rate of Democratic crossover was 17.6 percent. Change in probability is the change in the probability of crossover voting associated with a shift from the minimum to the maximum value of the independent variable, holding all other variables at their mean values.

*$p < .05$
**$p < .01$
***$p < .001$

the Democratic field (there were three Democratic gubernatorial candidates but only one in the Senate race). As hypothesized, greater liberalism is associated with an increased probability of crossover; greater partisanship is associated with a declining probability of crossover. The effect of liberalism was quite strong: the associated change in predicted probability is .34. Voting intention on Prop 226 is also significant and in the expected direction: a pro–Prop 226 stance, meaning a vote against unions, was negatively associated with crossover voting. In general, Republicans are more likely to remain loyal when they are more conservative, more partisan, and antagonistic to unions, a traditional Democratic constituency. Interestingly, gender is again significant: even after controlling for "political" variables, women were more likely than men to cross over and vote for Boxer.[23]

The results for Democratic crossover voting for Senator, presented in column two of table 5.5, again confirm our theoretical expectations. Liberalism and partisanship have significant negative effects on the probability of a crossover vote. The coefficient for the vote on Prop 226 is again significant and in the hypothesized direction: a vote against unions was associated with a greater likelihood of a Democratic crossover vote to Fong or Issa. The coefficient for education, as in the analysis of Democratic crossover for Governor, is significant and negative. Among Democrats, a higher level of formal education was associated with a declining propensity to cross over and vote for a Republican candidate for Senator. The changes in predicted probability again underscore the power of liberalism and partisanship as predictors of defection.

Crossover voting thus derives from relatively weak party ties, sympathy with the ideological orientation of the other party, and membership in demographic groups generally linked to support for the opposition. This pattern of associations suggests that most crossover voting is sincere voting or hedging. If raiding were prevalent, crossover voting should be concentrated among strong partisans and others with an interest in sabotaging the other party's nomination process. Instead, just the opposite holds true.

Crossing Over Consistently? Synthesizing Electoral and Individual Motivations

Thus far, two sorts of motivations for crossover voting have emerged. First, the aggregate level of crossover voting tends to increase when voters confront an uncompetitive race in their own party but a competitive race in the other party. Thus, the percentage of Republicans crossing over into the Democratic gubernatorial primary was much higher than the percentage of Democrats crossing over to Lungren. Second, the multivariate analysis of individual behavior shows that the strength of partisanship and ideological self-identification consistently influence the decision to cross over. Taken together, these two sets of findings suggest that crossover voting depends first on the choice structure. Weak partisanship or ideological distance from the party's core beliefs does not necessarily lead to crossover voting. Likewise, the mere presence of asymmetric competition stimulates crossover voting mainly among those voters who are already predisposed to defect from their party or, at the least, who find it wise to hedge their bets.

Further evidence for the confluence of electoral and individual attributes comes when we analyze the "consistency" of crossover voting—whether respondents crossed over in either the gubernatorial or senate race, or whether they crossed over in both races. We thus cease treating crossover voting in the gubernatorial race and crossover voting in the senatorial race as independent acts.

The incidence of consistent crossover voting—that is, in both the Governor's and U.S. Senate races—is quite small. For example, among Republicans who crossed over in the gubernatorial race, only 30 percent crossed over to vote for Boxer in the Senate race. Among Democrats who crossed over in the Senate race, only 18 percent crossed over to Lungren in the gubernatorial race.[24] Altogether, only 4.3 percent of Republican identifiers and 1.7 percent of Democratic identifiers were consistent crossover voters, demonstrating the important role of factors such as the competitiveness of each party's contest. Confronted with a competitive Democratic gubernatorial primary, a sizable number of Republican voters crossed over to Davis, Checchi, or Harman; by contrast, confronted with an uncompetitive Democratic senatorial primary, very few of these gubernatorial crossover voters preferred Boxer as well.

However, a simple descriptive analysis of the demographic and political attributes of consistent crossover voters demonstrates something more: as one would expect, these voters are even further out of step with their party than are those who crossed over in just one of the races. Table 5.6 shows that consistent crossover voters in both parties tend to be weak partisans and ideological misfits when compared to voters who either did not cross over or who crossed over in only one race. For example, only 11.6 percent of Republicans who crossed over in both races were strong partisans, as compared to 26.7 percent of Republicans who crossed over in one race and 43.6 percent of those who did not cross over at all. Those who crossed over twice were also less conservative and less supportive of Prop 226. Similarly, the Democrats who crossed over in both races were weaker partisans, less liberal, and more supportive of Prop 226.

This suggests that individual attributes and electoral circumstances combine to encourage crossover voting. Within each party, there exists a subset of voters with a predisposition to defect. In a sense, the party identification of consistent crossover voters in particular was an error in judgment. The blanket primary allowed them to find their true homes. Thus, these voters

TABLE 5.6 Characteristics of Consistent and Inconsistent
Crossover Voters

	Strong Partisan	Conservative	Supported Prop 226
Republican crossover			
None	43.6%	64.2%	79.3%
One race	26.7	48.1	71.2
Both races	11.6	33.3	56.6
Democratic crossover			
None	39.5	12.9	48.3
One race	24.6	20.2	58.3
Both races	20.6	26.5	77.4

SOURCE: Field Institute, Field Polls, February–May 1998 (San Francisco: The Field Institute, 1998).

were almost surely acting sincerely. However, defection is not a given; instead, it is inspired by the nature of the race itself. In particular, competitive races tend to attract crossover voters, especially when their own party's race is a foregone conclusion.

THE EFFECT OF THE PRIMARY VOTE ON THE GENERAL ELECTION VOTE: DO CROSSOVERS RETURN HOME?

The previous analysis clearly indicates a limited incidence of raiding in the 1998 California blanket primary. However, that finding does not speak to the relative incidence of sincere voting and hedging. One way of disentangling these motivations is to examine how crossover voters in the primary election behaved in the November general election. Sincere voting in the primary means that one chose one's favorite candidate, regardless of his or her party affiliation. Such voters should stick with this choice in the general election rather than return to their partisan home. By contrast, hedging is motivated by risk aversion. Hedgers vote for their second choice in the primary in order to reduce the chances of the worst-case scenario—a general election victory for their least-liked opposition candidate.

Accordingly, crossover voters who persisted in their partisan disloyalty, such as Republicans who voted for Davis in both the primary and general elections, are deemed sincere, while the primary crossover voters who returned to their own party in November may have been hedging in the primary. We say "may have" because the phenomenon of returning home could also indicate sincere voting. Suppose a Republican crossed over to vote for Checchi in the gubernatorial primary but then cast a vote for Lungren in the general election. The primary vote would be hedging, if Checchi were his or her most favored Democratic candidate but Lungren the first preference overall, but it would be an act of sincere voting if this Republican actually preferred Checchi above everyone else, and Lungren was simply his or her second choice. With the present data, it is difficult to distinguish hedging from sincere voting among crossover voters who voted for Checchi or Harman rather than Davis and Issa rather than Fong. But we can provide a reasonable, if inexact, estimate of the relative prevalence of these two voting strategies.

The data in this analysis come from the last preelection Field poll in October 1998. This poll not only asked voters their intended vote in the general election, but also their vote in the primary, if they stated that they had in fact voted in the primary. Naturally, such a recall measure is problematic. People tend to overstate their participation and may not accurately remember their primary vote, which occurred five months before. In this sample, more voters reported that they voted for the candidate who won the primary election than reasonably could have done so—evidence of the familiar bandwagon effect. According to this poll, Davis won the "recall" primary with 76 percent of the vote, instead of the 51 percent he actually garnered. Similarly, Matt Fong's vote share increased to 74 percent of the Republican "recall" electorate, whereas he actually won 45 percent.[25]

While both margins of victory were significantly inflated, there was a much more modest bias in respondents' recollections of crossover voting. Sixteen percent of the gubernatorial voters recalled crossing over against their party registration, as did 14 percent of senatorial voters.[26] These rates are similar to those from both the pre-primary Field polls and the *Los Angeles Times* exit poll. For example, according to the exit poll, 17.5 percent of voters crossed over in the gubernatorial race and 15 percent crossed over in the Senate race. The recall questions can thus help identify the motivations behind crossover voting, despite the uncertainty about how the aggregate recall bias toward Davis and Fong affects the individual results.[27]

If crossover voting was largely sincere, most Republican crossovers in the gubernatorial primary should have supported Davis in the general election, and Democratic crossovers in the Senate race should have supported Fong in the general election. Table 5.7 shows just that. The top panel shows that 63.3 percent of Republican crossovers stuck with Davis in November. The bottom panel presents a comparable result: 64.6 percent of Democratic crossovers stuck with Fong in November. This tendency indicates another similarity between the blanket primary and the general election. In a sense, the blanket primary is a preview, or even a first stage, of the general election campaign.[28]

General election preferences among crossover voters depended somewhat on their primary vote choice. Table 5.7 shows that, while only 25.4 percent of Republicans who voted for Davis in the primary returned to

TABLE 5.7   General Election Preferences

Among Republican Crossovers for Governor

	Percentage of Crossovers Who . . .	
Primary Vote Choice	*"Returned Home" in General Election*	*Also Crossed Over in General Election*
Davis	25.4%	74.6%
	(44)	(129)
Checchi	66.7	33.3
	(40)	(20)
Harman	46.7	53.3
	(7)	(8)
TOTAL	36.7	63.3
	(91)	(157)

Among Democratic Crossovers for Senator

	Percentage of Crossovers Who . . .	
Primary Vote Choice	*"Returned Home" in General Election*	*Also Crossed Over in General Election*
Fong	22.5%	77.5%
	(27)	(93)
Issa	70.5	29.5
	(31)	(13)
TOTAL	34.5	64.6
	(58)	(106)

SOURCE: Field Institute, Field Poll, October 1998 (San Francisco: The Field Institute, 1998).

NOTE: Weighted *N*s appear in parentheses.

their party, 46.7 percent of Harman voters and 66.7 percent of Checchi voters did so. A similar pattern emerges in the Senate race: Democratic voters who supported Fong in the primary were much more likely to stick with him in the general (77.5 percent did so) than were Issa voters, most of whom (70.5 percent) returned to the Democratic Party and supported Boxer in the general. Whether this pattern of voting represents hedging or sincere voting cannot be stated with precision.

However, it is possible to generate some minimum and maximum estimates of sincere voting and hedging. In the Governor's race, the hedgers include, at the minimum, everyone who supported Davis in the primary but not in the general.[29] Let us assume, for the moment, that Checchi and Harman voters who returned home were expressing their sincere prefer-

ence in both the primary and the general; that is, these Republicans preferred a (losing) Democratic candidate in the primary, but Lungren in the
general election. If this assumption is true, these voters should not be
counted as hedgers. Thus, hedging is limited to those voters who voted for
Davis in the primary but Lungren in November (i.e., 17.7 percent [44 of
248] of the Republican crossover voters analyzed in table 5.6). The maximum proportion of sincere crossover voters is thus 82.3 percent. At the
maximum, the hedgers include every Republican who returned home in
the general election—36.7 percent of the Republican crossover voters (91
of 248).[30] This leaves a minimum of 63.3 percent sincere crossover voters.
In the Senate race, similar computations among Democratic crossover voters generate nearly identical results: the minimum rate of hedging is 16.5
percent, and the maximum is 35.4 percent.

Thus, it appears that crossover voting in both of these races was largely
sincere. First, a variety of evidence suggests that raiding was scarce. Crossover voters tended to support the winning candidate in each party's primary, and their preferences followed the overall trend as the primary campaign wore on. Furthermore, multivariate analyses show that crossover
voting is most prevalent among voters with a predisposition to support the
other party, not among the strong partisans and ideologues who would
most likely perpetrate electoral mischief.

Second, the relationship between the primary and general election vote
demonstrates that, at the most, hedging occurred among just over a third
of crossover voters, meaning the majority of these voters were sincere. This
estimate must be treated with some caution, given the vagaries of how respondents remembered their primary vote choices. Nevertheless, it seems
reasonable to conclude that California's electoral reform did not radically
affect voting behavior. It merely allowed voters to express their true preferences earlier in the campaign.

CONCLUSION

A broad array of evidence indicates that crossover voting in the June 1998
blanket primary was largely sincere. Party mischief was minimal; moreover,
crossover voting did not affect the outcome of the gubernatorial and U.S.
Senate races. Therefore, this election was no apocalypse for the parties.
Neither was it an Eden for the blanket primary's proponents: 1998 did not
produce moderate, centrist candidates in these races. The blanket primary's most important impact may be how it prefigures the general election. Those involved in the 1998 campaign expressed a similar sentiment.
Davis's campaign manager, Garry South, has said, "For all practical purposes, the general was over on primary night, barring some cataclysmic

event or huge mistake on our part" (Lubenow 1999, 147). Doing well over-all, not just among the registered voters of one's own party, thus can be critical. If this is so, an additional set of research questions emerges. How do the results of the primary election affect voters' perceptions of the via-bility of the candidates who emerge? Moreover, at an institutional level, how does the need to fuse partisan and more general appeals even before the primary shape the nature of campaigns and campaigning?

APPENDIX: VARIABLE CODING

Dependent Variable

Crossover Voting | Coded 1 if a respondent intends to vote for (or stated that they voted for) a candidate of the opposing major party, as defined by the respondent's party identification (or registration), and 0 otherwise.

Independent Variables

Strength of Partisanship | Coded 1 (independent) to 4 (strong partisan). This was constructed by "folding" the standard, seven-point party identification scale.

Liberalism | Coded 1 (strong conservative) to 7 (strong liberal).

Prop 226 Vote | Coded 1 (yes) and 0 (no). A yes vote indicates support for Prop 226, which mandated that unions get the permission of members before spending their dues on political purposes, such as advertisements during campaigns.

Prop 227 Vote | Coded 1 (yes) and 0 (no). A yes vote indicates support for Prop 227, which was designed to re-structure, and largely do away with, bilingual education in California public schools.

Gender | Coded 1 (female) and 0 (male).

Protestant, Catholic, Latino, Black, Asian | Coded 1 if respondent identifies as a member of religious/ethnic group, and 0 otherwise.

Age | Coded 1 (18–24), 2 (25–29), 3 (30–39), 4 (40–49), 5 (50–59), 6 (60 and older).

Education | Coded 1 (eighth grade or less), 2 (some high school), 3 (high school graduate), 4 (trade/vocational school), 5 (1–2 years of college), 6 (3–4 years of college, no degree), 7 (college graduate), 8 (5–6 years of college), 9 (master's degree), 10 (graduate work past master's).

Income   Coded 1 (under $20,000), 2 ($20–40,000), 3
                      ($40–60,000), 4 ($60–80,000), and 5 (more
                      than $80,000).

Union Member   Coded 1 if respondent or a member of respon-
                      dent's family is a union member, and coded 0
                      otherwise.

NOTES

We thank Liz Gerber and Bruce Cain for their helpful comments. Mark DiCamillo of the Field Institute and Susan Pinkus of the *Los Angeles Times* graciously made available the data analyzed here.

1. Naturally, crossover voting occurs up and down the ballot, in well-publicized statewide contests as well as in local elections, such as those for the State Assembly and Senate. Cain (1997) has suggested that crossover voting may even be more prevalent in down-ballot races, and Cohen, Kousser, and Sides (1999) find comparable levels of crossover voting in 1998 California legislative races and Washington State Senate elections under its blanket primary. Though the Field Institute poll included questions about lower offices, such as Attorney General, in its pre-primary surveys, it did so only intermittently. Furthermore, such questions typically produce a great deal of missing data, since many respondents have no opinion about these races, especially months before election day. For example, in the April 1998 Field poll, 62.5 percent of respondents did not express a preference for Attorney General, even after the names and party affiliations of the candidates were read twice.

2. In the closed primary, all voters could vote for propositions and nonpartisan offices, but only those registered with political parties could vote in their party's contest.

3. In California, the official designation is "Decline-to-State."

4. As John McCain's experience in the 2000 presidential primary demonstrates, these voters can be crucial to a major-party candidate.

5. The Field poll uses the conventional measure of party identification with an initial question and then a two-stage partisan probe. The first question asks, "Generally speaking, do you usually think of yourself as a Republican, a Democrat, an Independent, or what?" The follow-up asks, "(If Republican or Democrat) Would you call yourself a strong (Rep/Dem) or a not very strong (Rep/Dem)? (If Independent, Other, or No Preference) Do you think of yourself as closer to the Republican or Democratic party?" One squabble in the literature on crossover voting centers on whether independence should include partisan "leaners" as well as pure independents. Hedlund and his colleagues (Hedlund, Watts, and Hedge 1982; Hedlund and Watts 1986) argue that they should not. However, given the compelling evidence presented in Keith et al. (1992), Wekkin (1988) argues that they should. We agree with the latter camp and thus define party identifiers as strong, weak, or leaning partisans.

6. Obviously, since all of these polls occurred before the election, they are not measuring crossover voting but *intended* crossover voting. In discussing results from the Field polls, we will occasionally remind the reader that this analysis concerns

only vote intention. However, in the interest of brevity, we will more often refer to the dependent variable simply as "crossover voting." Later we also analyze the *Los Angeles Times* exit poll conducted on the day of the primary, which enables us to examine actual reported voting behavior.

7. These estimates of the magnitude of crossover were generated using only those respondents who expressed a preference for a gubernatorial candidate.

8. There was more of a discrepancy between the magnitude of crossover voting by identification and by registration when independents were included. For example, in the Governor's race, the difference was roughly 7 percent (21.8 percent vs. 28.6 percent). This larger discrepancy derives from the greater number of independents as defined by party registration (15.5 percent of the pooled Field poll sample) compared to the number of independents by party identification (11.2 percent). However, since we focus primarily on the measures of crossover that exclude independents, this discrepancy is not presently significant.

9. We calculated the percent voting for candidates of the other party using the last pre-election Field poll in each election year from 1984 to 1996. In each of these years the last preelection Field poll deviated no more than two percentage points from the actual election results, and the outcome of each race was predicted correctly.

10. In a general election, hedging as defined here cannot occur, since there is no future election in which the hedger can return to his or her own party. However, voters may not vote sincerely in a general election if they vote for their second choice because their first choice is likely to lose. In doing so, voters avoid "wasting" their votes.

11. The composition of voters in the 1998 primary and in past general elections was also similar. Looking at likely voters in the last Field poll before the primary and general elections, we found nearly identical distributions of liberals and conservatives, as well as Democrats and Republicans (data not shown). This complements the earlier finding that primary voters are not much different from primary nonvoters (Ranney and Epstein 1966; Robeck 1984).

12. This is a collapsed version of the standard, seven-point party identification scale, with leaners included as partisans.

13. The results from the May 1998 Field poll are a bit problematic because the poll did not include Frank Riggs, who won roughly 10 percent of the vote, among the Republican candidates. Fong's actual winning margin was 45 percent to 40 percent.

14. The numbers of both decline-to-states and minor-party registrants who participated in the Republican primary were too modest to affect the outcome, even if they had all voted for Issa (data not shown).

15. Evidence from a *Los Angeles Times* poll of October 1997 suggests the possibility of policy-driven crossover. When asked which party could do a better job of handling issues ranging from the economy to education and immigration, between 7 and 27 percent of Democrats and Republicans felt that the other party would do a better job.

16. However, since both the gubernatorial and senatorial races featured female candidates, we do not have variation by contest. Analysis of more offices and of other elections would provide a richer understanding of this issue.

17. Union membership captures whether the respondent or someone in the respondent's family is a union member.

18. When estimating these logit models, we analyze only partisans, and thus this measure takes on only three values in reality.

19. However, Lungren nominally opposed Prop 227 and, according to his campaign staff, sought to run a campaign that would attract minority voters (see Lubenow 1999).

20. We performed several replications to test the robustness of the results. The first includes only the last three Field polls in the sample, since the first poll, which mentioned potential candidates (e.g., Riordan and Wilson) who never ran, may have produced anomalous results. The next replication includes only the sample from the May 1998 Field poll, conducted just before the election when vote preferences presumably had solidified. The third replication includes only those respondents who identified themselves as likely voters, since they might have a different motivation for crossing over. The last replication employs a new dependent variable, the measure of crossover voting using respondent's party registration instead of party identification. In general, the results of all these replications are highly consistent with the reported results. We footnote any discrepancies below.

21. For the most part, the replications confirm these results, although the effect of partisanship wanes in the first replication (March–May polls only). Interestingly, in the second replication, which includes only the poll closest to the primary election, a yes vote on Prop 227 is a significant predictor of crossover voting. As expected, its effect is negative: a vote for the proposition (i.e., against bilingual education) is associated with a declining probability of crossover voting among Republicans.

22. The replications produce comparable results. One difference is that the effect of ideology increases when the May 1998 poll is analyzed separately, as does the effect of union membership, somewhat curiously. The effect of education wanes to a statistically insignificant level in this replication.

23. The replications largely confirm these results, except that in the May 1998 version only ideology is statistically significant.

24. These numbers come from the same Field poll dataset analyzed in the previous section.

25. One reason for the observed recall bias is that the Field question only listed the major candidates. The senatorial recall question, for example, did not list Frank Riggs or "other Republican candidate" as one of the options. On election day, Riggs received 10 percent of the votes for Republican candidates.

26. We rely on party registration here because the November Field poll did not include the standard questions about party identification.

27. We described above how during the primary campaign similar trends in candidate preference emerged among crossover and loyal party voters, and we took this as evidence of sincere voting. There were also similar trends in recall bias among crossover and loyal voters, suggesting that the same factors shaped the memories of both types of voters. Seventy percent of Republicans who claimed to have voted for a Democratic candidate in the primary recalled voting for Davis, as did 76 percent of Democrats, and 90 percent of decline-to-states. (For both Republicans and Dem-

ocrats, the magnitude of the bias is about 20 percent above their respective election day tallies.) In the Senate race, the direction of bias, when it existed, was the same across voters, regardless of their partisanship.

28. Overall, 92 percent of voters who voted for a Democrat or Republican in the gubernatorial primary voted for the same party's nominee in the general election. In the senatorial race, 95 percent voted for a candidate of the same party in both elections.

29. In making this assumption, we ignore the possibility that a voter may have changed his or her mind during the general election campaign and come to support Davis over Lungren. Given the large and constant lead Davis maintained over Lungren during the campaign, such a switch does not appear very common.

30. To be crystal clear: this percentage comes from adding up the number of voters who returned home (44 + 40 + 7 = 91) and dividing it by the total number of Republicans who said they crossed over in the gubernatorial primary (91 + 157 = 248).

REFERENCES

Abramowitz, Alan; John McGlennon; and Ronald Rapoport. 1981. "A Note on Strategic Voting in a Primary Election." *Journal of Politics* 43: 899–904.

Adamany, David. 1976. "Crossover Voting and the Democratic Party's Reform Rules." *American Political Science Review* 70: 36–41.

Cain, Bruce E. 1997. "Report on Blanket and Open Primaries." Expert testimony in *California Democratic Party et al. v. Jones* 984 F. Supp. 1288 (1997).

Cohen, Jonathan; Thad Kousser; and John Sides. 1999. "Sincere Voting, Hedging, and Raiding: Testing a Formal Model of Crossover Voting in Blanket Primaries." Paper presented at the 1999 Meeting of the American Political Science Association, Atlanta, GA.

DiCamillo, Mark. 1998. "Californians Vote in the State's First Blanket Primary." *Public Affairs Report* 39, no. 5: 1, 4–5.

Hedlund, Ronald, and Meredith Watts. 1986. "The Wisconsin Open Primary, 1968 to 1984." *American Political Quarterly* 14: 55–73.

Hedlund, Ronald; Meredith Watts; and David Hedge. 1982. "Voting in an Open Primary." *American Political Quarterly* 10: 197–218.

Keith, Bruce E., et al. 1992. *The Myth of the Independent Voter.* Berkeley: University of California Press.

Lubenow, Gerald C., ed. 1999. *California Votes—The 1998 Governor's Race: An Inside Look at the Candidates and Their Campaigns by the People Who Managed Them.* Berkeley: Institute of Governmental Studies Press.

Miller, Warren E., and J. Merrill Shanks. 1996. *The New American Voter.* Cambridge, MA: Harvard University Press.

Ranney, Austin, and Leon Epstein. 1966. "The Two Electorates: Voters and Non-Voters in a Wisconsin Primary." *Journal of Politics* 66: 598–616.

Robeck, Bruce. 1984. "The Representativeness of Congressional Primary Voters." *Congress and the Presidency* 11: 59–67.

Southwell, Patricia. 1991. "Open versus Closed Primaries: The Effect on Strategic Voting and Candidate Fortunes." *Social Science Quarterly* 72: 789–96.

Wekkin, Gary. 1988. "The Conceptualization and Measurement of Crossover Voting." *Western Political Quarterly* 41: 105–14.

———. 1991. "Why Crossover Voters Are Not 'Mischievous Voters': The Segmented Partisanship Hypothesis." *American Politics Quarterly* 19: 229–47.

CHAPTER SIX

Should I Stay or Should I Go?

Sincere and Strategic Crossover Voting in California Assembly Races

R. Michael Alvarez and Jonathan Nagler

INTRODUCTION

There are at least two important questions about voter behavior in California's blanket primary. The first is, *How many* voters took the opportunity to cast a ballot for a candidate of a party different than that of the voter's registration or identification? The second question is, *Why* did these crossover voters decide to defect from their own party's nomination campaign and to support a candidate from another party?

In this chapter, we focus on these two questions at the Assembly district level. We examine Assembly district crossover voting for a number of reasons. First, there are eighty Assembly districts in California, and with the large number of races, we are given a unique laboratory in which to study crossover voting in many diverse geographic, political, and strategic contexts. Second, Assembly districts are the lowest level of statewide representation in California politics; thus, if strategic politicians and their advisors were going to attempt to coordinate crossover voting, it would be easiest to attempt in an Assembly race, given the relatively smaller size of these electorates.

The introduction to this volume defined several types of crossover voting behavior:

1. *Sincere* crossover voting occurs when a person votes for a candidate of another party because he likes that candidate better than any of the candidates in his own party primary. Thus, a sincere crossover voter has evaluated all of the candidates running for nomination in all parties and has decided to vote for the candidate he most prefers, regardless of that candidate's party affiliation.

2. *Hedging* is a form of strategic crossover that occurs when crossover

voting is motivated by the fact that the voter is faced with a situation in her party where the winner is certain, either due to incumbency or to a very strong candidate in that party. The voter thus crosses over to vote in the other party's primary, since that primary is more competitive and thus the voter's ballot might have greater influence in that race than in her own party's race.

3. A second type of strategic crossover, which we call *impact voting*, is another form of hedging. Impact voting occurs in one-party districts when a voter from the minority party casts a ballot in the dominant-party primary because she is certain that the nominee of the dominant party will win the general election and thus wants her vote to have some influence or impact on which dominant-party candidate will win the general election and represent her own interests.

4. *Raiding* is strategic crossover in which voters support a weak candidate in the opposing party's primary so that their own party's candidate will have a better chance of winning in the general election.

Thus the empirical questions we will answer by examining Assembly races are: (1) How much crossover is there? (2) How much crossover is sincere? (3) How much crossover is strategic? and (4) Of the strategic crossover, how much is raiding? The next section outlines our study, which was designed to answer these questions.

We conducted an exit poll on election day, June 2, 1998, in five different Assembly races statewide. After discussing the Assembly races and our rationale for picking these particular races, we present our analysis of crossover voting in these Assembly races. While we find relatively significant amounts of crossover voting in some races, we conclude that almost none of it is motivated by a malicious intent to raid. Where we are able to classify intent, the amount of strategic voting among those crossing over varied considerably. We chose the five Assembly districts in our study because of their high potential for strategic crossover voting; thus, the overall amount of strategic crossover is probably significantly lower than in these districts.

STUDY DESIGN

To determine the extent of crossover voting in Assembly races and the underlying motivations for this crossover behavior, we conducted an exit poll of approximately 3000 California voters spread throughout five Assembly districts as they left the polls on June 2, 1998. The five different Assembly districts fit into three distinct classifications—each defined by a unique strategic context that allowed us to answer different questions about the extent of and motivations for crossover voting in Assembly races:

- *Type 1 Districts: Competitive Primary in a Dominant Party in an Electorally Safe District.*   Type 1 districts allow us to examine whether voters in the nondominant party will cross over to vote in the competitive primary of the dominant party. We expect the crossover voting in such districts to be motivated by impact voting. We selected Assembly Districts 9 (Sacramento) and 75 (East San Diego County). Assembly District 9, in the city of Sacramento, was an open seat in the primary election, in a heavily Democratic district, where five Democrats and two Republicans were contesting each party's nomination. On the other hand, Assembly District 75, in East San Diego County, was considered a safe Republican seat, with three strong Republican candidates battling for an open seat. There was one Democrat on the ballot in Assembly District 75.
- *Type 2 Districts: Competitive Primary in One Party in an Electorally Competitive District Likely to Be Hotly Contested in the Fall.*   Type 2 districts allow us to see if voters in the party with the uncompetitive primary engage in strategic crossover. These voters should be most likely to engage in hedging behavior. We selected Assembly Districts 53 (South Bay, LAX) and 61 (Pomona and Montclair). District 53 ranges from LAX to the South Bay in Los Angeles County. This was a competitive district, with an open Assembly seat. Seven Democratic candidates and one Republican participated in the primary. In Assembly District 61, which is mainly in San Bernardino County and partly in far eastern Los Angeles County, there was another open Assembly seat in what was likely to be a closely contested district in the fall. There were two Democratic candidates in the race (with one, Nell Soto, a clear frontrunner) and four well-matched Republican candidates.
- *Type 3 District: Majority-Minority District.*   We were interested in studying a majority-minority district because we wanted to examine whether racial and ethnic minority candidates and voters were in any way adversely affected by the open primary, or would behave differently than whites. We selected Assembly District 49 (East Los Angeles and Monterey Park). This district is heavily Latino (45 percent) and Asian (11 percent), and is considered a strong Democratic seat. Here also there was an open Assembly seat, with five Democratic candidates in the primary and two Republicans.[1]

In each of the Assembly Districts, we selected at least eight polling places, and the interviews were all conducted by professional interviewers on election day.[2] Our exit poll instrument was two pages long, copied on the front and back of one sheet of paper; it was self-administered. The first page of the survey instrument contained brief demographic questions, questions about vote choice in the Assembly race and either the gubernatorial or U.S.

Senate race, and the partisan identification of the voter. Partisan identification was based on what the respondents "usually thought of (themselves) as"; thus, we were measuring partisan identification, not partisan registration. Since the primary purpose of the survey was to measure the *intent* of voters, this is the more appropriate partisanship measure (see chapter 5 by Sides, Cohen, and Citrin in this volume). The first page also contained a series of questions vital for our analysis of crossover voting motivations. First, voters were asked to rate candidates on a 1–10 scale, where 1 meant they disliked the candidate, and 10 meant they liked the candidate. Then voters were asked to rate the chances that these same candidates, if nominated, would win the general election in November, again on a 1–10 scale, where 1 meant that the particular candidate was "not likely to win," and 10 meant that the candidate was "very likely to win." Voters without an opinion were asked not to mark anything for a particular candidate. The entire sample of voters in each Assembly race was asked to complete these two sets of rating questions for all Assembly candidates; half of the sample was asked to rate the gubernatorial candidates and the other half was asked to rate the U.S. Senate candidates. The back side of the instrument contained questions asking voters to evaluate the open primary, to state how they had voted on three propositions, their opinions on issues, and additional demographic information.[3] Respondents were able to request questionnaires in English, Spanish, and Chinese, and bilingual interviewers were sent to precincts with large Latino and Asian populations.

Thus, using our exit poll data, we can operationalize a simple measure of crossover voting. Given a voter's stated partisanship and the vote he cast in the Assembly race, we define crossover voters as those who cast a ballot for an Assembly candidate who was running for the opposite party's nomination. Given that we limit our analysis to Democratic and Republican Assembly races, this means that a crossover voter is either a Democrat who voted for a Republican Assembly candidate or a Republican who voted for a Democratic Assembly candidate.

Among the subset of crossover voters, we want to understand their motivations for crossing over. We refer to sincere voters here as sincere crossers. We refer to hedgers and impact voters as strategic crossers; they are not voting for their first choice, but are trying to ensure that they have the best slate of candidates to choose from in the general election. Raiders are neither voting for their first choice nor trying to have the best set of candidates to choose from in the general election. We used our exit poll data to determine the motivations for crossover voting. Using the information from the two rating scales, we could determine whether crossover voters were sincere crossers, strategic crossers, or raiders. Since not all voters were able to rate all candidates, nor were all voters able to estimate the probability that each candidate would win the general election, we are not able to classify all voters into the different categories. Thus the sample we work with here is smaller than the sample we report for overall crossover results. This means we are almost certainly *overstating* the amount of strategic voting, especially the amount of raiding.[4] To engage in raiding requires that voters know *precisely* the information we are asking. If a voter is not able to determine the likelihood of different candidates winning the general election, then they are not able to engage in raiding.

In the next section we present the results from our exit poll on crossover voting in these five Assembly districts. In the subsequent section we examine the motivations underlying the crossover voting. We conclude with a summary of our results and a discussion of whether the crossover vote had an impact in any of these Assembly races.

CROSSOVER IN ASSEMBLY RACES

We begin by presenting, in table 6.1, an overview of our crossover voting results. We present the proportions of voters in each Assembly race who reported a crossover vote, with the first row presenting the rate of Democratic crossover into Republican races, the second row presenting the Republican crossover into Democratic races, and the last row giving the overall crossover voting rate in that Assembly district.

Our two Type 1 districts were Districts 9 and 75. District 9 was considered a safe Democratic seat and District 75 was considered a safe Republican seat. What we see in both cases in terms of voter crossover is quite consistent with our expectations. In District 9's safely Democratic seat, there is very little Democratic crossover into the Republican races; rather, most of the crossover voting is by Republicans crossing over to vote in the Democratic race (28 percent of Republicans crossed over in this race). In District 75's safely Republican seat, there was heavy Democratic crossover into the Republican race (41.2 percent), and (as expected) there was very little Republican crossover into the Democratic primary (5.6 percent).

Both of our Type 2 districts (Districts 53 and 61) were thought to be strongly competitive, and we expected to see crossover voting in both directions. But in both of these districts, crossover voting was actually lower than in each of the Type 1 districts. In both Districts 53 and 61 the Democratic crossover was quite low (5.7 percent and 10.7 percent respectively), while it was higher for Republicans (23.5 percent and 15.1 percent respectively).

In Assembly District 49, our Type 3 district, notice that virtually none of the Democrats in this strongly Democratic district crossed over into the Republican race. Republican crossover in this district was very heavy, how-

TABLE 6.1   Crossover Voting, by Assembly District

	AD 9 (Type 1)	AD 75 (Type 1)	AD 53 (Type 2)	AD 61 (Type 2)[a]	AD 49 (Type 3)
Democratic crossover	5.2%	41.2%	5.7%	10.7%	1.5%
Republican crossover	28.0	5.6	23.5	15.1	85.9
TOTAL CROSSOVER	12.7	25.6	12.6	12.3	17.1

[a]This district was expected to be a Type 2 district; it turned out to be more like a Type 1 race.

ever, with 85.9 percent of the Republican voters in our sample reporting a crossover vote for one of the five Democratic candidates in this party primary.[5]

Turning now to a more detailed discussion of each Assembly race, we present the results for each race in table 6.2. This table is organized with the partisanship of the voters in the rows, and the candidate vote shares in the columns (the number identifying with each party [PID] is given in the first column).

Beginning with the first panel in table 6.2, Assembly District 9 in Sacramento offered Republicans two reasons to cross over. First, the Democratic race was expected to be much closer than the Republican race; thus, a vote in the Democratic primary was more likely to influence the outcome of the primary. Second, the district is a safe Democratic district, where the winner of the Democratic primary is likely to actually represent the district. Republicans who wanted to be involved in selecting their representative would have to vote in the Democratic primary. This is exactly what we see: Republicans crossed over at a rate of 28 percent, while only 5.2 percent of Democrats crossed over to vote in the Republican primary. This suggests that much of the Republican crossover may have been sincere crossover, or crossover by impact voters. However, from the aggregate data alone, specific motivations are impossible to infer.

State Assembly District 75 in San Diego County was similar. It was a safe Republican seat, and the action in the primary was on the Republican side, with three candidates running. We observed what we would expect: 41.2 percent of Democrats crossed over into the Republican race; while only 5.6 percent of Republicans crossed into the Democratic race. Again, these Democrats could have been sincere or hedgers.

Assembly District 53 in Los Angeles was expected to be competitive between the two major parties in the general election. But in the primary only the Democratic side was contested. Again, crossover occurred as expected, with 23.5 percent of Republicans crossing over into the competitive Democratic primary, and only 5.7 percent of Democrats crossing over into the uncompetitive Republican primary. Here we would infer that the Republicans crossing over were either sincere or hedgers.

In Assembly District 49—East Los Angeles and Monterey Park—there was a tightly contested race between two prominent Latina Democrats and one well-known female Asian candidate. Most Democrats stayed within their party primary, since a mere 1.5 percent reported crossing over to vote for the Republican candidate. Republican crossover here was extremely high: 85.9 percent of Republicans crossed over. Again, since this was a district where the Democratic nominee was sure to win in November, we would expect this crossover to be motivated by sincere voting or impact voting.

Assembly District 61 in Los Angeles and San Bernardino County was expected to offer a similar scenario. The district was expected to be competitive in the general election, the Republican race was highly contested, and the Democratic race was expected to be one-sided. However, the Democratic race turned out to be more competitive than we expected when we chose the district (Soto beat McLeod by 53.2 percent to 46.8 percent). Here crossover was closer: 15.1 percent of Republicans and 10.7 percent of Democrats crossed over.

Thus our expectations of where we would see crossover voting based on the strategic circumstances in a district were confirmed. However, it is not possible to precisely infer individual motivations from aggregate data, since several different motivations could be consistent with the same observed patterns. Thus, while these numbers *suggest* some strategic behavior, we pursue the question of motivation in the next section using the same individual-level survey responses.

MOTIVATIONS FOR CROSSOVER VOTING

One of the central elements of a blanket primary is that it gives voters more opportunities to engage in strategic behavior. Here we examine voters' intent. While the context of each Assembly race *suggests* why voters crossed over, the only true way to know their intent is to find out their preference rankings of the candidates and their perceptions as to each candidates' chance to win the general election. This is why our exit poll asked respondents to rate the candidates on a 10-point scale and to say how likely they thought each candidate was to win the general election. Given those two pieces of information from each voter, we can infer whether or not they were behaving sincerely or strategically. Moreover, if they were behaving strategically, we can determine whether they were acting as raiders or as one of the two more benign types of strategic voters: hedgers or impact voters.[6]

TABLE 6.2 Voting Results in Five Assembly Districts

Voting in Assembly District 9 (Sacramento)

| | PID | Republicans | | Democrats | | | | Republican and Democratic Crossover |
		Boreman	Dismukes	Gracechild	Huffman	Pernell	Steinberg	
Democratic	253	3.6%	1.6%	21.7%	17.0%	21.3%	34.8%	5.2%
Independent	56	5.4	16.1	23.2	7.1	12.5	35.7	—
Republican	125	24.0	48.0	4.8	1.6	5.6	16.0	28.0
Other	20	5.0	5.0	5.0	5.0	15.0	65.0	—
TOTAL	454	9.5	16.3	16.5	11.0	15.6	31.1	12.7

Voting in Assembly District 49 (East Los Angeles, Monterey Park)

| | PID | Republicans | | Democrats | | | | Others | Republican and Democratic Crossover |
		Imperial	Bruesch	Chu	Martinez-Baker	Messina	Romero		
Democratic	343	1.5%	5.0%	21.6%	10.8%	12.8%	44.9%	3.5%	1.5%
Independent	85	27.1	4.7	25.9	5.9	11.8	11.8	12.9	—
Republican	78	10.3	12.8	34.6	6.4	9.0	23.1	3.9	85.9
Other	19	5.3	0.0	15.8	5.3	10.5	21.1	42.1	57.9
TOTAL	525	7.1	5.9	24.0	9.1	12.0	35.4	6.5	17.1

Voting in Assembly District 53 (South Bay, LAX)

| | PID | Republicans | Democrats | | | | Others | Republican and Democratic Crossover |
		Eggars	Nakano	Pinzler	Wirth	Zedler		
Democratic	263	5.7%	32.3%	15.2%	11.4%	21.3%	14.1%	5.7%
Independent	134	55.2	13.4	6.7	3.0	3.7	17.9	—
Republican	166	60.2	18.1	0.0	2.4	3.0	16.3	23.5
Other	20	20.0	5.0	15.9	0.0	5.0	55.0	45.0
TOTAL	583	33.1	23.0	8.9	6.5	11.5	17.0	12.6

Voting in Assembly District 61 (Pomona, Montclair)

	PID	Republicans				Democrats		Others	Republican and Democratic Crossover
		DeMallie	Skropos	Thalman	Wickman	McLeod	Soto		
Democratic	214	0.9%	6.5%	1.9%	1.4%	37.9%	41.1%	10.3%	10.7%
Independent	87	31.0	27.6	16.1	6.9	5.8	6.9	5.8	—
Republican	112	32.1	22.3	11.6	2.7	7.1	8.0	16.1	15.1
Other	11	18.2	0.0	18.2	18.2	0.0	9.1	36.4	63.6
TOTAL	424	15.8	14.9	7.8	3.3	22.2	24.5	11.6	12.3

Voting in Assembly District 75 (East San Diego County)

	PID	Republicans			Democrats	Others	Republican and Democratic Crossover
		Anderson	Price	Zettel	Debus		
Democratic	153	4.6%	3.9%	32.7%	45.1%	13.7%	41.2%
Independent	280	31.1	22.5	36.1	1.8	8.6	—
Republican	120	20.9	21.7	35.0	5.6	16.7	5.6
Other	21	19.1	0.0	9.5	0.0	71.4	28.6
TOTAL	574	21.4	16.6	34.0	14.1	13.9	25.6

NOTE: Proportion of total crossover (30.2%) is the total number of Democratic and Republican crossover voters (111) divided by the number of Democrats and Republicans voting (273; i.e., total votes minus the independents and other party votes).

Voters were classified as sincere if they crossed over to vote for a candidate they preferred over all other candidates in their own party. Voters were classified as strategic crossers if they preferred a candidate in their own primary to the candidate they crossed over to vote for. Voters were classified as raiders if they preferred a candidate in their own primary to the candidate they crossed over to vote for, *and* there was a candidate available in the primary they voted in whom they recognized as having a better chance of winning the general election than the candidate they voted for. Because of ties among the ratings of candidates on the 10-point scale, some voters could not be uniquely categorized, and we report them as a separate "sincere or strategic" category.

In table 6.3 we can see that most crossover voting was in fact sincere. In Assembly District 75 at least three-fourths of Democratic crossover and at least one-quarter of Republican crossover (though there was virtually none) was sincere. It is surprising that so much of the Democratic crossover here was sincere, since it was a situation ripe for strategic behavior by Democrats: the Democratic primary was not competitive, and the district was almost certain to be won by the Republican in November. In Assembly District 53 at least 87.2 percent of Republican crossover was sincere, and as much as 66.6 percent of Democratic crossover was sincere. While we would expect the Democratic crossover here to be sincere—these voters were leaving a competitive Democratic primary to vote in an uncompetitive Republican race—we would not have expected the Republican crossover to be sincere. These voters were leaving an uncontested race to vote in a contested race. In Assembly District 61 at least 82.4 percent of Republican crossover was sincere, and as much as 87 percent of Democratic crossover was sincere. This should not necessarily be a surprise, since the general election was expected to be competitive, and it turned out that both primaries had competitive races. Thus voters had little incentive for strategic behavior. In Assembly District 49, at least 70.1 percent of Republican crossover was sincere, and as much as 85 percent may have been sincere. And this is a district where we would expect Republicans to engage in strategic voting because it is a safe Democratic district. Yet few Republicans actually crossed over, and over half of those crossed over to vote for a candidate they preferred to the Republican alternatives. However, again we observe that inferences from context are misleading: voters we might think were behaving strategically were actually behaving sincerely.

Finally, we turn to the question of raiding. Did voters engage in strategic crossing over designed to nominate weak candidates for the opposing party? In three of the four State Assembly races in which we could classify people, the percentage of raiders among any partisan group was never more than 6.7 percent. In one district, Assembly District 49, 9.0 percent

TABLE 6.3   Classification of Sincere and
Strategic Intent among Crossover Voters

Assembly District 49

	Party Identification of Crossover Voters	
	Democratic	*Republican*
Sincere; sincere crossers	20.0	70.1
	(1)	(47)
Sincere or strategic	0.0	14.9
	(0)	(10)
Strategic crossers	80.0	0.0
	(4)	(0)
Raiders	0.0	9.0
	(0)	(6)
Non-classifiable crossover	0.0	6.0
	(0)	(4)
TOTAL SUBSAMPLE	5	67

Assembly District 53

	Party Identification of Crossover Voters	
	Democratic	*Republican*
Sincere; sincere crossers	33.3	87.2
	(5)	(34)
Sincere or strategic	33.3	7.7
	(5)	(3)
Strategic crossers	26.7	0.0
	(4)	(0)
Raiders	6.7	5.1
	(1)	(2)
Non-classifiable crossover	0.0	0.0
	(0)	(0)
TOTAL SUBSAMPLE	15	39

Continued on next page

of Republican voters could be classified as raiders. Thus raiding is clearly a rare event.

Because the questionnaire for Assembly District 9 omitted Darrel Steinberg from the list of candidates for voters to rate, we could not analyze raiding in that district as we did in the other four.[7] However, we can still draw inferences about the behavior of most voters. First, this is a safe Dem-

TABLE 6.3—*Continued*

Assembly District 61

	Party Identification of Crossover Voters	
	Democratic	*Republican*
Sincere; sincere crossers	0.0	82.4
	(0)	(14)
Sincere or strategic	87.0	11.8
	(20)	(2)
Strategic crossers	0.0	0.0
	(0)	(0)
Raiders	0.0	5.9
	(0)	(1)
Non-classifiable crossover	13.0	0.0
	(3)	(0)
TOTAL SUBSAMPLE	23	17

Assembly District 75

	Party Identification of Crossover Voters	
	Democratic	*Republican*
Sincere; sincere crossers	76.2	28.6
	(48)	(2)
Sincere or strategic	15.9	57.1
	(10)	(4)
Strategic crossers	3.2	14.3
	(2)	(1)
Raiders	1.6	0.0
	(1)	(0)
Non-classifiable crossover	3.2	0.0
	(2)	(0)
TOTAL SUBSAMPLE	63	7

NOTE: Table entries give the percentage of crossover voters fitting into each category of intent. The numbers in parentheses give the number of voters in the category. The data in this table are based only on the voters who were able to rate all of the candidates and give their estimate of the likelihood of all candidates winning the general election.

ocratic district, so it is hard to imagine any strategic reason for Democrats to vote in the Republican primary. This may explain why only 5.1 percent of them crossed over at all. Second, while 28.0 percent of Republicans crossed over, 12.0 percent of Republicans voted for a Democratic candidate other than Steinberg. Of those 12.0 percent, 86 percent of them voted for a candidate they preferred to either Republican. This suggests that they were sincere voters.

CONCLUSION: DID CROSSOVER VOTING MATTER?

In only one of the five Assembly races we studied—Assembly District 61—was there enough crossover voting to have had an impact on the outcome of either party's primary nomination. In the Republican race, DeMallie won with 19.2 percent of the actual election's total vote; his closest rival was Skropos (15.5 percent of the total vote). In this race, 15.1 percent of the Republicans crossed over to vote in the Democratic races. If these Republican crossover voters had to vote for one of the four Republican candidates, our predictive model (presented in table 6.4) states that 15.4 percent would have supported DeMallie and 84.6 percent would have voted for Skropos.[8] Adding these crossover voters to the DeMallie and Skropos vote columns from our exit poll sample, though, would give DeMallie a 33.9 percent to 32.1 percent victory over Skropos in this race among Republican voters. Given the sample size, this is essentially a statistical dead-heat. Thus Skropos's chances were compromised by the blanket primary.[9]

The second race in Assembly District 61 in which crossover voting might have mattered was the Democratic campaign between the two frontrunners McLeod and Soto. Here, 12.0 percent of the Democrats crossed over to vote in the Republican primary. Our predictive model states that 36.8 percent of these Democratic crossover voters would have supported McLeod in a closed primary and that 63.2 percent would have voted for Soto in a closed primary.[10] By adding these votes to each candidate's vote total from our exit poll sample, we end up with Soto receiving 46.1 percent of the Democratic vote to McLeod's 41.1 percent (with the remainder going for "other"). Soto still wins this primary election.

Not only do we find little evidence that crossover voting could have changed any of the five Assembly races we studied, we have found generally low levels of crossover voting in the Assembly races. Furthermore, very little of the crossover voting we observe in any of these different races is motivated by strategic reasons. Instead, crossover voting in these races is overwhelmingly sincere—Californians in these Assembly Districts were crossing over to support candidates they sincerely liked more than the candidates who were seeking nomination in their own party.

These results are generally consistent with the conclusions we reached in earlier analyses of crossover voting in Washington State primaries and in presidential primaries (Alvarez and Nagler 1997) and in other analyses of the June 1998 primary in California (Alvarez and Nagler 2000a). In all of these studies, we find that most crossover voting is motivated by sincere considerations, and that very little of such voting is motivated by a desire

TABLE 6.4   Multinominal Logit Estimates for Assembly District 61 Voting

Independent Variables	Probability of Supporting:					
	DeMallie	McLeod	Skropos	Thalman	Wickman	Other Candidates
Females	0.41	−0.13	0.02	−0.96	0.00	−0.63
	(0.44)	(0.35)	(0.40)	(0.58)	(0.65)	(0.40)
Age	0.07	0.03	−0.50	−0.16	−0.80	−0.27
	(0.22)	(0.17)	(0.20)	(0.26)	(0.35)	(0.20)
Latinos	−1.20	−1.30	−1.80	−2.10	−0.77	−0.40
	(0.68)	(0.55)	(0.71)	(1.10)	(0.91)	(0.52)
Hispanics	−1.90	−0.34	−1.10	−2.20	−0.62	−0.29
	(0.59)	(0.37)	(0.46)	(0.84)	(0.69)	(0.42)
Prop 226	0.54	0.57	1.10	−0.13	1.20	0.28
	(0.41)	(0.34)	(0.38)	(0.52)	(0.61)	(0.40)
Prop 227	0.46	0.30	0.12	0.84	0.54	−0.24
	(0.45)	(0.34)	(0.40)	(0.62)	(0.65)	(0.40)
Ideology	1.60	−0.21	0.78	1.50	1.20	0.69
	(0.27)	(0.19)	(0.23)	(0.33)	(0.37)	(0.22)
California economy	−0.10	0.27	−0.09	−0.09	0.16	0.33
	(0.25)	(0.19)	(0.23)	(0.32)	(0.37)	(0.21)
Jobs and economy	0.05	0.39	−0.12	0.23	0.07	−0.18
	(0.47)	(0.35)	(0.42)	(0.58)	(0.68)	(0.41)
Crime	−0.79	−0.10	−0.45	−1.90	−0.27	−0.54
	(0.44)	(0.35)	(0.40)	(0.59)	(0.65)	(0.40)
Experience	−0.12	0.29	0.45	0.10	0.79	0.59
	(0.57)	(0.43)	(0.50)	(0.71)	(0.80)	(0.48)
Abortion	−0.69	−0.19	−0.67	0.16	−1.60	−1.10
	(0.76)	(0.60)	(0.75)	(0.83)	(1.40)	(0.88)
Bilingual education	−0.26	−0.39	−0.45	−0.04	0.09	−0.32
	(0.49)	(0.41)	(0.46)	(0.57)	(0.69)	(0.44)
Special interests	1.00	1.00	1.20	1.20	−0.30	0.20
	(0.51)	(0.42)	(0.48)	(0.59)	(0.91)	(0.52)
Health care	−0.76	0.45	−0.26	−0.14	−0.19	−0.31
	(0.48)	(0.35)	(0.42)	(0.58)	(0.70)	(0.42)
Environment	−2.30	−0.33	−1.50	−0.64	0.52	0.40
	(1.10)	(0.48)	(0.74)	(0.83)	(0.84)	(0.53)
Cutting taxes	0.92	−0.002	0.17	0.27	−0.22	−0.41
	(0.44)	(0.36)	(0.41)	(0.55)	(0.70)	(0.44)
New leaders	−0.28	0.28	0.25	−0.61	0.98	0.09
	(0.53)	(0.41)	(0.47)	(0.71)	(0.69)	(0.47)
Constant	−5.50	−0.76	−1.30	−4.60	−4.90	−1.80
	(1.40)	(0.94)	(1.10)	(1.80)	(1.90)	(1.10)

NOTE: Soto is the baseline or comparison category in this model; thus the coefficients are interpreted as giving the relative impact of each predictive variable on the probability that a voter would choose any of the Assembly candidates relative to the probability that they would choose Soto.

to raid the other party's primary. The main motivation for crossover voting, in fact, stems from incumbency; when an incumbent is in a primary election, there is usually high crossover for the incumbent candidate.

Outside of crossover voting for incumbents, though, why is there so little crossover voting? More to the point, why is there so little strategic crossover voting? We believe that there is a simple explanation: strategic crossover voting requires a great deal of voter coordination (Cox 1997). That is, to be a strategic crossover voter requires a fair amount of information about both the dynamics within your own party and the other party primaries *and* about what is likely to happen in the general election. To be successful, strategic crossover needs to be coordinated on certain candidates—and it is difficult for voters on their own to engage in such coordination. Only when political elites, the mass media, or candidate campaigns provide these coordination cues will there be high levels of strategic voting and will this strategic voting sway the election outcome. Thus the important question really should be, Under what circumstances will elites or candidates be willing and able to undertake the costs of voter coordination in blanket primary elections?

NOTES

We wish to thank Tony Quinn for his help with identifying all of the Assembly Districts in our studies.

1. When we selected this district we expected it to be a Type 2 district; however, the Democratic race ended up being more competitive than we had anticipated (53.2 percent to 46.8 percent).

2. The interviewers were from Creative Data, Inc. They conducted a total of 2,977 successful interviews: 609 in Assembly District (AD) 9, 573 in AD 49, 644 in AD 53, 492 in AD 61, and 659 in AD 75.

3. The survey instrument was extensively pretested; for details of the pretesting or for copies of the survey question forms, please contact the authors at rma@usc.caltech.edu.

4. We assume that voters do not base their candidate evaluations on their expectations of the candidate's winning. We do not believe that voters would have any reason to do so, given the design of the survey instrument: voters willing to engage in strategic behavior are not likely to be bashful about it on an anonymous, self-administered survey.

5. Twenty-three percent of the registered voters in this district were Republican in 1998.

6. However, because distinguishing between hedgers and impact voters requires us to make distinctions between a candidate having "virtually no chance" and a race being "sufficiently close," we cannot ascertain whether the crossers who are not raiding are hedgers or impact voters. Thus we refer to them simply as "strategic crossers."

7. Steinberg's name was inadvertently omitted from questions 5, 8, and 9. To analyze voting in the district, we assumed that voters listing "other" as their vote choice voted for Steinberg based on the reported vote in our sample and what we know of the actual vote on election day.

8. These percentages are based on eleven of the seventeen Republican crossover voters for whom we have complete information and for whom we can make an accurate vote prediction.

9. Our counterfactual analysis is based on earlier academic work of ours in which we have developed techniques for determining how voters might have behaved had the set of candidates or parties which they could choose from in a particular election been different (Alvarez and Nagler 1995, 2000b). Our technique for answering this type of question is straightforward. We begin with a well-specified model that predicts which party or candidate each voter in our survey sample would select from the full and actual set of parties or candidates in the particular election. (By "well-specified," we mean a predictive model which includes as much information about each voter as possible, both demographic and political information. This ensures that we will have the most accurate predictions possible about the behavior of voters.) We estimate the parameters of this predictive model and use them to produce predictions for how much each voter likes or prefers each party or candidate. We can then remove parties or candidates from the set available to each voter in a hypothetical election and examine how all (or how subsets of the electorate) would behave under these restricted choice conditions. Our procedure in this analysis follows the same steps. We first estimate multinomial logit models which predict how much each voter in our exit poll sample likes or prefers all of the candidates in this race. We then examine only the crossover voters to see which candidate they would have preferred in their own party had they not been able to cross over on election day. Based on this counterfactual example, we compute the percentages of votes each candidate would have received in a hypothetical closed primary. The important assumptions which we make in this analysis are (1) that the same types of voters who turned out in the blanket primary would also have turned out had the previous closed primary system been used and (2) that voter preferences for candidates within their own party would have been the same had the closed primary been held instead of the blanket primary. The predictive model we employ uses the voter's gender, age, and racial or ethnic identification as demographic predictor variables. We also use the voter's opinions about Propositions 226 and 227, their ideological stance, their opinions about the state of the California economy, and their notions of what the most important issues were in this election. The multinomial logit results for candidate choice in Assembly District 61 appear in table 6.4. The Assembly District 61 voter choice model correctly predicts 34.4 percent of the voter choices, with a 50 percent correct prediction rate for Soto, 45.3 percent for McLeod, 42.0 percent for DeMallie, 22.7 percent for Skropos, 15.2 percent for Thalman, 7.1 percent for Wickman, and 0.1 percent for others.

10. These percentages are based on nineteen of the twenty-three Republican crossover voters for whom we have complete information and for whom we can make an accurate vote prediction.

REFERENCES

Abramson, P. R.; J. H. Aldrich; P. Paolino; and D. Rohde. 1992. "Sophisticated Voting in the 1988 Presidential Primaries." *American Political Science Review* 86: 55–69.

Alvarez, R. Michael, and Jonathan Nagler. 1995. "Economics, Issues, and the Perot Candidacy: Voter Choice in the 1992 Presidential Election." *American Journal of Political Science* 39: 714–44.

———. 1997. "Analysis of Crossover and Strategic Voting." Expert Witness Report, *California Democratic Party v. Jones.*

———. 2000a. *The Expressive American Voter.* Unpublished typescript. Pasadena, CA.

———. 2000b. "A New Approach for Modeling Strategic Voting in Multiparty Systems." *British Journal of Political Science* 30: 57–75.

Bartels, L. M. 1985. "Expectations and Preferences in Presidential Nominating Campaigns." *American Political Science Review* 79: 804–15.

———. 1988. *Presidential Primaries and the Dynamics of Public Choice.* Princeton, NJ: Princeton University Press.

Cain, B. E. 1978. "Strategic Voting in Britain." *American Journal of Political Science* 22: 639–55.

Cox, Gary W. 1997. *Making Votes Count: Strategic Coordination in the World's Electoral Systems.* New York: Cambridge University Press.

Galbraith, J., and N. Rae. 1989. "A Test of the Importance of Tactical Voting: Great Britain, 1987." *British Journal of Political Science* 19: 126–36.

Niemi, R. G.; G. Whitten; and M. N. Franklin. 1992. "Constituency Characteristics, Individual Characteristics, and Tactical Voting in the 1987 British General Election." *British Journal of Political Science* 22: 229–54.

Southwell, P. 1991. "Open versus Closed Primaries: The Effect on Strategic Voting and Candidate Fortunes." *Social Science Quarterly* 72: 789–96.

CHAPTER SEVEN

Peeking Under the Blanket

A Direct Look at Crossover Voting
in the 1998 Primary

Anthony M. Salvanto and Martin P. Wattenberg

Before California's blanket primary went into effect in 1998, its proponents argued that the new system would produce more moderate candidates: with all voters now able to vote in any contest, they reasoned, candidates with broader appeals would win. Opponents of the new system saw it as an infringement on a party's right to choose its own nominees. They feared that Democrats' nomination fights could now be unfairly influenced—perhaps even determined—by registered Republicans, and vice-versa. Minor-party contests might be especially vulnerable; with their low vote totals, they could easily be flooded by voters from the major parties. Moreover, many opponents argued that the new rules could advantage incumbents, whose name recognition would draw voters from outside the party in numbers that their challengers could never match.

All of these predictions—whether hopeful or fearful—rested on one key idea: that voters *would* move back and forth across party lines in significant numbers. In this chapter we take a direct look at voting behavior in the blanket primary and examine whether or not this was the case. We show how much crossover voting actually occurred, and we address why it occurred, including the electoral conditions that encouraged or discouraged it. We also consider the critical issue of whether crossover voting could potentially change electoral outcomes, either because it favors a certain type of candidate or because the vote choices of party members differ from those of crossover voters.

Our data consist of more than one-quarter million actual absentee ballots cast in the 1998 primary election in Los Angeles County. With the actual ballots, we can provide a complete and accurate picture of voters' selections across the entire range of contests. The ballots are anonymous, but each does contain the party registration of the voter who cast it, so this allows us to show precisely where and when partisans crossed over.

CROSSOVER VOTING: WHAT WE EXPECT

We consider three possible reasons behind crossover voting. These reasons correspond to the three motivations for crossover voting discussed in the introduction to this volume. First, as an example of *sincere* crossover voting, voters may cross party lines to support an incumbent when one is on the ballot. This is a form of sincere crossover voting in the sense that the voter prefers the incumbent to the other candidates by virtue of the former's incumbency status. We may attribute this preference to available information: incumbents enjoy a strong advantage in name recognition (Jacobson 1992), particularly in local and district-level contests. This factor might play an especially large role in a blanket primary, as voters who are faced with a long list of candidates might simply gravitate to the most recognizable name. By and large, incumbents also have more money and more avenues through which to communicate with the voters, and (if they are popular) they are likely to have supporters among nonpartisans and members of the other party. For these reasons, we expect to see large numbers of voters crossing party lines to vote for incumbents.

Electoral competition may suffer as a result of such behavior. Opponents of the blanket primary argued that the new system would greatly benefit incumbents. To the extent that voters engage in this sort of crossover voting, incumbents draw votes not only from supporters in their own party but also from *any* other voters who might approve of their performance, or who simply recognize their names. Meanwhile, candidates challenging incumbents for a nomination could rarely hope to match that influx of votes from outside their party. We expect that incumbents, when challenged, will receive the vast majority of all the crossover votes cast in the race.

A second hypothesized reason behind crossover voting is that voters might be drawn to where the action is: they might cross party lines to vote in competitive nomination fights whenever their own party offers an uncontested or noncompetitive race. This voting would not necessarily be sincere, as their most preferred candidate might still be the one running unopposed in their own party, but the chance to cast a meaningful or even decisive vote in the competitive race could provide enough incentive to make them cross (Downs 1957). In the language of the introductory chapter, these voters are engaging in strategic *hedging*. Such voting could also be inspired by a heavier flow of campaign information emanating from the close races, which usually produce more advertising and more news stories—thus making more information available. Information leads to participation: people cast ballots in contests when they feel they know something about the race, and shy away from races when they feel uninformed (Vanderleeuw and Utter 1993; Bowler, Donovan, and Happ 1992; Darcy and Schneider 1989). Overall, we expect to find many people drawn toward competitive races, especially when their own party does not offer one.

In a more general way, a lopsided flow of information could spur crossover voting among registered partisans who live in districts dominated by the other party. These voters would likely be exposed to a steady stream of political information from the other party—and the blanket primary would now give them a chance to act on it. We expect to see them do so.

Under a blanket primary system, voters also have the chance to use their votes in a malicious way: they could try *raiding* into another party in an attempt to sabotage outcomes there. This is the third possible motive behind crossover voting that we consider. Registered members of one party can, conceivably, study the other party's candidates and try to pick out the weakest one—that is, the one with the least chance of winning the general election. These partisans could then cross party lines in the primary and vote for that weak candidate in an attempt to throw the nomination to her. If they prove successful, then their own party's candidate would face that weaker nominee in November.

Although it represents an insincere vote choice, such strategic behavior might sound like an irresistible, even ingenious, idea for party loyalists. Indeed, many opponents of the blanket primary feared that this type of sabotage would unfairly swing some election results. Yet we expect that raiding in a blanket primary system will be very rare. First, the amount of political knowledge required to engage in such behavior is very high, and probably beyond the level of most voters. It would involve not only learning about candidates in the other party, but also making savvy predictions about their long-term fortunes. Second, without a massive and coordinated effort from thousands of voters, any single person considering a raiding strategy would probably come to see it as a wasted vote. If she did not fully anticipate like-minded fellow partisans acting in concert, then her vote would be squandered on a weak candidate from another party who was probably certain to lose.

DATA SOURCES

The absentee ballots examined in this chapter offer a unique insight into crossover voting. There were more than two hundred and fifty thousand absentee ballots cast in L.A. County in the June 1998 primary election, which constituted more than 20 percent of all the ballots cast in the election. The absentee ballots were reasonably representative of the full election-day canvass. (See the appendix and table 7.10, at the end of this chapter, for details and a note on our collection methods.) This means that our comparisons of vote choices between party members and crossover voters should reasonably reflect the pattern in the whole electorate.

One possible limitation with the absentee ballots, however, is that absentee voters fill out ballots early in the campaign. They would therefore have been at a disadvantage in planning strategic votes, because information that could have aided in that planning—such as media coverage of campaigns and the reporting of poll results—intensifies closer to election day. Thus, whatever amount of strategic voting we see here may represent the minimum found in the election. This factor could be offset, however, by the fact that absentee voters had plenty of time with the ballot in hand and perhaps used it to consider all their options. That extra time could also mean that absentee voters were the least likely (all else being equal) to pick the first candidate on a list whose name they recognized. Hence, the amount of crossover voting to support incumbents found among absentee voters was probably at least matched by the overall electorate. The final vote tallies support this conjecture as well.

A second possible limitation with the absentee ballots is that we cannot measure any possible campaign-specific effects that could have affected voters' decisions, such as a vote-by-mail drive in a particular district. However, we compensate for this possible limitation by examining more than fifty state and local contests and by observing voters across a range of electoral scenarios. Our conclusions about how voters behaved in any given electoral scenario (e.g., with the presence of an incumbent or of a competitive race) are drawn from crossover rates in a number of such cases.

OVERALL PATTERNS OF CROSSOVER VOTING

We begin the analysis by showing the overall patterns of voting in the sample. Table 7.1 shows how voters distributed their votes among the parties across eleven major offices. It shows the breakdown of votes cast by each of four types of voters: registered Democrats, registered Republicans, registered minor-party members, and nonpartisans (decline-to-states).

In the case of Democrats and Republicans, a plurality of voters cast votes only for candidates of their party of registration. However, the majority of registered partisans split their tickets in some way. For instance, 28.6 percent of Democrats mixed in some Republican votes, and another 10 percent selected at least one minor-party candidate. Registered Republicans were even more prone to cross party lines, with more than 37.8 percent selecting some Democrats and another 10 percent selecting minor-party candidates as well as Democrats.

Among nonpartisan voters, about one-quarter stayed loyal to a single party throughout. Some of these voters were probably people with strong

TABLE 7.1   Patterns of Party Voting for
Eleven Major Offices, by Party Registration

Pattern	Party Registration			
	Democrat	Republican	Nonpartisans	Minor Parties
Democrats only	45.6%	2.7%	9.6%	14.1%
Republicans only	2.0	40.5	16.8	5.9
Third parties only	0.2	0.2	0.8	5.1
Democrats and third parties only	11.5	0.9	8.2	18.0
Republicans and third parties only	0.6	6.5	3.3	8.4
Democrats and Republicans only	28.6	37.8	37.4	19.6
Democrats, Republicans, and third parties	10.6	10.8	22.0	27.7
Skipped all eleven offices	0.9	0.7	1.8	1.2
TOTAL	100.0%	100.1%	99.9%	100.0%

NOTE: Figures are percentages of each voter type casting a given vote pattern. (Figures may not total 100 percent due to rounding.)

party affiliations who preferred not to officially declare themselves. Thus, the new rules gave them a chance to participate in a primary for the first time. However, the vast majority of nonpartisans split their tickets, and did so predominantly between the two major parties.

Just 5.1 percent of all voters registered with a minor party selected only minor-party candidates. It was not as if they had no one to vote for: most minor parties fielded candidates in all the major statewide races and in many of the district-level races. Most of those candidates ran uncontested, however, which may suggest that minor-party members were more concerned with the contested races or incumbents elsewhere than they were with giving their party a larger share of the overall vote.

All of this ticket-splitting made the ballot patterns of this primary election look remarkably like a general election. To illustrate this, table 7.2 shows the distribution of votes in this election compared to the same county in the 1994 general election. (The 1994 data also come from the Los Angeles County Registrar and reflect a random sample of election-day ballots.) The percentages show a very similar pattern: voters' propensity to split their tickets, and the way in which they did so, was nearly the same under this new primary format as it was in the 1994 general election. Crossover voting may well be routine behavior for voters any time they are given choices among many parties.

TABLE 7.2   Patterns of Party Voting for Eleven Offices in
1998 California Primary and 1994 General Election

Pattern	1998 Primary	1994 General
Democrats only	26.7%	20.5%
Republicans only	17.1	16.5
Third parties only	0.3	0.5
Democrats and third parties only	7.4	8.8
Republicans and third parties only	3.2	4.9
Democrats and Republicans only	32.6	30.6
Democrats, Republicans, and third parties	11.9	18.0
Skipped all eleven offices	0.9	0.3
TOTAL	100.1%	100.1%

NOTE: Figures are percentages of ballots showing a given pattern. (Figures may not total
100 percent due to rounding.)

This finding helps to shed light on the motivations behind crossover voting. The patterns in table 7.2 suggest that on the whole, voters were not acting maliciously toward the other party in their crossover voting, because the voting trends in this primary looked so much like they did in a general election. In a general election voters have no incentive to try to sabotage the other party because there is no second, subsequent election for them to influence. More direct evidence in support of this conclusion comes later, when we examine specific vote choices.

CROSSOVER VOTING AND STATEWIDE RACES

In order to show the conditions under which voters crossed party lines, we can examine voting behavior by party affiliation for the eight statewide offices that were on the 1998 ballot. Table 7.3 shows the amount of crossover voting by registered Democrats and Republicans, as well as how non-partisan voters cast their votes. The figures show that the highest rates of partisan crossover for any one party occurred among registered Republicans voting for Democrats in the races for Governor and Controller. In each case, about 27 percent of registered GOP voters crossed party lines. These two races illustrate the two most viable explanations for partisan crossover: the appeal of a hotly contested race in the Governor's contest, and the appeal of a popular incumbent in the Controller's race. In both cases, crossover voting was no doubt stimulated because of the lack of any real contest in the other party.

In the Governor's race, the Democratic nomination fight was a highly visible contest between Gray Davis, Al Checchi, and Jane Harman. Although Davis pulled away at the end, the race had been considered close through-

TABLE 7.3   Major Partisan Defections and the Nonpartisan Vote
for Eight Statewide Elections

	Percentage of Other Party Crossing into:		Percentage of Nonpartisans Voting in:	
	Democratic Race for:	Republican Race for:	Democratic Race for:	Republican Race for:
Governor	26.9%	8.7%	62.6%	24.0%
Lieutenant Governor	10.2	12.9	37.3	33.1
Secretary of State	6.0	17.9	25.8	37.9
Controller	27.0	5.2	54.1	16.8
Treasurer	11.1	9.5	40.0	28.5
Attorney General	15.3	12.3	40.5	29.8
Insurance Commissioner	10.4	17.6	34.9	35.5
U.S. Senator	12.1	15.4	40.0	44.4

out the early phase of the campaign. Television advertising was heavy and started early, with Checchi leading the charge with a barrage of TV ads. By contrast, the Republican side saw no real contest, as Dan Lungren wrapped up the nomination easily. Lungren's clear path to the nomination meant that he did not need to spend as much on advertising, and he held off doing so until later in the campaign season. Thus Republican voters probably saw more of the Democratic candidates than they did of their own, and many found reason to vote for one of them. One simple reason may have been to make their vote count for more by casting it in a contested race.

In the Controller's race, Kathleen Connell clearly benefited from incumbency, facing no heated competition from within her own party. On the other side, there was no contest among Republicans to draw the attention of voters. Thus, Republican voters who felt Connell was doing a fine job were free to cross party lines and vote for her. There is no way to tell conclusively from these data to what degree name recognition alone was a factor, but given the lack of a campaign on the Republican side, one can reasonably suspect that it was strong. To a lesser extent, crossover voting in the Secretary of State's race was also skewed, this time to the Republican side. This is likely a result of the same phenomenon, as Bill Jones was a well-known Republican incumbent, while Democrats had no nomination contest.

The figures for nonpartisan voting support these patterns and conclusions. Almost two-thirds of nonpartisans voted for a Democrat in the gubernatorial race. These voters decided to weigh in on the Democratic side

TABLE 7.4   Comparison of a Democratic Nonminority District
(HR 29) to a Republican District (HR 28)

	Percentage of Other Party Crossing into:		Percentage of Nonpartisans Voting in:	
	Democratic Race for:	Republican Race for:	Democratic Race for:	Republican Race for:
Governor	+6.6%	−5.2%	+5.6%	−2.1%
Lieutenant Governor	+4.0	−12.1	+7.9	−11.0
Secretary of State	+1.3	−6.2	+9.7	−7.7
Controller	−3.1	−2.6	+3.9	−0.4
Treasurer	+2.5	−4.7	+4.7	−3.6
Attorney General	+3.5	−6.7	+6.3	−4.8
Insurance Commissioner	+2.3	−8.4	+8.8	−5.7
U.S. Senator	+4.8	−9.7	+17.4	−20.6

NOTE: Figures are percentages in Democratic area minus percentages in Republican area.

of the Controller's race by a sizeable 54 to 16 percent margin over the Republican side. The fact that nonpartisans, like their partisan counterparts, chose to cast ballots on the Democratic side of the gubernatorial race is further evidence that voting did not involve strategic sabotage attempts. Nonpartisans would generally have no incentive to sabotage one party or the other, and their voting patterns and the partisan voting patterns mirror each other. These findings point squarely to the impact of a contested race and to campaign and information effects as the main causes of crossover voting.

Information effects may not be confined to individual races; they may also affect the overall rate of crossover voting. We hypothesized that a registered partisan, living in a district dominated by a different party, might receive more information about that party and be more inclined to cross into it. As an example of this, table 7.4 compares crossover voting rates in the statewide races in two congressional districts, one heavily Democratic (but nonminority) and the other heavily Republican. The figures reflect the percentage difference between crossover voting in the Democratic and Republican districts. They show that Republicans were more likely to cross over if they lived in the Democratic district; Democrats were more likely to cross over when they lived in the Republican district. The right side of the table, meanwhile, gives the difference in crossover among nonpartisans. It is clear that these voters were more likely to vote in accordance with the partisanship of the district in which they lived, probably because they were more exposed to information about these campaigns.

ELECTORAL SCENARIOS: CROSSOVER IN DISTRICT ELECTIONS

By examining specific district-level races, we can gain further insight into when and why voters cross party lines. There were a variety of electoral scenarios spread among the dozens of district races in 1998. For example, some had contested races in only one party, some had incumbents facing challengers, while others had incumbents running unopposed, and so forth. In this section, we set up some of those various scenarios as comparative cases, and use them to examine the electoral conditions under which voters cross party lines. We use three types of district-level offices in the analysis: U.S. House, State Assembly, and State Senate.

Races with Incumbents

We begin with table 7.5, which explores the drawing power of an incumbent and shows when partisans are willing to cross party lines in order to vote for one. Included here are all districts in which an incumbent was running for renomination in one of the major parties. The behavior of registered Democrats and Republicans is considered in the table. Significantly, when one party had an incumbent on the ballot, and the other party offered a competitive race for its nomination (defined here as a final margin between candidates of 10 percent or less), a full 30.8 percent of that party's registered members still crossed over to support the incumbent. This stands as a testament to the power of incumbency in district elections, at least in comparison to the drawing power of a competitive race. Nearly one-third of registered partisans left their own party even though a battle for the nomination raged within it—a battle that their vote could have helped decide.

Name recognition, especially given the long, pooled list of candidates on the 1998 ballot, may have played a role in this result. It is also possible that voters saw the contested race in their own party as meaningless anyway, because the eventual winner would probably lose to the incumbent in the general election. However, such reasoning would still not directly compel a partisan voter to cross the party line: why not put up your party's best candidate, anyway? The preference for the incumbent over all others was therefore most likely a sincere choice. The number of voters crossing over when their own party offered no real contest for the nomination was roughly identical at 27.1 percent, and more than half of all registered partisans defected to vote for the incumbent when their own party offered no candidate at all. This result probably reveals as much a cause as an effect: incumbents in these districts were probably seen as so widely popular that no one from either party bothered to mount a challenge.

This strong drawing power for incumbents will certainly be seen by some

TABLE 7.5   Drawing Power of Incumbents:
Conditions under Which Partisans Crossed

	Other Major Party Offered:		
	Competitive Race	No Viable Contest or One Candidate	No Candidate
Mean percentage crossing to vote for incumbent	30.8%	27.1%	56.7%
N of cases	(2)	(22)	(7)

NOTE: Figures are percentages of voters casting ballots in the race. Districts used include U.S. House, State Senate, and State Assembly.

as cause for concern. Some opponents of the blanket primary format predicted that precisely this kind of voting pattern would emerge, and would help incumbents overcome challenges from within their own party. Our data indicate that crossover votes flow disproportionately to incumbents and raise their overall vote totals above the number of tallies received from registered voters within their own party. Candidates challenging the incumbent for the nomination, meanwhile, generally do not attract these crossover votes. Their resources, which are usually far more limited, are probably strained simply by trying to reach the voters in their own party, never mind additional potential crossover voters from the other party. They undoubtedly cannot match an incumbent's name recognition throughout the district, either. (Of course, some challengers will be well-funded or have great personal resources, but this is not often the case.) Hence the blanket primary, by allowing those crossover votes, could further disadvantage anyone who wants to challenge an incumbent for a party's nomination.

There is potential for an indirect incumbency advantage to emerge from this scenario as well. Incumbents, helped by crossover voting, could increase their share of the total primary electorate and perhaps even collect more than 50 percent of it. That could translate into easier fund-raising for the general election: the incumbent could trumpet these results to potential contributors as a sign of a coming victory in the general election, and by so doing gather even more money for the November contest. If this were to occur, the other party's nominee would need to gear up for a general election in which he was not only pitted against an incumbent, but against one with an even greater monetary edge.

Competitive Races

When one party offers a competitive race for its nomination while the other does not, we expect voters to gravitate toward it: their votes are more mean-

TABLE 7.6   Drawing Power of a Competitive Race:
Conditions under Which Partisans Followed the Action

	Other Party Offered:		
	No Incumbent	Incumbent	Competitive Race
Mean percentage crossing to follow the action	41.7%	6.7%	16.0%
N of cases	(8)	(2)	(1)

NOTE: Figures are percentages of voters casting ballots in the race. Districts used include U.S. House, State Senate, and State Assembly.

ingful when cast in a close race, and these heated contests generate more media and campaign activity to catch their interest.

In table 7.6, we consider districts where voters had the chance to cross over into such a race. It clearly shows that voters did seize the opportunity to vote in competitive races—*except when an incumbent was present.* In open-seat districts where both parties offered candidates but only one of those parties had a competitive race (again, defined as one in which the final vote margin was less than 10 percent), 41.7 percent of registered partisans left their own party to join the action in the other. Yet, when voters were faced with a choice between an incumbent in their own party and a competitive race in the other, they stayed put: only an average of 6.7 percent crossed party lines. This is the flip side of the effect shown in table 7.5. Incumbents were clearly bigger draws than competitive races when put head-to-head. In only one case did voters see a heated race in each party in an open-seat district, so it is hard to draw generalities from this. However the number of voters crossing in that district was but a sliver of those seen crossing in other districts; a contest in their own party kept partisans largely at home in this circumstance.

Strategic Sabotage?

Next we assess whether voters undertook strategic attempts to raid, or sabotage, other parties. The absentee ballots do not allow us to study candidate preference rankings such as those used by Sides, Cohen, and Citrin (chapter 5) and Alvarez and Nagler (chapter 6; both in this volume) to assess raiding, so we infer motivation from actual vote choices and the strategic context in which they took place. To do this, we compare the actual candidate choices made by registered partisans when they crossed into the other party with the vote choices of the party's own faithful. We make these comparisons in races where conditions were ripe for strategic sabotage to

TABLE 7.7   Votes of Potential Partisan Raiders in Districts
Where an Incumbent Faced Opposition

District	Party of Incumbent	Percentage of Other Party's Registered Voters Crossing Over ("Raiding")	Percentage of Partisan "Raiders" Voting for Incumbent	Incumbent's Support in Own Party	Incumbent's Margin
HR 26	D	84.0%	80.4%	74.9%	33.3%
HR 28	R	32.7	95.5	87.6	88.8
HR 37	D	32.8	83.9	76.5	41.2
HR 38	R	39.1	91.9	82.8	72.2
HR 41	R	31.7	36.5	23.3	−23.9
AD 55	D	30.2	41.3	56.1	19.7
AD 57	D	35.2	46.7	63.7	39.6

NOTE: Figures are percentages of all voters casting ballots in the race.

occur: contested races involving an incumbent ought to have provided opposing partisans with a prime—and highly visible—opportunity for sabotage. With the other party's incumbent facing challenge, these partisans could cross into that party's primary and vote for the challenger. If these efforts helped the challenger win the nomination, it would mean that their own party would not be up against the incumbent in November—and thus would have a better chance to win the office.

The data in table 7.7 indicate, however, that the behavior of crossover voters depends more on the incumbent's overall standing in the district than it does on any sinister strategies. Note that in the first four districts listed, overwhelming numbers of the crossover partisans voted for the incumbent in the opposite party. In these districts, the incumbents were strong in their own party as well, drawing huge numbers of their own partisans and winning by large margins. In districts where incumbents were on the ropes in their own party, however, they did not get the support of crossover partisans. The three districts listed at the bottom of table 7.7 (HR 41, AD 55, and AD 57) had incumbents with much lower levels of support among voters in their own party, and the levels of support from crossover partisans largely mirrored this trend. There were no districts in which an incumbent was the overwhelming choice of his own party while crossover partisans rushed in en masse to back a different challenger.

All this amounts to more evidence that widespread raiding simply did not occur. When an incumbent was popular in a district, that popularity was sweeping and crossed party lines; when an incumbent was in trouble, he or she was in trouble everywhere.

TABLE 7.8   Voting for Fong versus Issa (U.S. Senate),
by Party Registration

	Countywide		Minority Districts	
	Fong	Issa	Fong	Issa
Democrats (19.3%)	51.9%	33.4%	56.2%	27.9%
Nonpartisans (8.0%)	59.2	26.2	67.4	18.7
Minor party (1.4%)	42.3	37.7	48.8	26.4
Republicans (71.3%)	44.6	40.8	46.7	37.5
Overall sample (100.0%)	47.1	38.2	51.9	32.3

THE CONSEQUENCES OF CROSSOVER VOTING

The electoral consequences of crossover voting depend very much on whether the preferences of partisans and crossover voters match. If they do not, it is possible that a blanket primary will produce different nominees than a closed system would have, even with all voters voting their sincere preferences.

One instance where this may have occurred was in the Republican U.S. Senate contest between Matt Fong and Darryl Issa. Table 7.8 shows how the votes were split among the different sets of voters who selected one of those candidates. Note that while Fong held a slight plurality among registered Republicans, 44.6 percent to 40.8 percent for Issa, registered Democrats who made a choice between the two were solidly in favor of Fong, 51.9 to 33.4 percent. Nonpartisans showed an even larger discrepancy. In the last two columns of the table, these figures are shown only for congressional districts with nonwhite majorities (districts 30–35 and 37). In these districts, the discrepancy between Republican and other voters was even larger.

Because this analysis is relegated to one county, we cannot prove that crossover voting *caused* Matt Fong to win his party's nomination. Yet these data do illustrate that there can be large differences between the preferences of a party's own voters and the preferences of voters who cross into that party's nomination contest. This indicates that the switch to the blanket primary format has the *potential* to change outcomes.

At the district level, the results were often similar. There were sometimes substantial differences between those in a party and those outside of it, and most of these were large enough to have swung the outcome of a close election. However, the difference was never large enough in these instances to have swamped the preferences of a major party and throw the nomination to a Democrat or Republican who did not have a plurality of support

TABLE 7.9   Where the Minor-Party Vote Came From

	Minor-Party Members	Nonpartisans	Democrats	Republicans
Assembly	10.1%	13.9%	45.5%	30.5%
U.S. House	8.4	14.6	46.6	30.4
U.S. Senator	13.9	15.3	45.9	24.9
State Senator	8.5	15.2	43.2	33.0
Governor	13.8	15.0	40.5	30.7
Lieutenant Governor	10.5	14.8	51.6	23.1
Secretary of State	14.6	8.9	51.8	24.7
Controller	11.0	14.4	40.7	34.0
Treasurer	11.0	14.7	45.2	29.1
Attorney General	7.1	10.5	52.7	29.6
Insurance Commissioner	9.2	14.3	41.4	35.2

NOTE: Figures are percentages of all votes cast in minor-party contests.

in her own party. This finding also holds in districts where there was no incumbent running. To examine the differences in voter preferences without incumbency effects, we considered eight districts where there was a contested race but no incumbent. In four of those districts, the percentage of partisans voting for the eventual winning candidate was more than ten points greater than the percentage of raiders doing so.

CROSSOVER INTO MINOR-PARTY CONTESTS

Minor-party candidates also appear frequently on the California ballot, and they may potentially be the most affected by the consequences of crossover voting. Discrepancies between the preferences of voters in and outside a party can readily have consequences for minor parties. As these parties draw very few total votes relative to the major parties, it takes far fewer crossover votes to swing an election within them. With this in mind, table 7.9 shows that the bulk of votes cast in a given minor party's race did not always come from voters registered in that party. In this election votes for minor-party candidates came very heavily from *outside* the minor parties. Only 13.8 percent of the minor-party vote for Governor, for example, came from registered members of a minor party, while most of it came from registered Democrats and Republicans. The pattern is very similar for all the statewide offices. This is not a concern when a minor-party candidate is uncontested, as was the case with most of the minor parties and most of the offices. However in some instances, such as in the Peace and Freedom party's contest for Governor, there were two candidates competing. It is entirely possible that, given the source of most minor-party voting, the candidates who emerged as their party's nominees were not always the ones most preferred by the party members.

CONCLUSION

One of the objectives of the blanket primary was to allow voters to split their tickets. It is very clear that voters took much advantage of that opportunity. The overall pattern of voting in this primary was in fact comparable to a general election. Voters seemed to treat this primary as if it were simply round one in a two-round election: they selected candidates of either party, just as they do in November. We found no evidence that crossover voting involved deliberate strategic attempts by voters to raid the opposite party by aiding its weakest candidate.

When registered partisans supported candidates from outside their own party, their voting patterns indicate that they did so for one of two reasons: to vote for an incumbent from another party, or to vote in a competitive race—especially when there was no contest in their own party. Both actions have potentially serious electoral consequences. The former could give incumbents an additional advantage, not just in the primary contests but also in fund-raising for the general election. The latter certainly has the potential to swing a close primary election.

A contest held under a blanket primary system is not assured the same outcome as would have occurred under a closed primary: we showed that the vote choices of those registered within a party can vary substantially from those of voters who cross over. This crossover effect may be of particular concern for minor parties, whose low vote totals make it easy for crossover voters to affect a nomination if the race is contested. In fact, so much of the minor-party vote came from crossover voting that this effect could be greatly magnified. The major parties are surely susceptible to this influence as well. It is entirely possible that with enough crossover voting, or a close enough election, a different nominee could emerge under blanket primary rules than would have under a closed primary system. We cannot say for certain that it happened in 1998, at least not in the areas studied here—but it could undoubtedly happen in some other election held under blanket primary rules. The potential may rise higher still as candidates learn from California's experience with this primary and become more savvy at targeting voters from other parties.

This potential change in outcomes is undoubtedly what the proponents of the blanket primary wanted to see happen, in the hope that the winning nominees would be more moderate. However, this also confirms some of the worst fears of the blanket primary's critics, as the ability of a party and its members to choose their own nominees could most certainly be influenced by this new system. Ultimately, the Supreme Court decided that such influence would constitute an infringement upon the rights of political parties.

APPENDIX: DATA AND SAMPLES

Through 1998 Los Angeles County used a punch-card tabulation system that could save digital images of each absentee ballot as it was processed. (The system has since been retired.) The Registrar of Voters was kind enough to make the absentee ballot images from the primary available to us for this project. These images, however, were stored by the computer only in raw hexadecimal form and had to be decoded back into voters' actual punches, while accounting for the candidates' positions rotating on the ballot. This extensive process was accomplished with a computer program that one of this chapter's authors, Anthony Salvanto, developed for the task. The authors are grateful to Vern Cowles and the staff at the Los Angeles County Registrar's Office, who made the images available to us and without whom this study would not have been possible. We are also indebted to Bill Detlof for his technical advice and to Chad Rosenberg for his programming assistance and tireless work during the decoding process.

REFERENCES

Bowler, Shaun; Todd Donovan; and Trudi Happ. 1992. "Ballot Propositions and Information Costs: Direct Democracy and the Fatigued Voter." *Western Political Quarterly* 45: 559–68.

Darcy, R., and Anne Schneider. 1989. "Confusing Ballots, Roll-off, and the Black Vote." *Western Political Quarterly* 42: 347–64.

Downs, Anthony. 1957. *An Economic Theory of Democracy.* New York: Harper and Row.

Jacobson, Gary. 1992. *The Politics of Congressional Elections.* New York: HarperCollins.

Vanderleeuw, James M., and Glenn H. Utter. 1993. "Voter Roll-off and the Electoral Context: A Test of Two Theses." *Social Science Quarterly* 74: 664–73.

TABLE 7.10   Absentee Sample Percentages Compared to Overall Percentages for Eight Statewide Offices, Major Partisan Candidates

Contest	Percentage of Popular Vote in Absentee Sample	Percentage of Popular Vote in County
Governor		
Davis	34.0%	36.9%
Harman	11.4	12.0
Checchi	14.5	18.1
Lungren	30.6	27.8
Lieutenant Governor		
Bustamante	37.9	43.3
Hentschel	15.0	14.2
Leslie	10.9	9.1
Mountjoy	15.3	12.2
Secretary of State		
Alioto	41.9	45.1
Jones	49.7	44.0
Controller		
Connell	65.1	65.3
Barrales	29.5	27.9
Treasurer		
Angelides	26.0	28.2
Robles	22.7	23.2
Goldsmith	14.2	12.0
Pringle	27.5	24.8
Attorney General		
Calderon	13.9	17.3
Lockyer	25.3	25.5
Schenk	10.2	12.3
Capizzi	13.6	12.8
Stirling	33.3	29.5
Insurance Commissioner		
Brown	21.3	22.6
Martinez	26.5	29.6
Quackenbush	46.5	40.3
U.S. Senator		
Boxer	51.3	52.0
Fong	21.6	18.9
Issa	17.5	16.5

PART THREE

Effects of the Blanket Primary

Crossing Over When It Counts

How the Motives of Voters
in Blanket Primaries Are Revealed
by Their Actions in General Elections

Thad Kousser

The way a voter behaves in a general election reveals much about the motivation behind that voter's choice in a blanket primary. A Californian who crossed party lines in the June 1998 blanket primary could have done so for two reasons. She might have been sincere, crossing over out of a true preference for another party's candidate over any that her own camp had to offer. Or perhaps she was being strategic, backing someone who was not her top choice in the primary in order to help secure a favorable general election match-up (the two possible forms of strategic voting, hedging and raiding, are described in the introductory chapter of this volume). One way to discover whether a voter acted sincerely or strategically in the primary is to see if she continued to cross over in November or swung back to support her own party's nominee.

In this chapter, I analyze the general election voting behavior of primary crossover voters to gain insight into their primary election motivations. Exploring this link yields lessons that may interest three different categories of political observers. First, anyone concerned with the normative implications of the blanket primary wants to know why voters cross over. If they do so because they sincerely prefer a candidate from the other party, they are more likely stick with that candidate (and remain a crossover voter) if they have the chance to do so in November. However, if they are being strategic when they cross over in the spring, they may not continue to cross over. So tracking crossover voters' general election choices reveals whether the blanket primary frees voters to voice their sincere preferences, or opens up primary elections to strategic manipulation.

Second, political scientists who study American elections have long been concerned that strategic voting in open and blanket primaries can erode party responsibility. If crossover voters are able to swing nomination battles, party labels in the general election may become muddled and meaningless, with elected leaders tied to no coherent party platform or grass-roots organization. Scholars have explored the links between crossover voting and party responsibility (Hall 1923; Berdahl 1942; Ranney 1951; Key 1964; Cohen and Sides 1998), prescribed changes in the laws governing primaries to increase responsibility (Harris 1951; American Political Science Association 1950), and even provided expert testimony about the effects of blanket primaries on responsibility (Cain 1997; Alvarez and Nagler 1997).

Third, candidates, political consultants, and party leaders want to know how vigorously they should court the other party's voters in the primary and, if they are successful, how much continued support they can count on in November. Many conjectures have been offered on this topic. The architect of California's Republican Assembly campaigns in 1998, Minority Leader Bill Leonard, predicted that "if you can convince someone to vote for you in the primary, they will stick with you in November" (Ingram and Vanzi 1998).[1] Was he right? If not, do primary crossover rates and the extent to which voters continue to cross party lines vary with the characteristics of the primary race in which a candidate is involved? Identifying any systematic patterns here can provide political strategists with useful information for deciphering California's latest, and short-lived, experiment with electoral reform.

This investigation tests the hypothesis—suggested by evidence from surveys and from statistical studies[2]—that some portion of those who cross over in blanket primaries are voting strategically. Strategic voters may be hedging their bets by voting for the most palatable candidate from the other major party, just in case their party's nominee loses in the general election.[3] The incentives for this type of behavior are greatest in two situations. First, voters might hedge if they think that their party's prospects in November are dim. For instance, Republicans might cross over to help a somewhat moderate Democratic candidate win that party's nomination in an East Los Angeles Democratic stronghold, but then return to the Republican fold in the general election. Consequently, strategic voters have an incentive to cross over into the primary of the dominant party, but not to stick with that party in November. Second, hedgers might cross into the more competitive primary (with more candidates in it), following the electoral action. If their party's race is uncontested, for example, Democratic voters may be tempted to make their vote count by crossing into the Republican party's more competitive primary, even when they intend to remain loyal Democrats in the general election. Strategic crossover voters, then, will abandon the winner of a highly competitive primary. By examining patterns in primary and general election crossover, this chapter investigates whether a significant number of California voters strategically hedge their bets in blanket primaries.

RESEARCH DESIGN

To know with complete certainty whether crossover voters stick with their primary picks in the general election, I would need reliable information—perhaps in the form of longitudinal survey data—that tracks the same individuals through an election cycle. This ideal dataset does not exist. However, in the 1998 California gubernatorial and senatorial races, something approximating this information is available. An October, 1998 *Los Angeles Times* poll asked voters which candidate they remembered voting for in the primary and whom they expected to back in the November election. In the Governor's race, 63 percent of the Republican voters who had supported one of the three Democratic primary contenders indicated their intent to support Democratic nominee Gray Davis in the general election. It seems, then, that most of these voters crossed over sincerely, although a sizable minority showed signs of strategic behavior. The U.S. Senate contest revealed a similar pattern, with 65 percent of the Democrats who crossed into the Republican primary sticking with nominee Matt Fong in November.

Although the poll provides a useful starting point, this chapter looks beyond these limited survey data. One problem with relying on the poll's findings is that it was taken only once, in October. Respondents had to recall whom they supported on June 2. It appears that some made mistakes, since their reported vote totals do not match up with actual election results (or perhaps the poll's sample was not representative of the electorate, which would cause additional problems). Also, respondents were forced to predict what their vote choice in November would be at a time when impeachment hearings made the Senate race especially volatile.

More important, focusing only on crossover behavior in California's two marquee contests does not tell the full story of the state's elections under the blanket primary. While some voters may know enough to vote strategically in the statewide races that receive heavy media attention, are any sufficiently informed to be strategic in state legislative contests? Do some types of primaries attract more crossover voters than others? Are voters who cross into another party's primary more likely to be sincere, and thus likely to stick with that party, when the primary has certain characteristics? To answer these questions, scholars need to know something about crossover voting in a large number of contests.

In the California Senate and Assembly combined, there were one hundred legislative races in 1998, ninety of which were contested by both major parties. These ninety cases provide a good comparison group. While each took place under the same rules, the races exhibit a large degree of variation in many potentially important aspects such as the degree of competitiveness and the seat's partisan slant. Unfortunately, reliable survey data does not exist for all ninety of these districts (see Alvarez and Nagler's 1998 analysis of five of them). However, in the appendix, I describe how an ecological inference procedure devised by King (1997) can be used to calculate crossover rates for both the primaries and general elections in all ninety contested seats.

In this case, King's method requires that I first measure the percentage of voters who participate in each district's Democratic primary. By definition, this percentage equals the proportion of voters who are registered Republicans multiplied by the Republican crossover rate, plus the proportion of registered Democrats multiplied by (100 percent minus the Democratic crossover rate). This is the equation for a line, and there is one line for every district. To estimate the point on each line where the district actually falls (and thus to discover the crossover rates for both party's voters), King's method employs two steps. First, realizing the crossover rates must fall between 0 percent and 100 percent, it places bounds on each district's location along its line. Second, the method plots every district's line on a single graph. It then assumes that each district's location falls somewhere on a bivariate normal distribution—geometrically speaking, a mountain—centered at the point where the lines most densely intersect. After finding the pinnacle of this mountain, the method estimates both crossover rates and confidence intervals around them.

I repeated this process to estimate general election crossover, replacing the percentage of voters who participated in the Democratic primary with the percentage supporting the Democratic nominee. While these applications of King's method require some questionable assumptions, they produce figures that are consistent with Alvarez and Nagler's survey estimates of primary crossover rates in five districts. The correlation between Alvarez and Nagler's survey findings and my ecologically inferred estimates measures 0.98 for Democratic crossover and 0.94 for Republican crossover rates. Though the estimates produced by the ecological inference are higher than the survey estimates by an average of 7.7 percent of voters, half of the estimates differed by 2.5 percent or less. With fairly reliable estimates for all ninety races, I can begin to compare crossover rates in primary elections with those from general elections. Admittedly, analyzing these district-level figures allows only limited inferences about individual behavior. Still, because the actions of sincere voters will produce different aggregate patterns than the choices of strategic individuals, some important cross-level inferences can be made here.

For instance, if all crossover voters in a race are voicing their sincere preferences, then those who crossed party lines in the primary will stick with the other party in the general election, provided that their favored candidate wins the nomination. November crossover rates will therefore be as high as primary crossover rates. There may be some drop-off in the rates if voters broke party ranks to back a candidate who eventually lost in the primary, but a nominee would be able to expect that close to 100 percent of his party's sincere crossover supporters would stick with him in November.

However, if voters are strategic, crossover support will be less "sticky." When voters hedge their bets by participating in the other primary while they actually prefer the nominee of their own party, they will reveal their sincere preferences by returning to their party's fold in the general election. If much of a candidate's crossover support comes from strategic voters, he can expect relatively few of these voters to stay with him when it counts.

Therefore, one way to find out whether voters are strategic or sincere is to see how much crossover support a candidate can expect to attract in November for every additional percentage point of the other party's members he captures in the primary. I call this measure—the projected percentage of continued crossover support—a "stickiness factor." A high stickiness factor indicates that a large proportion of the voters who crossed into a party's primary support that party's nominee in the general election. Stickiness is low when voters switch back to their own party in November. This factor should change with the characteristics of a primary race. I expect that certain types of primary races attract relatively high numbers of strategic crossover voters. An analysis of legislative races in both Washington and California suggests that many of the voters who cross into the primary of the party that has the most candidates or an overwhelming registration edge in the district are likely to be strategic. These "hedgers" are drawn toward the more competitive race or the one that is likely to produce the district's eventual representative (Cohen, Kousser, and Sides 1999). To confirm these findings, I will compute different stickiness factors for different types of races. If I find that the factor changes significantly in the predicted directions, this can provide further evidence for the hypothesis that strategic crossover voters (who show their true colors in the general election) are where one expects to find them.[4]

EMPIRICAL ANALYSIS

This section begins with some basic statistics describing the ecologically inferred crossover rates (which are fully reported in table 8.7 in appendix A), and then estimates multivariate models of crossover stickiness. On average in California's 1998 legislative primaries, 21.7 percent of registered Democratic voters crossed into Republican races while 24.0 percent of Republicans participated in Democratic primaries. These rates are slightly higher than those observed recently in Washington State,[5] perhaps because

California voters were eager to try out the new blanket primary. In California's general election, the estimated mean crossover rates drop to 11.5 percent for Democrats and 16.9 percent for Republicans.

Two things could account for this decrease. One explanation is that nearly all of the new crop of voters who only participated in the general election (see note 4) remained strictly loyal to their parties. Were this the case, the November crossover rate would drop even if every voter who crossed party lines in the primary remained a crossover voter: the denominator of the rate would grow while its numerator stayed the same. But since survey evidence shows that the November-only voters in this election were comparable ideologically to those who took part in the primary as well,[6] it is unlikely that they all remained loyal partisans. A more plausible interpretation of the drop is that it shows a sizable minority of crossover voters returning to support their parties in the general election. In other words, it seems that they acted strategically in the primary. In a pattern similar to the one revealed by survey evidence from the Governor's and Senate races, only about 53 to 70 percent of primary crossover voters demonstrated their sincere intentions by sticking with the other party's nominee in legislative contests.

Neither crossover rates nor the level of stickiness appear to be constant across legislative districts. Close races with many candidates and contests within the dominant party, when there is one, draw in huge portions of the other party's membership. For instance, consider Senate District 20, an open seat in Los Angeles's San Fernando Valley with a strong Democratic registration advantage. While an estimated 60.1 percent of registered Republicans crossed over to take part in the hotly contested Democratic primary, only 3.9 percent of Democrats participated in the Republican race. Other races of this type show a similar pattern. Yet the crossover voters attracted to these races, while numerous, are also more likely to be strategic than voters who cross over away from the action or into a minority party's primary. In SD 20, only an estimated 19.0 percent of Republicans crossed party lines again in the general election. Democratic crossover, though low to begin with, actually increased to 5.3 percent. Table 8.1 illustrates these points more generally by examining the relationship between the competitiveness of primaries and crossover rates in both the primary and the general election.

Looking first at the primaries, the table shows that crossover rates fluctuate dramatically, with voters following the action into competitive primaries.[7] For example, although only about one in ten Democrats will cross over away from their party's contest when it is the closer race, well over a third of Democrats will vote in the Republican primary if it is more competitive. The same pattern holds true for Republican voters. The way that crossover rates are clearly tied to the closeness of primaries indicates that

TABLE 8.1   Mean Crossover Rates under Different Primary Conditions

	Democratic Primary Is Closer	Both Primaries Are Equally Close	Republican Primary Is Closer
Rate of Democratic crossover into Republican primary	10.4%	19.9%	35.6%
Democratic crossover rate in general election	8.2	11.7	14.1
Rate of Republican crossover into Democratic primary	37.5	22.5	13.8
Republican crossover rate in general election	18.6	17.7	13.7

many voters are being strategic. Why would a sincere crossover voter, interested in voicing her true preference rather than figuring out where her vote counts the most, care which race was tighter?

Patterns in general election crossover appear to support this conclusion. While a smaller percentage of partisans break party ranks in November in every type of election, the drop in crossover rates is especially large when a competitive primary has attracted many crossover voters. When the race for the Republican nomination is closer, Republican crossover measures 13.8 percent in the primary and remains steady at 13.7 percent in the general election. Yet in cases with a more competitive Democratic primary, Republican crossover plummets from 37.5 percent in the spring to 18.6 percent in November. These crossover voters seem to demonstrate their insincerity by returning to the Republican fold in the general election.

Examining the relationship between crossover rates and the edge in registration that one party has in a district reveals a similar pattern. Figure 8.1 shows a fairly tight correspondence between registration and Republican crossover in the primary: Republican voters are much more likely to cross party lines in solidly Democratic districts. The temptation to cross over (i.e., hedge) is strongest when the other side's dominance in the district is so great that capturing its nomination is tantamount to a victory in November. Consequently, hedgers in such cases should cross over in large numbers in the primary but then vote sincerely with their party in the general election. Figure 8.2 provides evidence that there are many hedgers who do indeed return to their party in November. This figure shows a much looser link between registration and general election crossover. Nominees from the dominant party can expect to attract many crossover voters in the primary, but they cannot plan to keep them.

Descriptive statistics alone cannot give a complete picture of how party strength and the competitiveness of primaries work together to shape

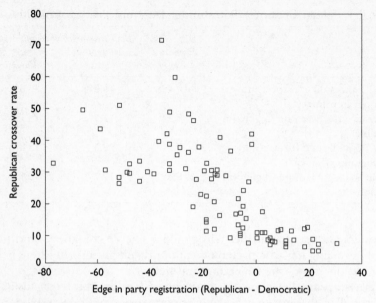

Figure 8.1. Estimated Republican crossover rate in the Democratic primary.

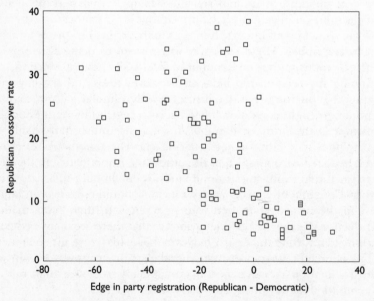

Figure 8.2. Estimated Republican crossover rate in the general election.

trends in crossover voting. For this, I turn to multivariate regression analysis. I construct models that use the level of crossover support received by each party in the primary, along with other potentially relevant electoral conditions, to predict how much cross-party backing that party's nominee will attract in the general election. This allows me to compute the "stickiness factor," the boost in November crossover that a nominee can expect for each additional percentage point of the other party's voters captured in the primary. In these regressions, the coefficient of the independent variable "Primary Crossover" represents the stickiness factor.

Since I am most interested in discovering how this factor changes depending on which party holds a registration edge and which primary is more competitive, I include interaction terms to see if the effect of Primary Crossover shifts with the characteristics of the races. To do this, I first built dichotomous variables that recorded whether or not the district was safely controlled by the Democratic or the Republican Party,[8] and whether there were more candidates in the Democratic or the Republican primary. I then include interaction terms, created by multiplying each of these four dummies by Primary Crossover, as explanatory variables in my models. Consequently, the coefficient for Primary Crossover alone gives the stickiness factor in districts with relatively even registration where each party fielded the same number of candidates in the spring.

I expect the models displayed in tables 8.2 and 8.3 to show that stickiness is highest in competitive contests for a weak party's nomination. These races are expected to draw mostly sincere crossover voters who stick with their primary choices in the general election. Close races in the dominant party's primary are expected to attract many strategic voters who return home in November, thus resulting in a small stickiness factor. Since I have no a priori theory about which type of district characteristic—party strength or primary competitiveness—should have the largest effect, I hypothesize that all interaction terms will be significant. This may not be the case, however. To avoid drawing distinctions between the stickiness of crossover voting where none exist, I begin by including all four interactions in an expanded model for each party and then eliminate those with coefficients smaller than their standard errors in a reduced model.

Both models include as independent variables the presence of incumbents and differences in campaign spending, which previous research has shown to be significant factors in explaining crossover voting.[9] Tables 8.2 and 8.3 present the results of ordinary least square regressions explaining general election crossover. I present results from models of Democratic and Republican crossover separately even though the rates in each district are generated by the same political conditions. These regressions, then, are best thought of as "seemingly unrelated regressions." Yet because the exogenous factors used in each model are functionally identical, they consti-

TABLE 8.2   Explaining November Crossover Rates
of Republican Voters

	Expanded Model	Reduced Model
Presence of a Democratic incumbent	3.55**	3.55**
	(1.70)	(1.70)
Presence of a Republican incumbent	0.16	0.16
	(1.40)	(1.50)
Difference in total primary spending	0.000005**	0.000005**
(Republican − Democrat)	(0.00)	(0.00)
Estimated Democratic crossover into	−0.15**	−0.15**
Republican primary	(0.07)	(0.07)
Estimated Republican crossover into	0.72***	0.72***
Democratic primary	(0.11)	(0.11)
Republican primary crossover ×	0.18***	0.18***
more competitive Republican primary	(0.07)	(0.07)
Republican primary crossover ×	−0.18***	−0.18***
more competitive Democratic primary	(0.06)	(0.06)
Republican primary crossover ×	−0.10**	−0.10**
safe Democratic seat	(0.04)	(0.04)
Republican primary crossover ×	0.002	
safe Republican seat	(0.16)	
Constant	3.90	3.90
	(3.40)	(3.40)
Adjusted R^2	.82	.83

NOTE: Entries are OLS regression coefficients, with standard errors in parentheses. Dependent variable is the percentage of Republican voters crossing party lines in the general election ($N = 90$).
  **$p < .05$
  ***$p < .01$

tute a special case of seemingly unrelated regressions in which ordinary least squares regression yields efficient estimators. Because patterns for each party's voters appear to differ, I estimate models of Democratic and Republican crossover separately.

INTERPRETATION OF QUANTITATIVE FINDINGS

These results indicate that the stickiness factor changes with the relative closeness of primary races and the advantage in registration that one party holds. Indeed, the expected effect of primary election crossover rates on November crossover varies in exactly the ways that hypotheses about strategic behavior led me to expect. In table 8.2, for instance, the coefficient on the "Safe Democratic Seat" interaction term is negative. This suggests that when a nominee's party holds a strong registration advantage in a

TABLE 8.3   Explaining November Crossover Rates
of Democratic Voters

	Expanded Model	Reduced Model
Presence of a Democratic incumbent	−0.76	−0.84
	(1.11)	(1.06)
Presence of a Republican incumbent	1.44	1.28
	(1.55)	(1.53)
Difference in total primary spending	−0.000002	−0.000002
(Republican − Democrat)	(0.00)	(0.00)
Estimated Republican crossover into	0.07	0.06
Democratic primary	(0.08)	(0.08)
Estimated Democratic crossover into	0.72***	0.70***
Republican primary	(0.09)	(0.09)
Democratic primary crossover ×	−0.21***	−0.21***
more competitive Republican primary	(0.04)	(0.04)
Democratic primary crossover ×	−0.002	
more competitive Democratic primary	(0.06)	
Democratic primary crossover ×	0.12	0.12
safe Democratic seat	(0.11)	(0.11)
Democratic primary crossover ×	−0.03	
safe Republican seat	(0.03)	
Constant	−4.00	−3.50
	(3.40)	(3.30)
Adjusted R^2	.84	.84

NOTE: Entries are OLS regression coefficients, with standard errors in parentheses. Dependent variable is the percentage of Democratic voters crossing party lines in the general election ($N = 90$).
**$p < .05$
***$p < .01$

district, that nominee should not expect to retain much support from the other party's voters who crossed over in the primary. Similarly, the negative coefficient on the interaction with "More Competitive Democratic Primary" indicates that most voters who crossed over to take part in a highly competitive primary when their party's contest was not close will return to their party's fold in the general election. These patterns are clearest in the behavior of Republican voters, but they also appear to be present in Democratic voting trends.[10]

The regression results from tables 8.2 and 8.3 are given substantive interpretation in tables 8.4 and 8.5. The coefficients of the interaction terms show how the stickiness factor shifts when different electoral conditions are met. By adding together the appropriate coefficients, I have created tables that display the stickiness factor for each party's voters in each type of election. For instance, the first row of table 8.4 can be used to predict the

TABLE 8.4   Behavior of Republican Crossover Voters

Type of District		Average Primary Crossover	"Stickiness Factor"	Total November Gain
If the seat is marginal or a safe Republican seat . . .	• and Republican race has more candidates	11.8% ×	0.90% =	10.6%
	• and primaries have same number of candidates	18.4 ×	0.72 =	13.2
	• and Democratic race has more candidates	23.0 ×	0.54 =	12.4
If the seat is a safe Democratic seat . . .	• and Republican race has more candidates	27.5 ×	0.80 =	22.0
	• and primaries have same number of candidates	31.1 ×	0.62 =	19.3
	• and Democratic race has more candidates	43.8 ×	0.44 =	19.3

NOTE: Results from model explaining 83 percent of variation in general election crossover rates; all differences significant at the .01 level. The "stickiness factor" represents the boost in November crossover that a nominee can expect for each additional percentage point of the other party's voters captured in the primary.

TABLE 8.5   Behavior of Democratic Crossover Voters

Type of Primary Election		Average Primary Crossover	"Stickiness Factor"	Total November Gain
If the seat is marginal or a safe Republican seat . . .	• and Republican race has more candidates	39.2% ×	0.51% =	20.0%
	• and primaries have same number of candidates	26.0 ×	0.72 =	18.7
	• and Democratic race has more candidates	20.3 ×	0.72 =	14.6
If the seat is a safe Democratic seat . . .	• and Republican race has more candidates	10.7 ×	0.63 =	6.7
	• and primaries have same number of candidates	7.1 ×	0.84 =	6.0
	• and Democratic race has more candidates	6.7 ×	0.84 =	5.6

NOTE: Results from model explaining 84 percent of variation in general election crossover rates. The "stickiness factor" represents the boost in November crossover that a nominee can expect for each additional percentage point of the other party's voters captured in the primary.

fortunes of a Democrat who won the nomination in a primary with relatively few candidates in a district that is not safely controlled by the Democratic Party. While this type of primary attracts on average only 11.8 percent of Republican voters, the Democratic nominee is expected to hold onto 0.90 percent of these Republican voters for every percentage point of crossover support captured in the blanket primary. This leaves the nominee supported by an expected 10.6 percent of Republican voters in November. By contrast, the bottom row of this table reports that the victor in a close Democratic primary in a solidly Democratic seat will attract 43.8 percent of Republicans but retain only 43.8 percent $\times$ 0.44 percent = 19.3 percent of them in the general election. The difference between these stickiness factors can be explained by voter motivations. I hypothesized that nearly all of the Republicans who crossed over in the type of race described in the first row did so sincerely. They continued to cross over, while the strategic voters who crossed over in races such as those described by the bottom row returned to back the Democratic nominee in November.

The message from these data is that California's new blanket primary enticed many voters to cross party lines strategically, and that strategic voting was most prevalent where one might expect it to be. But there is more to the story than this. Nominees care not just about how many crossover voters they keep in November, but about how many they can attract to boost their chances in the primary. To give some sense of this, tables 8.4 and 8.5 also report the mean percentage of crossover support attracted to each type of primary, and the percentage expected to stick around in November.[11] Again, the pattern observed here matches up with hypotheses about strategic voting. Since sincere voters cross over only when they prefer one of the other party's candidates, the level of sincere crossover voting should not fluctuate with district characteristics that do not systematically affect voter preferences. Any significant fluctuations in the crossover rate can likely be attributed to strategic behavior. Indeed, these tables show that crossover rates are especially high when a close competition or one party's overwhelming strength tempts strategic voters to cross party lines in the primary. But the lower stickiness factors for these races reveal that many crossover voters return to support their own party's nominee in the general election, when crossing over really counts.

CONCLUSION

Taken together, these findings point out a striking irony: in the situations that allow a party to attract the most crossover voters, few of these voters will stick around in November. This leaves candidates, party strategists, and political consultants faced with a difficult dilemma. Should candidates in the party with the closest primary expend resources to capture the tantalizing prize of crossover voters when half of their cross-party support might evaporate in the general election? My analysis provides no hard and fast rules for practitioners about how to balance this trade-off. It does, however, highlight two practical lessons for blanket primary participants. First, no one can afford to ignore crossover voting when planning a primary strategy, because, especially in certain kinds of races, there will be much of it. Second, once a candidate has gained the nomination, she can look back at the type of primary in which she was victorious as a guide to how many crossover supporters she can expect to stick around in November.

These findings also contain lessons for academics studying voter behavior and those concerned with the normative aspects of political reform. Most important, both the clear patterns in primary crossover rates and the relationship of these rates to general election crossover show that a considerable number of voters are being strategic. This supports Abramowitz, McGlennon, and Rapoport (1981) and Wekkin's (1991) findings that crossover voters can help determine the outcome of a primary, and Cohen, Kousser, and Sides's (1999) conclusion that this behavior often has strategic motivations. Alvarez and Nagler's (1998) analysis of a 1998 California poll found that only 10 percent or so of crossover voters in legislative races voted strategically. The large differences in crossover rates and stickiness factors between types of primaries seen in this analysis suggest that in some races, at least, strategic voting is much more common than that.

What are the normative implications of this strategic behavior? By definition, strategic voters are not casting a ballot for their top choice. Other research indicates that they are hedging their bets, supporting the candidate from the other party who provides the most palatable alternative to their own party's nominee. Those evaluating the blanket primary might not find anything insidious in hedging. They should note, though, that the frequency of this strategic behavior allows voters to help choose the other party's nominee when their sincere allegiances still lie with their own party. Survey evidence from San Diego's Assembly District 75 shows that Democratic crossover voters provided more votes for the eventual Republican nominee than Republicans did (Alvarez and Nagler 1998). The findings of this chapter indicate that more than half of these voters switched back to the Democratic nominee in November, revealing that they had crossed over strategically.

APPENDIX A: MEASURING CROSSOVER RATES
THROUGH ECOLOGICAL INFERENCE

To estimate the percentage of Democrats and Republicans who cross over in legislative primaries and general elections, this chapter relies on a method of ecological inference (King 1997). While valuable, it is important to recognize that this method is not without its critics (Rivers and Tam 1997; Tam 1997a, 1997b). Here I briefly discuss the application of King's method to the question of crossover voting, first undertaken by Alvarez and Nagler (1997) and Cohen and Sides (1998), and present crossover estimates.

Knowing only the number of Republican and Democratic voters in each district and the vote totals for each party, a researcher needs to make inferences about the number of Republicans who vote for a Democratic candidate (and vice versa). The first step of King's procedure, the method of bounds, uses logic quite similar to the reasoning employed by Hall's (1923) analysis of Wisconsin primaries. Hall reports that in 1918, while 192,145 primary voters cast their ballots in favor of Republicans, general election results suggest that there were only 155,799 Republicans in the active electorate that year. Democrats must have provided some of the Republican primary votes. The fact that only 112,576 Democrats turned up in the general election sets an upper bound on how many Democrats voted in the Republican primary. These bounds imply that Democratic crossover in this race fell between 36,346 and 112,576.

King's method constructs a "tomography plot," with lines in this case representing each California district. The *x*-axis gives the proportion of Democrats voting for a Democratic candidate and the *y*-axis gives the proportion of Republicans voting for a Democratic candidate. King assumes that the crossover values are most likely to lie at the pinnacle of a "mountain" (taking the shape of a truncated bivariate normal distribution) that is located where the lines are most densely bunched. His ecological inference procedure yields point estimates of voting rates across all districts derived from the mountain's pinnacle and a confidence interval mapped by the mountain's contour lines. King's method then uses a simulation procedure to calculate district-level estimates of crossover rates.

Using EzI, a program designed to compute King's model, I computed crossover rates in the ninety contested California Assembly and Senate races in 1998.[12] I conducted separate runs of the program to estimate crossover in the primaries and in the general election. Some of the assumptions made in both cases to provide input for EzI introduce substantive concerns in addition to the statistical criticisms of ecological inference. To calculate crossover rates, EzI needs to be fed the number of Republicans and Democrats who show up at the polls as well as the number of ballots cast for candidates from each party. While election returns give exact measures of the latter figures, researchers need to find a proxy for the partisan breakdown of the electorate that actually turns out. The proxy that I employ here—Democratic and Republican registration as a percentage of major-party registration—is imperfect. In many elections, Republicans go to the polls at a rate higher than that of registered Democrats.

TABLE 8.6   Estimates of Crossover Vote,
with 95 Percent Confidence Interval

	Democratic Crossover			Republican Crossover		
	Lower	Estimate	Upper	Lower	Estimate	Upper
Primary election	13.0%	21.7%	35.1%	11.2%	24.0%	41.6%
General election	6.0	11.5	19.9	8.8	16.8	27.9

The assumption that there is no turnout differential in this case, though, seems tenable. In part because of a large mobilization by organized labor to defeat a major anti-labor initiative, Proposition 226, Democratic participation in the primary did not lag behind Republican turnout, as it often has. General election turnout rates were also nearly equal.[13] Another flaw of this proxy is that it assumes that every voter is a member of one of the major parties. Since 9.5 percent of those who cast a ballot for a major-party candidate in the 1998 primary belonged to a minor party or had no declared party affiliation, the EzI procedure slightly overestimates primary crossover rates. In the general election, this figure was 8 percent (*Los Angeles Times* exit poll). The nonaffiliates in each district are functionally assigned a party identification based on the major-party breakdown, and some are counted as crossover voters if election returns diverge from party composition patterns.

Tam (1997a) warns of another potential problem with this application of ecological inference. King's ecological inference model assumes both that the parameters (crossover rates, here) are uncorrelated with the regressors (registration figures) and that the lines in the tomography plot are all "related to one common mode" (Tam 1997a). Since I found that crossover does vary with the partisan leanings of a district, and since the tomography plot for this application does appear to be bimodal, I recomputed the estimates using the model extensions described in chapter 9 of King (1997). Specifically, I provided information about the relative competitiveness of primary races expressed in two different ways to the EzI program.[14] The estimates were fairly robust to these changes. Estimates from each run of EzI correlated with analogous estimates at .95 or higher, and none of the means differed by more than 4 percent. Because the original crossover rates most closely match the survey data from five districts collected by Alvarez and Nagler (1998), I use these figures in my analysis.

Aware of the statistical and substantive challenges to the ecologically inferred crossover rates, one should not place great credence in the precise point estimates that EzI provides. Yet just as a weatherman will predict temperatures in a five-day forecast, this chapter reports and analyzes these figures because they represent a "best guess" about the direction and magnitude of voting trends. Table 8.6 provides an average over all legislative districts of the percentage of Democrats and Republicans who crossed over to vote in the opposing party's primary and those who supported the other party in the general election. It also reports the mean lower and upper edges of the 95 percent confidence interval surrounding each estimate in order to quantify the level of uncertainty that this application of King's method entails.[15] Table 8.7 (pages 160–63) reports estimated crossover rates in each contested Senate and Assembly district in 1998, with districts grouped by party registration advantages and the competitiveness of the primaries.

APPENDIX B: CROSSOVER BEHAVIOR IN THE
MARCH 2000 PRIMARY

Thad Kousser and John Sides

Using the same techniques employed earlier in this chapter, this addendum (and its tables, beginning on page 164) analyzes California's March 2000 primary elections to answer two basic questions. First, how many voters crossed over into the other major party's primary? Second, how many could be expected to continue to cross over in the general election?

Table 8.10 reports primary crossover rate estimates for both Republican and Democratic voters in each of the ninety-seven Senate and Assembly contests that both parties contested in 2000. Tables 8.8 and 8.9 group these races into the same categories used in tables 8.4 and 8.5. Average crossover rates into districts from each category in 2000 are quite similar to the 1998 averages. To estimate expected general election crossover, we used the "stickiness factors" computed for each type of race in 1998. If the relationship between primary crossover, the dynamics of each race, and general election crossover remains stable from one electoral cycle to the next, these predictions will be useful. Estimated November crossover rates in each district are reported in table 8.10.

TABLE 8.7 Estimates of Crossover Rates in Each California 1998 Election

Seat	Major-Party Nominees in General Election (Democratic Nominee vs. Republican Nominee)	Estimated Crossover in Primary Races		Estimated Crossover in General Election Races	
		Democrats to Republican Race	Republicans to Democratic Race	Democrats for Republican Nominee	Republicans for Democratic Nominee
Democratic Primary Had More Candidates, Safe Democratic Seat					
SD 8	Speier vs. Tomlin	4.4%	49.3%	2.6%	34.1%
SD 10	Figueroa vs. Gough	5.5	46.7	5.7	22.8
SD 20	Alarcon vs. McCaulley	3.9	60.1	5.3	19.0
SD 26	Murray vs. Key	1.4	49.7	1.1	31.0
AD 7	Wiggins vs. Sanchez	8.6	38.4	6.8	16.8
AD 9	Steinberg vs. Dismukes	5.6	40.1	6.7	16.5
AD 18	Corbett vs. Nowicki	6.1	39.1	11.3	13.4
AD 23	Honda vs. Du Long	5.9	42.3	3.6	25.5
AD 31	Reyes vs. Jackson	22.7	19.4	14.3	11.7
AD 47	Wesson vs. Leonard	2.6	43.7	2.5	22.2
AD 49	Romero vs. Imperial	2.5	71.8	5.2	17.1
AD 50	Firebaugh vs. Miller	2.8	51.3	2.3	30.9
AD 55	Floyd vs. Eslinger	5.0	33.0	10.9	13.9
AD 57	Gallegos vs. Gonzales	8.1	38.2	4.7	23.7
AD 58	Calderon vs. Nunez	7.2	29.7	6.4	15.4
AD 62	Longville vs. Escobar	5.6	48.7	7.9	14.5
Democratic Primary Had More Candidates, Not a Safe Democratic Seat					
SD 4	Desio vs. Johannessen	36.8%	12.8%	24.6%	6.5%
SD 28	Bowen vs. Knott	10.1	33.1	5.4	23.1

SD 32	Baca vs. Ulloa	9.3	30.9	7.7	16.2
AD 15	Brydon vs. Leach	29.5	11.9	22.0	6.8
AD 20	Dutra vs. Zager	15.1	20.8	10.8	11.2
AD 30	Florez vs. Prenter	33.3	12.1	16.0	10.3
AD 53	Nakano vs. Eggers	8.2	39.2	5.0	25.3

Primaries Had Equal Number of Candidates, Safe Democratic Seat

SD 16	Costa vs. Palmer	9.7%	30.8%	3.2%	32.2%
SD 24	Solis vs. Taylor	6.1	32.8	3.9	26.0
SD 30	Escutia vs. Robertson	7.8	27.3	4.8	20.7
AD 12	Shelley vs. Fitzgerald	7.1	30.2	2.9	26.1
AD 13	Migden vs. Bernard	6.2	29.8	2.5	25.2
AD 14	Aroner vs. Udinsky	6.3	30.6	2.7	23.1
AD 16	Perata vs. Marshall	8.5	28.2	6.8	17.6
AD 19	Papan vs. Ferguson	8.3	36.6	3.4	30.4
AD 42	Knox vs. Davis	7.5	30.9	3.3	30.3
AD 45	Villaraigosa vs. Hedrick	5.8	33.7	2.7	29.4
AD 46	Cedillo vs. Kim	6.0	29.8	3.7	22.7
AD 48	Wright vs. Woodes	3.5	32.9	0.7	25.2
AD 51	Vincent vs. Acherman	9.7	26.5	4.9	15.8
AD 79	Ducheny vs. Kinz	7.2	35.7	3.1	29.0

Primaries Had Equal Number of Candidates, Not a Safe Democratic Seat

SD 2	Chesbro vs. Jordan	29.5%	15.1%	16.3%	9.3%
SD 12	Canella vs. Monteith	33.5	13.6	23.2	7.5
SD 18	O'Connell vs. Klemm	8.8	42.5	4.0	38.6
SD 34	Dunn vs. Hurtt	25.6	15.5	13.2	11.6
SD 36	Swift vs. Haynes	31.1	12.0	16.4	8.0
SD 38	Arkelian vs. Morrow	33.8	9.4	15.3	5.8
SD 40	Peace vs. Divine	9.1	37.1	3.9	34.2

Continued on next page

TABLE 8.7—Continued

Seat	Major-Party Nominees in General Election (Democratic Nominee vs. Republican Nominee)	Estimated Crossover in Primary Races		Estimated Crossover in General Election Races	
		Democrats to Republican Race	Republicans to Democratic Race	Democrats for Republican Nominee	Republicans for Democratic Nominee
AD 1	Strom-Martin vs. Crump	12.6%	22.7%	6.2%	18.5%
AD 8	Thomson vs. Thompson	11.8	28.1	6.8	19.7
AD 17	Machado vs. Smart	10.3	29.2	4.1	33.6
AD 21	Lempert vs. Atherly	7.1	41.3	3.6	37.5
AD 22	Alquist vs. Kawczynski	10.6	29.4	5.3	25.5
AD 25	Firch vs. House	41.1	9.6	32.6	4.6
AD 26	Cardoza vs. Hollingsworth	11.2	30.7	5.0	22.5
AD 28	Styles vs. Frusetta	39.8	11.6	28.7	5.7
AD 32	Tucker vs. Ashburn	46.1	7.7	38.7	4.0
AD 34	Figueroa vs. Olberg	42.1	8.8	28.5	5.3
AD 36	Calderon vs. Runner	38.1	8.9	24.0	5.7
AD 41	Kuehl vs. Jhin	12.1	29.1	5.7	20.3
AD 44	Scott vs. LaCorte	15.0	24.6	7.2	18.9
AD 56	Havice vs. Hawkins	24.1	16.5	14.4	10.1
AD 59	Christiansen vs. Margett	27.4	12.1	14.1	8.7
AD 66	Hockersmith vs. Thompson	29.0	13.0	14.7	8.0
AD 69	Correa vs. Morrissey	34.3	14.3	15.3	10.8
AD 71	Badger vs. Campbell	36.9	7.8	20.5	5.1
AD 72	Legas vs. Ackerman	35.6	7.7	23.6	4.9
AD 74	Fitzgerald vs. Kaloogian	25.3	12.4	11.9	9.6
AD 77	Carlson vs. Baldwin	35.0	11.3	23.8	6.4
AD 80	Acuna vs. Battin	38.0	10.2	26.8	6.1

Republican Primary Had More Candidates, Safe Democratic Seat

AD 6	Mazzoni vs. Weiner	9.3%	27.8%	4.8%	22.1%
AD 27	Keeley vs. Chavez	13.3	23.3	5.4	22.2
AD 40	Hertzberg vs. Hammans	9.5	31.3	4.5	28.8

Republican Primary Had More Candidates, Not a Safe Democratic Seat

SD 6	Ortiz vs. Quackenbush	18.1%	19.6%	7.9%	17.7%
AD 2	Sullivan vs. Dickerson	48.8	8.8	20.0	7.2
AD 3	Gruendl vs. Aanestad	47.6	7.4	11.1	11.8
AD 4	Norberg vs. Oller	47.5	6.9	23.5	4.8
AD 5	Davis vs. Cox	38.9	9.1	22.1	7.4
AD 10	Gravert vs. Pescetti	39.2	11.5	10.4	10.4
AD 24	Stokes vs. Cuneen	50.3	9.4	33.8	5.6
AD 33	Sanders vs. Maldonado	52.8	7.8	25.8	5.9
AD 35	Jackson vs. Mitchum	28.3	17.1	11.2	11.5
AD 37	McGrath vs. Strickland	35.6	11.4	10.9	10.8
AD 43	Wildman vs. Repovich	16.1	22.0	3.9	32.6
AD 54	Lowenthal vs. Alban	42.3	10.8	14.6	11.3
AD 60	Wong vs. Pacheco	47.4	8.0	18.6	7.9
AD 61	Soto vs. Demallie	25.0	17.3	8.7	15.3
AD 65	Quinto vs. Granlund	40.1	8.5	19.1	7.1
AD 67	Fennell vs. Baugh	58.5	6.8	12.6	9.3
AD 68	Matsuda vs. Maddox	46.1	9.6	12.3	9.1
AD 73	Wilberg vs. Bates	55.1	5.5	24.4	4.6
AD 75	Debus vs. Zettel	56.2	5.6	26.0	4.1
AD 76	Davis vs. Admire	11.7	27.3	3.2	34.8
AD 78	Wayne vs. Roesch	17.0	17.7	4.8	26.5

TABLE 8.8   Behavior of Republican Crossover Voters (March 2000)

Type of District		Average Primary Crossover		"Stickiness Factor"		Total November Gain
If the seat is marginal or a safe Republican seat . . .	• and Republican race has more candidates	11.6%	×	0.90%	=	10.5%
	• and primaries have same number of candidates	16.5	×	0.72	=	11.9
	• and Democratic race has more candidates	19.8	×	0.54	=	10.7
If the seat is a safe Democratic seat . . .	• and Republican race has more candidates	32.3	×	0.80	=	25.8
	• and primaries have same number of candidates	29.4	×	0.62	=	18.2
	• and Democratic race has more candidates	43.6	×	0.44	=	19.2

TABLE 8.9   Behavior of Democratic Crossover Voters (March 2000)

Type of Primary Election		Average Primary Crossover		"Stickiness Factor"		Total November Gain
If the seat is marginal or a safe Republican seat . . .	• and Republican race has more candidates	37.6%	×	0.51%	=	19.2%
	• and primaries have same number of candidates	26.8	×	0.72	=	19.3
	• and Democratic race has more candidates	19.8	×	0.72	=	14.3
If the seat is a safe Democratic seat . . .	• and Republican race has more candidates	5.5	×	0.63	=	3.5
	• and primaries have same number of candidates	5.6	×	0.84	=	4.7
	• and Democratic race has more candidates	3.8	×	0.84	=	3.2

TABLE 8.10   Estimates of Crossover Rates in 2000 California Elections

House	Seat	Estimated Crossover in Primary Races		Predicted Crossover in General Election Races	
		Democrats to Republican Race	Republicans to Democratic Race	Democrats for Republican Nominee	Republicans for Democratic Nominee
Senate	1	40.2%	10.2%	16.8%	7.0%
Senate	3	6.3	28.1	2.5	23.9
Senate	5	15.6	20.3	5.4	19.8
Senate	7	22.2	15.2	9.6	14.4
Senate	9	3.1	31.1	0.1	26.2
Senate	11	13.6	24.1	6.6	22.8
Senate	13	6.5	32.1	2.9	26.4
Senate	15	40.8	11.2	27.0	4.0
Senate	17	41.5	8.5	27.4	4.0
Senate	19	46.9	8.6	20.0	4.6
Senate	21	9.7	34.0	5.3	27.0
Senate	23	3.1	54.3	2.3	27.3
Senate	25	3.6	31.3	1.3	17.1
Senate	27	15.2	20.2	7.5	19.7
Senate	29	21.2	15.2	12.2	8.9
Senate	31	35.5	9.9	23.3	5.9
Senate	33	40.2	7.8	25.1	3.5
Senate	35	32.0	10.8	20.8	7.1
Senate	37	50.1	9.0	21.6	4.5
Senate	39	13.9	20.6	6.6	20.2
Assembly	1	8.2	30.8	3.3	28.4
Assembly	2	51.4	8.6	34.3	2.5
Assembly	3	40.0	8.2	26.3	3.9
Assembly	4	39.9	9.0	25.0	4.4
Assembly	6	3.8	45.6	2.3	23.4
Assembly	7	8.6	26.4	4.3	22.5
Assembly	8	9.7	24.6	4.0	23.7
Assembly	9	7.7	24.6	3.5	21.6
Assembly	10	30.7	12.7	20.1	8.6
Assembly	11	6.5	36.5	4.0	19.0
Assembly	12	5.0	27.0	1.4	23.4
Assembly	13	3.8	28.4	−0.3	29.6
Assembly	14	4.3	28.6	0.9	24.6
Assembly	15	35.3	9.7	23.0	5.7
Assembly	16	3.3	31.7	1.1	23.1
Assembly	17	15.8	17.2	8.6	13.9
Assembly	18	5.6	31.9	2.2	26.4
Assembly	19	5.2	37.8	2.2	30.1

Continued on next page

TABLE 8.10—*Continued*

House	Seat	Estimated Crossover in Primary Races		Predicted Crossover in General Election Races	
		Democrats to Republican Race	Republicans to Democratic Race	Democrats for Republican Nominee	Republicans for Democratic Nominee
Assembly	20	9.0%	26.9%	3.6%	25.5%
Assembly	21	11.3	18.8	5.6	15.7
Assembly	22	10.5	26.6	4.6	25.1
Assembly	23	3.1	51.0	2.1	25.9
Assembly	24	20.8	16.3	7.7	15.4
Assembly	25	41.9	9.8	17.6	6.5
Assembly	26	8.4	30.0	3.3	27.8
Assembly	27	8.0	27.2	2.9	25.8
Assembly	28	21.7	16.0	12.7	12.2
Assembly	29	50.5	6.8	33.5	1.4
Assembly	30	8.9	28.9	3.6	27.0
Assembly	31	9.9	27.6	5.4	23.1
Assembly	32	55.9	7.3	37.3	1.0
Assembly	33	51.1	7.3	34.0	1.6
Assembly	34	52.3	7.9	22.6	3.2
Assembly	35	9.9	27.7	4.2	20.9
Assembly	36	38.1	9.5	25.0	5.2
Assembly	37	27.4	15.7	17.9	8.4
Assembly	38	34.2	10.4	13.9	8.2
Assembly	39	4.1	36.2	1.2	29.3
Assembly	40	6.0	30.3	1.1	30.8
Assembly	41	9.6	24.5	4.7	15.7
Assembly	42	2.5	54.4	1.8	27.5
Assembly	43	14.1	21.0	7.6	16.9
Assembly	44	9.9	24.7	4.9	15.7
Assembly	46	4.0	32.9	0.9	27.3
Assembly	47	4.2	24.0	0.6	21.7
Assembly	48	3.1	26.4	−0.2	23.3
Assembly	50	7.3	25.6	3.2	22.3
Assembly	51	3.5	36.2	1.6	19.3
Assembly	52	8.0	25.6	2.1	26.7
Assembly	53	9.8	31.5	4.4	28.6
Assembly	54	17.6	18.5	5.4	21.5
Assembly	55	2.0	50.2	1.1	25.7
Assembly	56	22.4	18.5	7.7	20.8
Assembly	57	3.6	46.8	2.3	23.9
Assembly	58	7.3	27.2	3.3	23.2
Assembly	59	52.5	7.2	22.6	2.6

TABLE 8.10—*Continued*

House	Seat	Estimated Crossover in Primary Races		Predicted Crossover in General Election Races	
		Democrats to Republican Race	Republicans to Democratic Race	Democrats for Republican Nominee	Republicans for Democratic Nominee
Assembly	60	47.8	9.3	31.8	3.6
Assembly	61	27.1	15.3	10.7	13.6
Assembly	62	6.7	29.9	2.9	19.6
Assembly	63	40.5	9.5	18.2	6.5
Assembly	64	34.3	9.9	22.4	6.0
Assembly	65	48.5	7.6	20.7	3.5
Assembly	66	58.2	5.6	25.4	0.2
Assembly	67	52.6	5.8	22.6	1.2
Assembly	68	38.8	10.8	25.6	6.0
Assembly	69	16.3	21.4	8.4	20.4
Assembly	70	29.7	10.5	17.9	7.0
Assembly	71	41.1	6.8	18.3	4.0
Assembly	72	64.1	5.9	28.2	−0.4
Assembly	73	39.9	7.6	26.2	3.5
Assembly	74	55.3	5.8	23.9	0.9
Assembly	75	41.4	6.9	18.5	4.0
Assembly	76	11.5	24.9	3.6	24.6
Assembly	77	35.0	9.2	14.2	6.9
Assembly	78	11.0	24.3	2.5	27.6
Assembly	79	4.2	44.8	1.8	39.1
Assembly	80	29.0	11.4	17.5	7.8

NOTES

1. When many Democrats who had crossed over to vote in the Republican primary returned to their party's candidates in the general election, Leonard's Republicans lost five Assembly seats, and Leonard lost his leadership post. Also quoted in the same article was former Democratic Minority Leader Richard Katz, who would go on to lose in a State Senate Democratic primary: "As a candidate, you feel like a lab rat or a guinea pig."

2. See Alvarez and Nagler 1998 and Cohen, Kousser, and Sides 1999.

3. Alvarez and Nagler (1998) and Cohen, Kousser, and Sides (1999) both find little evidence of raiding in blanket primaries and thus conclude that hedging is the dominant form of strategic crossover voting. The approach taken in this analysis, however, cannot distinguish between the two forms of strategic behavior.

4. When attempting to test this hypothesis, the first thing one should realize is that the electorate grows (in most cases, it doubles) between the general election and the primary. Consequently, the general election crossover rate is the average of the crossover rate for voters who participate in the primary and the general election and the rate for those who turn out only in November. The latter rate should not be influenced by the characteristics of a primary that drive some primary voters to cross over strategically. They do not care about how many candidates were in each primary, and in the general election can no longer hedge their bets to give a palatable candidate from the other party the nomination. Therefore, the crossover rate for "November-only" voters should be invariant to primary characteristics. If I find patterns linking types of primaries to general election crossover rates, then, I can reasonably conclude that they are patterns in the stickiness factor of those who participated in both the primary and general elections.

5. Cohen, Kousser, and Sides (1999) find that it is more like 20 percent in Washington.

6. *Los Angeles Times* exit polls count the number of moderates in both elections at 43 percent.

7. A more competitive primary is defined here as one in which one major party fields more candidates than the other. This larger candidate field signals to voters, who may know little about a race other than what they see on the ballot, that the primary with the most candidates will be the closest one.

8. "Safe" is defined as a 20 percent lead in registration for the Democrats or a 10 percent lead for Republicans. The need for this asymmetry, which results from higher Republican turnout and loyalty rates, is demonstrated in J. Morgan Kousser (1996). While many political strategists consider seats in which the parties have smaller registration edges to be safe, I use these levels to capture voter perceptions. Changing the levels to 10 percent and 5 percent, respectively, does not change any of the regression results.

9. See Alvarez and Nagler (1998); Cohen, Kousser, and Sides (1999).

10. One reason why these effects might be less clear in models of Democratic crossover—indicating that strategic voting was less common among these voters—is that Democrats generally hold an electoral advantage in California (46.7 percent of registered voters are Democrats, compared to the 35.6 percent who are Republicans). This means that there were fewer Republican strongholds in which Demo-

cratic voters might be tempted to hedge their bets, and fewer races with more Republicans then Democrats.

11. Since the ecological inference technique that I use here cannot pinpoint which particular candidate benefits from crossover voting, these figures simply show how large a pool of the other party's voters the set of candidates has to draw from in the primary.

12. The program used here is version 2.20 of EzI for Windows 95, written by Kenneth Benoit and Gary King, which can be downloaded easily from King's home-page at http://GKing.harvard.edu. Races in which one major party failed to field any candidates are dropped from these datasets, because voters driven into another primary by a lack of any options in their own party's primary cannot properly be said to cross over.

13. According to the *Los Angeles Times* exit poll, 48.3 percent of primary voters in 1998 were registered Democrats and 40.2 percent were Republicans, while the Secretary of State reports that overall party registration was 46.7 percent Democratic and 35.6 percent Republican. In the general election, a *Times* exit poll estimated the partisan breakdown as 48 percent Democratic and 39 percent Republican.

14. I included this variable first as a dichotomous measure, as suggested in King 1997 (174), and then as a continuous variable.

15. When I recomputed the regressions reported in tables 8.2 and 8.3 using both the upper and lower bounds of this confidence interval, the direction and significance levels of the coefficients were unchanged.

REFERENCES

Abramowitz, Alan; John McGlennon; and Ronald Rapoport. 1981. "A Note on Strategic Voting in a Primary Election." *Journal of Politics* 43: 899–904.

Alvarez, R. Michael, and Jonathan Nagler. 1997. "Analysis of Crossover and Strategic Voting." Expert testimony in *California Democratic Party et al. v. Jones* (1997).

———. 1998. *Preliminary Report on June 2, 1998, Exit Poll.* Riverside, CA: Alvarez and Nagler Political Research Group.

American Political Science Association, Committee on Political Parties. 1950. "Toward a More Responsible Two-Party System." *American Political Science Review* 44 (supp.).

Berdahl, Clarence A. 1942. "Party Membership in the United States." *American Political Science Review* 36: 16–50, 241–62.

Bernstein, Dan. 1998. "Blanket Primary Erases Party Lines." *Sacramento Bee,* June 7, A1.

Cain, Bruce E. 1997. "Report on Blanket and Open Primaries." Expert testimony in *California Democratic Party et al. v. Jones,* 984 F. Supp. 1288 (1997).

"California Journal's District-by-District Analysis: Assembly." 1998. *California Journal* 29 (May): 39–54.

Cohen, Jonathan; Thad Kousser; and John Sides. 1999. "Sincere Voting, Hedging, and Raiding: Testing a Formal Model of Crossover Voting in Blanket Primaries."

Paper presented at the 1999 American Political Science Association meetings, Atlanta, Georgia.

Cohen, Jonathan, and John Sides. 1998. "The Incidence and Importance of Crossover Voting in a Blanket Primary: Washington State Senate Elections, 1986–1996." Institute for Governmental Studies: Working paper 98-6.

DiCamillo, Mark. 1998. "Californians Vote in the State's First Blanket Primary." *IGS Public Affairs Report* 39 (September): 1, 4–5.

Freedman, D. A., et al. 1998. "On 'Solutions' to the Ecological Inference Problem." Technical Report No. 515, Statistics Department, University of California, Berkeley (April).

Hall, Arnold Bennet. 1923. "The Direct Primary and Party Responsibility in Wisconsin." *Annals of the American Academy of Political and Social Science* (March): 40–54.

Harris, Joseph P. 1951. *A Model Direct Primary Election System: Report of the Committee on the Direct Primary.* New York: National Municipal League.

Ingram, Carl, and Max Vanzi. 1998. "Campaign Expenses Soar for First 'Blanket' Primary." *Los Angeles Times,* May 8, 1998: 3.

Jones, Bill. 1998a. *1998 California Primary Election: Campaign Receipts, Expenditures, Cash-On-Hand, and Debts for State Candidates and Officeholders.* Sacramento.

———. 1998b. *Report of Registration: September 1998.* Sacramento.

———. 1998c. *Statement of Vote: Primary Election, June 2, 1998.* Sacramento.

———. 1998d. *Preliminary Returns from General Election 1998.* Sacramento.

Key, V. O. 1964. *Politics, Parties, and Pressure Groups.* 5th ed. New York: Thomas Y. Crowell.

King, Gary. 1997. *A Solution to the Ecological Inference Problem: Reconstructing Individual Behavior from Aggregate Data.* Princeton, NJ: Princeton University Press.

Kousser, J. Morgan. 1996. "Estimating the Partisan Consequences of Redistricting—Simply." *Legislative Studies Quarterly* 21 (November): 521–41.

Ranney, Austin. 1951. "Toward a More Responsible Two-Party System: A Commentary." *American Political Science Review* 45: 488–99.

Rivers, Douglas, and Wendy Tam. 1997. "Yet Another Solution to the Ecological Regression Problem." Unpublished ms. Available on the Political Methodology server: http://wizard.ucr.edu/polmeth.

Rocca, Helen M. 1927. *Nominating Methods, with Special Reference to the Direct Primary.* Washington, D.C.: National League of Women Voters.

Tam, Wendy. 1997a. "Iff the Assumptions Fit . . ." Unpublished ms. Available on the Political Methodology server: http://wizard.ucr.edu/polmeth.

———. 1997b. "Structural Shifts and Deterministic Regime Switching in Aggregate Data Analysis." Unpublished ms. Available on the Political Methodology server: http://wizard.ucr.edu/polmeth.

Trounstine, Phillip J. 1998. "Political Labels Don't Stick in Open-Primary Season." *San Jose Mercury News,* February 22, 1998: C1.

Wekkin, Gary D. 1991. "Why Crossover Voters Are Not 'Mischievous Voters': The Segmented Partisanship Hypothesis." *American Politics Quarterly* 19 (April): 229–47.

CHAPTER NINE

Candidates, Donors, and Voters in California's Blanket Primary Elections

Wendy K. Tam Cho and Brian J. Gaines

In March of 1996, by a 59.5 percent to 40.5 percent vote, California voters approved Proposition 198, thereby changing the state's primary election law from closed to open. A large majority of citizens undoubtedly consider electoral law to be exceptionally esoteric, even less worthy of attention than normal party politics. By contrast, professional politicians quite sensibly take great interest in electoral mechanisms, as is evident from the heated arguments at the elite level that preceded and, especially, followed Proposition 198's passage. In this chapter, we do not directly take sides on the merits and demerits of the "blanket" primary. Nor do we thoroughly dissect the logic of arguments advanced by Proposition 198's friends and foes. Instead, we proceed by addressing their claims empirically: did opening the primaries have any of its anticipated consequences? We compare California's 1998 elections with those of 1992, 1994, and 1996 in search of significant, systematic changes in the behavior of candidates, voters, and campaign contributors. Our main conclusion is that these actors were slow to react to new strategic opportunities. Changes in political behavior may have manifested themselves had the Supreme Court not overturned California's Proposition 198 in June of 2000; people require time and practice to understand a new electoral system.

The chapter proceeds as follows. We begin by reviewing the debate that surrounded Proposition 198. Our goal is to extract hypotheses about the anticipated effects of a blanket primary law from arguments made by proponents and opponents in the Proposition 198 campaign. We then examine data from recent elections (both primary and general) to assess how accurate these hypotheses were. Specifically, we compare the 1998 election to its immediate predecessors. In examining the hypotheses, we focus on issues related to participation and campaign contributions. Finally, we conclude with some general discussion about when changes in electoral law should or should not be expected to affect outcomes.

In trying to identify what effects the change in California's primary rules (or, indeed, any change in electoral law) ought to have had, a natural way to start is by reviewing who promoted the change and who opposed it. In the next section, then, we consider what effects the pro– and anti–Proposition 198 forces highlighted in the spring 1996 campaign. We then turn attention to 1998's legislative races, especially the contests for the U.S. House, to evaluate these hypotheses against the first run of the blanket primary system in California.

HYPOTHESES ABOUT BLANKET PRIMARIES

Prior to its debut in June of 1998, the blanket primary was regarded as something of a wild card by disinterested observers. In a preview of the election, *CQ Weekly Report* summarized, "Most pollsters and political consultants have been unable to predict how the new system will affect election results" (Birtel 1998, 1373). In the absence of expert consensus, a natural place to find hypotheses about the likely effects of Proposition 198 is the "official" debate provided to voters by the Secretary of State in the voters' handbook. In this official state publication, opponents and proponents of each initiative present short statements in support of their positions. The state then circulates these pamphlets with ballots.[1] Each side can also rebut the other side's claims, so this exchange provides the interested voter with a four-part debate on the merits of the policy at hand. The debate on Proposition 198 was not atypical, in that the arguments made on both sides were a blend of specific claims with a somewhat clear logic, vague and probably untestable points, and plentiful rhetoric. Again, in this chapter we will not dwell on the task of elucidating the logic behind the various positive and negative claims made about blanket primaries. Instead, we will regard these propositions as worthy of investigation and proceed directly to evaluating their empirical veracity.

Supporters of Proposition 198 broached three direct and two indirect arguments. Their direct arguments were that the switch to a blanket primary would "give voters a choice," "increase voter participation," and "restore healthy competition." One of their indirect arguments was that the blanket primary was not an untried experiment: other states had already adopted such laws (and, implicitly, had thereby succeeded in improving something about their politics). California's "closed" primary system was said to be broadly incompatible with Californians' tastes for independence. Further, Proposition 198's opponents were described as "hard liners" in both major political parties who opposed the blanket primary because it would weaken their own powers and the powers of the "special interests" that support them.

In the rebuttal to the anti–Proposition 198 claims, the proponents stressed the value of having a choice. The ability to choose from all candidates was said to have a number of beneficial results: it makes elected officials more responsive to voters and not to party chairmen; it encourages candidates to address the issues rather than simply to make partisan appeals; it gives control to the voters and takes it away from special interest groups; and it strengthens the parties by increasing participation and by allowing candidates from both parties to be elected with broader bases of voter support.

The opponents of Proposition 198 adopted a not atypical style of rhetoric and repetition in their argument. The word "No" occurs seven times in the initial one-page brief, four times in capital letters and three times with exclamation points. They stressed that only voters who are registered with a political party *should* be able to take part in picking that party's flag bearers, but were light on justifications for this position. Their most explicit argument was that "self-serving politicians," "special interests and political consultants" would abuse the blanket system. Mention of "massive checkbooks" implied that the blanket primary might ultimately prove to be far more expensive than its closed counterpart. And, somewhat prophetically, they raised the specter of the "badly drafted" initiative "clogging up" the courts.

In their rebuttal to supporting arguments, the opponents raised one other issue, that the blanket primary would exacerbate convergence of the parties. In this claim, they seem to have been agreeing with those proponents who contended that the blanket primary offers advantages to moderate candidates, while, of course, disagreeing on the normative status of this feature.

In all, we extracted the following testable hypotheses about the blanket primary from the voter's handbook.

- Turnout could be higher, both because of direct expansion of voting opportunities for a significant portion of the eligible electorate and because (as asserted next) races could be more competitive.
- Races—both primary and general—could, on average, be more competitive.
- Nonpartisan registration could soar, as voters were freed from artificial attractions to party registration.
- Moderate candidates could enjoy better results, leading to (more) convergence of parties.
- Primary campaigns could become more substantive and issue-based.

- Spending could increase, and special-interest spending could increase dramatically.

We will not examine all of these hypotheses in this chapter. Some are examined in other chapters of this volume (see, e.g., Gerber's chapter 10 on candidate moderation). Others, such as those concerning the amount of substance in campaigns, would require extremely time-consuming content analysis of speeches, TV advertisements, newspaper coverage, and so forth.

Instead, we focus on the hypotheses related to voter participation and campaign finance. First, did voter turnout increase in 1998? Second, were the races in the primary or the general systematically more competitive? Third, is there evidence that financial contributions and campaign spending were different under the new regime? Did candidates spend more, on average? Did their expenditures become more front-loaded? Did contributors give more to campaigns? Did the timing of contributions shift to the primary election?

These are not, of course, unrelated questions. High turnout, high spending, and close races are frequent companions (e.g., Cox and Munger 1989). It is generally true that close elections are marked by higher turnout and by higher spending than are landslides. What is not obvious is what is cause and what effect. The closeness of the final election is undoubtedly affected by candidates' campaign choices, donors' decisions, and citizens' selections, in a complicated, interactive, multistage process. Fortunately, to answer our central query—Did the introduction of the blanket primary change political behavior?—we need not grapple with the many facets of strategy in elections all at once. Instead, we will examine various electoral issues in sequence, without attempting to delineate a precise causal logic.

Voter Participation

Figure 9.1 shows rates of registration and turnout trends for California for all election years since 1944, when the legislative and presidential primaries were first synchronized.[2] For all four series, the denominator is voting-age population. Figures for registration include nonpartisan registrants, and turnout is measured by the total number of ballots cast. Not surprisingly, citizens are more likely to register and to vote in general elections than in primaries, year in and year out. The gap is especially pronounced in voting. The general election turnout figure displays a familiar saw-tooth pattern also evident in national data: presidential-election years always draw larger shares of the electorate to the polls than do midterms. That effect is much less obvious or regular in primary elections. Finally, both turnout series exhibit (familiar) negative trends over the postwar era, while the registra-

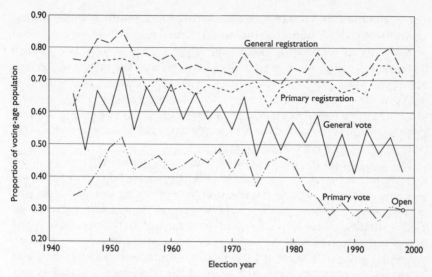

Figure 9.1. Turnout and registration in primary and general elections in California, 1944–98.

tion series are fairly flat since about 1960, and even display a small upturn in the 1990s.

What is of immediate interest is whether the blanket primary delivered on the promise of increasing voter participation. Primary turnout in 1998 was 29.8 percent, just slightly lower than the 31.1 percent in 1996. If one compares prior midterms, though, 1998 represents a positive swing. The years 1986, 1990, and 1994 saw primary election turnout rates of 28.1 percent, 28.0 percent, and 26.2 percent, for an average of 27.4 percent. Hence, one can interpret 1998 as having shown a roughly 2.4 percent surge in primary turnout. Note, however, that this surge did not carry over to the general. Also note that the blanket primary almost automatically guaranteed some rise in turnout, since it expanded voting opportunities for about 1.8 million voters who were registered, but not affiliated with any party. These voters could have made the trip to the polls under a closed system, but they were not permitted to participate in partisan primary races, so only ballot initiatives and local elections beckoned. Without a breakdown of participation by registration status, we cannot say definitively if the new primary law increased participation rates in any partisan subgroup, or simply expanded the reasons to show up for a new bloc of voters, who then participated in about the same numbers as did others. Quick calculations show that the numbers are, at least, consistent with this latter interpretation. If about 27.4 percent of registered partisans turned out to vote in the

1998 primaries, that would account for roughly 5.7 million votes, leaving about five hundred thousand votes unaccounted for. If those were the votes of nonpartisan registrants, that would imply a 27.2 percent nonpartisan turnout at the primary. It is possible, of course, that the effects of the new openness in the primary were more complicated. But the aggregate data are consistent with a simple account, that turnout increased only in a mechanical sense, by fully admitting another set of citizens into the primary electorate. There is no obvious sign in the aggregate data that the blanket primary energized party registrants.

Did the change in primary law increase registration? Figure 9.1 shows that primary registration rose dramatically in 1994, and then slipped downwards in 1996 and 1998. But the main effect of letting independents participate more fully in primaries could be a rise in nonpartisan registration. Voters with fairly weak attachments to parties might, in the past, have opted to register with parties all the same, in order to maintain access to primary ballots for partisan offices. At 1.86 million, nonpartisan registration was at its highest ever total in 1998. As a share of the voting age population, this is about 9 percent. But while the trend is upwards, 1998 does not exhibit a sharp or dramatic rise. Nonpartisan registration has been increasing slowly since 1988, and the 1998 value is consistent with a mildly positive slope over these six elections, suggesting that it did not increase by an unexpectedly large amount.

Survey data, comparisons with other states, and investigation of turnout and registration values at the county and congressional-district level with controls for such factors as closeness of the races, might flesh out this picture. However, without this more elaborate analysis, it does not appear that Proposition 198's immediate impact on participation rates was very dramatic, and so we will turn our attention to other forms of (possibly strategic) behavior. The next section turns to another of the previously delineated claims about the impact of the blanket primary by discussing candidate entry and competitiveness.

Candidates and Competitiveness in the Spring and Fall

Evaluating the competitiveness of a race is a deceptively complicated task. After the fact, one can easily observe how close a given election turned out to be. Under plurality rule, the margin of victory is an adequate measure of competitiveness in two-candidate races, and multicandidate contests are only a little more difficult to characterize. But a larger issue is that all after-the-fact measures ignore campaign dynamics completely. Implicitly or explicitly, one invokes some variety of rational expectations assumption when taking the final observed closeness as an indicator of how competitive was a race at the outset and over the course of the campaign.[3] If one's interest lies in, say, voter expectations, subjective *ex ante* closeness is much more important than objective, *ex post* closeness. The obvious difficulty in developing a more nuanced measure of closeness is that it requires very fine data: multiple opinion polls, preelection surveys, real-time expert surveys, and so on. Fortunately, our concern here is with the election outcome per se. Claims about competition made in the Proposition 198 debate were advanced about outcomes. So one can simply compare the final tallies in 1998 with those from closed primary elections to see whether or not the expected increase in competition transpired.

Tables 9.1 and 9.2 show descriptive statistics on California's primary and general elections in the 1990s. The tables contain a large amount of information, and do not instantly convey a simple story. But the trends apparent on inspection run counter to the suggestion that 1998 might have been a year of close races. The ultimate in noncompetitive elections is the uncontested race. In all four 1990s elections, some seats have been completely abandoned by one of the major parties, and others have seen one or both major party nominations won without any challenge. Considering the two major parties' contingents separately, 1998 saw more, rather than fewer, uncontested races than its predecessors. More than half the districts had no more than one Republican candidate, and nearly three-fourths saw no competition for the Democratic nomination. In a blanket primary, there is a clear incentive for voters to participate in a race in which there is actual competition, since, despite the appearance of competition in a multicandidate ballot, any candidate unchallenged within her party is guaranteed to advance to the general election (provided she secures at least one vote). Strategic-minded Californians, though, were thwarted by a paucity of genuine races. In only one district did more than one candidate seek any of the minor parties' nominations: there were two Libertarians running in the First District. In twenty-nine of the fifty-two districts, at least one of the major parties' nominations was contested, but only eight seats saw races on both sides.[4]

Were those races that did involve competition closer than usual? On the Republican side, the election that stands out as most competitive in this set is 1992. The average number of candidates, the average "effective" number of candidates, and the victors' margins over second-place finishers are generally similar for 1994, 1996, and 1998.[5] By contrast, 1992 is an unusually close election in all these respects. The Democratic picture is more striking still: 1998 is the odd election out, but it is less, not more, competitive than the others. Fewer total candidates competed in open and Republican-held seats, the vote was more concentrated in those seats, and margins of victory were abnormally high (in open and in Republican-held seats), or else unchanged (in Democratic-held seats). In short, by a variety of measures, to the extent that the 1998 primaries stand out, it is for their reduced

TABLE 9.1 Competitiveness of Primary Elections to U.S. House in California, 1992–98

| | | | Republican Primary | | | | | Democratic Primary | | | | |
| | | | Uncontested Races | | Contested Races | | | Uncontested Races | | Contested Races | | |
Year	Status	n	No Candidates	One Candidate	$\bar{N}$	$\bar{N}_e$	Average Margin	No Candidates	One Candidate	$\bar{N}$	$\bar{N}_e$	Average Margin
1992	Republican incumbent	16	0	2	2.7	2.1	38%	1	7	3.6	2.9	21%
	Democratic incumbent	21	3	9	3.2	2.6	16	0	14	2.4	1.6	60
	Open	15	1	3	6.1	4.1	11	0	2	5.7	3.6	20
1994	Republican incumbent	20	0	9	2.5	1.8	49	0	8	2.5	2.2	26
	Democratic incumbent	29	2	9	2.8	2.2	27	0	15	2.3	1.5	60
	Open	3	0	1	4.5	2.5	22	0	0	4.0	2.5	12
1996	Republican incumbent	25	0	16	2.1	1.6	54	0	17	2.8	2.2	28
	Democratic incumbent	24	0	9	2.7	2.3	28	0	18	2.2	1.5	57
	Open	3	1	0	2.0	1.5	58	0	0	6.0	3.8	15
1998	Republican incumbent	22	0	13	2.8	1.6	64	5	13	2.0	1.6	46
	Democratic incumbent	26	4	11	2.6	2.1	28	0	20	2.2	1.5	61
	Open	4	0	1	3.9	2.7	20	0	0	2.6	1.7	50

NOTE: For 1998, the columns headed Republican Primary and Democratic Primary show the Republican field of candidates and the Democratic field of candidates, in open primary.

TABLE 9.2   Competitiveness of General Elections to U.S. House
in California, 1992–98

Year	Status	n	Uncontested Races		Contested Races		
			No Republican	No Democrat	$\overline{N}$	$\overline{N}_e$	Average Margin
1992	Republican incumbent	15	0	0	3.5	2.2	19%
	Democratic incumbent	21	2	0	3.4	1.9	38
	Open	16	0	0	3.9	2.2	20
1994	Republican incumbent	20	0	0	3.4	1.9	32
	Democratic incumbent	29	2	0	1.9	1.9	28
	Open	3	0	0	2.7	2.0	16
1996	Republican incumbent	25	0	0	4.3	2.1	24
	Democratic incumbent	25	0	0	3.3	1.8	41
	Open	2	0	0	5.0	2.3	6
1998	Republican incumbent	21	0	5	3.3	1.9	30
	Democratic incumbent	26	4	0	3.2	1.7	50
	Open	5	0	0	4.2	2.1	18

competition. Neither friends nor foes of Proposition 198 predicted that the blanket primary would make the primaries less close, but where they seem to have changed at all, this was the nature of the change.

The general election results are not as clear. Again, 1998 saw unparalleled numbers of uncontested races, which runs directly contrary to the prediction of closer competition. Where there were contested races, on the other hand, there is no general trend in either the number of candidates or the victors' vote margins. These data, in short, do not suggest that 1998 was an unusually competitive year in California's general election races for the U.S. House.

Of course, the change in primary election law is not the only feature that sets 1998 apart from prior election years. The national environment has varied over the four 1990s elections, and such factors as the number of incumbents retiring, how parties qua parties were faring in popularity, and so on may be important explanations of the results described in tables 9.1 and 9.2. We separated seats according to their incumbency status for that very reason, but it might also be useful to set California into national context to evaluate whether or not its U.S. House races were, in any sense, more competitive in 1998. Accordingly, we reconsidered the general election data for the U.S. House using a fixed-effects panel data model designed to decompose election returns into normal district vote, incumbency advantage, candidate quality effects, and national partisan swings.[6] The virtue of this model is that it separates all of the major forces that shape election returns, allowing one to distinguish between such phenomena as rising incumbency advantage, gerrymandering, secular change in normal vote, and so forth. We estimated the model shown below for 1992 through 1996, and then again for 1992 through 1998, and compared the estimated de-trended district normal vote parameters for California. Did the 1998 returns, once purged of candidate effects and national trends, render California's district normal votes more or less competitive, on average? Our basic model is:

$$y_{it} = \mu_i + \eta_t + \beta' \mathbf{x}_{it} + \varepsilon_{it}$$

where y_{it} is the Democratic share of the two-party vote in congressional district i and election t, $\mathbf{x}_{it}$ is a matrix of incumbency and candidate-quality indicator variables, with the corresponding β coefficients estimating various forms of incumbency and quality-challenger advantage, and η_t and μ_i are parameters to be estimated, capturing national swings and district normal votes, respectively.[7]

Consider California's First District, a marginal seat that has twice changed party hands in the 1990s. When applied to the 1992–96 returns, our model estimates a (de-trended) normal Democratic vote of 50.4 percent there, implying that the seat is almost exactly a toss-up in expectation. Adding the 1998 returns revises this estimate upward to 54.4 percent, suggesting substantially less competitiveness. By contrast, the same figures for the Second District (a Republican stronghold continuously held by Wally Herger in the 1990s) are 38.0 percent and 40.0 percent, respectively. Hence, incorporating 1998 returns increases our measure of expected competitiveness for that district, which is, by either value, a fairly safe Republican seat. Both of these changes were exceptional in their magnitudes: no district saw a larger gap in the two normal vote estimates than did the First, and the median change in California was just under 1 percent. Our interest here is in whether the normal votes shifted to being more or less competitive across the state. Averaging over all fifty-two California districts, the net change brought about by characterizing the present California electoral map on the basis of 1992–98 general election returns rather than 1992–96 general election returns is a small increase in competition. The mean absolute value of (50 percent—estimated-normal-vote) using 1992–96 is 10.0 percent. Adding 1998 lowers this value to 9.7 percent. The medians are, respectively, 9.5 percent and 9.1 percent.

These numbers suggest a very small aggregate movement towards greater competition. However, two final points merit mention. The comparable values for the remainder of the country are similarly signed, but higher: the average change across all other states was from 9.5 percent to 9.1 percent (means) or 8.3 percent to 7.8 percent (medians). Second, differences in estimated incumbency- and experience-advantage parameters were far more striking. The specification that fits the data best resulted in incumbency advantages of 6.5 percent (1992–96) or 7.5 percent (1992–98) and experience bonuses of 1.7 percent (1992–96) or 2.1 percent (1992–98) for challengers and open-seat candidates. These estimates are based on national data, and so they resist any interpretation as being induced by primary law changes. They do, however, begin to explain how descriptive data in table 9.1 can be reconciled with the apparent increase in closeness as measured in normal vote. The 1998 election was a good one for incumbents, and so some of the decline in competition detectable in the 1998 results reflects an increase in estimated incumbency advantage once the 1998 returns are added to the 1990s data set (see also chapters 4 and 7 in this volume by Baldassare and by Salvanto and Wattenberg, respectively). Beneath the incumbency effects, normal party competition tightened just slightly in California, but not by quite as much as it did in the rest of the country. On balance, it seems fair to conclude that the blanket primary probably did not itself immediately cause closer or more competitive contests in either the primary or the following general election. This nonresult seems to hold even when one controls for candidate effects and the national political climate in 1998.

Campaign Finance

In examining competitiveness, we focused on the ultimate result of the electoral process. It is possible, of course, for various aspects of electoral behavior to change without substantially altering the outcome. A change in electoral law might, for example, induce various alterations in strategy or behavior that offset one another. We have already examined mass participation, candidate entry, and vote dispersion, and 1998 did not distinguish itself from years past on these fronts. However, we have yet to consider a set of actors especially likely to be sensitive to changes in the institutional environment: campaign contributors. These actors are especially likely to react quickly to electoral law change because they are generally elite figures who pay more attention than most to politics and the electoral process. Moreover, the contributors are not the only players in campaign finance. Instead, campaign finance involves three kinds of actors: candidates for offices, individual members of the public who make financial contributions, and elite contributors such as PACs and parties. The distinction between the latter two, at least implicitly, underlies much of the rhetoric about "special interests" so popular in the debate on Proposition 198. When the primary system changes, all of these actors may have incentives to change their behavior in order to capitalize on the new rules. Hence, this political venue seems particularly prone to exhibiting immediate change following the opening of the primary.

For candidates, the blanket primary seems most likely to affect this first-stage (primary) strategy. Under closed rules, candidates craft appeals to their own partisans, perhaps with one eye to the general election and the potential for primary election pronouncements and stands to recur as issues. Open rules allow candidates to court a larger and presumably more diverse electorate. If nothing else, the change ensures that there are more potential supporters to woo. This form of expanding the electorate is clearly different from enlarging geographic districts. For example, television markets do not grow simply because more voters in a fixed area become potential supporters. But some of the costs of basic campaign communication, such as sending direct mailers, ought to be related to the size of the electorate. In California, most races for U.S. House seats are, in fact, mail-oriented. For this reason alone, opening primaries could increase the amount of money raised and spent.

We might expect the consequences of the larger potential electorate base to vary for candidates in different types of strategic situations. Since the results of the blanket primary remain the same—that is, the leading vote-getters from each party advance to the general—the change in the primary law is not necessarily great. Candidates in marginal seats face virtually the same situation. The more competitive the general election is expected to be, the more alluring the primary is for ambitious candidates. Hence, one expects competitive, expensive races in both major-party nomination battles, *ceteris paribus*. It is not evident that admitting independents or permitting cross-party voting should alter this situation.

By contrast, in seats in which one party is not usually competitive in the general election, there are incentives for voters to increase their influence by voting in the other party's more consequential election.[8] Hence, candidates in safe districts could face new uncertainty under the blanket primary system because of the expanded electorate. This uncertainty does not translate to the general election, which remains a foregone conclusion. But the larger and more diverse electorate might come into play in the primary races in a way that sometimes increases the competition. So, while a candidate such as Maxine Waters, a liberal Democrat with a very safe seat, will win any election over a Republican, she must contend with other Democrats for the nomination. To the extent that independent and Republican primary voters are disinclined to vote for her and more inclined to vote for any candidate who is more moderate, her reelection chances (and the chances of candidates like her) should fall under a blanket system. Adding non-Democrats to the potential Democratic nomination electorate should only make relatively extreme, safe-seat Democrats vulnerable, assuming that many will prefer to participate on the Democratic side in the primary when the Republican is basically not electable in the general. And, of course, parallel logic would apply to safe Republican seats.

Our first look at the data on California campaign finance in the 1990s

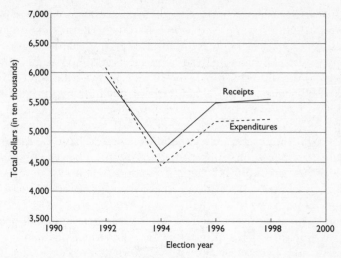

Figure 9.2. Total receipts and expenditures in U.S. House races, 1992–98.

is an overall picture of campaign receipts and disbursements. Figure 9.2 displays total receipts and expenditures over the 1992–98 election years. Figure 9.2 is most striking for its lack of strikingness. The year with the blanket primary, 1998, seems to fall well in line with our expectations of a year without any significant changes in electoral law. Though 1992 seems to be a high outlier, the high expenditures that year were due largely to Michael Huffington, who spent $5.4 million in personal funds on his campaign for a House seat. Without that one extreme value, 1992 expenditures fall well within the expected pattern. Candidates, apparently, did not spend much more money in 1998 than they had in previous years. If figure 9.2 suggests any puzzle, it is why spending was abnormally low in 1994.

Figure 9.3 displays total PAC contributions in California's U.S. House races between 1978 and 1998. Much like the receipts and expenditures plot, this graph is not very striking. PAC funding seems to be on the rise, and the 1998 value fits comfortably within the general pattern. If we anchor the dollar at its 1988 valuation and adjust the other years for inflation, the pattern is the same, and the trend is even less spectacular. This time, the only plausible candidate for outlier status is 1992: PAC funding increased by over 50 percent between 1990 and 1992. The 1.2 percent rise from 1992 to 1994 paled in comparison. Even the 10.7 percent rise from 1994 to 1996 was not as striking. Most important for present purposes, the 8.1 percent increase in 1998 is well in line with previous trends. Hence, while PAC funding did increase following the change in primary law, the change was neither unusually large nor outside the expected pattern. The Proposition 198 campaign rhetoric about special interests, then, seems to be

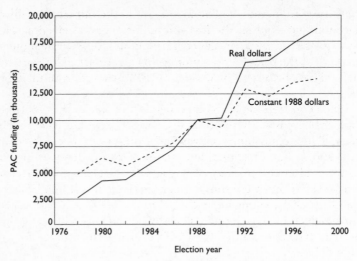

Figure 9.3. Total PAC funding of U.S. House races in California, 1978–98.

unfounded. PAC funding has increased slowly over recent elections, and 1998 was not an unusual year in this regard.

Special-interest money is, of course, only one component of campaign finance. Individual contributors also have incentives to change their behavior and contribution patterns. Initially, determining whether individual contributors have changed their behavior may seem to be an easy task, but the rules underlying campaign contributions are surprisingly complicated. It is thus not trivial to determine how individual contributors have reacted to the new primary. At the outset, a simple hypothesis to test is that the new primary system has resulted in contributions being shifted to the earlier part of the election cycle. After all, in order to see one's favored candidate in the general election, one needs to ensure that this candidate emerges from the primary election, now with a potentially larger electoral base. One way to make this more probable is to pile money into a candidate's war chest early.

There are three ways in which one might observe individual contributors shifting their activities toward primary elections. Because of FECA limitations, contributors are limited to giving a total of $2,000 during an election cycle, $1,000 in the primary and $1,000 in the general election, where each contribution is earmarked for a specific election. However, many contributors simply want to contribute the maximum amount to a certain candidate. Hence, while these contributors earmark $1,000 of their total $2,000 donation for the primary election, they do not necessarily want the candidate to spend $1,000 in the primary and $1,000 in the general. If the candidate were Maxine Waters, for instance, she could use her money most effectively by spending the maximum amount in the more competitive primary election and none in the less competitive general election. Hence, one way to gauge increased primary contributions is to separate money that is earmarked for the primary from money that is earmarked for the general. This method has obvious problems and will almost certainly result in flawed estimates.

Since each contribution is accompanied by the date of the contribution, a method that bypasses these problems is to separate the data by the primary date. Those contributions given before the primary can be counted as contributions that were intended for use in the primary, while contributions given after the primary obviously were not meant to be primary donations, even if they were thus earmarked. It is, in fact, not unusual for candidates to receive money *after the general election* that is earmarked for the primary election. This money is clearly not meant to be spent directly in a primary bid, and candidates are free to use this money to pay off campaign debts.

A final option for the researcher is to combine the first two approaches, placing the contributions into four categories: given before the primary and earmarked for the primary; given after the primary but earmarked for the primary; given before the primary but earmarked for the general; and given after the primary and earmarked for the general. This last option, while not flawless, provides a good compromise between the other options.

We present the results of our analysis in table 9.3. The dependent variable in these models is the proportion of all individual contributions that was both earmarked for and given before the primary election.[9] The only exception is the column labeled "1996 (June)," where the dependent variable is the proportion of funds that were contributed before June 2, 1996. In 1996, the primary date was moved forward to March in what turned out to be a futile bid to increase California's influence in the races for presidential nominations. The primary in all of the other years occurred in June. We used this modified dependent variable for 1996 to simulate an unchanged primary environment for that year. The data in column 1 comprise all contributions from the period 1992–98. For subsequent columns, the data are year-specific.

The independent variables in the models are the number of candidates in the primary, a dummy variable indicating if there was at least one quality opponent in both the primary and general, a dummy variable indicating whether the seat was open in the general, a measure of district partisan advantage, and a dummy variable indicating whether the election involved a blanket primary. Candidate quality is operationalized simply: any individual who has ever held any electoral office is a quality candidate (Jacobson 1987). The variable labeled "District partisan advantage" is a signed difference between our estimate of the district's normal vote and 50 percent.[10]

TABLE 9.3 Timing of Individual Campaign Donations, 1992–98, U.S. House, California Delegation

	1992–98	1992	1994	1996	1996 (June)	1998
Intercept	0.491**	0.545**	0.463**	0.479**	0.616**	0.550**
	(0.025)	(0.046)	(0.044)	(0.054)	(0.053)	(0.057)
Number of candidates in primary	−0.008	−0.022	0.018	−0.015	−0.023	−0.034
	(0.008)	(0.012)	(0.018)	(0.024)	(0.23)	(0.026)
Quality opponents in primary	0.040	0.002	0.016	0.135	0.114	0.035
	(0.053)	(0.070)	(0.108)	(0.164)	(0.163)	(0.171)
Quality opponents in general	−0.098**	−0.080	−0.164**	−0.089	−0.070	−0.094
	(0.030)	(0.056)	(0.054)	(0.071)	(0.070)	(0.064)
Blanket primary	0.008					
	(0.027)					
Open seat in general	−0.018	0.056	−0.022	−0.141	−0.144	−0.112
	(0.039)	(0.059)	(0.111)	(0.126)	(0.125)	(0.079)
District partisan advantage	0.882**	1.160**	0.872**	0.413	0.578*	0.943**
	(0.135)	(0.252)	(0.227)	(0.308)	(0.307)	(0.306)
N	412	91	95	92	92	81
R^2	.32	.39	.49	.16	.19	.38

NOTE: The table reports OLS regression estimates. The dependent variable is the proportion of primary contributions. Standard errors are in parentheses.
*$p < .10$
**$p < .05$

The sign is positive if the district generally favors the party of the candidate in question and negative if that candidate's party's normal vote falls below 50 percent. Our observations are all major-party candidates who competed in the general elections.

The model that pools the data for 1992 through 1998 indicates that the change to a blanket primary system did not significantly alter what proportion of individual contributions were given for the primary election, since the blanket primary dummy variable is not significant. Contrary to the arguments of both the proponents and the opponents of Proposition 198, the new primary system apparently had little effect on the timing of contributions. This is a striking result that runs counter to initial expectations and preelection rhetoric. It is also striking in that the results indicate that the 1996 election, *not* the 1998 election, is the outlier. As we can see from table 9.3, the differing proportion of contributions intended for the primary can be explained by the same variables for each year except 1996. For 1996, none of the independent variables explains the variation in contribution timing. Moreover, the R^2 value is significantly lower for both 1996 models than it is for any of the other years.

As noted previously, the most obvious difference between the 1996 election and the others is that 1996 saw a much earlier primary date. So, while the change in primary type did not have a significant impact, the timing of the primary apparently does. Timing, then, trumps institutional design in its ability to alter the proportion of funds available for use in the primary. This claim is further bolstered when we note that the results in the column labeled "1996" are less similar to the results of other years than the results in the column labeled "1996 (June)." In the latter column, we artificially "moved" the 1996 primary date to June to coincide with the other years. That is, we counted all donations prior to June 2, 1996 as primary donations. Further analysis is warranted, but this preliminary inspection suggests that timing is at least as significant as the details of the electoral formula.

Lastly, one might expect individual contributors to behave differently in different types of races. In other words, the funding dynamic may be dissimilar between races for safe seats and competitive races. Certainly candidates running in safe seats generally receive less funding than candidates running in competitive districts. Their constituents and supporters understand that they simply do not need the money. However, the change to the blanket primary may have altered this strategic situation in the aforementioned manner.

In order to test this hypothesis, we separated the data into two sets: safe seats and competitive seats. We defined a competitive seat as one in which the normal Democratic vote was either above 60 percent or below 40 percent. We then ran regressions with the same independent variables that were reported in table 9.3. Again, the 1998 elections did not distinguish themselves from the other years. Hence, safe district or not, 1998 was not a banner year for change in campaign donations.

CONCLUSION

As a general matter, identifying the precise effects of various features of electoral law proves difficult. Neither the formal, deductive nor the empirical, inductive literatures on the effects of election law is particularly rich with consensus findings. Debating the veracity, logic, and applicability of Duverger's law, a fairly simple and high-level claim, has kept scholars occupied for decades. Not coincidentally, politicians do not often introduce self-interested reforms in electoral procedures, even when they unambiguously have the power to do so. They may fear a public backlash from too obviously loading the dice, or they may regard electoral institutions as too unpredictable to be manipulated easily. Certainly, examples of changes in electoral law that either failed to produce the predicted outcomes or even backfired by producing unanticipated consequences are not hard to find. In recent years, Italy, New Zealand, and Israel have all made major changes in their national election rules without achieving their respective goals. New Zealand's politics have become less stable, not more so; Italy managed to accentuate its already exceptional partisan fragmentation; and Israel perversely increased the influence of very small parties.

Compared to those efforts, California's alteration of primary election rules was minor. The laws governing general elections were unchanged, and the primary was still based on plurality rule. Should the introduction of fully open (blanket) primary rules have been expected radically to alter the elections, directly at the primary stage or indirectly at the general stage? We regard this "open" question as an open question. Here, we have not dwelt on the logics of optimal behavior under the old and new rules. Instead, we have shown that the most publicized predictions about how the new rules would play out in terms of voter turnout, competitiveness, and campaign finance do not seem to have been realized in the first (and only) trial. There does not seem to have been much change in turnout, so, conditional on the behavior of elites (that is, decisions to run, and campaign styles), the masses do not seem to have changed behavior in this regard. The primary elections were not especially close—they may even have been a little less close than normal. Neither did they feed into newly competitive general elections.

Campaign finance is a complicated world, and inferences about changed behavior are, again, perilous, given that one can provide supply- or demand-side explanations for any trend. Moreover, the supply side includes sophisticated elite actors like PACs as well as ordinary citizens acting on small scales and in (relative) isolation. Again, though, our preliminary analysis revealed little change, rendering moot the question of whose actions should be regarded as most likely to have caused the (nonexistent) change. Campaign expenditure and campaign contributions, in total, do not seem to have been off-trend for the blanket primary year. Nor was there any detectable shift in the timing of the donations. Based on one run, we see no sign that the blanket primary encourages front-loading one's spending, not even in seats dominated by one party. PACs seem to have been important in 1998, but not much more important than they already were in 1996, 1994, or 1992.

Our conclusion from this analysis, then, is that the blanket primary was a barely noticed and largely irrelevant innovation in California. We should close, though, by hedging our bets in two ways. First, there may be some respects in which the opportunities to cross over or otherwise support another party that a blanket primary presents did make a difference. For example, we eschewed analysis of the ideologies of candidates here, and so we cannot rule out that the potential broadening of the primary electorates did encourage moderation by some of the candidates. Second, election law, it is worth reiterating, is arcane. There is good reason to believe that equilibria may not be quickly discovered. It may take several elections for even elite actors to catch on to the subtle features of a change in rules. It has, after all, taken scholars many decades to formalize properties of election rules—two hundred years elapsed between Condorcet's paradox and the Gibbard-Satterthwaite Theorem! So it may be premature to declare the rules governing primary type irrelevant. One must observe a series of runs under the blanket primary rules to know how behavior settles. Of course, the Supreme Court has now ensured that there will be no such series. Nonetheless, California's experiment in electoral law change is ongoing, and so will remain of interest to political scientists, journalists, and other political junkies, who can celebrate this variance in election law even while carefully qualifying any conclusions they draw about its consequences.

NOTES

Thanks to Mike Alvarez, Bruce Cain, and Elisabeth Gerber for valuable comments. Gaines began work on this project while visiting the Department of Applied Economics at the Katholieke Universiteit Leuven, and thanks KUL for its hospitality. Oana Armeanu, Paul Diperna, and Rebecca Harris provided helpful research assistance.

1. The relevant provisions of the Elections Code date from the Political Reform Act of 1974.

2. The data plotted in figure 9.1 are taken from Jones 1998a, vi, and Jones 1998b, v.

3. Even professional election observers sometimes forget that landslides such as

the 1980 American presidential election or the 1987 British general election were regarded by journalists and academics alike as close calls right up to election night.

4. An interesting fact about voter behavior—but an unimportant fact with regard to final outcomes—is that minor-party support soared in 1998. Since independents decline to register not only with major parties, but also with minor parties, there is no reason to expect them to favor small parties disproportionately. Yet, the minor-party primary vote went from about 0.9 percent in 1996 to about 5.3 percent in 1998. It fell in only eight districts, and rose in the other forty-four, despite the almost complete lack of actual competition for these nominations in the U.S. House districts (most statewide-office races featured two Peace and Freedom Party candidates).

5. The "effective" number of candidates is an index that weights the number of actual candidates according to their vote shares, so that strong candidates count far more than do very weak ones. We used the most common such measure in the voting literature, the Laakso-Taagepera index (1979), computed district by district. The averages shown in tables 9.1 and 9.2 are computed as:

$$\bar{N}_e = 1/n \; \Sigma_i \; [(\Sigma_j \; V_{ij})^2 / (\Sigma_j V_{ij}^2)]$$

where V_{ij} is the number of votes won by candidate j in district i, and there are a total of n districts in the state (or, as applicable, n districts in which there is some competition).

6. The normal vote is rooted in a conception of elections being subject to short-term and long-term forces. The former include regional swings to and from given parties on the basis of timely issues as well as district-level forces particular to given elections. Prominent in this latter category are any candidate effects, such as an incumbency advantage or a friends-and-neighbors advantage a candidate enjoys in his or her hometown or region. The major long-term determinant of election returns is the normal vote, the expected breakdown of vote shares when the parties field comparable candidates and there are no election-specific tides favoring one party or the other.

7. See Gaines and Rivers (1994) for technical details on this model and its derivation. Gaines (1998) uses a similar model to analyze British elections, while Levitt and Wolfram (1997) adopt the same basic approach in their analysis of incumbency advantage in the U.S. House. In this application, we omitted Louisiana data completely (because of its odd electoral law and paucity of general elections); dropped all uncontested races; excluded two districts—South Carolina's Second and Florida's Twenty-First—from the first run because they had no contested elections in those three general elections; and dropped Vermont's at-large district, where a non-major-party Representative (Bernie Sanders) was both the incumbent and the winner in all four 1990s elections.

8. We have in mind a voter's subjective sense of influence rather than the miniscule objective probability of one's vote actually counting by making or breaking a tie.

9. The primary dates were June 2, 1992; June 7, 1994; March 26, 1996; and June 2, 1998. Analysis shows that models with this version of the dependent variable yield coefficients that lie between the coefficients obtained by the other two methods (i.e., using only the earmarking information, or using only the timing information to identify those contributions intended for the primary).

10. Our method of estimating the normal vote is described in the preceding section.

REFERENCES

Birtel, Marc. 1996. "Ballot: 'Jungle Primaries' Adopted . . . Reclassifying Lions Rejected." *Congressional Quarterly Weekly Report* 54, no. 13 (March 30): 902–3.

———. 1998. "Changing Demographics Keep Orange County in Play." *Congressional Quarterly Weekly Report* 56, no. 21 (May 23): 1371–74.

Block, A. G., and Claudia Buck, eds. 1997. *California Political Almanac 1997–1998.* 5th ed. Sacramento, CA: California Journal / State Net.

Cox, Gary W., and Michael C. Munger. 1989. "Closeness, Expenditures, and Turnout in the 1982 U.S. House Elections." *American Political Science Review* 83, no. 1 (March): 217–31.

Dubin, Michael J. 1998. *United States Congressional Elections, 1788–1997.* Jefferson, NC: McFarland.

Elving, Ronald D.; Inces Pinto Alicea; and Jeffrey L. Katz. 1992. "Boxer and Feinstein Victorious in 'Year of the Woman.'" *Congressional Quarterly Weekly Report* 50, no. 23 (June 6): 1621–31.

Gaines, Brian J. 1998. "The Impersonal Vote? Constituency Service and Incumbency Advantage in British Elections, 1950–92." *Legislative Studies Quarterly* 23, no. 2 (May): 167–95.

Gaines, Brian J., and Douglas Rivers. 1994. "Incumbency Advantage in the House and Senate." Working ms. Stanford University.

Gerber, Elisabeth R., and Rebecca B. Morton. 1998. "Primary Election Systems and Representation." *Journal of Law, Economics, and Organization* 14, no. 2 (October): 304–24.

Jacobson, Gary C. 1987. *The Politics of Congressional Elections.* 2d ed. Glenview, IL: Scott, Foresman.

Jones, Bill. 1998a. *Statement of the Vote: Primary Election, June 2, 1998.* Sacramento, CA: Office of the Secretary of State, Elections Division.

———. 1998b. *Statement of the Vote: General Election, November 3, 1998.* Sacramento, CA: Office of the Secretary of State, Elections Division.

Laakso, Markku, and Rein Taagepera. 1979. "'Effective' Number of Parties: A Measure with Application to Western Europe." *Comparative Political Studies* 12, no. 1 (April): 3–27.

Levitt, Steven D., and Catherine D. Wolfram. 1997. "Decomposing the Sources of Incumbency Advantage in the U.S. House." *Legislative Studies Quarterly* 22, no. 1 (February): 45–60.

"March 26 California Primary Results." *Congressional Quarterly Weekly Report* 54, no. 13 (March 30): 908–11.

McGillivray, Alice V. 1995. *Congressional and Gubernatorial Primaries 1993–1994.* Washington, D.C.: Congressional Quarterly.

"Primary Results." 1998. *Congressional Quarterly Weekly Report* 56, no. 23 (June 6): 1547–52.

CHAPTER TEN

Strategic Voting
and Candidate Policy Positions

Elisabeth R. Gerber

One of the most debated questions about the blanket primary is whether it advantages candidates with ideologically moderate or ideologically extreme policy positions.[1] This question directly addresses the issue of political representation. If moderate candidates benefit from the blanket primary, in the sense of having a higher probability of being nominated and elected, then we expect the interests of citizens sharing their centrist or moderate views to be better represented in the policy process. If ideologically extreme candidates benefit from the blanket primary, we expect citizens with extreme views to benefit instead.

Two views regarding the effects of the blanket primary on candidate policy positions prevail. One view, which is central to the arguments made by proponents of the blanket primary, is that the blanket primary advantages moderate candidates (see California Secretary of State 1996). By opening participation in the primary to voters outside a candidate's party, the blanket primary system forces candidates to compete for the ideological center of the electorate. Candidates with more moderate positions, or who can move to the center, receive greater support and prevail. A second view, often advanced or implied by opponents of the blanket primary, is that it advantages extremist candidates (California Secretary of State 1996). By allowing participation by members of the other party, the blanket primary invites "raiding" or "sabotage" by ideologically motivated partisans. These voters nominate weak candidates in the other party and their own ideologically polar candidate prevails.

In this chapter, I assess these two alternative views of primary election dynamics in light of the experience of the June 1998 California primary. First, I sketch out the logic of each view. Second, I review existing evidence about the relationship between primary election systems, candidate strategies, and candidate policy positions. Third, I test hypotheses about the effects of primaries on candidates' positions with election returns and case study evidence from the 1998 California gubernatorial, congressional, and state legislative races.

TWO VIEWS OF PRIMARY ELECTION DYNAMICS

The two views of primary election dynamics agree on the basic structure of primary elections. Both sides see primary elections as the first phase in a multistage election process. Primary election laws define the rules of participation; that is, they define which voters are permitted to participate in candidate nominations. Both sides agree that under closed primaries, participation in the primary is limited to registered members of that party. Under blanket primaries, participation is extended to all registered voters, including partisans, independents, and members of other parties.[2]

Where the two views differ is on their interpretation of the consequences of extending participation to all voters. Specifically, they differ in their expectations of how voters will behave in blanket primaries and how candidates will respond. As discussed in the introduction to this volume and the several chapters on voter behavior, voters in blanket primaries can engage in several forms of crossover voting—sincere crossover, hedging, and raiding. All three forms of crossover voting are difficult or impossible under closed primaries, since voters would need to anticipate their desire to cross over long before the election and re-register under a new party label. In some closed primary states, such as New York, voters must re-register a full year before the election. In California prior to 1998, the registration period was twenty-nine days—shorter but still potentially prohibitive for most voters (Bott 1991). Low rates of re-registration in closed primary states suggest that crossover voting in these systems rarely occurs. By contrast, voters in open primary systems (both traditional open and blanket) can decide to cross over at the polls, requiring no precommitment to one or the other party. Voters in blanket primaries are even less constrained by party and can cross over race by race.

The first view of primary election dynamics argues that of the three types of crossover behavior, sincere crossover and hedging will prevail. This is not to say that voters will never engage in raiding; rather, the argument is that most voters are not sufficiently informed to engage in such sophisticated behavior. Raiding requires voters to calculate (1) which candidate would pose the weakest challenge to their favored candidate; (2) whether that candidate can win the primary; and (3) whether that candidate will lose the general. Further, even if they are sufficiently informed to figure out how to raid the other party's primary, voters are likely to be risk-averse and may not vote for a candidate they dislike, even if it means increasing the possibility that the candidate they really like wins. Hence, under this first view, most crossover behavior is by centrist independents and moderates voting across party lines for their preferred candidates.

From the candidates' perspective, extending participation in the primary to centrist independent and moderate voters creates advantages for centrist and moderate candidates. Extending participation means shifting the primary electorate median voter toward the ideological center. In other words, the blanket primary median is closer to the ideological center than the closed primary median. Hence, moderate candidates with policy positions close to the median will prevail, resulting in the nomination of more conservative Democrats and more liberal Republicans compared to their closed primary counterparts.[3] I refer to this prediction as the "moderation hypothesis."

The second view of primary election dynamics argues that of the three types of crossover behavior, the effects of raiding will prevail. This view recognizes the possibility that some voters, especially independents and moderates, may engage in sincere crossover voting and hedging, drawing candidates to the ideological center. However, they also argue that voters will sometimes face strong incentives to engage in raiding. The most favorable situation for raiding is when one party's primary is uncontested. Voters from that party waste their vote by casting it for their party's presumptive nominee. The question then becomes which candidate they should vote for from the other party. Voters ask if they are better off voting for the more preferred candidate in the other party (i.e., hedging), leading their top two candidates from the two parties to face off in the general election, or voting for the less preferred candidate in the other party (i.e., raiding), leading their most preferred candidate to face his or her weakest opponent. In the end, voters' choices will depend on their preferences relative to the candidates, their attitudes toward risk, and the several candidates' electoral prospects. As discussed above, critics of this view argue that voters are simply not well enough informed to behave in such a sophisticated manner. Defenders counter by pointing out the potential for candidates and campaign organizations to help voters coordinate their behavior.

From the candidates' perspective, the possibility of strategic crossover greatly complicates matters. On the one hand, extending participation to independents and members of other parties means shifting the primary electorate median voter toward the ideological center, as noted above. On the other hand, if some voters engage in raiding, it is no longer clear whose preferences become decisive. Hence, the question candidates must ask is: What types of voters are likely to cross over? To the extent that ideologically extreme voters cross over strategically, benefiting extremist candidates, this view results in what I refer to as the "polarization hypothesis."

To illustrate the logic of voter choice in blanket primaries, consider a

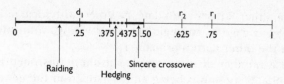

Figure 10.1. Example of crossover voting.

very simple example in which there are two parties, called D and R. Each party has a "front-runner" candidate designated as d_1 and r_1, respectively. For simplicity, I assume that only one party's primary (arbitrarily, the R party) is contested by candidate r_2. I simplify the example by assuming that all voters have single-peaked policy preferences (i.e., that they are risk-neutral); that voters' ideal points are uniformly distributed over the uni-dimensional space [0,1] (hence the general election median voter's ideal point is located at .50); and that all voters with ideal points to the left of .50 are registered with the D party and all voters with ideal points to the right of .50 are registered with the R party. Voters are forward looking, in the sense that they seek to maximize the expected utility of their primary election vote by considering how it will impact their general election choices.[4] To begin, I set $d_1 = .25$ and $r_1 = .75$ and assume that the R party's primary is contested by a moderate candidate whose ideal point is $r_2 = .625$. I illustrate the configuration of voter and candidate preferences in figure 10.1.[5]

In figure 10.1, since the D party primary is uncontested, voters whose ideal points are closest to d_1 need not "waste" their votes in the uncontested D party primary, as they would under closed primaries. Rather, they can vote for one of the R party candidates. The question is, which one? Voters know that if r_1 wins the primary, d_1 and r_1 will meet in the general. Since d_1 and r_1 are equidistant from the general election median (at .5), r_1 will win the general election with prob = .50. If r_2 wins the primary, r_2 will beat d_1 with certainty. Therefore, all voters who prefer a lottery between d_1 and r_1 to a win by r_2 will vote for r_1. This will be the case for voters with ideal points from 0.00 up to .375. These voters have ideal points that are closer to d_1 than to r_2 and so prefer a primary outcome that gives d_1 some chance of victory in the general election. Voters to the right of .375 receive higher utility from r_2 than from the lottery, and so they vote for r_2. Since in this example the number of r_2 voters is greater than the number of r_1 voters, r_2 wins the primary and then the general.

This example is constructed to illustrate all three types of crossover voting. Voters with ideal points between .4375 and .5 engage in sincere cross-over, voting for their most preferred candidate, r_2. Voters with ideal points between .375 and .4375 engage in hedging—they most prefer d_1, but prefer r_2 over the other R party candidate, r_1. Voters with ideal points between 0.00 and .375 engage in strategic crossover voting, voting for a weaker candidate in the other party's primary, r_1.

Note that a number of the example's assumptions, such as the front-runner candidates' positions being equidistant from the general election median voter's ideal point, are critical to generate the precise predictions about r_2 winning the primary and the general. If we relax some of these highly restrictive assumptions—for example, if we allow candidates to take more extreme or more moderate positions, or for more than one challenger to enter, or for the number of D and R voters to be different, or for voters to be risk-averse, or for turnout to be probabilistic or uncertain—then optimal voter strategies and candidate responses become much more difficult to determine.[6] The point of the example is not to make specific predictions about winning candidate positions, but rather to illustrate how all of these variables interact.

EVIDENCE OF CROSSOVER VOTING, CANDIDATE ENTRY, AND POLICY POSITIONS

Several recent studies have analyzed the effects of primary election laws on candidate strategies. Gerber and Morton 1998 compare the ADA scores of U.S. Representatives elected under different primary systems.[7] They show that winning House candidates elected from open, blanket, and nonpartisan primaries are more moderate (that is, Democrats are more conservative and Republicans are more liberal) than otherwise similar candidates elected from closed primaries. They also find that the greatest share of moderates are not elected from the most open systems, but rather from semiclosed systems. They conjecture that in semiclosed systems, where new voters and independents can participate, but not members of other parties, incentives for sincere crossover and hedging clearly dominate. In other words, Gerber and Morton's evidence suggests that while sincere crossover, hedging, and raiding all are important in blanket primaries, the moderating effects of sincere crossover and hedging prevail. In a related study, Grofman and Brunell (2001) show a higher proportion of mixed-party U.S. Senate delegations in open primary states, suggesting that voters are trying to moderate the net ideology of the delegation by electing Senators of different parties.

Together, these studies provide evidence that is consistent with the moderation hypothesis and contrary to the polarization hypothesis. They imply that, on average, the moderating effects of sincere crossover voting and hedging dominate the polarizing effects of raiding. As a result, moderate candidates tend to prevail in open primaries. These results are consistent with the findings in the five chapters in this volume on voter behavior

(Sides, Cohen, and Citrin, chapter 5; Alvarez and Nagler, chapter 6; Salvanto and Wattenberg, chapter 7; Kousser, chapter 8; and Petrocik, chapter 14). All of these analyses find evidence of substantial sincere crossover and hedging, and very little evidence of raiding.

There is, however, some compelling evidence to the contrary. King (1998) shows that party organizations are less cohesive and candidate positions show greater variance in open primary states. He argues that under open primaries, candidates have an incentive to "specialize," focusing on one or a few issues and appealing to ideological subgroups in the electorate. In other words, he finds that candidates may be more moderate *or* more extreme under open primaries, depending on the issues they promote. Further empirical research is required to assess the generality of this claim.

CANDIDATE MODERATION
IN THE CALIFORNIA BLANKET PRIMARY

I now consider the candidate moderation and polarization hypotheses in light of evidence drawn from the 1998 California primary and general election. Did primary and general election winners hold moderate or extreme policy positions relative to those of their challengers? Did they hold more moderate or more extreme policy positions than their counterparts previously elected under closed primaries? Did the competitive circumstances of the race matter? That is, were more moderate candidates nominated and elected in contested races? Uncontested races? Open seats? Was the moderation effect more important in some races than in others? Was the polarization effect more important in some races?

Governor's Race

The Governor's race represented a prime opportunity for crossover voting. Incumbent Governor Pete Wilson was prohibited from running due to term limits. In the Republican primary, former State Attorney General Dan Lungren ran unopposed,[8] while in the Democratic primary, three candidates— former Lieutenant Governor Gray Davis, former U.S. Representative Jane Harman, and businessman Al Checchi—competed for the nomination.[9] With the Republican nomination virtually unchallenged, Republican voters were free to cross over into the highly competitive and uncertain Democratic primary.

When they crossed party lines, however, Republican voters faced a field of three ideologically similar, centrist candidates. Harman's record in the U.S. Congress distinguished her as one of the most pro-business, fiscally conservative Democrats in the House.[10] Checchi's lack of political experience made his ideological position more difficult to assess, but even after he committed to running as a Democrat, he repeatedly emphasized his centrist, pro-business positions and downplayed any ties to Democratic ideals. Davis's campaign promised a bipartisan, pragmatic, non-ideological, problem-solving approach to policy, which he has faithfully executed since his election. Thus, Republicans hoping to raid the Democratic primary to advantage Lungren would have been hard pressed to identify the most liberal candidate. Republicans hoping to hedge with the most moderate Democrat could have chosen any of the above.

Nor did crossover voting into the contested Democratic primary appear to result in the nomination of a weak opponent to Lungren. Davis raised nearly $26 million in campaign contributions (California Secretary of State 1998a) and ultimately beat Lungren by nearly 20 percentage points in November (California Secretary of State 1998b). If raiders targeted Davis as the weakest Democratic candidate, it looks like they seriously miscalculated.

This is not to say that the blanket primary had no effect on campaign dynamics or the relative strength of the several candidates. Some of their centrist positioning may, in fact, have been the result of electoral pressures from the center felt during the blanket primary. Further, the fact that three moderates entered the Democratic primary and emphasized their centrist positions may reflect their beliefs that centrist candidates had a greater chance of winning the blanket primary. In fact, Checchi's campaign manager admitted that they saw the blanket primary as a unique opportunity for a candidate without traditional party ties to appeal to independents and moderate Republican crossovers (Institute of Governmental Studies 1999). However, it is clear that the blanket primary was not, at least in this case, decisive. Other factors, such as Checchi's lack of political experience, Harman's inability to mobilize financial support, and Davis's more convincing appeal as an "incumbent-like" challenger seemed to dominate any moderating effect of the blanket primary (see chapter 4 by Baldassare and chapter 7 by Salvanto and Wattenberg in this volume on the importance of incumbency in the 1998 elections).

U.S. Senate Race

The U.S. Senate race presented similarly favorable circumstances for crossover voting. In the Democratic primary, incumbent Barbara Boxer ran virtually unopposed, while former State Treasurer Matt Fong and businessman Darrell Issa competed for the Republican nomination.[11] So, in the same way that Republicans were able to cross into the competitive Democratic primary for governor, Democrats could employ their votes in a race where they might actually count—the Republican primary—while their incumbent Senator was assured of the Democratic nomination.

As in the Governor's race, however, it was less than clear which Republican Senate candidate was the more moderate and hence the more attractive to sincere crossover voters and hedgers. Issa, like Al Checchi in the gubernatorial primary, lacked political experience and spent much of the early part of the campaign staking out his ideological turf. Toward late spring, an image began to emerge of a candidate who was quite conservative on social issues and liberal economically. Fong, by contrast, tried to portray himself as more liberal on social issues and conservative on economic issues, although his endorsement by conservative Christian organizations undermined this image to some extent. Hence, it is safe to say that while the Republican primary candidates took different positions on the issues, neither was obviously more attractive to centrist independents and crossover voters.

Where the candidates did clearly differ is on their political records and ties to the political parties. Issa, like Checchi, had no prior political experience. In previous elections, when voters were in the mood to take out their frustrations about a sagging economy on incumbent politicians, this outsider status might have worked to Issa's advantage. In 1998, however, voters were in quite a different mood: incumbents and experienced politicians won up and down the ballot in both the primary and the general (see Baldassare, chapter 4; Salvanto and Wattenberg, chapter 7). To make matters worse, Issa's lack of ideological discipline and inconsistency of policy positions, no doubt a result of his political inexperience, were interpreted by the media as the mark of an erratic and unpredictable candidate. Thus, the lack of partisan ties and ideological rigidity—which should have helped Issa attract support from sincere crossovers and hedgers—failed to carry the day in 1998.

Where Issa lacked political experience, Fong was viewed as a traditional, mainstream party candidate. He was a long-term member of the Republican party. His mother was the very popular (Democratic) Secretary of State for many years. Fong served as a member of the state Board of Equalization and then as State Treasurer. Over many years of public service, Fong established himself as an expert on taxes and fiscal policy, and promised to make reform of the tax code one of his top legislative priorities as Senator (California Secretary of State 1998d). Hence, while it is impossible to know how voters weighed the relative importance of policy positions and political experience, it is clear that Issa was not able to capitalize on his independent status as a party outsider to defeat Fong in the primary.

To the extent that Fong benefited from having greater political experience than his primary competition, and perhaps from being perceived as more moderate ideologically, he was no match for Boxer in the general election. Exit polls show that most of the Democrats that crossed over for Fong in the primary returned to their party in the general and supported

Boxer (see Kousser, chapter 8 in this volume). Thus, Fong's marginally greater appeal to moderates in the primary failed to translate into a lasting base of support. And in the end, perhaps the most ideological candidate from either party won the U.S. Senate seat.[12]

U.S. House Races

It is more difficult to generalize about the effects of the blanket primary on candidate positions in legislative races because (1) electoral circumstances vary greatly from race to race, and (2) much less is known about most candidates, especially those who lose in the primary. Furthermore, since House incumbents are reelected at an extremely high rate, there is very little competition in most House general election races and hence little opportunity for the primary to make much difference in terms of electoral outcomes.[13] Nevertheless, there are at least three types of races in which we might expect crossover voting to affect winning congressional candidates' policy positions. The first type is the open-seat race. In open seats, there are no incumbents, and so challengers have a real chance of winning. However, open seats often generate competition in both parties, and so voters may be reluctant to cross over if their own party's nomination is contested. The second type of race in which the blanket primary may matter is the contested-challenger primary. In such races, only one party is seriously contested, leaving members of the incumbent's party free to cross over into the challenger's primary. However, since challengers rarely beat incumbents in the general election, any effects on candidate positions in the primary are unlikely to translate into election outcomes in the general. The third type of race in which the blanket primary may matter is when a vulnerable incumbent faces a challenge from within his or her own party. These challenges are rare. When they do occur, they may signal to potential crossover voters that the seat is up for grabs and that their votes could matter.

Table 10.1 reports the primary election candidates, primary nominees (single asterisk), and general election winners (double asterisk) for each open seat, contested-challenger, and contested-incumbent race in 1998. I describe the results of these races in detail below.

Open Seats.   There were four open House seats in 1998 due to incumbent retirements: Congressional District (CD) 1, CD 3, CD 34, and CD 36. In addition, three seats were filled in special elections in the spring of 1998 due to incumbent retirements or deaths, and although their occupants were listed on the ballot as incumbents, they were rematched with their primary competitors again in June (CD 9, CD 22, and CD 44). I refer to these races as "quasi-open" seats. I discuss these races in this section because

TABLE 10.1 Primary and General Election Candidates,
U.S. House Elections, California Delegation, 1998

District	Democratic Candidates	Ideology	Republican Candidates	Ideology
Open and Quasi-Open Seats				
CD 1	Mike Thompson**	M	Mark Luce*	—
	Jim Hennefer	—		
CD 3	Sandy Dunn*	M	Barbara Alby	C
	Bob Dean Kent	—	Doug Ose**	M
CD 34	Grace Napolitano**	L	Ed Perez*	—
	James Casso	L		
CD 36	Janice Hahn*	—	Steve Kuykendall**	M
			Rudy Svorinich	—
			Susan Brooks	—
			Robert Pegram	C
CD 9	Barbara Lee**	L		
CD 22	Lois Capps**	M	Tom Bordonaro*	C
			James Harrison	M
CD 44	Ralph Waite*	—	Mary Bono**	C
CD 46	Loretta Sanchez**	M	Robert Dornan*	C
			Lisa Hughes	—
			James Gray	M
Contested-Challenger Primaries				
CD 10	Ellen Tauscher (I)**	M	Charles Ball*	M
			Donald Amador	C
			Gordon Blake	C
CD 15	Dick Lane*	M	Tom Campbell (I)**	M
	Connor Vlakancie	—		
CD 17	Sam Farr (I)**	L	Bill McCampbell*	M
			Mark Cares	—
CD 20	Cal Dooley (I)**	M	Devin Nunes	M
			Cliff Unruh*	C
CD 24	Brad Sherman (I)**	M	Randy Hoffman*	M
			Joe Gelman	C
			William Westmiller	C
Contested-Incumbent Primaries				
CD 41	Eileen Ansari*	—	Jay Kim (I)	C
			Gary Miller**	C
CD 43	Mike Rayburn*	—	Ken Calvert (I)**	C
			Joe Khoury	C
CD 45	Patricia Neal*	L	Dana Rohrbacker (I)**	C
			Charmayne Bohman	M

C = conservative, I = incumbent, L = liberal, M = moderate.
* Nominees.
** Winners.

I do not expect these "incumbents" to enjoy the same electoral advantages as their colleagues who had been in office since at least 1996. One additional seat matched freshman incumbent Loretta Sanchez and former ten-year incumbent Robert Dornan, who was defeated in 1996. I discuss the Sanchez-Dornan race in the "Open Seats" section because I expect each candidates' "incumbency" status to negate the advantage of the other. I also refer to this race as a "quasi-open" seat.

As mentioned above, we expect little crossover voting in open seats when both parties compete for the nomination, since members of both parties will be concerned, first and foremost, with their own party's nomination. However, in 1998, only one of the eight open or quasi-open seats was contested by both parties, so crossover voting is a real possibility.

Of these eight open or quasi-open seats, moderate candidates were elected in five races.[14] In CD 1, moderate former State Senator Mike Thompson beat Jim Hennefer in the primary and Republican Mark Luce in the general. In CD 3, both parties nominated moderates, and Republican Doug Ose beat Democrat Sandy Dunn in the general. In CD 36, moderate Steve Kuykendall beat a field of three other Republicans for the nomination and defeated Democrat Janice Hahn in the general. In the Twenty-Second District, Democrat Lois Capps faced no primary opposition and defeated conservative Tom Bordonaro in the general. And moderate Democrat Loretta Sanchez beat conservative Republican Bob Dornan in CD 46. Extremist candidates were elected in three districts. In CD 34, liberal Democrats Grace Flores Napolitano and James Casso met in the primary, with Napolitano advancing to the general and easily defeating Republican Ed Perez. In CD 9 and CD 34, liberal Democrat Barbara Lee and conservative Republican Mary Bono, respectively, faced the same opponents they had defeated in special elections just months before and won easily. Hence, these open-seat races provide some preliminary support for the moderation hypothesis.

A closer look at the open-seat races, however, reveals that circumstances were ripe for crossover voting—sincere, hedging, or raiding—in only five races (CD 1, CD 22, CD 34, CD 36, and CD 46). In these five races, only one party held a contested primary. All five produced moderate general election winners, but only two produced moderate winners in the contested primary (Democrat Mike Thompson in CD 1 and Republican Steve Kuykendall in CD 36). The nomination and election of these moderates suggests that in these races there may have been substantial sincere crossover and hedging. Note, however, that other factors besides the blanket primary, including superior political experience, campaign resources, and key endorsements, also played important roles in all of these races.

Contested-Challenger Races. House incumbents are rarely challenged in the primary (in 1998, three House incumbents from California faced serious primary challenges from their own party—see below). The most common scenario is a contested primary to nominate the challenger. In these races, the outcome of the incumbent's primary is virtually certain and members of the incumbent's party are free to participate in the contested challenger's primary. We therefore expect any effects of crossover voting to manifest predominantly in the contested-challenger primaries. Of course, the outcome of these contested-challenger primaries rarely affects general election outcomes, since congressional incumbents are reelected at extremely high rates. Nevertheless, other less direct effects of crossover voting into the challenger's primary may still be felt in the general election, particularly if such crossover voting results in a challenger who can force the incumbent to address new issues or take new positions on old issues.

In the 1998 California primary, fourteen congressional races witnessed some competition in the challenger's party's primary. In three of these races, there was also significant intraparty competition in the incumbent's own primary. However, since challengers are virtually assured of losing in the general, these contested-challenger races rarely attract strong candidates with well-developed policy positions. Moreover, even if they have well-developed positions, challengers can rarely mobilize sufficient resources to run professional campaigns that effectively disseminate information about the candidate's positions to voters. This means that during the election, potential crossover voters have little information on which to base their voting decisions. After the election, analysts have little information with which to classify candidates' positions. Recognizing these information problems, I therefore focus on the contested-challenger primaries with "serious" candidates. I define these as races in which at least one candidate received at least 20 percent of the total primary vote. There were five such races in 1998.

Moderates were nominated in four of the five contested-challenger primaries with serious candidates. In two races, there was one candidate who was clearly moderate and two who were clearly conservative, and the moderate was nominated in both races. In the Republican primary in CD 10, relatively moderate Charles Ball defeated conservative primary challengers Donald Amador and Gordon Blake; in the Republican primary in CD 24, moderate Republican Randy Hoffman defeated conservatives Joe Gelman and William Westmiller. In the other two races, none of the challenger primary candidates were clearly liberal or conservative, and moderate candidates Dick Lane (CD 15 Democratic primary) and Bill McCampbell (CD 17 Republican primary) were nominated. Thus, in all four of these races, conditions were ripe for crossover voting, and moderate candidates were nominated, providing evidence that is consistent with the moderation hypothesis. In the fifth race, the CD 20 Republican primary, Cliff Unruh, the more conservative of the two candidates, was nominated. While this outcome is more consistent with the polarization hypothesis, observers note that the moderate candidate's age (twenty-four years old) was probably more of a detriment than his policy positions (Hoffenblum 1998b).

Contested-Incumbent Races. Congressional incumbents rarely face challenges from within their own party. When they do, the challenge usually results from extraordinary circumstances such as the incumbent's involvement in a scandal. The three intraparty incumbent challenges in 1998 (CD 41, CD 43, and CD 45) are cases in point. In all three races, the conservative Republican incumbent was involved in a major personal or political scandal. In CD 41, incumbent Jay Kim was defeated by a conservative opponent Gary Miller. In CD 43, incumbent Ken Calvert prevailed over a conservative opponent, Joe Khoury. In CD 45, incumbent Dana Rohrbacker prevailed over his moderate opponent Charmayne Bohman. Due to the extraordinary circumstances in each of these races, however, I hesitate to generalize from these outcomes about the effects of the blanket primary.

State Assembly Races

The State Assembly races provide even more opportunities to analyze the effects of the blanket primary on candidate positions. Due to term limits, there were many open seats and contested races for State Assembly in 1998. This should translate into ample opportunities for studying all types of crossover voting.

Due to the lack of reliable information on candidate positions in some low-profile races, I again restrict my analysis to the contested Assembly primaries with "serious" candidates who received at least 20 percent of the total vote cast for all primary candidates. I was able to obtain information about the winning candidate in thirty-four of thirty-seven such races. For each race, I obtained information on the winning candidate's ideology (conservative, moderate, liberal); party (Democratic or Republican); type of race (open seat, challenger's party, incumbent's party); and district ideology (safe D, strong D, split, strong R, safe R).[15] For sixteen races, I was also able to identify the losing candidate's ideology.[16] I report these raw data for 1998 in table 10.2.

One advantage of analyzing the Assembly primaries is that there were a sufficient number of contested races to conduct statistical analyses to test the moderation and polarization hypotheses directly. To test whether the blanket primary resulted in more moderate or more extreme candidates, I need to compare the results in these races to the results in races with a

TABLE 10.2 Characteristics of Winning Candidates,
California State Assembly Races, 1998

District	Party	Race Type	Winner's Ideology	Second-Place Candidate's Ideology	Third-Place Candidate's Ideology	District Ideology
2	Rep.	Open	M	C		Safe R
3	Rep.	Open	C	C		Safe R
4	Rep.	Inc.'s party	C			Safe R
5	Rep.	Open	M	C		Safe R
7	Dem.	Open	L			Strong D
9	Dem.	Open	L	L		Strong R
10	Rep.	Open	M	C		Strong R
15	Dem.	Chal.'s party				Strong R
18	Dem.	Open	L	M		Safe D
20	Dem.	Open	M			Strong D
20	Rep.	Open	M			Strong D
23	Dem.	Inc.'s party	L			Safe D
24	Rep.	Inc.'s party	M	C	C	Strong R
29	Rep.	Open	C		M	Safe R
30	Dem.	Chal.'s party	L			Split
33	Rep.	Open	M			Safe R
35	Dem.	Open	M			Split
35	Rep.	Open	M			Split
37	Rep.	Open	C		M	Safe R
47	Dem.	Open	M			Safe D
49	Dem.	Open	M	L	L	Safe D
50	Dem.	Open	L	L		Safe D
53	Dem.	Open				Split
54	Rep.	Open	M			Split
54	Dem.	Open	M			Split
55	Dem.	Inc.'s party	M			Safe D
57	Dem.	Inc.'s party	L			Safe D
60	Rep.	Open	M			Split
61	Rep.	Open	C			Split
62	Dem.	Open				Strong D
65	Rep.	Inc.'s party	C			Safe R
67	Rep.	Inc.'s party	C	M		Strong R
68	Rep.	Open	C	M		Safe R
73	Rep.	Open	C	C		Safe R
75	Rep.	Open	M	C		Safe R
76	Rep.	Chal.'s party	C	M		Strong D
78	Rep.	Chal.'s party	M			Split

different primary system. The obvious comparison is to the contested Assembly primaries under the closed primary in 1996. The 1996 and 1998 primaries were quite similar in many ways. There were about the same number of contested primaries in both years, and all of the pre-term-limits members were termed out of the Assembly by 1996.[17] There were also some important differences, however. Most important, 1996 was a presidential election year, while 1998 was a mid-term election. However, the hotly contested open-seat Governor's race in 1998 may have reduced some of these differences by increasing salience and turnout in 1998. Table 10.3 reports Assembly candidate characteristics for 1996.

Table 10.4 compares the percentage of contested Assembly primaries won by moderate candidates in 1996 (under the closed primary) and in 1998 (under the blanket primary). The first row shows that moderates won half of all contested primaries in 1998, compared to 37 percent in 1996. A one-tailed difference of proportions test produces a p-value of .12, indicating that we can reject the null hypothesis that the proportions of moderate winners in the two elections are the same (or that the 1996 proportion is higher) with 88 percent confidence. A two-tailed difference of proportions test produces a p-value of .24. While these tests fail to achieve the standard 95 percent level of confidence, due largely to the small number of races in both election years (forty-one in 1996, thirty-four in 1998), they do indicate some support for the moderation hypothesis.

To test the robustness of the moderation effect, subsequent rows in table 10.4 break down the races in a number of ways. We see that the percentage of open-seat and challenger party primaries won by moderates is higher in 1998. Both moderate (i.e., less liberal) Democrats and moderate (i.e., less conservative) Republicans were more likely to win in 1998. These results are starker when the winner faced an extreme challenger and when voters in the district were moderate.

These comparisons indicate that, while the moderation effect holds across the various subsamples of races, there are also important differences in the overall level of candidate moderation in the different races. In other words, factors such as race type, party, presence of an extreme challenger, and district ideology appear to affect the probability that moderates will be nominated, independent of the effect of the blanket primary. To test this more complete model of candidate policy positions, I ran a multivariate logistic regression analysis. Table 10.5 reports the results of this analysis. The dependent variable is whether or not a moderate was elected in each race. The logit coefficients report the effect of each independent variable on the log of the odds ratio, that is, on the log of the ratio of the probabilities that a moderate candidate is and is not nominated.

The logit coefficients in column 2 (Model 1) show that once we control for the other factors that affect the probability of nominating a moderate

TABLE 10.3 Characteristics of Winning Candidates,
California State Assembly Races, 1996

District	Party	Race Type	Winner's Ideology	Second-Place Candidate's Ideology	Third-Place Candidate's Ideology	District Ideology
1	Dem.	Open	L	M	L	Split
1	Rep.	Open	M	M		Split
4	Rep.	Open	C			Safe R
8	Dem.	Open	M			Split
8	Rep.	Open	M			Split
9	Dem.	Open	L	M		Safe D
11	Dem.	Open	L			Safe D
14	Dem.	Open	L	L	L	Safe D
15	Rep.	Open	C	M		Strong R
16	Dem.	Open	M	L		Safe D
19	Dem.	Open	L		M	Safe D
22	Dem.	Open	M			Strong D
22	Rep.	Open	M		C	Strong D
23	Dem.	Open	L	M	L	Safe D
26	Dem.	Open	M			Split
26	Rep.	Open	M	C		Split
27	Dem.	Open	L			Strong D
27	Rep.	Open	M	C		Strong D
28	Rep.	Chal.'s party	C			Split
30	Rep.	Inc.'s party	C	M		Strong R
32	Rep.	Open	C	M		Safe R
36	Rep.	Open	C	M	C	Safe R
38	Rep.	Open	C	M	M	Safe R
39	Dem.	Open	L	L		Strong D
40	Dem.	Open	L			Strong D
43	Rep.	Open	M		C	Split
44	Rep.	Open	C			Split
48	Dem.	Open	L	L		Safe D
51	Dem.	Open	L	L	L	Safe D
52	Dem.	Open	L	L		Safe D
53	Rep.	Chal.'s party	M	M		Split
54	Dem.	Chal.'s party	L	M		Split
55	Dem.	Open	M			Safe D
56	Rep.	Open	C		C	Split
64	Rep.	Open	M	C	M	Safe R
67	Rep.	Inc.'s party	C	C	M	Strong R
71	Rep.	Open	C	C		Safe R
74	Rep.	Inc.'s party	C	M		Strong R
76	Rep.	Chal.'s party	C	M		Split
78	Dem.	Open	M	L		Split
78	Rep.	Open	M	C		Split

TABLE 10.4 Percentage of Contested California Assembly Primaries Won by Moderates

	1996	1998	$p < z$ (1-tailed)	$p < |z|$ (2-tailed)
All	37%	50%	.12	.24
Open	41	58	.10	.20
Challenger's party	25	33	.40	.81
Democrats	32	46	.20	.40
Republicans	41	52	.23	.45
Extreme challenger	42	60	.18	.36
Moderate district	48	63	.18	.36
Vote margin (VM)	18.66	21.03	.26	.52
VM—Open seats[a]	18.65	16.31	.28	.56
VM—Challenger's party[a]	21.25	16.25	.29	.59
No. of candidates[a]	3.61	3.51	.40	.80
No. of candidates—Open seats[a]	3.88	3.88	.50	1.00
No. of candidates—Challenger's party[a]	2.25	2.00	.31	.62

[a]Average value lower in 1998; hence 1-tailed test is $p > z$.

TABLE 10.5 Moderates Nominated in Contested Assembly Primaries, Logit Estimates

Independent Variable	Model 1	Model 2	Model 3
Blanket	1.02**	0.99**	0.45
	(0.54)	(0.54)	(0.83)
Open seat	1.67**	1.74**	1.20
	(0.69)	(0.70)	(1.24)
Moderate district	1.49**	1.46**	1.53
	(0.55)	(0.56)	(0.89)
Democrats		−0.39	−1.73**
		(0.54)	(0.89)
Extreme challenger			2.23**
			(0.98)
Constant	−2.92**	−2.78**	−3.59**
	(0.86)	(0.88)	(1.47)
Pseudo-R^2	.13	.14	.26
N	75	75	46

NOTE: Asymptotic standard errors are in parentheses.
*$p < .10$, 1-tailed test
**$p < .05$, 1-tailed test

candidate, our confidence in the effect of the blanket primary increases substantially. The coefficient on the blanket primary variable (scored 1 for 1998 and 0 for 1996) is positive with a t-ratio of 1.88. This translates into a p-value of .03 for a one-tailed t-test with 71 degrees of freedom and a p-value of .06 for a two-tailed t-test. The coefficients on the open-seat dummy (scored 1 for open seats, 0 otherwise) and the moderate district dummy (scored 0 for safe Democratic and safe Republican districts, 1 otherwise) are both positive and significant. Thus, the blanket primary, open seats, and moderate districts all result in a higher probability of moderates being elected.

Model 2 adds a dummy variable scored 1 if the race is a Democratic primary and scored 0 otherwise. The negative coefficient is small relative to the other estimated effects and not significant. Thus, once we control for primary type, race type, and district ideology, Democrats are no more likely to elect moderates than Republicans. Finally, Model 3 adds a dummy variable indicating whether the winner faced an extreme challenger. The coefficient on the extreme challenger variable is positive and significant, indicating that moderates are more successful when they face extreme challengers.[18] Inclusion of the extreme challenger variable increases the size and significance of the Democratic primary dummy. However, it also decreases the size and significance of the blanket primary variable. Further research, perhaps analysis of elections in other blanket primary states, is necessary to determine whether these effects are due to limited observations or some other considerations.[19]

Since logit coefficients express the estimated effect of each explanatory variable on the log of the odds ratio, they are difficult to interpret on their own. Therefore, it is common to report how the independent variables of interest affect the predicted probabilities of the event (in this case, of nominating a moderate candidate), holding constant the values of the other independent variables. I therefore convert the coefficients from column 2 into predicted probabilities. Table 10.6 reports the predicted probabilities of nominating moderates associated with closed and blanket primaries, under various combinations of race type and district ideology.

The main finding from table 10.6 is that for all combinations of race type and district ideology, the probability of nominating a moderate candidate is higher under the blanket primary. In the least favorable setting—when there is an incumbent running and the district is safe Democratic or safe Republican—the probability of nominating a moderate increases from .05 under a closed primary to .13 under a blanket primary. In the most favorable setting—where the race is an open seat and the district ideology is moderate—the probability of nominating a moderate increases from .56 under a closed primary to .78 under a blanket primary.

TABLE 10.6   Predicted Probabilities of Nominating Moderates,
Based on Model 1 Logit Estimates

Blanket	Open Seat	Moderate District	Z	P
0	0	0	−2.92	.05
0	0	1	−1.43	.19
0	1	0	−1.25	.22
0	1	1	0.24	.56
1	0	0	−1.90	.13
1	0	1	−0.41	.40
1	1	0	−0.23	.44
1	1	1	1.26	.78

SUMMARY AND CONCLUSION

One of the most debated questions about the blanket primary is whether it would result in the nomination and ultimate election of moderate or extreme candidates. The potential advantages enjoyed by such candidates result from strategic voter behavior. Under the blanket primary, the costs of engaging in three types of voter behavior—sincere crossover, hedging, and raiding—are all substantially lowered. If voters engage primarily in sincere crossover and hedging, the blanket primary advantages moderate candidates. If voters engage primarily in raiding, the blanket primary advantages extreme candidates.

Analyzing the results of the 1998 California races for Governor, U.S. Senate, U.S. Congress, and State Assembly, I find some evidence for the moderation hypothesis and little evidence for the polarization hypothesis. At the top of the ballot, the blanket primary did not seem to have a major effect on election outcomes. Other factors, such as incumbency (or an incumbency-like appeal), seem to have been more important. If anything, the U.S. Senate race provides some evidence for the polarization hypothesis, since the least moderate Senate candidate was elected. The blanket primary seemed to make some difference in the competitive U.S. Congressional primaries, with moderates prevailing more often than extremists. And it clearly made a difference in the State Assembly races, leading to the nomination of a significantly greater number of moderates in 1998 compared to 1996. This is not to say that raiding never occurred or that extreme candidates never benefited from crossover voting made possible by the blanket primary. Rather, the evidence strongly suggests that the overall net effect of the blanket primary was to produce more moderate candidates.

NOTES

1. By "moderate" candidates, I simply mean those with centrist policy positions. Thus, moderate Democrats are relatively conservative, and moderate Republicans are relatively liberal. By "extreme," I mean far to either the liberal or conservative end of the ideological spectrum.

2. The other forms of primary elections used in the United States are the open and semiclosed. Twenty-three states use open primaries. In open primaries, participation is open to all registered voters, but each party has a separate ballot, and voters are restricted to participating in a single party's nominations in a given election. Eight states use semiclosed primaries, which are an intermediate form that allows independents and/or new voters to participate but not members of other parties. Louisiana uses a nonpartisan "primary," in which any candidate who receives a majority of the total vote automatically wins the office. If no candidate receives a majority, the top two vote receivers from any parties meet in a runoff (see Bott 1991).

3. It is also possible that existing candidates will change their policy positions. In Downsian fashion, candidates may move away from their hard-core partisan constituencies and converge towards the center to compete for the favor of the sincere crossovers and hedgers (Downs 1957). This "move" towards the center may occur either as existing candidates change their positions to adapt to the new electoral environment, or as new candidates enter with more moderate positions.

4. I also assume that all voters turn out, and that all actors know all aspects of the example.

5. This example is deliberately simplistic to illustrate the basic dynamics of voter choice under open or blanket primaries. I consider the consequences of relaxing some of the most restrictive assumptions, such as the voter distribution and candidate positions, below.

6. See Gerber and Morton 2001 for a more detailed examination of this basic model.

7. ADA scores are voting indices constructed by the liberal interest group Americans for Democratic Action. They indicate the proportion of times the legislator cast a liberal vote on selected bills. Gerber and Morton use ADA scores as indicators of legislators' ideology.

8. In fact, three other Republican candidates were listed on the ballot. However, none was ever considered a real threat to Lungren and, in the end, none received more than 4 percent of the vote.

9. Three other Democrats were listed on the ballot. All received less than 1 percent of the party vote.

10. Harman's 1996 ADA score was only 60 (with 100 being the most liberal), placing her among the most conservative Democrats in the House (Block and Buck 1997, 390).

11. One other Democratic candidate won 7.85 percent of the party vote. Four other Republican candidates were also listed on the ballot. One received 10.36 percent of the party vote, and the others received less than 2 percent each (California Secretary of State 1998c).

12. Boxer's 1996 ADA score was a perfect 100 (Block and Buck 1997, 341).

13. It is possible, of course, that candidates' retirement decisions are tied in part to strategic considerations related to the blanket primary. See Kiewiet and Zeng 1993 on strategic retirements.

14. My assessment of candidate policy positions is based on information from several sources, including candidate statements and election materials, newspaper coverage, and political consultant Allan Hoffenblum's *California Target Book,* a careful race-by-race assessment of state legislative races used extensively by campaign professionals. The *Target Book* is produced and updated throughout the election cycle. I thank Mr. Hoffenblum for his generosity in providing me access to the *Target Book.*

15. As with the U.S. Congressional races, I relied primarily on candidate statements, election materials, newspaper reports, and Hoffenblum's *California Target Book* to assess winning candidates' positions and district ideology.

16. In most cases, this information was available for the second-place candidate. In a few, it was also available for the third-place candidate.

17. Candidates who predated term limits, instituted in 1992, may have an incumbency advantage not enjoyed by post-term-limits candidates. Therefore, comparisons between 1998 and years prior to 1996 are severely suspect.

18. An alternative explanation posits the opposite causal story; that is, strong moderate candidates attract ideologically extreme challengers.

19. Reliable data on challenger policy positions were available for only forty-six races (thirty in 1996, sixteen in 1998).

REFERENCES

Block, A. G., and Claudia Buck. 1997. *California Political Almanac.* Sacramento, CA: State Net.

Bott, Alexander. 1991. *Handbook of United States Election Laws and Practices.* New York: Greenwood Press.

California Secretary of State. 1996. *Ballot Pamphlet.* Sacramento.

———. 1998a. *California General Election Campaign Receipts, Expenditures, Cash on Hand, and Debts for State Candidates and Officeholders (July 1, 1998 through December 31, 1998).* Sacramento.

———. 1998b. *Statement of the Vote: Primary Election, June 2, 1998.* Sacramento.

———. 1998c. *Statement of the Vote: General Election, November 3, 1998.* Sacramento.

———. 1998d. *Ballot Pamphlet.* Sacramento.

Downs, Anthony. 1957. *An Economic Theory of Democracy.* New York: Harper and Row.

Gerber, Elisabeth R., and Rebecca B. Morton. 1998. "Primary Election Systems and Representation." *Journal of Law, Economics, and Organization* 14, no. 2: 304–24.

———. 2001. "Electoral Institutions and Party Competition: The Effects of Nomination Procedures on Electoral Coalition Formation." Unpublished working paper. University of California, San Diego.

Grofman, Bernard, and Thomas L. Brunell. 2001. "Explaining the Ideological Differences Between Two U.S. Senators Elected from the Same State: An Institutional Effects Model." In Peter F. Galderisi, Marni Ezra, and Michael Lyons, eds.,

Congressional Primaries and the Politics of Representation. Lanham, MD: Rowman & Littlefield.

Hoffenblum, Allan, ed. 1996a. *California Target Book, March 1996*. Los Angeles: Allan Hoffenblum and Associates.

———. 1996b. *California Target Book, May 1996*. Los Angeles: Allan Hoffenblum and Associates.

———. 1998a. *California Target Book, Final Primary Edition*. Los Angeles: Allan Hoffenblum and Associates.

———. 1998b. *California Target Book, General Election Edition*. Los Angeles: Allan Hoffenblum and Associates.

Institute of Governmental Studies. 1999. Transcript, 1998 Governor's Race Conference. Berkeley, CA: n.p.

Kiewiet, D. Roderick, and Lanche Zeng. 1993. "An Analysis of Congressional Career Decisions." *American Political Science Review* 87: 928–41.

King, David C. 1998. "Party Competition and Polarization in American Politics." Paper presented at the Annual Meeting of the Midwest Political Science Association, Chicago.

CHAPTER ELEVEN

Openness Begets Opportunity
Minor Parties and
California's Blanket Primary

Christian Collet

The blanket primary will maim, if not destroy, third parties.
FROM PLAINTIFF'S OPENING BRIEF FILED IN
CALIFORNIA DEMOCRATIC PARTY
ET AL. V. JONES (1997)

Relatively speaking, the 1990s were prosperous times for minor parties in California. Since the decade began, the number of minor parties qualified for the state ballot doubled, from three to six; the number of alternative candidates mounting campaigns for Congress grew from 33 in the 1990 elections to 77 in 1998 (from 0.7 to roughly 1.5 candidates per district); and the proportion of statewide voters not registering with the Republicans or Democrats grew from 11 to 18 percent. Minor-party candidates won nonpartisan races in Berkeley, Davis, Santa Monica, Simi Valley, and Santa Cruz; and in 1996 the Green party won a majority on the council of the northern coastal city of Arcata. The coup de grâce occurred on April Fools' Day 1999, when voters in the East Bay Area's Sixteenth Assembly district elected Audie Bock, a Green, over heavily favored and financed former Oakland Democratic Mayor Elihu Harris. Bock, a first-time candidate and political novice, became the first minor-party candidate to win a State Legislative seat since 1917.[1]

In spite of these successes, the passage of Proposition 198 cast some uncertainty on this otherwise bullish epoch for alternative politics. After the measure passed in March 1996, the following questions emerged: How would the blanket primary affect minor parties? Would they be helped, or hurt, by the reform? While most of the attention focused on Proposition 198's impact on major parties and the new emancipation given to voters, minor parties were left wondering how the initiative would alter, if at all, their quest for political legitimacy. Some joined Republicans and Democrats in fervent philosophical opposition to the blanket primary. But others remained conspicuously quiet, preferring to take no outright position on a reform whose impact could conceivably be beneficial to their strategic electoral goals.

This chapter addresses the impact of the state's blanket primary on California's minor parties—and the question of whether minor parties might have benefited from the reform. In order to shed light on this, I examine the electoral performance of minor-party candidates in 1998 relative to the last gubernatorial election in 1994. As well, I consider the attitudes of candidates and party leaders themselves toward the reform as revealed in a survey and personal interviews. Lastly, I compare the experience of minor parties in California with those in Washington and Alaska, the two states that currently have blanket primary systems.

Historical evidence suggests that while the reform provides the *potential* for outsider mischief, as opponents contend, such instances are rare. Rather, I conclude that the answer to the question of whether the blanket primary helps or harms minor parties depends on the goals of the parties themselves. If minor parties in California merely aspire to persist as insular "ideological entities," then the blanket primary may be considered harmful, since the "openness" of the format allowed for infiltration of outside voters in the nomination process and may have produced less ideologically pure candidates. However, if the goal of minor parties is to gain more visibility for their candidates and issues, the primary's openness could have offered a significant opportunity for them to advance their electoral position in California.

THE PLAINTIFF'S ARGUMENT AGAINST THE BLANKET PRIMARY

The minor parties that joined the Republican and Democratic plaintiffs in *California Democratic Party et al. v. Jones*—namely the Libertarian party (LP) and the established wing of the Peace and Freedom party (PFP)[2]—focused on how the blanket primary would violate their First Amendment right to association. Simplified, the plaintiffs' argument went as follows: minor parties are "explicitly ideological entities" that are distinctive in their distance from the political mainstream occupied by the Republicans and Democrats; as such, they are small, have relatively few supporters, and are particularly sensitive to the influence of outsiders. If the blanket primary were to be imposed, minor parties would likely receive scores of votes from other party and decline-to-state registrants. This would mean that the act of nomination—one of the primary functions of a political party—would be decided almost completely by non–party members.

The plaintiffs focused on the fact that since minor-party primaries usually involve fewer voters (in the case of legislative races, often in the hundreds) a small number of votes are usually enough to decide the party's nomination. A closely contested primary run under a blanket format would therefore almost certainly be decided by "outsiders"—a clear infringement, they argued, of associational rights. Since minor parties rarely have the resources to educate non–party members about their candidates or their platforms, they would suffer from having nominations determined by voters who, in their contention, are completely ignorant of the choices they had made.

The implication of this argument is that minor parties could have their nominations stolen by so-called outsiders who are completely unfaithful to party principles or who, because of personal circumstances, might embarrass the party. Imagine, for example, what could happen if O. J. Simpson were to run on an LP ticket in an overwhelmingly African-American district, or if David Duke were to run for the American Independent party nomination in a northern Central Valley district. In both cases, the dubious celebrity nominees would likely win with factional support from voters outside the parties; in both cases, the parties, lacking the resources to advertise on behalf of the preferred nominee, would be helpless to prevent the ignominy from occurring. The taint of nominating such a candidate could be devastating to a party that is not otherwise known or well established in the electorate.

Since such instances of embarrassment are relatively rare and anecdotal (I shall discuss this below), the plaintiffs' empirical evidence focused on (1) demonstrating the small number of votes that have decided contested minor-party primaries in the past and (2) how the vote for minor-party candidates would dramatically increase under the blanket system. Though there was no way of knowing just how much, and under what conditions, crossover voting would likely occur for minor-party candidates, Richard Winger, the publisher of *Ballot Access News,* offered the following speculation for the plaintiffs:

> In my opinion, if the new California primary law goes into effect, the vote for minor-party candidates in primary elections will be *much* higher than it has been in the past. The new voters will not be party members. As a general proposition, I believe that minor-party members voting in their own primary will be outnumbered by non–party members. Even where they are not outnumbered, the proportion of non–party voters will be very high—much, much higher than in major-party primaries. ("Appellant's Opening Brief," filed in *CA Dems. v. Jones,* 36–39)

Such a dramatic increase implies that the votes of party registrants would be swamped by the votes of independents and registrants of other parties—and would overwhelm the preferences of supposed "party members."

The defendant, namely the office of Secretary of State Bill Jones, claimed that Winger's contention was "without foundation." "Nothing suggests that crossover voting in minor-party primaries will be widespread, much less negatively impact the parties or their candidates" (Appellee's and Inter-venor's Brief, *CA Dems v. Jones,* "No Harm to Minor Parties," 42–43). As a result, the defendant argued that concerns raised by plaintiffs—the potential stealing of party nominations and weakened and / or embarrassed parties—are not significant enough to "rise to the level of protected associational interests." Minor parties are not competitive, claimed the defendant, but expressive; as the Supreme Court has determined in previous cases, elections are about the process of casting ballots, not the advertisement of alternative political ideas.

THE HISTORY OF MINOR PARTIES IN CALIFORNIA PRIMARIES

There were a number of ironies in the plaintiffs' argument. One was that they portrayed themselves and other minor parties as small, impotent, ideological entities while simultaneously arguing that they were significant enough for court protection. They also put themselves in the awkward position of contending that getting more votes in a primary election is somehow a *bad* thing, an idea that runs counter to most conceptions of party formation and electoral competition. Indeed, it seems safe to assume, most would expect any political party (particularly a small one) to rejoice at the opportunity to win additional supporters—any time, any place.

Perhaps the hardest point the plaintiffs had to sell was the fact that minor parties were somehow affected significantly by primary elections when, historically, such intraparty challenges have been rare. Indeed, between 1960, when the practice of party cross-filing ended in California, and 1996, there were just ninety cases where more than one minor-party candidate contested for the same statewide, Board of Equalization, congressional, or state legislative seat (see figure 11.1).[3] In 1998, there were just seven such contests, compared to eighty-six for the major parties.

Of the ninety-seven, more than a third (thirty-three) occurred in 1970 as a result of a factional split in the conservative American Independent party (AIP). The party with the highest number of competitive primaries in this period, however, has been the socialist PFP (forty-three since 1970). The other minor parties in the state—the LP (eleven since 1980), the Greens (two occurring in 1994), the Natural Law party (one in 1996), and the Reform party (also one in 1996)—have scarcely seen challenges from within.

Most intraparty challenges in California's minor parties have occurred at the congressional (seventeen) or state legislative level (forty-seven). Taking these races together, this constitutes 61 percent of all intraparty primaries. But it is worth noting that there has been a contested race in every gubernatorial election since 1970 and in five out of the last six U.S. senatorial elections. For whatever reason—greater exposure driving can-

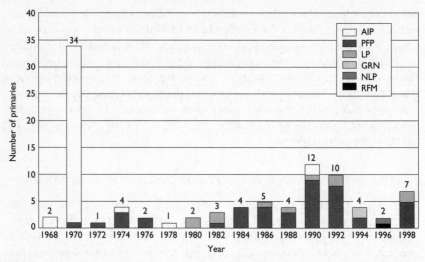

Figure 11.1. Contested minor-party primaries in California, 1968–98 (presidential primaries excluded). Source: California Secretary of State, *Statement of the Vote.*

didate ambition or perhaps greater stakes revealing party divisions[4]— high-profile offices have more consistently seen contests for minor-party nominations.

When minor parties do have "competitive" primaries, they generally do not live up to their name. The average margin of victory in eight minor-party gubernatorial primaries between 1968 and 1996 was 17.8 percent; for Lieutenant Governor, the margin was 22.9 percent. Races have been equally lopsided at lower levels. In congressional races, the victor has, on average, won by 16 percentage points; in races for the Assembly, the margin has been an average of 20 percentage points.

When looking at the raw vote totals, things appear to be much more competitive. Minor-party primaries under the closed system were decided by a relative handful of votes, as the Proposition 198 plaintiffs demonstrated. This was due to two factors: the generally low level of minor-party registration (which can fall to the low hundreds in some Assembly districts) and the low level of turnout among most minor-party registrants.[5] Of the ninety contested minor-party primaries between 1968 and 1996, thirty were decided by fewer than fifty votes, and nine were decided by ten votes or less. Two primaries at the legislative level in 1970 were decided by a single vote. Overall, the average number of votes that separated intraparty contestants in statewide primaries was 2,112; for congressional and legislative races, it was a mere 72 votes.

WHAT HAPPENED IN 1998?

In 1998, as the plaintiffs expected, things changed dramatically for minor-party candidates—especially those running in down-ballot races. In table 11.1, I juxtapose the average primary vote totals for selected offices in the 1968–96 period to the totals for the seven intraparty contests that occurred (five in the PFP, two in the LP) in 1998. The comparisons are staggering. In some races, such as those for Secretary of State and Insurance Commissioner, the vote was twenty to thirty times higher than the twenty-eight-year average. But races for Lieutenant Governor, Congress and the Assembly nonetheless saw increases in the vote that ranged from eight to eleven times greater than what had been seen under the closed primary system.

It is worth noting, however, that the increases in voting were smallest at the top of the ticket. In the gubernatorial PFP primary in 1998 between Marsha Feinland and Gloria de La Riva, just 37,077 votes were cast—about three times more than the average in eight previous gubernatorial races in the 1968–96 period (11,695). But the total number of votes cast for the two candidates was only about half of the party's statewide registration (71,620).

We continue to see evidence of increased minor-party voting in table 11.2. The mean candidate percentage of the total vote more than tripled in major statewide races and increased anywhere from sevenfold up to twelvefold for down-ballot races. Looking at the minor parties individually, the only potential "loser" (in terms of vote share) from the blanket primary may have been the AIP, which actually received a lower percentage of the vote in the 1998 gubernatorial race than when the primary was closed in 1994. The drop may reflect some of the softness in the AIP's registration, since it is widely thought that many California voters inadvertently register with the "American Independent Party" under the belief that they are registering as independents (i.e., decline-to-state). Still, the party's vote percentage more than quadrupled in U.S. House races and doubled in Assembly races.

The biggest "winner" (in terms of increased vote share) from the blanket primary would appear to be the Green party, whose percentages increased from 0.5 to 3.4 percent in congressional races and from 0.7 to 4.1 percent for Assembly races. LP and PFP candidate percentages also rose dramatically with the expansion of the primary electorate. But not as much as the Greens, who, conceivably, have a broad appeal to progressive crossover voters and others concerned with environmentalism and social justice.

While tables 11.1 and 11.2 unequivocally show an increase in voting for minor parties in 1998, questions remain about its impact. Who benefited the most and under what conditions? Generally speaking, excluding races where a major-party contestant was lacking, the minor-party vote in a given

TABLE 11.1   Average Number of Votes in Contested Minor-Party
Primaries, 1968–96 versus 1998

	1998	1968–96 Average	Increase
Governor	37,077	11,695	3:1
N =	1	8	
Lieutenant Governor	141,128	12,865	11:1
N =	1	5	
Secretary of State	127,609	6,357	20:1
N =	1	2	
Attorney General	137,946	—	—
N =	1	0	
Insurance Commissioner	159,307	5,400	30:1
N =	1	1	
U.S. Congress	4,343	536	8:1
N =	1	16	
State Assembly	3,469	314	11:1
N =	1	33	

SOURCE: California Secretary of State, *Statement of the Vote* (Sacramento, 1968–96 and 1998).

TABLE 11.2   Mean Minor-Party Candidate Percentages of the Total
Vote in California Primaries, by Party, 1994 and 1998

	Governor		U.S. Senate		U.S. House		California Senate		California Assembly	
	1994	1998	1994	1998	1994	1998	1994	1998	1994	1998
AIP	0.4	0.3	0.4	0.4	0.5	2.2	—	—	0.6	1.2
Green	0.1	1.5	0.2	—	0.5	3.4	—	—	0.7	4.1
LP	0.3	0.8	0.3	1.2	0.3	2.4	0.4	3.4	0.4	3.3
NLP	—	0.2	—	0.4	—	1.8	—	3.0	—	2.4
PFP	0.1	0.3	0.1	0.9	0.2	2.0	0.2	3.4	0.2	3.5
Reform	—	—	—	0.8	—	1.1	—	—	—	2.0
TOTAL	0.2	0.7	0.2	0.8	0.3	2.2	0.3	3.4	0.4	3.0

SOURCE: California Secretary of State, *Statement of the Vote* (Sacramento, 1994 and 1998).
NOTE: Means are controlled for percentages garnered in races without a major-party contestant. Intraparty primary candidate percentages were averaged. Neither the Reform party nor the Natural Law party was qualified for the ballot in 1994.

congressional or legislative race tended to be higher for candidates who had an ethnic surname or were female. It was also higher in districts where a competitive primary was lacking in one of the major parties. As table 11.3 shows, the few female and ethnic minor candidates who ran in 1998 did noticeably better than their white male counterparts—suggesting the ac-

TABLE 11.3   Mean Minor-Party Candidate Vote in 1998 U.S. House, State Senate, and State Assembly Primaries

	U.S. House	California Senate	California Assembly
Candidate was . . .			
Female	2.6%	3.5%	3.1%
Male	2.1	3.4	2.9
Candidate had . . .			
A Latino or Asian surname	4.6	—	3.4
No ethnic surname	2.7	—	3.0
Major-party competition			
Seat had one uncontested Republican or Democratic primary	3.1	3.4	2.4
Seat had two contested Republican and Democratic primaries	1.7	3.1	1.6
Minor-party candidates in race			
1	3.5	3.5	3.1
2	2.4	2.9	1.9
3	2.0	—	1.8
Total minor-party registration in district was . . .			
Above average (> 5.1%)	3.1	3.3	2.0
Below average (< 5.1%)	2.9	3.5	2.3
Total decline-to-state registration in district was . . .			
Above average (> 12.6%)	2.4	3.3	3.1
Below average (< 12.6%)	2.1	3.4	2.8

NOTE: Means are controlled for percentages garnered in races without a major-party contestant.

tivity of crossover voters. Candidates who ran in seats where there was no competition for either the Republican or Democratic nominations also did better, and those who did not face any competition from other minor-party candidates also got a higher percentage of the vote. However, a minor-party candidate's success in the 1998 primaries appears to have had little to do with either the total minor-party registration in the district or the independent, decline-to-state registration. This would suggest that a good portion of crossover votes for minor-party candidates came from those registered with the major parties.

The minor-party vote exploded under the blanket primary, as the Proposition 198 plaintiffs, and many other observers, expected. But did the vote exceed what minor-party candidates normally receive in a general election? According to figure 11.2, no. In the gubernatorial and U.S. senatorial race,

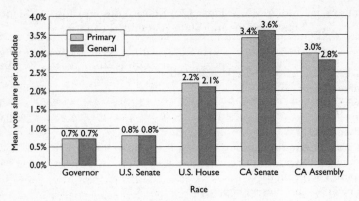

Figure 11.2. Comparison of mean minor-party candidate vote for primary and general election, 1998 (controlled for uncontested races).

the mean vote share per candidate was exactly the same in both the primary and general election (0.7 and 0.8 percent, respectively). Candidates for U.S. House and California Assembly races saw higher percentages, on average, in the primary, but the difference was negligible. In the instance of State Senate races, the mean percentage actually increased slightly in the general.

Given the congruity in the vote in the spring and fall elections, it seems as if the increase in minor-party voting under the blanket primary may have been a function of general election supporters being able to cast an earlier ballot for their preferred minor-party candidate. In other words, a minor-party candidate's *primary* election constituency under the blanket primary may, in fact, have reflected his or her *general* election constituency and hence his or her "normal" share of the vote. If this was the case, it undercuts, to some degree, the assertion that candidate selection under a blanket system is made by outsiders with no familiarity with the party or its candidates.

THE PEACE AND FREEDOM PARTY'S EXPERIENCE WITH CALIFORNIA'S BLANKET PRIMARY

Along with the influence of nonregistrants in the nomination process, minor-party plaintiffs raised concerns about the blanket primary being used for mischievous purposes. Though it remained unknown to many, such an instance occurred in 1998 in the PFP, the minor party known for having the most primaries and the one that had the most in 1998. The story of their experience with the blanket primary in California is instructive, giving observers insight into how the change in primary rules can particularly affect minor parties—for better and for worse.

As the only explicitly socialist party active in California politics, the PFP has traditionally had difficulties with envious parties attempting to "raid" its nomination procedures. This, along with a reputation for passionate political infighting, has fueled many primary battles over the years. Tom Condit, a longtime Bay Area activist in the PFP who lost a bid to be the party's candidate for Insurance Commissioner in 1998, explained that the PFP has had more contested primaries for two reasons: (1) because "a small party is a natural target for 'takeover bids' " and (2) "a lot of people in PFP take their politics very seriously and are willing to fight over them." He explained that, prior to 1980, "candidates were mostly picked by consensus within the ranks of party activists." But in 1980, the Communist Party "asked if we would be upset if they ran Gus Hall in our presidential primary. People who thought that the excitement of contested primaries might attract more interest to the party opened the Pandora's Box and it hasn't been closed since."[6]

Marsha Feinland, a gubernatorial candidate who, like Condit, lost in a contested PFP primary in 1998, agreed:

As a small party, we are particularly vulnerable to challenges by other groups that want to use our ballot line. . . . Specifically, the Communist Party, the Socialist Party, the Internationalist Workers Party, the New Alliance Party, and the Workers World Party have all sought to run people for office as Peace and Freedom Party. Some of these groups have worked as active PFP members, while others have just tried to "raid" PFP.

Thus the PFP has seen its secured position on the ballot serve as a lure for nonqualified left parties who want to run candidates. According to Jan B. Tucker, a "second-generation member" of the PFP who has been with the party since its inception in 1968, many groups over the years—communists, socialists, and even libertarians in the early 1970s—have used the PFP's "ballot access as battle ground." This, he contends, is because the PFP has not been organizationally strong and active in campaigns, but has served only as an insular and ideological "ballot status party." This has given "leftist invasions," in Tucker's terms, the incentive and opportunity to continually attempt to influence the PFP's nomination procedures.

In 1998, however, the party's battles did not come from external invasion, but from insurrection—led by Tucker himself. Dissatisfied with the established wing of the PFP led by Condit and Feinland, and with the party's perceived electoral weakness—"our party's structure resembles the organizational principles of the Marx Brothers more closely than those of Karl Marx," he once wrote—Tucker formed an alternative slate of candidates to challenge the officially endorsed party slate. Support for the blanket primary and more democratic reforms was at the heart of Tucker's dissention. But his biggest gripe was that the PFP too often "ran nothing but white males" (from the Bay Area) and that the party needed to offer a more diverse slate of candidates in order to make inroads with the state's voters.

Conscious of the strategic possibilities available in the blanket primary, Tucker assembled a slate of two Latinos and two women (whom Condit contends were "a group of [Tucker's] friends and acquaintances, none of whom had previously been active in the [PFP]") to appeal to potential crossover voters. Along with gubernatorial candidate Gloria La Riva (who was endorsed by, but not an official part of, the slate), two of Tucker's candidates won PFP nominations. But most significantly, especially in light of the data in table 11.3, all of the three candidates on the PFP ballot with purely Latino surnames—including one not on the Tucker slate—were victorious.

Though the division between the Tucker slate and the established wing of the party did not result in the type of embarrassing scandal that opponents of Proposition 198 feared, the PFP has suffered since the election. Failing to gain 2 percent of the vote in any of the statewide offices for which it ran in 1998, the PFP was subsequently disqualified from the state ballot. As of this writing, it is mounting a drive to register roughly fourteen thousand more voters to get back on the ballot for 2002.[7] Ironically, the party that had staked out an official position against Proposition 198—and had seen itself torn asunder by the new primary—turned to using the reform as part of its sales pitch to gain more registrants. "Your party registration," read the Party's official website in late July 1999, "will not affect your right to vote for whichever candidate you prefer in either the primary or general election" (www.peaceandfreedom.org, July 26, 1999). Tucker and other PFP members have since joined the Green party.

THE BLANKET PRIMARY AS A STRATEGIC RESOURCE

The experience of the PFP would seem to justify the fears that some minor parties had regarding the blanket primary. But, during the March 1996 campaign of Proposition 198 and the subsequent lawsuit, one party—the Reform party—remained optimistic. It did not offer an official position, nor did it join the plaintiffs in the suit. Tacitly, however, it gave lukewarm backing to the blanket primary. The roots of the party's support were consistent with its own populist philosophy; following the Ross Perot mantra, the party believed that empowering independent voters and bringing more people into the political process took precedence over the self-interest of parties. Michael Farris, who was chairman of the fledgling California Reform party at the time, argued, like Tucker, within his party to take a more "pro-active position" in supporting the "broader public interests" involved in Proposition 198. In the end, however, "certain administrative internal party stuff" kept them from doing so.

Populist arguments aside, the Reform party's position regarding the blanket primary reflected more pragmatism than the positions taken by the other minor parties involved in the lawsuit. A new party, less rooted in ideology and more familiar with mainstream politics, the Reform party sensed the strategic opportunities offered by the blanket primary and felt as if it could advance its position in California politics.

How? First of all, a blanket primary system may encourage minor parties and their candidates to actually "run" for office—and to do so earlier in the election season. The typical campaign of a minor-party candidate is low-budget and casual. A 1994 survey of minor-party candidates found that most of the respondents performed few of the basic electioneering activities associated with running for office, like walking precincts or posting signs (Collet 1997). With the closed competitive primary consisting, in many instances, of competition for just hundreds of party voters, there is hardly inspiration for candidates to go beyond committee meetings and run an active campaign.

The "openness" offered by a blanket primary, however, gives minor-party candidates incentive to run "early and often" in order to be heard. Farris himself was an interesting example. Running in Assembly District 37, he told me that, as the lone alternative party candidate in the race, he gained some leverage by garnering early endorsements and by being able to compete earlier in the year with his opponents. Something worked; he received 3.5 percent in the fall after getting 2.8 percent in the primary. Overall, a total of fifteen statewide, thirty U.S. House, and twenty-eight state legislative candidates increased their vote share, like Farris, in the general. A fourth gained more than 1 percent—a significant gain for a small-party candidate.

A related benefit is that a blanket primary may encourage minor parties and their candidates to campaign to the general electorate. Tucker, complaining about the alleged insularity of the PFP, believed the blanket primary would have been instrumental in forcing the party to get its message out to voters statewide. "Those who actually campaign will do well." He continued to explain his belief that the blanket primary would have compelled minor parties to be more than "ballot status" parties: "It forces them to get out and do things that they have never had to do, revolutionary things like campaigning around the state, contacting voters . . . walking precincts." Condit, Tucker's adversary, tended to agree. When asked about how the blanket primary would change campaigning for the PFP, he replied by saying that "if I run for statewide office again, I will begin my campaign outreach to the general electorate much earlier. That isn't easy to do, of course, given the limited resources of our party, but I think it is necessary."

An ancillary benefit for the minor parties is that broader competition under a blanket primary can inspire moderation on issues and positions.

Certainly, minor-party candidates will thrive, as they have throughout history, on the votes of the dissatisfied and the marginal—and many future candidates and parties will concentrate on that infinitesimal segment of the electorate. However, a candidate or party that is ambitious and wants to make inroads with independents or major-party voters may wish to moderate some positions. As the blanket primary took the power of nomination out of the hands of a few insiders, candidates were encouraged to abandon the narrow and sometimes insular world of minor-party politics and engage the mainstream electorate. This was a step toward shaking the "fringe" label, and enhancing the credibility of their candidacies and their ideas.

A fourth potential benefit for minor parties is that a good showing in the primary can put the major parties on the defensive *before* the general election—and thus increase the minor parties' role as "spoilers" *during* the election. Under a closed system, it is generally not until after the election that anyone even notices the performance of the minor-party candidates. Media and private polling tend to ignore minor-party candidates; even if they are included in polls, their minuscule vote percentages are subject to large sampling errors that render the data almost meaningless.

Under a blanket system, the primary election is a straw poll of sorts. It reveals the strengths and weaknesses of all serious contenders for office—particularly those who do not have an intraparty opponent—months before the general election campaign. If a major-party candidate is in trouble, or a minor-party candidate does surprisingly well, the latter are in a position to directly influence the tone and dynamics of the campaign. A strong primary showing for one or more minor-party candidates will likely attract media attention that can result in more funds and volunteer support. Such strength then forces the major-party candidates to engage the minor-party candidates (when, under normal circumstances, they probably would not), include them in candidate debates, and otherwise treat them as legitimate opponents. Not only does this result in much-needed resources that aid long-term party building, but it gives the minor parties a direct line of communication with the voters for the purpose of selling themselves and their ideas.[8]

Along this line, a blanket primary can give minor parties the opportunity to influence the policy debate. Unless there are some extraordinary factors at work, as there were in the 1998 election of Audie Bock, minor-party candidates will probably not be able to defeat major-party candidates. The resource disparities are too great. However, with earlier visibility and the opportunity to participate actively in the general election, there remains a possibility for minor-party candidates to score another kind of victory: the acceptance of their ideas.

Throughout history, minor parties have served as the incubators of new policy initiatives, while the major parties, sensing the potential electoral power of these ideas, have been all too quick to absorb them. Republicans, for example, seized on the slavery issue brought to the fore by Free-Soilers, and many New Deal programs adopted by the Democratic Party found their roots in progressive and socialist minor-party movements (Mazmanian 1974, 81–82). In more recent times, Ross Perot and the Reform party forced both major parties to pursue a balanced national budget and reforms in entitlement spending and campaign finance.

Similarly, a major-party candidate who runs weakly in a blanket primary may be forced to adopt a minor party's issues as a strategic measure to prevent defeat in the general election. Consider a moderate Democrat running in a marginal coastal district who saw a Green candidate receive 7 percent of the vote in a blanket primary. The Democrat, in order to prevent heavy vote siphoning and a Republican upset, may adopt more Green positions during the campaign in order to preserve victory. Likewise, a moderate Republican might adopt more antitax or reduced government positions if he or she saw a strong Libertarian performance.

A final strategic benefit for minor parties is that the potential for greater support and competition may give them greater opportunity to attract high-quality candidates. Insofar as a blanket primary diminishes the importance of party labels and fosters a free-for-all battle for votes, ambitious, independent-minded candidates may be more likely to run on a minor-party ticket. Major parties, because of their mainstream legitimacy and embedded organizational apparatus, will almost always be the first choice for an aspiring politician looking for a vehicle. Running as an independent, because of heavy access restrictions and the inability to compete in the primary, will almost always be the last choice. Hence, minor parties can serve as a plausible alternative—by offering a ballot position and the ability to circumvent a tough contest for a major-party nomination. Minor parties may thus become a more attractive option to visible outsider politicians and those who simply want the opportunity to compete with the establishment candidates.[9]

CANDIDATES SENSE THE OPPORTUNITIES

Minor-party candidates seemed to sense the potential benefits of the primary and, as a result, supported it. A statewide survey distributed to all candidates who ran in partisan offices in the 1998 primary reveals that the blanket primary received its strongest support from minor-party candidates—with the exception of those running for LP nominations—as well as centrist candidates in the major parties (see table 11.4).[10] Overall, 83 percent of all non-LP minor-party candidates in the sample said the blanket primary was "a good reform," while 10 percent said it was a failure. More than four of every five respondents who said the primary was a failure were Libertarians. Worth noting is the fact that majorities of candidates from

TABLE 11.4 Candidate Attitudes toward the Blanket Primary, by Party

	Republicans			Democrats			LP	Other Minor Parties
	Lib./Mod.	Cons.	Total	Lib.	Mod./Cons.	Total		
Percentage who believe the blanket primary . . .								
Is a good reform	62%	44%	47%	24%	57%	43%	27%	83%
Is a failure	31	48	45	53	17	33	50	10
Doesn't make much difference either way	8	9	8	24	26	25	23	7
Position on the blanket primary (10-point scale)[a]								
Percentage giving scores of . . .								
6–10 (support)	62%	44%	47%	17%	54%	47%	27%	77%
0–4 (opposed)	31	52	48	61	29	43	58	19
5 (neutral)	8	4	5	22	17	19	16	3
Mean	5.9	4.8	5.0	3.2	6.4	5.1	3.6	7.3
(S.D.)	(4.2)	(4.1)	(4.1)	(3.1)	(4.2)	(4.0)	(3.4)	(3.2)

NOTE: Columns may not equal 100 percent due to rounding.
[a]Actual question worded as follows: "On a scale of 0 to 10, with 0 being very strongly opposed and 10 being very strongly in support, how would you rate your position on the open/blanket primary?"

minor parties like the Greens and the PFP, who officially opposed Proposition 198, nonetheless felt that it was a "good reform."[11] When asked to rate their position on the blanket primary on a 10-point scale, 77 percent of non-LP minor-party candidates gave it a ranking above 5, resulting in a mean of 7.3. On this measure, moderate Republicans (62 percent) and Democrats (54 percent) were also supportive. LP candidates remained the most opposed, with 58 percent giving a score below 5.

The survey also reveals strong beliefs among all minor-party candidates about the electoral benefits of the blanket primary. While 41 percent of Republicans and 39 percent of Democrats believed the primary "helped [them] win more votes," 74 percent of LP and 68 percent of other minor-party candidates believed the same. Just 2 percent of LP and 7 percent of other minor-party candidates believed the primary "hurt them and cost [them] votes." Roughly two in five major-party candidates, along with one in every four minor-party candidates, said the blanket primary "didn't make much difference either way."

Overall, 74 percent of non-LP minor-party candidates agreed that the blanket primary "[helped] the alternative (or minor) parties." LP candidates, however, were divided (46 percent). Just 29 percent of major-party candidates agreed, and many expressed uncertainty regarding the impact of the blanket primary system on the minor parties.

EXPERIENCE IN WASHINGTON AND ALASKA

How has the imposition of the blanket primary in other states, namely Washington and Alaska, affected minor parties and their candidates? In the former, the blanket primary plays a unique role and has a greater immediate impact. In order to qualify for the general election in Washington, minor-party candidates must receive at least 1 percent of the vote in the primary, a requirement that would likely prevent most from ever advancing to the fall campaign under a closed primary. But with the blanket primary, minor-party candidates are able to draw votes from the entire electorate. In many ways, minor parties in Washington get the best of both worlds. Unlike nominations in major parties, minor-party nominations, under state law, are closed and determined by convention (preventing any minor-party contested primaries). But minor-party candidates are able to receive votes from the entire electorate in the election itself—which greatly enhances their odds of meeting the 1 percent threshold needed to advance to the fall election. "I doubt that we would have ever achieved major-party status with a closed primary," said Paul Telford, Washington chair of the Reform party. Before losing their access in 1998, the Reform party was legally recognized in Washington as a major party—akin to the Republicans and Democrats.

Given the access and advancement requirements, Washington has not had any notable experiences where minor-party nominations have been raided. Telford explains that even if such a thing were to occur in Washington, it "would take a concerted effort to have a big impact—and the word would get out. How could party manipulators get a lot of people to do this without everybody hearing about it?"

Alaska is a different story. With 58 percent of voters registered as something other than a Republican or Democrat, the state has been a hotbed of minor-party activity. Currently, there are three minor parties active on the ballot, and Alaska is one of four states to have elected an independent governor since 1990 (Walter Hickel).

Libertarians in Alaska have had a poisonous experience with the blanket primary. In 1986, the party had two contestants for its gubernatorial nomination, Mary O'Bannon and Ed Hoch. Hoch received the support from party insiders because O'Bannon was wanted by state authorities for selling fraudulent advertisements. But O'Bannon won the nomination in the blanket primary, presumably because her female name was attractive to crossover voters. With a wanted fugitive as their nominee, the LP failed to get the 3 percent of the general election vote needed to retain its status as a "recognized political party" along with the Democrats and Republicans. Since then, the LP has had to file petitions every election year in order to run candidates for office (personal correspondence, Richard Winger, July 23, 1998; see www.gov.state.ak.us/ltgov/elections/partysta.htm, August 3, 1999).

Since the decline of the LP in Alaska, other minor parties have emerged. Among the most significant is the Alaska Independence Party (AKIP), a libertarian-conservative party predicated on "Alaska First" issues and the right to vote on secession from the United States. Like the LP, the AKIP has had problems because of the blanket primary. Yet their official position has been one of tolerant support of the system. This, says AKIP Chairman Mark Chryson, is due to some deference to the widespread independence of Alaskan voters and the fact that the AKIP really has not been hurt by the process. Chryson, who as a candidate was himself once stung by an uninvited intraparty primary challenge, said, "We don't really have enough candidates to where [the blanket primary] is an issue. We can deal with it. But myself, I would like to see us go to a convention to select candidates. But we don't have the money, organization or resources to do so."

On the one hand, says Chryson, "it does create havoc," but on the other, it gives many AKIP party registrants (who are dispersed throughout remote areas of Alaska) an opportunity to vote in elections from which they would normally be excluded. The lack of a widespread slate of AKIP candidates would mean that they would not have a chance to vote until the November election. In 1998, the AKIP officially remained tolerant of the blanket primary, but passed an official party resolution against candidates who have "attempted to use the Party in order to further their self-serving ends."

WEIGHING PRACTICAL BENEFITS
AGAINST PRINCIPLED OPPOSITION

One of the classic divisions within a political party is the conflict between pragmatism and purity—or, in other words, the extent to which a party is willing to compromise its ideological principles in order to make electoral gains. In the case of major parties, the result is self-evident: pragmatists almost always prevail because the imminent goal is to win offices. But in the case of minor parties, the goals are not always as clear-cut.

On the one hand, many within California's minor parties are conscientious about the need to win votes (at least enough to maintain ballot access); on the other, the parties are "explicitly ideological entities" that serve primarily to express discontent and articulate alternatives to the establishment. While it may fly in the face of most conventional thinking, some members of minor parties do not aspire to major-party status. And some, particularly the LP and the PFP, pride themselves on being "parties of principle," by maintaining their philosophical purity and ideological consistency on a variety of issues—regardless of the repercussions at the polls.

This means that the purity versus pragmatism conflict lies at the heart of most internal decisions made by minor parties. As such, it colors our response to the central question: Does a blanket primary system help or hurt minor parties? When one takes the purist view—as do most Libertarians and the established wing of the Peace and Freedom party—one is indeed inclined to opposition. The system clearly offers the potential for mischief by inclined outsiders or dissatisfied insiders. The number of votes deciding minor-party nominations increased dramatically in 1998, and it appears as if there is some potential for candidates with female or ethnic names to draw nonregistrant support—regardless of whether the candidate has the endorsement of the party. Insofar as party organizations are weakened by the fact that their nomination decisions can be influenced by others, minor parties may suffer under a blanket primary system.

When one focuses on the electoral imperative, the practical benefits offered by the blanket primary for minor parties are manifest. Earlier involvement in the campaign and wider exposure to the voters can bring much-needed attention to a candidate and his or her party's issues. And gaining the exposure in June, rather than November, of an election year means that minor parties can actually become *pre facto* rather than *post facto* spoilers. With the June election serving as a straw poll for the strength of the major-party candidates before the fall election, the blanket primary gives minor parties an opportunity to reveal citizen dissent before the campaign begins—and a real opportunity to be heard once it does. With more voice comes more attention and, potentially, more incorporation of minor-party ideas into the political agenda. And with the incorporation of more ideas comes legitimacy. Candidates and other party pragmatists seem to sense this and offer the blanket primary support.

Regardless of who is right, purists or pragmatists, minor parties can agree on one thing: in order to survive, they must adapt to the electoral system. Under a closed primary, minor parties can maintain a quiet existence as fringe ideological entities—as long as they have enough votes or registered members. But, as we saw under California's short-lived experience with a blanket system, strategic opportunities grow as elections become more open. Rather than "maiming" or "destroying" them, a blanket system can entice a minor party toward the mainstream, heighten its visibility, and raise its electoral stakes. Following Plunkitt of Tammany Hall, those parties who are able to see their opportunities under a new system—and take 'em—are likely to be rewarded.

NOTES

1. Independents have won recent elections to the State Senate (e.g., Quentin Kopp in San Francisco's Eighth District and Lucy Killea in San Diego's Thirty-Ninth). An incumbent Democratic Assemblyman, Dom Cortese, switched his party affiliation in 1996 to the Reform party, but lost a bid for election to San Jose's Thirteenth State Senate District under that banner, garnering just 8.8 percent. In 2000, Bock was defeated for reelection, earning 22 percent of the vote as an independent.

2. The Green party of California also opposed Proposition 198, although it was not named as a plaintiff in the case. Their opposition, according to Michael Monnot, the Green "liaison to the Secretary of State" (essentially their de facto party chair, since the party does not have a traditional organizational hierarchy), was based less on the right-to-association argument, but on the "belief that this was a weak reform, and that there are far better alternatives." "Generally," Monnot told me, "the Green party does not believe that political parties should be weakened (which seems to be the goal of 198), but that there should be better ballot access for small parties, and that they should have a better chance at representation through a proportional election system."

3. Between 1960 and 1966, there were no contested minor-party primaries. The figure cited here excludes presidential primaries and twenty-seven cases where Green party candidates ran against "none of the above" between 1992 and 1994, as per their party rules.

4. There are at least two potential reasons why statewide races would be prone to attracting multiple minor-party challengers. Along with the attention and leadership distinction that is given to a top-of-the-ticket nominee, a statewide candidate can retain her party's ballot access by receiving 2 percent of the vote.

5. Libertarians are the exception to a general trend of low turnout among minor-party registrants. In 1994 statewide races, for example, the LP had an average abstention rate among its registrants of 19 percent, versus 24 percent for the Greens, 40 percent for the PFP and 53 percent for the AIP. The Reform and Natural Law parties had yet to qualify for the ballot.

6. This and all subsequent quotations in this chapter are taken from personal interviews conducted June through August 1998 by the author.

7. The party was unable to qualify for the 2000 elections.

8. There is a counterargument that would suggest that the blanket primary gives the major parties a "heads up" on a potential upset and the time to redouble their efforts to prevent it from occurring. Regardless, it seems as if minor parties would benefit from the increased exposure.

9. Pat Buchanan's campaign for the Reform party presidential nomination in 2000 is a good example.

10. These data derive from the "California Blanket Primary Candidate Opinion Survey," a mail questionnaire that was distributed to every candidate who appeared on ballots for statewide constitutional office, U.S. Senate, U.S. House, Board of Equalization, State Senate, and State Assembly in the primary election, June 2, 1998. Candidate addresses were collected from the Secretary of State's website at http://Primary98.ss.ca.gov. Questionnaires were mailed on September 9, and completed replies arrived through the cutoff date, October 31, 1998. Overall, 735 questionnaires were distributed and 179 completed, usable forms were received. Subtracting 13 "undeliverable" questionnaires that did not make their destination (change of address, etc.) from the total, the project ended with a response rate of 25 percent. The results presented in this chapter are raw and unweighted, and are subject to the self-selection biases that are inherent in mail surveys. They are not intended to be reflective of a scientifically drawn, random sample of candidates or candidate opinions.

11. Eighty-six percent of the PFP candidates in the survey, along with 50 percent of Green candidates, said the blanket primary was a "good reform," with just 14 and 17 percent, respectively, saying it was a failure. Consistent with the "official" Green position mentioned in note 2, 33 percent of Green candidates said that the primary didn't make much difference—the highest percentage among any subgroup.

REFERENCES

Appellee's and Intervenor's Brief. 1997. *California Democratic Party et al. v. Jones.* "No Harm to Minor Parties."

Collet, Christian. 1997. "Taking the 'Abnormal' Route: Backgrounds, Beliefs, and Political Activities of Minor Party Candidates." In Paul S. Herrnson and John C. Green, eds., *Multiparty Politics in America.* Lanham, MD: Rowman and Littlefield.

Mazmanian, Daniel. 1974. *Third Parties in Presidential Elections.* Washington, D.C.: Brookings Institution.

CHAPTER TWELVE

Thinner Ranks

Women as Candidates
and California's Blanket Primary

Miki Caul and Katherine Tate

Despite recent gains, women remain numerically underrepresented among elected officials in the United States at both the state and national levels. In 1997, women made up only 12 percent of the House of Representatives and 9 percent of the U.S. Senate. Rates of female officeholding across the fifty state governments vary considerably, with Kentucky and Alabama having the fewest women serving in their state legislatures at 5 to 7 percent and Colorado and Washington having the most at 40 percent. In California, women make up 18 percent of the state Senate and one-quarter of the Assembly (Field and Sohner 1999). While the proportion of women serving in California's state government is only slightly higher than the average proportion of women in U.S. state governments, California is currently one of only two states in the union with two female U.S. Senators, Dianne Feinstein and Barbara Boxer. Moreover, with ten women in the state's fifty-two-member U.S. House delegation, women also make up a slightly higher percentage (19 percent) than for the nation as a whole.

Increasing the descriptive representation of women is important because female elected officials raise and promote issues that are distinct from those emphasized by their male counterparts (Thomas 1993; Thomas and Welch 1991; Dodson and Carroll 1991). In addition, in districts where a woman is elected, female voters are more likely to be interested in and participate in politics, and to have a greater sense of political efficacy and competence (High-Pippert and Comer 1998). The underrepresentation of one-half of the population not only limits the diversity of parliaments but also runs counter to one way that representative democracies may be evaluated, on the basis of whether their elected leadership reflects the society from which it is drawn in terms of salient political cleavages such as race, gender, ethnicity, region, and class.

Research on women's political representation in legislatures has established that the method of election has a profound effect on the numbers of women elected to political office. A change in the method of election, therefore, is likely to alter women's election opportunities and the resultant gender composition of the elected body. California's recent and short-lived adoption of the blanket primary, had it survived its test in the Supreme Court, may have had a negative effect on female officeholding in the state. Broadly, we hypothesize that the implementation of a blanket primary system weakens the role of parties in selecting candidates and increases the costs of elections. Raising the cost of statewide races in states such as California, where campaign costs are high, may mean that fewer viable female candidates will emerge and win.

Specifically, the blanket primary may reduce a woman's chances to advance to the general election because with a weaker role for the major political parties, the individual candidate's resources become more important. Candidates in the blanket primary generally need more resources such as personal financial support, PAC contributions, contacts, and ties to businesses and unions. As a group, women are less likely to have these personal resources. The blanket primary raised the financial and personal bar for candidates, and—had its influence persisted— Californian women might have been less well descriptively represented in their state government relative to women in other states.

THE EFFECTS OF ELECTION METHODS ON FEMALE CANDIDATES

A large empirical literature exists that explains why so few women are elected to democratic governments and why so few are found among the political elite. Although no one thus far has examined the impact of political primary systems on rates of female officeholding, this literature can help us anticipate the likely impact of a blanket primary system on female officeholding.

Research demonstrates that for three decades, women have been as likely as men to win seats in the U.S. House of Representatives once candidate status is taken into account. Although a significant minority of the U.S. population considers women to be less "emotionally suited" to run for political office, no evidence indicates that voter hostility toward female candidates impedes their elections. Nor is there empirical evidence to support claims of a conspiracy of the predominantly male political elite or systematic inadequacies in women's campaigns as barriers to their election (Carroll 1985; Darcy, Welch, and Clark 1994). Further, in a study of the 1980 congressional candidates, Uhlaner and Schlozman (1986), controlling for the type of race and incumbency, found that female candidates raised as much money as their male competitors. Although female candidates in the

1980s received fewer votes per dollar spent, by the 1990s, female candidates in open-seat House elections reaped the same electoral returns for their campaign resources (Green 1998).

Specifically, women fare as well as men in primary races. In a study of women in open-seat primaries for the House from 1968 to 1990, Burrell (1992) concludes that relative to men, women acquire as many votes, that they are *not* substantially older candidates, and that they are just as likely to have previous experience in public office. Rather, as established in research on general elections, the small proportion of women who win primaries is largely due to the paucity of women who run in primary elections. In both Democratic and Republican House primaries, voters had the opportunity to cast their vote for a woman in less than a quarter of the races between 1968 and 1989 (Burrell 1992). Yet by 1990, that proportion had risen to one-third of House primaries.

If the low levels of victorious women are a result of few women stepping forward to run for office, then we might ask, What structures encourage women to run in other countries where levels of women's representation are higher? As noted earlier, the electoral system has an important effect on rates of female officeholding. In general, proportional representation (PR) systems, where parties list their set of candidates, produce more women in parliament than plurality systems do (Duverger 1955; Rule and Zimmerman 1994). PR systems in countries such as Iceland, Sweden, Austria, and Switzerland have legislatures that are, on average, 20 percent female compared to single-member district countries including the United States, the United Kingdom, and Canada, whose national governments are only 10 percent female (Darcy, Welch, and Clark 1994, 142). Rule (1987) concludes that the method of election, when compared with socioeconomic and educational indicators, is the strongest indicator of women's parliamentary representation in advanced industrial democracies. Winner-take-all, single-member district systems, researchers believe, are less likely to run a woman because the parties perceive that they may lose the seat to a male competitor (Lakeman 1994). In party-list PR systems, in contrast, parties are more likely to add women to the list in order to broaden their appeal and balance the ticket. The perceived risk with a female candidate decreases when a female is part of a group, rather than the sole candidate.

Although there are several names for each office on the ballot and more than one nominee from that list advances to the general election, the blanket primary system is still essentially a plurality rule, single-member district system. Because the candidate with the most votes from each party advances to the general election, the blanket primary is clearly not a proportional system.

Political parties in other established democracies generally both recruit and nominate their candidates (Norris 1997; Lovenduski and Norris

1993). Often candidates are selected from the ranks of internal party officials and activists. As such, candidates are required only to have worked loyally for the party for some years, rather than being required to have their own personal resources. In contrast to most other party-based political systems, however, candidates in the United States must take the initiative to step forward themselves, raise their own money, and manage their own campaigns. It is not uncommon for U.S. candidates running for top national and state seats to be unknown to their state and national party chapters.

The weak role that political parties play in the nominating process in the United States puts American women at a distinct disadvantage relative to their European counterparts. After all, as Darcy, Welch, and Clark describe, political parties "have been the key for women's advancement to public office in the proportional representation nations. . . . in which women hold between 20 and 40 percent of the parliamentary seats. In these countries, the political parties have committed themselves to electing more women"(1994, 186). In fact, even among single-member district electoral systems, countries such as Australia, Canada, and New Zealand, where the political parties intend to elect more women, have in fact achieved higher levels of women in their national legislature than have the United States or the United Kingdom (Inter-Parliamentary Union 1997).[1] Darcy, Welch, and Clark (1994) show that greater centralized control over the candidate selection process helps women. The stronger the role that parties play in controlling candidate nominations, the greater the proportion of women elected in government.

Similarly, Matthews (1984) shows that the weakening of political parties and the entrepreneurial style of primary nominations have hampered women's candidacies. Evidence from state and city elections suggests that stronger parties may increase political opportunities for women. Broadly, female city council members are more likely to pursue higher office under certain circumstances. In particular, women are more likely to enter races that are legally partisan (Bledsoe and Herring 1990). Women running from a partisan council have an expected success rate nine times higher than that of women running from a nonpartisan council. Deber's (1982) research on women in congressional races in Pennsylvania reveals that those who won were more likely to have received organizational backing from a major party organization. She concludes that weak political parties "may thus hamper efforts by outgroups such as women to penetrate the political system by denying them access to the one ready-made source of political resources (organizational, financial, and electoral) which could be used to help a marginal candidate win election" (1982, 479).

In his seminal work, V. O. Key (1949) theorized that where parties play little or no role, those who have their own resources are more likely to pursue and win office. According to Matthews, "Private wealth can be a distinct asset to a legislative career, particularly in entrepreneurial political systems, where candidates must raise their own campaign resources" (1984, 549).

In primary systems where candidates generally self-select, personal resources are essential. The competition stimulated in races where parties have less control may discourage the entrance of less advantaged groups who do not possess the "personal political capital" necessary to run for public office. Personal political capital consists of resources accumulated by a candidate that lead to an advantage in the campaign, such as personal wealth, social position, professional career, and ties to strong pressure groups (Guadagnini 1993). Because women as a group are less likely to possess these resources, they are at a disadvantage relative to potential male competitors. The heavy reliance upon large sums of campaign money, especially the use of personal wealth, may preclude many potential female candidates from entering a nomination race.

As a group, women average lower incomes than men, and are less likely to have contacts with other elected officials (Verba, Schlozman, and Brady 1995, 260–61). In addition, women are not as well represented in the prestigious occupations that are the most common springboards to office in the United States. The most heavily represented occupation in the U.S. Congress is law (Matthews 1984). Although women are increasing their proportion of law school enrollments, it will be another generation or two before women represent an equal share of U.S. lawyers. In 1989, women made up only 20 percent of the legal profession. Verba, Scholzman, and Brady (1995) demonstrate that it is in these professional occupations (where women are far less likely to be) that citizens learn their most basic civic skills. In sum, Darcy, Welch, and Clark (1994) conclude that the concentration of women in "pink-ghetto" occupations that are not traditionally the springboards for political careers severely handicaps women, because these careers do not offer the prestige, business contacts, or wealth that are necessary in a campaign.

Taken together, the bulk of the empirical research suggests that political parties play an integral role in increasing women's numerical representation (Lovenduski and Norris 1993; Darcy, Welch, and Clark 1994; Caul 1999). While a strong empirical case has yet to be made for the claim that strong political parties lead to higher levels of women's representation, most scholars agree that weakening the control of parties will impede the growth of female representation in legislative office. Even political parties themselves have recognized their link to women's representation. In numerous democracies, many parties have adopted measures directly intended to increase the proportion of women in office. By 1995, eighty-four parties in thirty-six nations worldwide had enacted candidate gender quotas. Further, one-quarter of those parties had implemented special training programs for female candidates (Inter-Parliamentary Union 1997).

Because the literature clearly indicates that parties were key in increasing women's representation in most of the nations where representation is high, we are led to expect that the weakening of parties through the implementation of blanket primaries will only further offset any trends favoring women's candidacies. Switching to a blanket primary may not necessarily place women at a greater disadvantage for winning primaries, but it might discourage more women from stepping forward to run.

The weakening of party control over the nomination process may deter potential female candidates in two ways. First, if female candidates do not receive the support of state party officials, they must pay for the resources on their own that the party organization usually provides, such as party workers, candidate research, and get-out-the-vote drives. Since as a group women lack the wealth and social status that men as a group possess, women are at a critical disadvantage in initially financing their own campaigns. Second, it is easier for parties to encourage and recruit female candidates for nomination if party committees and conventions have more control in the nomination process. Strong parties can prepare and train potential candidates, compensating, therefore, for women's relative disadvantage to men in terms of the personal resources that they are able to bring to the campaign.

THE NUMBER OF FEMALE CANDIDATES IN RECENT STATE PRIMARY ELECTIONS

As many had predicted, the 1998 inauguration of California's blanket primary was the most expensive in California state history: a record $50 million was spent. In the gubernatorial primary the only woman in the race, Democrat Jane Harman, lost in a three-way race to her male competitors. Harman received only 12.3 percent of the vote to Al Checchi's 12.7 percent, while Gray Davis won with 34.9 percent. Harman had enough preexisting "personal political capital" to enter the race and offer a strong challenge to her contenders. Harman, as well as Checchi, both millionaires, contributed heavily to their own campaigns. Davis, who had close ties to the teachers' union and other large unions, received greater interest group support.

In the same election year in the Senate primary, San Diego Mayor Susan Golding originally entered the race. As a moderate supporter of abortion rights who received "high marks overall," Golding, many analysts believed, was the Republicans' best chance at defeating Barbara Boxer in the general election. However, Golding dropped out of the race citing fund-raising problems. Thus, the top contenders in the Republican primary—Darrell

Issa, a multimillionaire car alarm manufacturer, who used his personal wealth to flood the media with advertisements, and Matt Fong, who as State Treasurer, entered the race with statewide name recognition—were both male.

Because the backing of the party appears to be important to increasing the number of women in primary elections, a comparison of the percentages of female candidates running under similar primary election methods may shed light on the impact of the blanket primary on women in California. In most established democracies elections are partisan, and parties, not voters, nominate the candidates. However, in the United States three other states utilize primary systems that are similar to the blanket primary system that was adopted in California: Washington, Alaska, and Louisiana (Cook and McGillivray 1997).

The blanket primary in Washington is nearly identical to the system that California adopted. However, the systems in Alaska and Louisiana vary in potentially important ways. In Alaska, the Republican candidates are not listed on the blanket ballot. The Republican primary is only open to registered Republicans and those who are undeclared. All other parties' candidates are listed on the same ballot, and all voters except registered Republicans can vote for these candidates. In Louisiana, all candidates are listed together on the ballot, and there is an added runoff component. If one candidate receives 50 percent of the total vote, she is automatically elected to office. If no candidate receives 50 percent, the two top finishers, regardless of party, advance to a runoff election. Because there are few cases of these distinct blanket-like primaries, for this analysis we will lump together races in these four states despite important differences, and refer to them as "blanket/nonpartisan." We then compare these to races in all other states, referring to them as "partisan."

We compare statewide races in 1994, 1996, and 1998. The results are shown in the appendix (table 12.2).[2] Of the one hundred Senate primaries, forty-two of the races included at least one woman candidate.[3] Of the eighty gubernatorial primaries, thirty-seven, or 46 percent, included at least one woman candidate. Similarly, in those three election years, of the ten primary elections that were blanket/nonpartisan, six races included at least one woman, of which female candidates won four.

These initial results do not support our hypothesis. On the basis of data from these three election years, blanket/nonpartisan primaries do not negatively affect the numbers of female candidates running relative to partisan primaries. Although there are very few cases of blanket/nonpartisan primaries, it does not appear that fewer women run in these primaries, nor are those women who run more likely to lose their races. Thus, contrary to our original hypothesis, it appears that the blanket/nonpartisan primary system does not directly impede the numerical representation of women.

DOES THE BLANKET PRIMARY AFFECT
THE TYPE OF FEMALE CANDIDATES WHO RUN?

The type of primary system utilized by states may be of little consequence for candidacies of women because even partisan primaries are not vehicles through which parties can exert much control over the recruitment of candidates. In other words, all primary types, whether partisan or nonpartisan, reduce the power of the party elites to select their own candidates. Even if the party perceives the need to promote and recruit female candidates behind the scenes, there may be few means by which to do so (Burrell 1993). Thus, relative to most established democracies, political parties in the United States have so little power to help recruit female candidates that the further weakening of parties in the nomination process is infinitesimal. The effects of a switch to a blanket/nonpartisan primary may be undetectable, considering the great degree to which a primary system disadvantages women in the first place.

It still may be that blanket/nonpartisan primaries attract female candidates with different characteristics from those who run in partisan primaries. The number of blanket/nonpartisan cases is too small to put this hypothesis to a rigorous test. However, it appears that in the statewide blanket/nonpartisan races, the women who run are likely to have the personal political capital that most female candidates lack. For example, Jane Harman in California was a member of Congress and entered the gubernatorial primary with a great deal of personal wealth. Likewise, Mary Landrieu, who advanced to the runoff election in the 1996 Louisiana Senate race, is the daughter of a prominent Louisiana politician.

In order to discern whether primary candidates in blanket/nonpartisan races have different backgrounds from candidates in partisan primaries, we collected data on the background of all candidates in Senate and gubernatorial elections in 1994, 1996, and 1998. The occupational background or the type of elected office previously held by each candidate was that listed in *Congressional Quarterly Weekly*. In addition, in order to determine whether the candidate brought substantial amounts of personal wealth to the primary race, we reviewed articles detailing the campaigns in the same magazine. If a candidate had previously held elected office, brought personal wealth or widespread name recognition to the campaign, or had special connections for fund-raising as a former state party chair, we considered that candidate to have accumulated substantial personal political capital before entering the primary race.

Table 12.1 presents the difference in the percentage of candidates in blanket/nonpartisan and partisan primaries who either brought personal wealth, enjoyed statewide recognition, or had previously held elected office. Excluding incumbents, in partisan primaries 61 percent of women

TABLE 12.1   Difference in Percentage of Candidates
Who Brought "Personal Political Capital" to
Nonpartisan and Partisan Primaries

	Percentage-Point Difference between Nonpartisan and Partisan Primaries
Both races	
Women	+27
Men	+1
Senate	
Women	+15
Men	+7
Gubernatorial	
Women	+36
Men	+5

NOTE: Entries represent the gender difference between the percentage of nonpartisan and partisan races in which candidates
brought personal wealth to the primary or had previously held elected
office. We report the percentage-point difference for Senate and gubernatorial primaries for 1994, 1996, and 1998.

and 44 percent of men held at least one of these qualifications, while in
nonpartisan primaries 88 percent of women and 45 percent of men
brought at least one. The difference between women in blanket/nonpar-
tisan and partisan primaries is twenty-seven percentage points. For male
candidates, the difference is only one percentage point.

Although the number of blanket/nonpartisan cases is quite small when
categorized by type of race, among Senate races more women in blanket/
nonpartisan races brought personal political capital than women in partisan races, by fifteen percentage points. For men the difference is only seven
percentage points. Among Gubernatorial races, more women in blanket/
nonpartisan primaries had at least one of the above qualifications, by thirty-
six percentage points, while the same difference for men is only five percentage points.[4]

When the same analysis is conducted, but the list of qualifications is
limited to holding *statewide* office or substantial amounts of personal wealth,
the results are similar. Excluding the incumbents, the difference between
blanket/nonpartisan and partisan primaries for women is forty-seven percentage points. In contrast, among male candidates the relationship is reversed—only 21 percent of men in blanket/nonpartisan primaries, compared to 39 percent of men in partisan primaries, brought personal
political capital.

Overall, it appears that women who run in blanket/nonpartisan primaries are different from women who enter partisan primaries. Women who step forward to run in blanket/nonpartisan primaries are significantly more likely to bring personal wealth or resources or to have held statewide or other elected office. The same relationship does not hold for men. Men in blanket/nonpartisan primaries do not bring as many of these qualifications to their races. Men with no other outstanding qualifications beyond a professional occupation step forward to run in partisan and blanket/nonpartisan primaries. In contrast, fewer women without some type of personal political capital step forward. When women do step forward to run in blanket/nonpartisan primaries, they have usually previously held elected office, many at the statewide level, or bring personal wealth or some other statewide fame to their races.

CONCLUSION

Although the existing research suggests that the blanket primary may reduce the numbers of women running for office, we found that the absolute numbers of women running in statewide races in recent years were the same in both partisan and blanket/nonpartisan primary systems. Because it generally functions as a self-nominating system, the American primary system, whether partisan, blanket, or nonpartisan, limits the number of female office seekers. Parties, in other words, cannot aggressively or effectively ensure that equal numbers of women and men are nominated for public office in either a partisan or blanket/nonpartisan system. Secondly, other reforms and trends may work to offset the negative consequence of blanket primaries on the number of women seeking office. In California, there are term limits for state office. Term limits have increased the proportion of open-seat contests, which improves the odds that a woman will be elected. Term limits are one reason women are entering state legislatures faster than they are entering the U.S. Congress.

Even offset by past reforms, the blanket primary may still have an impact on female officeholding because it increases the personal cost of running for public office. Fewer women will have the qualifications necessary to make a credible bid for public office under a blanket primary system like the one adopted in California. We found some evidence for this in our examination of statewide primaries held over the last three election cycles. The types of women running in the partisan and blanket/nonpartisan nominating contests were very different. Female candidates in the blanket/nonpartisan systems were better qualified than their counterparts running in partisan contests. They were generally wealthier, or established political officeholders, or had name recognition because of family ties. Moreover, the fact remains that gender-role expectations regarding family life discourage many women from pursuing public office and leadership positions. These beliefs are changing, but remain quite powerful as ceilings on the career ambitions of women. Thus, unless directly invited and supported by a political organization to run for office, fewer women than men, because of how they are socialized, will take the initiative and declare their own candidacy for public office. Gender-role expectations may also explain why we found no systematic differences in the qualifications of the men running in both the partisan and blanket/nonpartisan systems. Women may feel that they need to establish superior qualifications or political connections to justify their candidacies when running in a blanket/nonpartisan system. Men, in contrast, may not feel the need to be extremely well qualified or positioned to run for public office.

Although women have made great strides in achieving greater equality in the labor force, they are still vastly underrepresented in the pool of business and economic elites from which political leaders are drawn. Campaign finance reform and, specifically, strict spending limits on campaigns and the public financing of campaigns, would open the candidate pool to individuals lacking personal wealth or the social connections that have almost become prerequisites for holding public office in the United States. In the end, our research and other studies reaffirm the central role that political parties play in increasing the numerical representation of women in democratic governments. The single most effective reform would strengthen the political party's role in the nominating process. Parties would be in a better position to ensure that our pool of candidates for public office resembled more closely the general population. California's Proposition 198 and similar measures weaken the role of the political party in the nominating process and make it harder for women, as a political minority, to compete for public office.

APPENDIX

TABLE 12.2   Women in Partisan and Nonpartisan Primaries: Senate and Gubernatorial Races, 1994–98

1994 Senate	
Total races	34
Races with at least one woman	18
Women who win	8
Nonpartisan races	1—Washington
Women in nonpartisan races	0
Women who win nonpartisan races	0
1994 Governor (plus 1993 New Jersey)	
Total races	37
Races with at least one woman	19

TABLE 12.2—*Continued*

Women who win	9
Nonpartisan races	1—Alaska
Women in nonpartisan races	0
Women who win nonpartisan races	0

1996 Senate

Total races	33
Races with at least one woman	12
Women who win	7
Nonpartisan races	2—Alaska and Louisiana
Women in nonpartisan races	2
Women who win nonpartisan races	1

1996 Governor (plus 1995 Louisiana)

Total races	10
Races with at least one woman	5
Women who win	5
Nonpartisan races	2
Women in nonpartisan races	2—Washington and Louisiana
Women who win nonpartisan races	1

1998 Senate

Total races	33
Races with at least one woman	12
Nonpartisan races	4
Women in nonpartisan races	2
Women who win nonpartisan races	2—both incumbents— California and Washington

1998 Governor (plus 1997 New Jersey)

Total races	36
Races with at least one woman	15
Nonpartisan races	3
Women in nonpartisan races	1
Women who win nonpartisan races	0

NOTES

1. Although minor-party primaries include women candidates, we limited our study to the Democratic and Republican party primaries.

2. We examined only the Democratic and Republican party primaries for these years.

3. Because the Republican primary in Alaska is partisan, it has been excluded

from the analysis. Therefore, the Alaskan 1994 gubernatorial and 1996 Senate primaries consist only of Democratic and other-party candidates, who are listed on the same multiparty ballot.

4. The same analysis was conducted with the incumbents included, and the results reveal the same relationship: women in nonpartisan races bring more qualifications. For both types of races, with the incumbents included for partisan primaries, 57 percent of women have at least one qualification, and 37 percent of men. In contrast, in nonpartisan primaries, 70 percent of women have at least one, as do only 43 percent of men. Among Senate races for partisan primaries, 52 percent of women and 30 percent of men had at least one qualification, while in nonpartisan primaries, 63 percent of women and 41 percent of men had at least one. And among partisan primaries in gubernatorial races, 61 percent of women and 44 percent of men had at least one qualification. In contrast, in nonpartisan elections, both of the two women who fell into this category had at least one qualification, while only 44 percent of the men brought the same.

REFERENCES

Bledsoe, Timothy, and Mary Herring. 1990. "Victims of Circumstances: Women in Pursuit of Political Office." *American Political Science Review* 84 (March): 212–23.

Burrell, Barbara. 1992. "Women Candidates in Open-Seat Primaries for the U.S. House: 1968–1990." *Legislative Studies Quarterly* 4 (November): 493–510.

———. 1993. "Party Decline, Party Transformation, and Gender Politics in the USA." In Lovenduski and Norris 1993.

Carroll, Susan J. 1985. *Women as Candidates in American Politics*. Bloomington: Indiana University Press.

Caul, Miki L. 1999. "Women's Representation in Parliament: the Role of Political Parties." *Party Politics* (January): 79–98.

Cook, Rhodes, and Alice V. McGillivray. 1997. *U.S. Primary Elections*. Washington, D.C.: Congressional Quarterly.

Darcy, R.; Susan Welch; and Janet Clark. 1994. *Women, Elections, and Representation*. 2nd ed. Lincoln: University of Nebraska Press.

Deber, Raisa. 1982. "The Fault Dear Brutus: Women as Congressional Candidates in Pennsylvania." *Journal of Politics* 44 (May): 463–79.

Dodson, Debra, and Susan J. Carroll. 1991. *Reshaping the Agenda: Women in State Legislatures*. New Brunswick, NJ: Center for American Women in Politics.

Duverger, Maurice. 1955. *The Political Role of Women*. Paris: United Nations Economic and Social Council.

Field, Mona, and Charles P. Sohner. 1999. *California Government and Politics Today*. New York: Addison Wesley Educational Publishers.

Green, Joanne Connor. 1998. "The Role of Gender in Open-Seat Elections for the U.S. House of Representatives: A District Level Test for a Differential Value for Campaign Resources." *Women & Politics* 19, no. 2: 33–53.

Guadagnini, Marila. 1993. "A 'Partitocrazia' Without Women: The Case of the Italian Party System." In Lovenduski and Norris 1993.

High-Pippert, Angela, and John Comer. 1998. "Female Empowerment: The Influence of Women Representing Women." *Women & Politics* 19, no. 4: 51–66.

Inter-Parliamentary Union. 1997. *Democracy Still in the Making: A World Comparative Study.* Geneva: Inter-Parliamentary Union.

Key, V. O., Jr. 1949. *Southern Politics in State and Nation.* New York: Knopf.

Lakeman, Enid. 1994. "Comparing Political Opportunities in Great Britain and Ireland." In Rule and Zimmerman 1994.

Lovenduski, Joni, and Pippa Norris. 1993. *Gender and Party Politics.* London: Sage.

Matthews, Donald. 1984. "Legislative Recruitment and Legislative Careers." *Legislative Studies Quarterly* (November): 547–85.

Norris, Pippa. 1997. *Passages to Power: Legislative Recruitment in Advanced Democracies.* Cambridge: Cambridge University Press.

Norris, Pippa, and Joni Lovenduski. 1995. *Political Recruitment: Gender, Race, and Class in the British Parliament.* Cambridge: Cambridge University Press.

Rule, Wilma. 1981. "Why Women Don't Run: The Critical Factors in Women's Legislative Recruitment." *Western Political Quarterly* 34: 60–77.

———. 1987. "Electoral Systems, Contextual Factors, and Women's Opportunity for Election to Parliament in Twenty-Three Democracies." *Western Political Quarterly* (September): 477–98.

Rule, Wilma, and Joseph Zimmerman. 1994. *Electoral Systems in Comparative Perspective: Their Impact on Women and Minorities.* Westport, CT: Greenwood Press.

Thomas, Sue. 1993. *How Women Legislate.* Oxford: Oxford University Press.

Thomas, Sue, and Susan Welch. 1991. "The Impact of Gender on Activities and Priorities of State Legislators." *Western Political Quarterly* 44, no. 2: 445–56.

Uhlaner, Carole Jean, and Kay Lehman Schlozman. 1986. "Candidate Gender and Congressional Campaign Receipts." *Journal of Politics* (February) 1986: 30–50.

Verba, Sidney; Kay Lehman Schlozman; and Henry E. Brady. 1995. *Voice and Equality.* Cambridge: Harvard University Press.

CHAPTER THIRTEEN

Targets of Opportunity
California's Blanket Primary and the Political Representation of Latinos

Gary M. Segura and Nathan D. Woods

What effect, if any, did the adoption of the blanket primary have on the political fortunes of California's Latino voters? Most Latino voters register and vote as Democrats, and the attachment of Latinos to the Democratic party has become stronger in recent years (Segura, Falcón, and Pachon 1997). Given their strong partisan attachments, it is conceivable that, because these voters are especially unlikely to cross over, the blanket primary meant nothing to the political future of California Latinos, and Latino politicians had little to gain or lose by the switch to this more open system.

While our evidence is extremely limited, since California's experience under the blanket primary was so brief, we argue the contrary. The adoption of the blanket primary served simultaneously to help solve the Republicans' "Latino problem" and the Latinos' "Republican problem" by providing a structural mechanism that would have allowed for the diversification and moderation of the Republican party, particularly on issues of interest to Latinos. Latinos could and did use the blanket primary in 1998 to help nominate Republican Latinos in competitive districts for the California Assembly, often against more conservative opponents.

In this chapter, we first briefly trace the background of Latino political power in California politics. We then outline the parameters of the "Latino problem" facing Republican strategists and suggest why Latinos should be interested in engaging the GOP, that is, in solving their "Republican problem," despite the existing differences. Finally, using data from the 1998 primary and focusing specifically on contested primaries in which Latinos sought the GOP nomination, we suggest that the blanket primary system had already begun to bear fruit for Latino political interests before it was overturned. We conclude with some thoughts about the potential for the Latino-GOP relationship under a blanket primary system.

CALIFORNIA'S LATINOS AND POLITICAL POWER

In addition to the passage of Proposition 198, the 1996 elections high-lighted a number of other important political developments. California's Democratic party retook control of the State Assembly. The surge in Dem-ocratic electoral fortunes was, in part, a result of surging Latino political participation. Latinos, indeed all minorities, turned out at higher rates in 1996, at least in part driven to the polls by their opposition to Proposition 209, which ended affirmative action practices in public employment, con-tracting, and education in California. Though Prop 209 passed decisively, the swollen Latino electorate helped send fourteen Latinos to the Assem-bly, and this new Democratic majority ultimately elected Cruz Busta-mante—a political moderate from California's Central Valley—to the Speakership, the first Latino Speaker in California history.

At the time of this writing, Latinos hold six seats in California's House delegation (11.5 percent), seven seats in the forty-member California State Senate (17.5 percent), and twenty seats in the Assembly (25 percent). Bus-tamante is now the Lieutenant Governor, and was replaced at the time as Speaker by another Latino, Antonio Villaraigosa.

Latinos' share of the California population (currently around 31 per-cent) has always exceeded their share of the electorate, with large numbers of noncitizens living in California. Nevertheless, the Latino share of the electorate climbed to 13 percent in the November 1998 election, up from only 9 percent just four years prior. And Latino political power has grown as a result. A telling example was the passage of Measure BB in the 1997 Los Angeles municipal election, a school bond initiative that many felt was badly needed, and the largest school bond passed in U.S. history. Latinos' support for Measure BB was higher than that of any other racial or ethnic group, which is perhaps not surprising, since more than 60 percent of all children in the Los Angeles Unified School District (and 44 percent of Los Angeles County residents) are Latinos.

CALIFORNIA'S REPUBLICANS AND THEIR "LATINO PROBLEM"

How exactly has this newfound electoral power affected party politics in California? The behavioral evidence is clear—Republicans face a growing electoral problem, one rooted in party policy and long-term demographic trends among California's Latinos, and perhaps nationwide. While much was made of George W. Bush's efforts and success at wooing Latino support and votes when he was governor of Texas, the national trends are less promising. Voter Research and Surveys (VRS) estimated that only 21 per-cent of Latinos voted Republican in the 1996 national election, down from a paltry 24 percent in the 1992 election. Estimates vary considerably across different polling organizations, but Ronald Reagan and George Bush regularly attracted between 30 and 40 percent of the Latino vote in the three presidential elections during the 1980s. Not since 1976 have Republicans fared so badly among Latinos.[1]

Republicans have long felt that they had a significant opportunity to make inroads into this population (Kosnin and Keysar 1995; Chavez 1996; de la Torre 1996; Rodriguez 1996). Latinos are a socially conservative and churchgoing population. The chief connection between Latinos (at least non-Cubans) and the Democratic party has been over economic issues. But growth in the Latino middle class has diversified economic views. Should economic progress continue, not only would the economic connection to Democratic policies wane, but the salience of economic issues vis-à-vis the more GOP-friendly social issues should also wane.

But the publicity and perceptions generated by the introduction and passage of Propositions 187, 209 and 227[2] have served to alienate Latinos from the GOP (Segura, Falcón, and Pachon 1997). Many Latinos in California felt that they were directly targeted by these measures, widely heralded and embraced by the GOP and, particularly, by former Republican Governor Pete Wilson.

How much trouble is the GOP in with California Latinos, and are the ballot propositions really to blame? In a 1996 preelection poll conducted by the Tomás Rivera Policy Institute (TRPI), only 14.5 percent of likely Latino voters indicated a preference for the GOP presidential candidate. More troubling to GOP electoral prospects is that among those recently enfranchised through the naturalization process or just entering the voting-age population, only 5.4 percent expressed a preference for Dole. In terms of party registration, 16.2 percent of likely voters and only 9.4 percent of newly enfranchised voters self-identified as Republicans.

Respondents to the TRPI study were asked how their sentiment might have shifted towards the political parties in recent times. Specifically, respondents were asked to evaluate that sentiment in the wake of significant public discourse on immigration, affirmative action, and welfare reform.[3] Fully 43 percent of all respondents reported feeling closer to the Democratic party, while only 6 percent reported feeling closer to the Republicans; the remainder reported either no shift (35 percent) or movement away from both parties (11 percent). Perhaps more important, in multivariate analyses predicting the magnitude and direction of change in partisan sentiment, concern over these issues was a powerful predictor of anti-GOP shifts, while income and religiosity, the supposed avenues of access for the GOP to Latino voters, remained insignificant (Segura, Falcón, and Pachon 1997).

Republicans are increasingly aware of and alarmed by this shift in sentiment and what it means for their electoral future. Reports recently generated by the GOP's own caucus staff in the Assembly show that only 11 percent of new voter registrants in the 1990s declared a Republican affiliation. The reports go on to cite "the GOP's inability to come to grips with the state's changing demographics, economics, and political trends" (Jeffe 1997).

The party has made some efforts at redressing this distance. Gubernatorial nominee Dan Lungren made considerable efforts in the 1998 election to attract Latino votes and devoted significant resources to Spanish-language advertising. He received about 27 percent of the Latino vote— not huge, but certainly an improvement over recent fortunes.

But a political party is not a single hierarchical structure, so changing strategy and rhetoric is not as simple as it is for a single decision-maker who chooses to do so. Even while the Assembly caucus staff was reporting its concerns, convention delegates to the statewide GOP convention were adopting resolutions supporting Proposition 227 (the anti–bilingual education initiative) despite what, to that point, had been a uniform reluctance on the part of many GOP officeholders and candidates to endorse the proposition. Former Congressman Bob Dornan's widely publicized fight to overturn his 1996 defeat by Loretta Sanchez (D–CA), and his decision to seek renomination for the seat, were additional sources of discomfort for party leaders hoping to reverse the party's slide among Latinos.

For the GOP to solve its "Latino problem" will require the party to put forward policy positions more friendly to Latino interests, disengage from wedge issue politics, and offer candidates more appealing to these new voters. Accomplishing this in a loosely structured party system where primaries, not party strategists, select nominees and drive the policy positions of candidates is a tough task, particularly if, as some suggest, ideologues dominate primary electorates.

Why should Latinos be concerned about the degree to which the GOP and its candidates seek their support? A clearly identified social group might be attracted in very high numbers to a single party by the parties' contrasting positions on the issues of high salience to the group. Once the pattern is established, however, the capture of that group by the party in question creates the likelihood that their support is taken for granted and their interests less primary. African-Americans and gays and lesbians are quite familiar with the political dynamics of having one party feel sure of the group's support, while the other party, adopting policy positions deemed to be contrary to the interests of the group, if not openly hostile, fails to represent a credible threat. To the extent that policy differences between the two parties on issues of salience to the group in question diverge, the threat of abstention is not credible either. It is in the long-term political interests of California Latinos and other political minorities to have both major political parties actively and aggressively courting their votes. This is not to say that party competition for a group's votes necessarily breeds responsiveness—only that the absence of competition dramatically reduces the incentives to cater to a constituency group's interests.

CALIFORNIA'S LATINOS AND THE BLANKET PRIMARY

How would a blanket primary make the GOP more attractive to Latino voters? First, the blanket primary changes the composition of party primary electorates. Efforts by the GOP leadership to present a more appealing image to Latino voters are undermined when the actual nominees continue to distance the GOP from Latino voters through their policy preferences and rhetoric. The nature of the pool of nominees, however, can be changed, at least in part, if the blanket primary system is used to good effect. Substantial crossover voting would, in theory, moderate primary electorates, thereby reducing the number of general election candidates or elected officials who feel comfortable openly expressing hostility to the interests of this significant voter bloc. Thus, while the GOP leadership takes steps to present a more appealing image to Latino voters, the blanket primary can serve to secure more appealing candidates less likely to engage in wedge issue politics or to adopt policies perceived to be as economically harmful to Latino interests.

Second, and more to the point of this chapter, Latinos could themselves cross over and thus ensure the nomination of a GOP candidate they find acceptable. Latinos lack influence in GOP position-taking precisely because they are a largely Democratic subgroup. Outside of ethnic-majority districts, no reasonable GOP primary candidate would devote significant resources or tailor issue positions to attract Latino votes since, as we have argued and the literature suggests, there are so few Latino GOP primary voters to be had under the closed primary. A blanket primary at least creates the possibility that this reality may change.

Under what conditions would we expect to see Latinos influence the outcome of GOP primaries? There are four specific hypotheses that arise from the logic we have just put forward. Two arise from what we see as necessary conditions for Democratic Latinos to vote in the GOP primary, and two pertain to factors that would affect the magnitude of such a trend. First, the district must be at least competitive for the GOP. Latinos will have little motive to engage in crossover voting in the primary if the general election is a sure win for Latino-friendly Democratic candidates. In districts with a very large majority of Latinos in the population or in which the outcome is securely Democratic, participation in the Republican primary— selecting a candidate sure to lose to one more amenable to the policy preferences of the relevant voters—is less valuable, *ex ante*. We should expect to observe lower levels of crossover voting by Latinos in these contexts. We would expect more crossover voting from Democrats in places where the parties are competitive or where the seat is considered safe for the GOP.

Second, the GOP primary must be contested. That is, *ceteris paribus,* we would expect little crossover voting by any Democratic group, including Latinos, when a potentially attractive GOP candidate faces no primary opposition.

Third, the absence of a contested Democratic primary, while not absolutely necessary, would certainly make crossing over more attractive to Latino voters because the Democratic nominee is secure, and Latino votes in the Democratic contest are unnecessary. By contrast, in elections in which the Democratic primary offers a meaningful contest, Latino voters may still perceive that there is more to be gained by voting in their own party's primary.

And finally, we expect Latinos to be most likely to engage in crossover voting when there is at least one Latino candidate seeking the GOP nomination. The literature on ethnic voting is well-developed, though the bulk of the work has been done on African-Americans. That work suggests that voters are partial towards candidates of their own subgroup (Karnig and Welch 1981; Sheffield and Hadley 1984; Grofman and Handley 1989) and are more likely to turn out if one is present on the ballot (Atkins, DeZee, and Eckert 1985; Tate 1991). It seems reasonable that, when controlling for other factors, Latinos are more likely to turn out and to vote across party lines for candidates with Hispanic surnames. Certainly, their candidacy must be viable. Stealth Latino candidates, with no money or name recognition, are far less likely to attract sufficient attention to garner much cross-party support.

DID LATINO CROSSOVER VOTING SHAPE OUTCOMES IN 1998?

With the very small number of cases to draw upon, it is difficult with aggregate data to show definitively that Latino crossover voting shaped outcomes in the 1998 primary. Using individual-level polling data would require valid samples of sufficient size in each of the districts affected, which are unfortunately not available. Aggregate data, however, do suggest that Latino engagement and overall voter interest in the GOP primaries increased when competitive Latino candidates appeared upon the primary ballot.

When Rod Pacheco was elected to the California Assembly from the Sixty-Fourth District in 1996, he became the only self-identified Latino Republican to serve in the Assembly since 1881, and only the third ever (Mendel 1998). In the 1996 elections, Pacheco was one of four Latino candidates in the GOP Assembly primaries, and one of three Latino nominees from the Republican party, two of which ran in districts so heavily Democratic that they stood no chance of winning the seat.[4]

By contrast, 1998 witnessed the election of four Latino Republican Assembly members, Pacheco and three freshmen colleagues. A total of nine Latino nominees carried the GOP banner into the general election (out of thirteen who sought GOP nominations).[5] Table 13.1 lists the Latino Republican candidates for the Assembly, along with some relevant district information regarding party registration and total vote in the 1998 primary.

A quick glance at the data reveals some interesting patterns. The most obvious is the substantial increase in voters going to the polls in nearly all of these districts. With the exclusion of Pacheco's district—where he ran unopposed by candidates of either party—the total number of primary votes cast increased between 7.5 percent and almost 68 percent, compared with total votes cast two years before. Statewide total votes cast increased only 2.1 percent across the state, an indication that these districts experienced unusually high increases in participation when compared to the rest of the state.[6] Certainly, some of this effect is due to other factors, including the absence of incumbents in a number of districts (where total vote increased an average of 34.3 percent) and the level of primary competition in either party.[7] But incumbent retirements due to term limits were as substantial in other districts as well, and the growth in total votes in the cases highlighted here dramatically exceeds the statewide mean. Finally, in Districts 27, 57, and 67, total votes increased an average of 30.5 percent in the primary despite the presence of incumbents.

Further, when we examine the data on GOP votes, it becomes clear that the level of participation in the GOP primary also increased substantially in the 1998 elections, even where there was no competition in the GOP primary to attract interest. In eleven of thirteen races fielding Republican Latino candidates, total GOP votes increased. The mean increase in contested seats was 43.8 percent from the comparable figures in the 1996 primary. More surprising, GOP votes increased by a mean of 17.3 percent in the uncontested races as well. In eight of the thirteen districts, including the four districts in which Latino nominees eventually won the seat for the Republicans, GOP vote grew at a rate higher than total vote.

But was this GOP turnout in districts with Republican Latino candidates higher than we might have expected? Across all thirteen districts with Latino GOP candidates, Republican vote share in the primary exceeded Republican registration by 16.7 percent. The comparable figure for the other sixty-seven districts without Latino primary candidates was 11.7 percent. This 16.7 percent also compares favorably with the 1996 primary, in which GOP vote exceeded registration by 12.2 percent in these same districts, and with the 1996 general election, in which the comparable figure was

TABLE 13.1 Turnout and Registration in Assembly Districts with Latino GOP Primary Candidates, June 1998

Candidate	AD	Share of GOP Vote	GOP % of Total Vote	GOP Registration	Democratic Registration	Latino % in 1997	Increase in Vote from 1996 Primary	Increase in GOP Vote from 1996
Paredes	5th	30.82%	64.80%	44.25%	40.13%	9.5%	+28.6%	+55.5%
Sanchez	7th	100.00	27.00	30.72	52.90	14.3	+11.6	−12.6
Vargas-Widmar	20th	40.26	40.73	31.37	47.68	17.0	+47.0	+51.5
Chavez	27th	51.60	34.80	29.94	49.46	15.2	+7.5	−0.6
Maldonado	33rd	44.33	72.60	43.80	39.98	25.7	+21.5	+44.2
Gonzales	57th	100.00	25.60	26.22	56.15	71.1	+67.8	+15.0
Nuñez	58th	100.00	24.60	23.65	62.48	70.0	+61.9	+25.5
Pacheco, Robert	60th	36.47	67.60	39.89	42.92	38.0	+34.8	+59.6
Escobar	62nd	100.00	21.56	27.66	57.98	47.7	+42.4	+5.3
Pacheco, Rod	64th	100.00	100.00	43.07	41.90	33.9	−9.7	+53.3
Rocha	67th	4.09	77.40	50.47	32.56	13.2	+16.2	+38.4
Gonzales	68th	5.56	69.60	43.39	39.10	30.5	+35.7	+58.1
Zettel	75th	45.14	75.70	50.10	29.59	11.8	+25.0	+43.5

10.4 percent. Though incumbent Rod Pacheco's lack of opposition inflates this figure, if we examined only those primaries with Latino candidates that were contested in 1998, GOP vote exceeded registration by a mean of 18.0 percent. This unusually high turnout in these specific GOP primary races, we suggest, is explained, at least in part, by the volume of crossover voting.

One might raise the objection that the single most important predictor of Democratic to Republican crossover voting would be whether the Democratic primary was contested, since such a contest would be likely to discourage raiding or hedging by Democrats. It is the case that in the seven primaries in which the Democratic race was contested, GOP vote exceeded registration by only 6.8 percent. But four of those seven races had no contest for the GOP primary. In the three cases where *both* parties' primaries were contested, GOP vote exceeded party registration by 18.9 percent. The comparable figure in the six districts with no Latino candidates where both parties had contested primaries was 14.5 percent.

To summarize, while this aggregate examination is limited in inferential power, a number of patterns emerge which seem to suggest that the presence of Latinos in the race altered the level of interest and participation. The races represented in table 13.1 experienced turnout growth that was considerably larger than the statewide number. The GOP vote exceeded party registration at a rate higher than in other comparable elections, and contested GOP races attracted considerably more voters even when Democrats had a contest of their own. And in seven of eight races where the GOP vote grew at a rate higher than total turnout, the Republican nominee went on to win the seat, and four of these nominees were Latinos.

HERE'S TO THE WINNERS!

Those Latino candidates that went on to become the four Latino Assembly members stand out from the others who ran for and / or received the GOP nomination. Several distinctions among the races are very clear, as presented in table 13.2.

First, consistent with our hypothesis that crossover voting is likely to be attractive only in contested primaries, turnout growth was stronger in the contested races. For the four cases here where the GOP primary was uncontested (but the Democratic primary *was*), GOP vote share *underperformed* GOP registration share by 2.4 percent. In the eight cases where the GOP primary was contested, vote share in the primary *exceeded* registration share by an average of 21.5 percent.[8]

Second, if Latino crossover voting was responsible for boosting the GOP's total share of the vote, it was those candidates who benefited the most from this crossing—where GOP vote share most exceeded their share of registration—that then went on to win the seat in the general election.

TABLE 13.2 Key Characteristics of Districts with Latino GOP Primary Candidates, June 1998

Candidate	AD	GOP Vote % Minus GOP Registration	District Type	Democratic Primary Contest	Latino % in 1997	Primary Election Outcome	Primary Margin of Win/(Loss)	General Election Result
Uncontested GOP nominees								
Sanchez	7th	−3.72%	Safe D	Yes	14.3%	Unopposed	N/A	L
Gonzales	57th	−0.62	Safe D	Yes	71.1	Unopposed	N/A	L
Nuñez	58th	+0.95	Safe D	Yes	70.0	Unopposed	N/A	L
Escobar	62nd	−6.10	Safe D	Yes	47.7	Unopposed	N/A	L
Contested GOP primary losers								
Paredes	5th	+20.55	Leans R	Yes	9.5	Lost	(14,951)	N/A
Vargas-Widmar	20th	+9.36	Safe D	Yes	17.0	Lost	(4,846)	N/A
Rocha	67th	+26.93	Safe R	Yes	13.2	Lost	(23,875)	N/A
Gonzales	68th	+26.21	Leans R	No	30.5	Lost	(11,134)	N/A
Contested GOP primary winners								
Chavez	27th	+5.14	Safe D	No	15.2	Won	978	L
Maldonado	33rd	+28.80	Leans R	No	25.7	Won	4,040	W
Pacheco, Robert	60th	+27.71	Leans D	No	38.0	Won	1,752	W
Zettel	75th	+27.60	Safe R	No	11.8	Won	8,821	W
Candidate unopposed by either party								
Pacheco, Rod	64th	+56.93	Leans R	No	33.9	Won		W

L = lost, W = won.

For the four primary candidates who ultimately lost, GOP vote share exceeded registration share by 20.8 percent. For the four primary candidates who received the nomination, GOP vote share exceeded registration share by 22.3 percent on average. And for the three of these four who went on to win the general election, the comparable figure is 28 percent.

Three types of Latino nominees emerged from the primaries spotlighted in tables 13.1 and 13.2. The first two are "sacrificial lambs," or candidates nominated to run under circumstances of near certain general election defeat. There are two types of sacrificial lambs—those nominated by virtue of running in heavily Latino districts and those nominated in heavily Democratic districts. Henry Gonzales in the Fifty-Seventh District and Albert Nuñez in the Fifty-Eighth fall into the first category. Those two districts' populations are 71.1 and 70 percent Latino, respectively. Latinos ran unopposed in both party primaries, and the Latino Democratic nominees won in nearly identical landslides in the general election with about 72 percent of the vote. Not surprisingly, and consistent with our hypothesis regarding safe districts and uncontested primaries, there is little evidence of crossover voting in the primary, since GOP vote totals in the primary hover just above the level of GOP registration.[9]

The second type of sacrificial lamb is one led to the purely partisan slaughter (as opposed to the ethnic one). Bob Sanchez (District 7), Phil Chavez (District 27), and Irma Escobar (District 62) each ran in heavily Democratic districts, facing GOP registration disadvantages of 22 percent, 20 percent and 30 percent less than Democratic registration respectively. Each of these candidates faced non-Hispanic Democrats, but the party registration disadvantage doomed all three to lose, each garnering only 30 to 35 percent of the general election vote.

Like Nuñez and Gonzalez, Sanchez and Escobar ran unopposed in the primary. In both instances, however, the Democratic primaries were contested, so there was little incentive for Democrats to cross over in the Republican primary, and, not surprisingly, Republican vote share was actually less than GOP registration.[10]

Of those nominated to run in the general election in these difficult districts, only Phil Chavez in District 27 faced primary opposition. Chavez faced a close race with Chuck Carter and won the nomination by only 978 votes. It is conceivable that Chavez's nomination was secured by crossover votes, and the district—around Monterey and Santa Cruz—is 15.2 percent Latino. Republican share of the total vote, however, exceeded party registration by just over 5 percent, but was actually lower than GOP vote share in both the 1996 and 1994 general elections and primaries. Given the GOP's overall performance compared to elections in the recent past, it is difficult to make a case that much if any crossover occurred. But with such a close vote margin, it is possible that enough Latinos crossed over to make the difference.

The final type of nominee includes those with a legitimate chance to win. The four winners in 1998 have substantially different stories to tell. Only Charlene Gonzales Zettel was nominated to run in a safe Republican district. The other three were nominated in districts where party registration was fairly competitive. Similarly, only Zettel ran in a district with a very small Latino population. The other three candidates ran in districts where the Latino population was large enough to make an electoral impact (ranging from 26 to 38 percent), but not so large as to guarantee a safe Democratic or safe majority-Latino seat. Unfortunately for the purposes of our inquiry—but fortunately for him—Rod Pacheco was lucky enough to face no opposition in either party, so it is impossible for us to speculate what effect the blanket primary might have had on his electoral fortunes. The remaining three faced primary opposition. That leaves us with three cases where the Latino candidate faced primary opposition in seats where the winner had a reasonable chance of being competitive or winning in the general election: Zettel in District 75, Abel Maldonado in District 33, and Robert Pacheco in District 60. Those cases are worthy of a closer examination.

The Thirty-Third Assembly District

Abel Maldonado's election in District 33 was not a simple undertaking. The primary campaign included a number of charges of unethical behavior regarding endorsements and the like, and some press reports suggested that his Republican primary opponents might not support him in the general election (Wilcox 1998a, 1998b).

Maldonado was not the most moderate candidate in the election, but was clearly the more moderate of the two leading candidates—the other being Rick Bravo, whose support came from the more conservative wing of the party. Bravo was also Latino, of Cuban and Ecuadorian ancestry.

This intraparty division is not new in the district, which covers Santa Maria, San Luis Obispo and Pismo Beach. A recent special-election GOP primary for Congress between Tom Bordonaro and Brooks Firestone produced a similar divide. Bordonaro, the more conservative of the two, won the nomination and went on to lose to Democrat Lois Capps in the general election.

Maldonado's campaign was the potential beneficiary of the dynamic we have described. There was no contest on the Democratic side, freeing voters to cross over at little cost. The district is over 25 percent Latino, up from just 20 percent since 1990. Crossover voting is key to any candidate's electoral chances since the GOP registration advantage over the Democrats is just under 4 percent.

On primary election day, GOP percent of the total vote exceeded registration by nearly 30 percent, a strong indication that crossover voting made a difference. Maldonado polled 44.3 percent of the GOP vote, while Bravo received 38.6 percent of GOP votes. The difference in real numbers was 4,040 votes out of over 71,000 GOP votes cast. Maldonado went on to beat Democrat Betty Sanders by almost 30,000 votes in the general election, receiving 60.4 percent of the vote.

The Sixtieth Assembly District

Robert Pacheco (who is unrelated to Rod Pacheco) was something of an underdog in this race. His closest competitor, Mike Radlovic, was the anointed party successor ("District by District Analysis" 1998), was well financed through personal wealth, and was the son of a prominent Republican party activist. He was described by the *California Journal* as a "businessman" and political "outsider" despite these connections. By contrast, Robert Pacheco was a former Walnut city councilman and had far more in the way of local ties and electoral experience.

The district, which includes all or parts of West Covina, Whittier, La Habra Heights, and Walnut, leans Republican, but only slightly; GOP registration exceeds Democratic registration by just over 3 percent. Again, the Democrats had no contest on their side, freeing voters to cross over. Pacheco's presence on the ballot, no doubt, attracted voters in a district that is now 38 percent Latino, up from less than 30 percent in the 1990 census.

GOP vote share in the June primary (67.6 percent) exceeded party registration (39.9 percent) dramatically. In terms of raw numbers, total vote increased almost 35 percent from the 1996 primary, and GOP vote increased almost 60 percent. Pacheco beat Radlovic 36.5 percent to 32.4 percent, a vote margin of only 1,752 votes out of 42,608 GOP votes cast. It seems highly likely that Latino crossover voting made a difference in this primary. Pacheco went on to defeat Democrat Ben Wong in a fairly close race, receiving 52.5 percent of the vote and outpolling Wong by less than 7,000 votes in a race where over 90,000 votes were cast. Having a Latino carry the banner for the GOP in this increasingly Hispanic district may have actually determined the ultimate outcome in a race Democrats thought they had a chance of winning ("District by District Analysis" 1998).

The Seventy-Fifth Assembly District

In contrast to the other two districts presented, Charlene Zettel's district (Poway, El Cajon, and Lakeside) is solidly Republican. The GOP enjoys a registration margin of over 20 points. In such a safe seat, we expect significant crossover voting, and the absence of a contest on the Democratic side in this primary only exacerbated that propensity.

Zettel, as a pro-choice Latina and member of the Poway School Board, was clearly the most moderate of the major candidates. Her opponents, Joel Anderson and Mark Price, were both white males from the business community with no political experience to speak of. Both were described by the *California Journal* as decidedly more conservative, and the race turned largely on these two competing for the conservative vote. The press accounts suggest that the campaign was expensive and nasty on the part of all three candidates, with charges and countercharges exchanged, most of which proved to be false (Braun 1998). Latinos make up only 11.8 percent of this district. Nevertheless, GOP vote share on election day was 75.7 percent, 6 percent higher than the 1996 primary vote share and over 25 percent above party registration. Zettel received 45 percent of the GOP vote, while Anderson and Price split the conservative vote and received 31.4 percent and 23.5 percent, respectively. The division among the conservatives was critical to Zettel, who outpolled Anderson by 8,821 votes. Nevertheless, the lone Democratic candidate polled only 18.6 percent of all votes, suggesting that, along with abstention, a significant number of Democrats crossed over. The lion's share of those votes went to the pro-choice Latina. Zettel went on to win the general election with 64.4 percent of the vote, more than doubling the number of votes received by her Democratic opponent[11] but substantially underperforming previous GOP vote tallies.[12]

Latino GOP Candidates Who Didn't Make the Cut

The four cases where Latino primary candidates failed to reach the general election warrant some attention. In two instances, the Latino candidates were never serious contenders. Felix Rocha, running in the crowded Sixty-Seventh District, polled only 3.2 percent of the total vote. Rocha placed last in a six-candidate GOP field that included both an incumbent (Scott Baugh) and a former holder of the seat (Doris Allen). The Democratic nomination was also contested. Republican share of the total vote was high (77.4 percent), an indication that some crossover voting occurred, though it likely benefited Allen. Though the district is 13.2 percent Latino, it is doubtful whether Rocha's candidacy attracted much attention within the community, though they may well be responsible for the 2,593 votes he managed to gather. The seat is safe for the GOP, which enjoys an 18 percentage point advantage in party registration.

A bigger surprise was Paul Gonzales in the Sixty-Eighth district. Gonzales, too, placed last in a crowded field of five GOP candidates. But the district is competitive, with Republican registration only 4.3 percent higher than Democratic. The Democratic half of the primary was uncontested, and the Latino population has climbed to 30.5 percent in recent years. Gonzales' 2,152 votes were an indication that his candidacy was never a significant factor in the district.

The more interesting cases come from Districts 5 and 20. In the Fifth, Sam Paredes placed second to Dave Cox. Despite a contest on the Democratic side, GOP total vote share was 10 points higher than in 1996 and 20 points higher than registration percentages. It is unlikely, however, that Paredes was the beneficiary of a significant crossover vote. As executive director of the Gun Owners of California, Paredes was decidedly not a moderate in the race. In addition, the district is only 9.5 percent Latino. Paredes lost the nomination by almost 15,000 votes.

Finally, in the Twentieth District, Linda Vargas-Widmar lost the GOP nomination to Jonelle Zager. Vargas-Widmar did manage to attract over 40 percent of the GOP votes cast, and the district's 17 percent Latino population may well have helped her. But the presence of a Democratic contest and the fact that District 20 is heavily Democratic (47.7 percent Democrat to 31.4 percent GOP) severely limited her chance of attracting enough crossover voters to make the difference.

We learn a number of important caveats from the four primary losses. First, not every Latino candidate is more moderate than his primary opposition, and while the attraction of a Hispanic surname might be significant, it is not alone sufficient to ensure competitiveness. Second, poorly funded campaigns with low name recognition cannot be compensated for merely through crossover balloting. Candidates who are not competitive in the first place can take little comfort in the hope that Latinos in the other party will vault them to victory.

GOP to Democratic Crossover

We have focused our discussion on Democratic to Republican crossover voting. It is reasonable to ask what, if any effect, the blanket primary had on Latinos running in Democratic primaries. Since most politically active Latinos are already voting Democratic, the level of crossover voting from the GOP for the benefit of Latino candidates is likely to be small.

Nevertheless, we looked at all Assembly races in which Latino Democrats sought the party's nomination in a contested primary. A total of eight districts had Latino candidates facing primary opposition. In six of those cases, however, it seems fairly clear that crossover voting was either not significant or had little effect. In Districts 30, 31, and 61, growth in GOP total votes exceeded growth in Democratic votes. In the first two cases, the margin of victory was sizable, making it even less likely that crossover voters had an effect on the outcome. In the third case, a hotly contested GOP primary held Democratic total vote close to Democratic share of two-party registration.

In the remaining three districts, other factors suggest that crossover voting had no effect. In District 50, all three Democratic candidates were Latino, and the district was strongly Democratic, where Democratic registration exceeded GOP registration by 53 percent. In Districts 57 and 58, there was substantial growth in Democratic votes. But given the nominees' margins of victory—the nominees received nearly 70 percent of the Democratic votes in the Fifty-Seventh and 83 percent in the Fifty-Eighth—and that GOP vote share was close to its share of two-party registration, it is highly unlikely that there was any crossover impact.

In two cases, however, there does appear to be some evidence that crossover voting affected Latino political fortunes. In the Forty-Ninth District, the Democratic vote more than doubled from 1996, while the GOP vote declined substantially. The Democratic primary attracted five candidates—three Latinos—and the Latino victor won by less than 3,000 votes over an Asian-American rival. By contrast, in the Sixty-Second District, which is only 47.7 percent Latino, though safely Democratic, the Democratic vote increased 57.2 percent compared to an increase of only 5.3 percent for Republicans, who underperformed their share of two-party registration. Two Anglos faced three Latino candidates. While apparent crossover benefited one Anglo candidate, who secured the nomination with 30 percent of the Democratic vote, the division in the 60.8 percent of the vote that went to the three Latino candidates likely played a pivotal role in determining the outcome.

As in our discussion of Democratic-to-Republican crossover voting, the number of contested Democratic primary races with Latino candidates from this one election is not sufficient to draw hard and fast conclusions about any long-term effects the blanket primary may have had on Democratic Latino candidates. Further, we do not examine whether the blanket primary had an effect on the Democratic party as a whole. Rather, our focus on Latino candidates suggests that the impact of Republican-to-Democratic crossover was small and mixed. In only two cases did aggregate evidence suggest that crossover *might* have played a role, and in one of those cases, it was to the detriment of the leading Latino candidate. In that latter case, division of the Latino vote among three candidates was likely more responsible for the loss. In short, the opportunity to cross party lines in the primary election seemed to have more significant effects for Latinos who were running in the Republican primaries than for those seeking Democratic nominations.

DISCUSSION AND CONCLUDING THOUGHTS

We began this enterprise with the question of whether the adoption of the blanket primary served Latino interests in the 1998 primary. We argued that since most Latinos are Democrats, evidence that Latinos made "use" of the blanket primary would be significant crossover voting for GOP candidates. We hypothesized that Latino crossover voting would occur when competitive Latino candidates contested GOP primaries in districts where they had a reasonable chance of winning, and in districts where the Latino population could contribute to that effort.

In the absence of individual-level evidence on the thirteen districts in which Latinos sought GOP Assembly nominations, we relied on aggregate evidence which, while not definitive, is at least suggestive that Latino voters made a difference in several GOP primaries, possibly changing the outcome in a few, and ultimately electing four moderate Latinos to the California Assembly in competitive or safe Republican districts.

Clearly, to the extent that this effect exists, it is not systematic—crossover voting can make a difference only when circumstances are ripe. First, for the blanket primary to present an opportunity to Latino voters requires *competitive* Latino candidates in the GOP which, itself, is likely endogenous to these processes. In other words, the very factors which have driven Latino voters into the Democratic fold have reduced the available pool of potential Latino GOP candidates. Without credible Latino candidates, the crossover opportunity we identify here is of limited use. Second, the outcome of the GOP primary has to matter. Electing Latino GOP nominees in a Latino-majority district is no trick, and nominating Latinos from the GOP to run in safe Democratic seats serves little purpose. Third, the district needs to have an electorally meaningful Latino population; otherwise even significant crossover voting is unlikely to change the outcome.

Nevertheless, the opportunity to elect competitive Latinos did manifest itself, and the opportunity appears to have been taken. As table 13.2 clearly showed, when the hypothesized circumstances were in place, crossover voting appears to have occurred at significant levels, and the competitive Latino candidates did well. The result is a GOP Assembly caucus that is less conservative and more ethnically diverse than at any point in its modern history. This change may well have served long-term Republican electoral interests, had the blanket primary rules remained in force. The irony, of course, is that this change occurred through a mechanism the party leadership opposed—the blanket primary. Had it survived, the blanket primary may have saved the Republican party from itself.

It is important to make clear what we have *not* argued here. We do not suggest that Latinos were uniquely more likely to cross over. In fact, if we suspect any intergroup difference, it would be a lesser propensity among Latinos.[13] The evidence presented elsewhere in this volume suggests substantial crossover voting. What we *do* mean to suggest is that Latino identity, either communicated in campaign materials or signified by surname, serves as one important avenue for drawing non–party members into a party's nominating process. Given the growing importance of the Latino electorate, this avenue might have been particularly important to the future competitiveness of the state's GOP.

The same dynamics might have served to help other minority and female candidates within the GOP as well. To the extent that identity politics trumps partisan preferences in the hierarchy of voter concerns, we could imagine that substantial crossover voting might have occurred among African-American, Asian-American, and especially female voters who identify with GOP primary candidates with like characteristics. This possibility, particularly in the case of female candidates, is certainly worth exploring. The likelihood of such an occurrence for other minority groups, however, is damped by the relatively rare instances of the GOP running candidates of like identity. Unlike Latinos, however, who now make up almost a third of the state's population, Asian-American and African-American voters are less frequently concentrated in sufficient numbers—and in electorally competitive or safe Republican districts—to affect outcomes. As California's demography continues to evolve, however, this possibility might well have grown substantially.

A few other observations are worth noting as well. First, we have confined our examination to the State Assembly for good reason. The dynamic we believe we have identified was clearly not replicated in the 1998 races for the State Senate or the U.S. House. There were no Latino candidates for GOP nominations to the State Senate. For the House, three Latinos ran for GOP nominations, two of them successfully. However, both nominees were unopposed and ended up losing in the general election in heavily Democratic majority-minority districts. The unsuccessful candidate mounted almost no campaign, received less than 2 percent of the total vote, and placed last in a field of four Republicans (including Bob Dornan) seeking the seat currently held by Loretta Sanchez (D–CA), who undoubtedly attracted nearly all Latino attention and votes in that hotly contested district.

Second, Latinos have shown themselves to be moderately successful at running in white districts in a way African-Americans have never been. None of the four Republican Latino Assembly members represents a majority-minority district, and two of the Latino Democrats in the Assembly are also from majority white districts. In the State Senate, three of the seven Latinos represent majority white districts.

Future research into blanket primary systems and their effects among Latinos might want to answer a number of questions for which our data are insufficient. First, can the relationships we hypothesized here be demonstrated both at the level of the individual voter and across a larger number of races? Second, does crossover voting begin to have spillover effects? It would be important if ethnic crossover voting in the primary is associated with the same types of increased ticket splitting in the general election, or even a slow drift into the other party, as demonstrated by Sides, Cohen, and Citrin (chapter 5) and Kousser (chapter 8) in this volume. Similarly, crossover voting in one race may well be associated with crossing over in other races. Third, crossover voting is hypothesized here as a function of the voters' identification with Hispanic-surnamed candidates. The propensity to engage in ethnically driven voting might decline vis-à-vis stronger party identification as the individual is more assimilated into the society. Should this be the case, crossover voting by Latinos may well be more common among the newly enfranchised naturalized citizens than among second- or third-generation Latinos whose partisan attitudes are more fully developed. Or, by contrast, the reverse might be the case if longer-term and second-generation Latino citizens become less uniform in their partisan preferences as they become more socially and economically diverse.

The evidence we presented in the first section of this chapter strongly suggested that the GOP was in very deep trouble among the state's Latinos. It may turn out that 1998 was the high-water mark of efforts to reverse the slide and attract Latinos to the GOP. And any effect we observed here was confined to races for the State Assembly. The party was clearly serious about the effort to attract more Latino votes, appointing a Latino as its political director and, more recently, electing Rod Pacheco as the GOP Assembly leader, though his tenure in that position turned out to be startlingly brief. But the very presence of these four Latinos in the Republican caucus serves to help the GOP's perception among Latinos and may well shape party policy into something less directly confrontational with the fastest growing segment of California's electorate.

The blanket primary could not, alone, make the GOP competitive among Latinos or moderate and diversify its group of elected officials. And it is not clear how the Democratic party might respond to such a challenge. To continue enjoying their advantage among Latino voters, Democrats might become more aggressive in recruiting Latino candidates in mixed and / or competitive districts or more specifically tailor their message to this specific audience. Given the dominance of the Democrats among Latinos and the successes of Latino Democratic politicians to date, it is difficult to imagine that party doing more. Nevertheless, our findings do suggest that the blanket primary may have provided a first step in making Republicans competitive for Latino votes.

NOTES

1. In 1976, only 18 percent of Latinos voted for Gerald Ford, according to the CBS News/*New York Times* exit polls. The same poll reported 37 percent support for Reagan in 1980, 34 percent for Reagan in 1984, and 30 percent for Bush in

1988. Other network-based polls offer different estimates, all of which are generally higher than CBS's estimates (de la Garza and DeSipio 1997).

2. Proposition 187 was adopted in November 1994 and withheld most state services, including education and health care, from undocumented immigrants. Proposition 209, passed in the 1996 general election, abolished all racial, ethnic, and gender preferences by government in hiring, contracting, and admissions, effectively ending most affirmative action programs in the state public sector. Proposition 227, passed in June 1998, mandated the elimination of bilingual education programs and their replacement with English immersion in California public schools. In all three cases, significant majorities of Latino voters opposed the measures.

3. At the time of the survey, Proposition 187 had been adopted, and the campaign over Proposition 209 was drawing to a close. The actual question was worded as follows: "There has been a lot of talk about affirmative action, immigration, and welfare reform in the last few years. As a result of the positions taken by the Republican Party and the Democratic Party, do you feel that you have moved closer to the Republican Party, closer to the Democratic Party, away from both parties, or have these issues had no effect on your feelings toward the political parties?"

4. The other two GOP nominees were in the Sixteenth and Fifty-Eighth districts. Democratic registration in the Sixteenth Assembly district exceeds GOP registration 65.6 percent to 14.2 percent. In the Fifty-Eighth, the comparable figures are 62.5 percent to 23.7 percent.

5. A total of twenty-eight Latinos held major-party nominations for Assembly seats in November 2000. Democrats succeeded in electing thirteen of their nineteen nominees, while the Republicans elected four of nine.

6. According to the California Secretary of State's office, total votes in the 1994 primary were 4,966,827, or 26.22 percent of the eligible population and 35.05 percent of the registered voters. In 1996, the numbers were 6,081,777, which represented 31.47 percent of the eligible population and 41.88 percent of registered voters. Turnout in 1998 was 6,206,618, 30.05 percent of those eligible and 42.49 percent of registered voters.

7. Assembly Districts 5, 7, 20, 33, 58, 60, 62, 68, and 75 had no incumbent seeking reelection.

8. Among the other sixty-seven districts where no Latino sought the GOP nomination, ten had no GOP contest, while the Democratic race was contested, and six had contests in both parties. GOP share of the vote exceeded GOP share of registration in the first type by an average of 2.1 percent and, in the latter cases, by 18.3 percent on average.

9. In District 57, GOP registration was 26.22 percent, while the GOP nominee went on to capture 27.93 percent of the vote. In District 58, GOP registration was 23.65 percent, while the GOP nominee received 27.97 percent of the vote.

10. Sanchez received 27 percent of the total primary vote in a district (Seventh) with 30.7 percent GOP registration. Escobar received 21.6 percent of the total primary vote in District 62, where GOP registration was 27.7 percent of registered voters.

11. The Libertarian and Natural Law candidates in this race combined for 7.7 percent of the vote, likely from more conservative GOP protest voters.

12. Incumbent Jan Goldsmith won the seat with 71.7 percent in 1996 and 70.0 percent in 1994.

13. Our expectations here are due to lower overall participation rates among Latinos and, given lower median levels of education, an electorate that is politically less aware.

REFERENCES

Abramowitz, Alan; Ronald Rapoport; and Walter Stone. 1991. "Up Close and Personal: The Iowa Caucuses and Presidential Politics." In Emmett H. Buel and Lee Sigelman, eds., *Nominating the President.* Knoxville: University of Tennessee Press.

Atkins, Burton; Matthew DeZee; and William Eckert. 1985. "The Effect of a Black Candidate in Stimulating Voter Participation in Statewide Elections." *Journal of Black Studies* 16, no. 2: 213–25.

Braun, Gerry. 1998. "Assembly Hopefuls Turning Mean with Last-Minute Mailers." *San Diego Union Tribune,* May 31, B1.

Cain, Bruce E. 1997. "Report on Blanket and Open Primaries." Expert testimony in *California Democratic Party v. Jones,* 984 F. Supp. 1288 (1997).

California Secretary of State. 1994, 1996, 1998. *Statement of the Vote.* Sacramento.

———. 1998. *Report of Registration.* Sacramento.

Chavez, Linda. 1996. "The Hispanic Political Tide." *New York Times,* November 18, A17.

Crotty, William, and John Jackson. 1985. *Presidential Primaries and Nominations.* Washington, D.C.: Congressional Quarterly Press.

de la Garza, Rodolfo O., and Louis DeSipio, eds. 1999. *Awash in the Mainstream: Latino Politics in the 1996 Elections.* Boulder, CO: Westview Press.

de la Torre, Adela. 1996. "Latinos Can't Be Taken for Granted; Republicans Alienate Many on Immigration and Bilingual Issues. Democrats Talk But Don't Always Deliver." *Los Angeles Times,* October 16, home edition, 9.

"District by District Analysis." 1998. *California Journal* 29, no. 7 (July): 43–46

Grofman, Bernard, and Lisa Handley. 1989. "Minority Population and Black and Hispanic Congressional Success in the 1970s and 1980s." *American Politics Quarterly* 17: 436–45.

Hedlund, R., and M. Watts. 1986. "The Wisconsin Open Primary 1968–1984." *American Politics Quarterly* 14: 55–73.

Hedlund, R.; M. Watts; and D. Hedge. 1982. "Voting in Open Primaries." *American Politics Quarterly* 10: 197–218.

Herrington, John, and Bill Press. 1996. "Argument Against Proposition 198." Secretary of State. Ballot Information. Sacramento.

Jeffe, Sherry Bebitch. 1997. "California Conservatism's Worst Nightmare Revealed." *Los Angeles Times,* August 17, home edition, 1.

Jewell, Malcolm. 1984. *Parties and Primaries: Nominating State Governors.* New York: Praeger.

Karnig, A., and S. Welch. 1981. *Black Representation and Urban Public Policy.* Chicago: University of Chicago Press.

Kosnin, Barry, and Ariela Keysar. 1995. "Party Political Preferences of U.S. Hispanics: The Varying Impact of Demographic Factors." *Ethnic and Racial Studies* 18, no. 2: 336–47.

Ladd, Everett. 1978. *Where Have All the Voters Gone?* New York: W. W. Norton.

Mendel, Ed. 1998. "Pacheco May Be Major GOP Inroad to Latinos." *San Diego Union Tribune,* November 6, A1.

Monardi, Fred. 1994. "Primary Voters as Retrospective Voters." *American Politics Quarterly* 22: 88–103.

Norrander, Barbara. 1989. "Ideological Representativeness of Presidential Primary Voters." *American Journal of Political Science* 33, no. 3: 570–87.

Ranney, A. 1975. "Turnout and Representation in Presidential Primary Elections." *American Political Science Review* 66: 21–37.

Rodriguez, Gregory. 1996. "California Latinos Make History, But Is the Democratic Party Home?" *Los Angeles Times,* November 10, home edition, 1.

Segura, Gary; Dennis Falcón; and Harry Pachon. 1997. "Dynamics of Latino Partisanship in California: Immigration, Issue Salience, and Their Implications." *Harvard Journal of Hispanic Policy* 10: 62–80.

Sheffield, James, and Charles Hadley. 1984. "Racial Crossover Voting in a Biracial City: A Reexamination of Some Hypotheses." *American Politics Quarterly* 12: 449–64.

Southwell, Priscilla. 1988. "Open versus Closed Primaries and Candidate Fortunes, 1972–1984." *American Politics Quarterly* 16, no. 3: 280–95.

Tate, Katherine. 1991. "Black Political Participation in the 1984 and 1988 Presidential Elections." *American Political Science Review* 85, no. 4: 1159–76.

Tomás Rivera Policy Institute. 1996. California Pre-Election Survey. Claremont, CA: Tomás Rivera Policy Institute.

Walker, Jack. 1988. "The Primary Game." *Wilson Quarterly* 12: 64–77.

Wekkin, Gary. 1988. "The Conceptualization and Measurement of Crossover Voting." *Western Political Quarterly* 41: 105–14.

Wilcox, Dave. 1998a. "Maldonado Tops Bravo." *San Luis Obispo County Telegram-Tribune,* June 3, A1.

———. 1998b. "Party Strife Distinguishes Assembly GOP Campaign." *San Luis Obispo County Telegram-Tribune,* June 4.

CHAPTER FOURTEEN

Candidate Strategy, Voter Response, and Party Cohesion

John R. Petrocik

Primaries, the advocates of party government insist, reduce the authoritativeness of party leaders, encourage unmanageable programmatic heterogeneity among the party's candidates and officeholders, threaten a candidate's general election success when they are divisive, and severely limit the role of party organizations—to name just a few of the harms commonly attributed to them.[1] The effects are worse with some forms of the primary, and are thought to reach their limit with blanket primaries, which potentially eliminate any party basis to a nomination.[2] Systematic evidence supporting these outcomes is not extensive. The correlation is mostly demonstrated by the coincidence of the putative weakening of the parties as the primary system was adopted throughout the United States. The coincidence of primaries with other social and political trends and events may never make it possible to develop conclusive evidence for their party-weakening consequences.

However, because primaries create opportunities for insurgent and anti-party forces, it is at least plausible that they have undercut party leaders and party cohesion. Moreover, the argument is not entirely speculative. Haeberle (1985), for example, provides evidence that candidates selected in closed primaries are more cohesive than those selected in open and blanket primaries. He found that members of Congress nominated in closed primaries had a party unity score of almost 73 percent, compared to those selected in open primaries, who averaged about 69 percent. Members selected through a blanket primary had the lowest party unity scores—just under 66 percent. Also, Sorauf's (1963) study of candidate selection in Pennsylvania found candidates to be more loyal to party programs when their selection and nomination involved significant party input.

This chapter reports additional evidence for how primaries, in this case the blanket primary, can weaken parties by reducing the influence of a party's core electorate in the selection of party nominees. The analysis uses survey data to illustrate how the blanket primary can be exploited by candidates to overcome the preferences of core party supporters. It focuses on the potential impact of crossover votes (a Democrat voting in a Republican primary, or vice versa) on nominations by examining whether an ambitious candidate can frame the primary choice in a way that will draw enough crossover votes to win a blanket primary.[3] Specifically, it examines whether a candidate can encourage enough crossover voting to overwhelm the preferences of party loyalists. It goes on to indicate why the strategy may have an impact on the programmatic cohesion of a party's officeholders.

The scenario that is examined argues that the effect of a blanket primary on party cohesion is a byproduct of the incentives it gives candidates to *solicit* crossover votes. These crossover-seekers present an ideological posture at odds with the majority of their party's supporters in order to create a winning coalition with votes from the other party's supporters. Such candidates present themselves as issue and policy moderates in order to attract a median voter who is well to the left or right (depending upon whether the primary contest is, respectively, Republican or Democrat) of the party's electorate in a closed primary. This outcome creates greater programmatic variability among each party's elected officials, since those elected with a crossover strategy have an incentive to protect their winning primary coalition with an issue position that appeals to the preferences of a significant fraction of independents and identifiers with the other party. The model assumes (on the basis of evidence reviewed below) that "raiding"—crossover voting that is motivated by a desire to nominate someone who will easily be defeated in the general election—will be trivial because most voters are crossing over to support the candidate they want to win the general election.[4]

The data do not directly test the effect of the type of primary on party cohesion. The assessment is indirect, with evidence of the blanket primary's effect on the party's programmatic orientation found in the ideological posture that candidates elected through crossover voting might need to maintain to assure their electoral security. The data establish only a few of the suggested effects. First, they demonstrate that crossover voting increases when voters are sensitized to the hopeless general election prospects of their party's candidate. Second they show that crossover voters will overwhelmingly support the more moderate candidate. Finally, the data illustrate that the "moderates" who cross over to vote in the other party's primary have dramatically different policy preferences than the "moderates" they join. Republican "moderates" are significantly more conservative than Democratic "moderates," or, viewed from the other side, Democratic "moderates" are significantly more liberal than GOP "moderates."

The hypothesized decline in party cohesion is a by-product of the (assumed) need for successful crossover-elected candidates to retain the support of programmatically distinct moderates. Whether candidates selected in a blanket primary are more moderate than winners in a partisan primary is not directly demonstrated (but see Gerber, chapter 10 in this volume). However, it is a more than plausible conjecture. Legislators tailor themselves to their districts in ways that improve their electoral security. A Democratic incumbent elected with the support of moderate Republicans cannot usually afford a record as liberal as a Democrat whose nomination and election were achieved with a loyal core of Democratic support. When many incumbents depend upon crossover support, the frequent outcome is a Democratic caucus with many moderates and conservatives and a GOP delegation containing moderates and liberals (see Froman 1963; Mayhew 1974; Fenno 1978). Adams's (1996) study of the consequences of changing the Illinois multimember district system to single-member districts capitalized on what amounts to a natural experiment that demonstrated that creating a more partisan electorate created more programmatically homogeneous party delegations in the Illinois legislature.

Why this might happen is better understood after a brief overview of the relevant features of the primary, particularly why the nomination process helps to decide which individuals and groups have the most influence with officeholders. That is addressed in the next section. The chapter then outlines a process by which crossover votes can be solicited by candidates who raise strategic considerations around the competitiveness of a district and the relative programmatic proximity of the candidates. The data address potential influences associated with voter motivations to cross over and the strategic calculations by candidates that increase or depress crossover voting. Finally, the chapter examines the policy and attitudinal orientation of "moderate" voters. The data demonstrate that moderates are a diverse group, and different in much the same way that leaning Democrats differ from leaning Republicans. These last data are used to speculate on how the blanket primary might affect the programmatic orientations of the parties.

THE POLITICAL INTENTION OF THE PRIMARY SYSTEM

When the direct primary was introduced late in the nineteenth century, the vast majority of elective offices—for Congress, state legislatures, city councils, county supervisors, sheriffs, and so forth—were not competitive (nor, of course, are they today). Electoral manipulation (gerrymandering, for example) and group traditions (the urban Irish were Democrats, while Midwestern Germans were Republicans) had created party bastions almost everywhere, and voters, then as now, loyally supported the candidates of their party.[5] Nomination assured election, and, in most cases, party leaders and political notables used personal loyalties and patronage to control the caucus and convention delegates who did the nominating. The result was officeholders who were more responsive to the party leaders—who could deny them renomination—than they were to an electorate that rarely defeated them in the general election.[6]

The reinforcing elements of this system of party government were separated by the direct nominating primary because it eliminated the support party leaders received from the electorate's partisanship. The nominating primary never asked voters to cross party lines. It allowed them to select preferred candidates *within* their party and then support them again in the general election.[7] It promised to weaken party leaders by increasing the chance of selecting candidates who were not beholden to party leaders for the nomination (Merriam 1908).

The hoped-for effects of the primary were not immediate. Slating, endorsements, control over money and other electoral resources, and the commitment and cohesiveness of party cadres gave party leaders continued influence over nominations. In time, however, the influence of traditional party leaders and notables was significantly reduced.

A Problem with Primaries

The grandest vision of the reformers went unrealized because primaries developed their own nominating elite: the few who bothered to vote in them. In the typical contemporary primary, turnout rarely exceeds 35 percent of the eligible electorate (it was 30.1 percent of the eligible electorate in the June 1998 California primary).[8] The problem with such low participation is the unrepresentativeness of those who take part. Primary voters are better educated than the median eligible voter, have higher incomes, are older, and are disproportionately white. A more relevant bias of primary voters is their higher-than-average level of political interest and motivation, greater concern with politics and government, and greater-than-average inclination to vote and work for candidates who share their preferences—and to oppose those who do not.

This traditional wisdom about the "bias" of primary electorates (dating, at least, to V. O. Key 1952) expects the most ideological elements of each party to be overrepresented in their primaries (Ranney 1972; for an example for California, see Costantini 1963). Candidates with strong policy views are especially attractive to such voters and the result, in this scenario, is ideologically ardent nominees. Party leaders and candidates tend to share the belief that primary voters are strongly motivated by ideology and opposed to political moderates. As a result, the would-be nominees, even when they are not personally inclined to take strong issue positions, often

TABLE 14.1   Policy Preferences of Primary and Nonprimary Voters, 1980

	Primary Voter		
	Yes	No	Difference
Unrestricted access to abortion			
Democrats	35%	35%	0%
Republicans	30	32	−2
Welfare attitudes			
Democrats	−29	−19	−10
Republicans	57	33	24
Helping minorities			
Democrats	0	11	−11
Republicans	59	48	11
General ideological identification			
Democrats	−21	−21	0
Republicans	62	54	8

NOTE: The numbers in the first two rows of the table report the percentage who support unrestricted access to abortion services. The values in the remainder of the table are percentage differences calculated by subtracting the percentage offering the liberal response from the percentage offering the conservative response. Negative values indicate a predominantly liberal response among the group. Positive values indicate a conservative response. For example, the "−29" for Democratic identifiers' attitudes on welfare issues means that they are 29 points more liberal than conservative on welfare issues.

feel that they must, and the preferences of the ideologically motivated get overrepresented as candidates—even moderate ones—make an effort to placate activists by supporting "hot-button" ideological issues.[9]

The accuracy of this traditional wisdom about primary voters is questionable. Some research found a substantial similarity between primary voters and the general electorate, at least in presidential primaries (Geer 1988). But the overall sense that primaries are largely controlled by ideologically extreme voters and unrepresentative interests remains the conventional wisdom, especially within the parties.[10] And it may have some merit. The data in table 14.1 provide some support for the belief that primary voters are more ideologically extreme than nonvoters, although the difference is not equally large for all four issues or similar between the parties.[11] The data show GOP primary voters to be more conservative than primary nonvoters on three issues; Democratic primary voters and nonvoters differ on two of them. A prudent conclusion is that differences probably exist, although they may not be of the magnitude or consistency presumed in the earliest research.

More important for the possible consequences of a blanket primary system is the large *interparty* difference. Republicans are—abortion opinions excepted—more conservative than Democrats, and the difference is greatest among those who turned out in the primaries. This fact is important for candidate strategy in blanket primaries and is what can contribute to lower *intraparty* cohesion.

The "Blanket Solution" to the Primary Problem

California's blanket primary was initially sponsored by Republican moderates as a solution to the presumed dominance of GOP nomination politics by ideological conservatives. The blanket primary was expected to draw more moderate voters into the primary and allow moderate Democrats, Republicans, and independents to rally in support of moderate candidates. In the reformer's scenario, the potential for moderate candidates to find substantial support among moderate voters would have cumulative consequences. It would lead moderate Democrats and Republicans to contest primaries that they would otherwise refuse to enter; while moderate voters, rejecting the ideological candidates, would provide the winning margin for them. The expected result was greater opportunity for candidates not committed to the ideological activists in the parties—in approximately the same manner that the original primary created opportunities for candidates not subservient to party leaders.

The blanket primary was a suggested remedy for other often-decried features of modern government. It was promoted as likely to increase turnout in primaries because it would allow those not registered as party supporters to take part (see California Secretary of State 1996). However, its prospect for reigning in the ideological extremists in both parties and the governmental gridlock they cause was its major selling point (see, for example, the *Los Angeles Times* editorial [1998] endorsing the proposition)— although the evidence that gridlock is unavoidable in divided government might also be questioned (see Mayhew 1991).

VOTERS IN PRIMARY ELECTIONS

In all elections, the records of the candidates' parties, their policy proposals, party association, and personal qualities provide the systematic criteria that determine the vote. Voters consider some or all of these factors, weigh them in various ways, and cast a vote. In a general election each is potentially germane.

The party factor is canceled in closed primaries since the candidates and voters share a party affiliation.[12] But a new variable, *viability in the general election,* complicates the utility calculations of any voter who considers it. Since the outcome of the general election can sometimes be estimated, a voter might not vote for the preferred candidate if that candidate is likely to lose the general election. In such a circumstance, the preferences of a voter may be best satisfied if the primary nominates a candidate with "imperfect" issue positions but a higher probability of winning the general election. A vote for the less preferred primary candidate invokes a *minimax* version of Downs's utility voting rule by voting for the most preferred primary candidate *with a reasonable chance to win the general election.*

Voters in Open and Blanket Primaries

In open and blanket primaries, the calculations of voters can be more complex, depending upon whether the voter is a loyalist supporting a candidate of his party, or a crossover to the other party's primary. Loyalists who support the candidate with the preferred policy proposals, record, and personal qualities are indistinguishable from maximizing voters in a closed primary. Similarly, loyalists who vote for the candidate with a better chance for general election victory than the candidate with the most preferred policies and record are indistinguishable from minimax voters in closed primaries.

The motives of crossover voters can be either *sincere* or *strategic,* and they do not fit so easily into a utility-maximizing model of voter choice. *Sincere crossover voters* are maximizers. Presented with an array of candidates, some representing their party, sincere crossover voters support the candidate they find the most attractive. Their vote supports the candidate they prefer over all others seeking nomination, and the candidate they support in the primary is the one they intend to vote for in the general election. *Strategic crossover voters* are of two types. *Raiders* (the term used in the introductory chapter) are the mirror image of minimax voters. While they may be committed to a candidate, they do not vote for that candidate. They vote for the opposition candidate likely to be the easiest to defeat in the general election, hoping to foist a sure loser on the opposition. They do not behave as minimax voters because there is nothing about their vote that can be defined as a strategy to avoid a victory by their least preferred candidate. Raiders are simply attempting to improve the prospects of their preferred candidate in the general election by creating an opponent who will maximize (1) loyalty among partisans of their party and (2) defections among partisans of the other party. *Hedgers* are crossover voters who have an ideological and motivation profile that is virtually identical to strategically motivated minimax voters in a closed primary. They would prefer to see their party's candidate win the general election; however, recognizing that outcome as unlikely, they vote to achieve the next best result—a victory by the opposition-party candidate who is closest to their ideological ideal.

The Incidence of Raiding

Raiding is not common. In virtually all previous research, sincerity and hedging were the typical motivations for crossing over, and its effect was largely limited to eroding or magnifying the margin of the victor (Southwell 1991; Geer 1986; Hedlund, Watts, and Hedge 1982; Lengle 1981; Hedlund 1977–78; Adamany 1976; and Ranney 1972). California voters in the two blanket primaries conducted prior to the overturning of Proposition 198 did not express the motivations of raiders. The *Los Angeles Times* exit poll analyzed by Sides, Cohen, and Citrin (chapter 5 in this volume) found 90 percent of Democrats and 82 percent of Republicans reporting that a sincere preference is the most likely reason one would cross over in a primary. Upwards of 75 percent of crossovers in the 1998 California blanket primary remained with their primary preference in the general election; obvious raiders represented barely 7 percent of the Democrats and 5 percent of the Republicans.

In short, although the crossover voting that we observe sometimes looks suspicious—it is typically at its greatest when only one of the parties experiences a competitive primary—the raiding threat is more apparent than real. Even when their party's nomination is uncontested and crossing over would give the ill-willed an opportunity to harm the general election chances of the opposition by nominating a weak candidate, the candidate supported by crossover voters is usually the one whose programmatic profile matches the voter's ideological and policy preferences.

Survey data from the 1998 Senate primary in Washington State corroborate data from presidential primaries.[13] The Washington U.S. Senate primary offered an ideal opportunity for raiding. The renomination bid of Patty Murray was unopposed; she was regarded by some as vulnerable to a strong Republican challenge; the GOP nomination was competitive. Yet the Democratic crossovers were not numerous, and their profile was not characteristic of raiders. Sixty-eight percent of those who planned to vote in the GOP Senate primary were Republican identifiers, 23 percent were independents, and only 9 percent were Democrats. More to the point, the overwhelming bulk of the crossovers were self-described moderates or conservatives; only 4 percent of all those who planned to vote in the GOP primary were Democratic or Independent liberals. Finally, and following the pattern observed in presidential primary voting (see, in particular, Southwell 1991; Hedlund and Watts 1986; Hedlund, Watts, and Hedge 1982), the crossovers—whether liberal or moderate, Democratic or independent—supported the candidate preferred by Republican identifiers. In the survey, the ultimate winner received 59 percent of the votes of Republican identifiers in the survey, 64 percent of independent votes, and 71 percent of Democratic votes. Crossover voting moved survey support for the winner from 59 percent (the vote of Republican identifiers—all that mattered had there been a closed Republican primary) to 61 percent in the blanket format, which included the preferences of avowed Democrats and independents.

Further, an attempt to raid the opposition party's primary would run into voter resistance to "dirty tricks" and probably produce enough notoriety and contrary behavior that the effort would backfire. The media's appetite for scandal and political maneuver makes it unlikely that elite-organized raiding could be hidden. The GOP governor of Wisconsin, Tommy Thompson, discovered this when he advised Republicans to vote in the Democratic presidential primary in 1988. At the time, George Bush was largely unopposed, virtually certain to win the Wisconsin primary, and assured of the nomination. The Democrats, by contrast, still had not settled the matter. Jesse Jackson and Michael Dukakis were competing for delegates. Thompson's suggestion that Republicans cross over and vote for Jackson produced a virtual firestorm of negative comment throughout the state.[14]

The rarity of raiding in high-salience elections does not preclude a significant political effect from crossover voting (which can be up to 40 percent; see Alvarez and Nagler 1997). The 2000 presidential primaries, for example, despite the attention and concern lavished on crossover voting, conformed to the historical pattern.[15] Democrats were slightly more than 5 percent of the vote in Republican primaries; Republicans identifiers contributed about 4 percent of the Democratic presidential primary electorate.[16] But while their numbers were not large, their candidate preference differed from that of party voters. The crossover vote in the Democratic primary was too small to yield a reliable estimate of the behavior of crossovers. But in six of the seven GOP primaries, where crossovers were sufficiently numerous to examine, the majority of their votes went to John McCain, while a majority of Republican identifiers voted for George Bush.[17] More meaningful were the large number of self-described independents (averaging almost 27 percent in the Republican primaries and 21 percent in the Democratic contests). In fifteen out of twenty-three GOP primaries, the independents preferred McCain to Bush. Independents voted for Bradley over Gore in twelve of eighteen Democratic primaries. In each case where McCain won, it was because of support from independents. Bush was the majority choice of Republicans in every contest except New Hampshire (where McCain carried all partisan groups in the GOP primary).

CANDIDATE STRATEGY IN PRIMARIES

What McCain might have accomplished with independents can be achieved when candidates are prepared to present a political persona that is attractive to independents and crossover voters. The generic election strategy requires candidates to persuade a majority of the voters that they best approximate the voter's ideal with regard to party affiliation, issue stance, and personal qualities. They announce policy positions, party affiliation, and record—hoping that a majority of voters will find these attributes close to some ideal point (the "positive" campaign). At other times they attempt to create dissimilarity between the voters and the opposition (the goal of "attack" or "comparative" campaign strategies). The candidate's strategy in a closed primary can exploit a minimax consideration by emphasizing the superiority of her policy prescriptions, record, personal traits, *and general election prospects*. This strategy attempts to persuade voters that no candidate with similarly satisfying policies has a greater probability of winning the general election.

Candidate Strategy in Open and Blanket Primaries

A candidate with an issue posture that appeals across party lines is exactly the kind of candidate envisioned by the blanket primary and approved by the political culture. Most important, the preconditions for a crossover-based campaign strategy are present. Like most other Americans, Californian's support for party institutions is weak—and has been for a long time (Field Institute 1983). Half of the respondents in this survey agreed that "parties do more to confuse voters than to provide clear choices in elections," and almost 70 percent agreed with the proposition that politics is too partisan and that the public suffers because the parties are at odds over almost everything. Less than 50 percent regarded the candidate's party to be an important aspect of their vote.[18] Also, few legislative districts are competitive. Redistricting, whether partisan or bipartisan, typically produces party bastions (Kousser 1996).

In the uncompetitive districts, where nomination virtually guarantees election, an open or blanket primary can present a way for an ambitious individual from the majority party to defeat the party's candidate with a moderation strategy. Announcements that create the moderate persona and endorsements from respectable groups with a reputation for "reasonable" choices must be cultivated in this strategy. The ambitious Democrat must be the moderate alternative to the "typical" liberal always elected in an uncompetitive Democratic district; the ambitious Republican must be the moderate alternative to the "typical" conservative always selected in a solidly GOP district. Campaign tactics for directly appealing to crossovers and independents (direct mail, for example) complete the linkage to voters who want to select the "best candidate."

The moderate-crossover strategy does not require voters to have strong ideological motivations. Indeed, the most issue-motivated voters are the least likely to cross over, since they are the most likely to reject the other party's candidates, even the moderate ones (see Petrocik 1979; Wright and Berkman 1986; Petrocik and Doherty 1996). The most likely crossover prospects are mildly interested in politics, motivated to select a "good" candidate, and receptive to the "moderate" posture of the candidate who is challenging an incumbent of the opposite party, who can be portrayed as "immoderate" (see Verba, Nie, and Petrocik 1979; Petrocik 1979; Wright and Berkman 1986; Zaller 1998). The moderate strategy of a challenger in the blanket primary is not vulnerable to accusations of unfair or "immoral" campaigning. The candidate can occupy the positively valued ground of moderation, while appealing to sincere sentiments among voters, who, in their turn, would respond to such appeals with full honesty.

This strategy mixes a global appeal to the median voter with a specific appeal directed at *hedgers*—those who recognize that their party's candidate might (or will) lose the general election and can be persuaded to seek the next best result in a victory by the opposition-party candidate who is closest to their ideal. In California's (and the nation's) weakly partisan climate, a candidate with a moderate persona might induce enough crossover voting to win. The spotlight of public attention will be directed at the nomination struggle in the majority party rather than to the pointless struggle (if there is a struggle) for the minority party's nomination. Minority-party supporters will be attracted because of the intensity of the battle, and in that exposure the candidate might create crossover appeal. How this would work is illustrated with the example below.

Would it work among voters? Some political observers assert that moderate Republicans benefited from crossover votes in four open-seat Assembly districts in 1998, fulfilling the hopes of the blanket primary's proponents (Quinn 1998). Higher than average crossover rates on behalf of the majority party were reported in uncompetitive State Assembly districts by Alvarez and Nagler (1997). There is also clear evidence of a moderation-crossover strategy in the 2000 GOP primary for State Assembly seats. In both cases, Republican-registered voters gave a majority of their votes to the candidate endorsed by the GOP establishment. However, Democratic crossovers and independents voted heavily for the victorious insurgents—who actively courted them (Wisckol 2000).[19]

Electoral Arithmetic for a Moderation-Crossover Strategy

The necessary arithmetic underlying the moderate candidate strategy is illustrated in table 14.2. In this district, 44 percent are registered Democrats, 30 percent are registered as Republicans, and 26 percent either declined to state a preference or are registered with a minor party. Democratic nominees have won the November election with more than 60

TABLE 14.2   A Crossover Strategy to Win a Primary

| | Voter Is Registered as: | | | |
Type of Candidate	Democrat	Independent	Republican	Total
Liberal Democrat	24%	8%	1%	33%
Moderate Democrat	17	8	9	34
Republican	2	8	20	30
Others	1	2	0	3
TOTAL	44	26	30	100

percent of the vote in every election since the lines were drawn in 1991.[20] In a closed primary (which can be approximated by looking at the vote among registered Democrats), the liberal Democrat is the expected nominee with about 57 percent of the primary vote, and the general election winner with, if past is prologue, about 60 percent of the vote.[21] But the liberal Democratic incumbent can be defeated in a blanket primary if a moderate Democrat can run well among Democratic voters and attract enough Republicans to forge at least a plurality of the votes cast for all Democratic candidates. In this example, the moderate Democrat wins with less than 39 percent of the Democratic votes (17 of 44 percent), a third of the independents, and a 30 percent crossover from Republicans. The margin is narrow (the arithmetic is in the table), but it sends the moderate to the general election, where the Democratic partisanship of the district virtually ensures victory. If the moderate Democrat attracted more of the independents and Republicans, the victory over the Democrat-preferred Democratic candidate would be even larger, or the required fraction of the Democratic vote would be smaller.

The following survey-based "experiment" shows that voters *can* be attracted to political moderates as the blanket primary proponents hoped they would.

TESTING THE EFFECT OF THE BLANKET PRIMARY

Prior to California's blanket primary in June of 1998, the Center for the Study of Society and Politics of the Institute for Social Science Research at UCLA conducted a blanket primary experiment in its annual Los Angeles County Social Survey.[22] The experiment included a question series designed to assess how much crossover voting might occur, who was likely to cross over, and whether crossover voters would respond to the appeal of moderate candidates in uncompetitive districts. It assumed that down-ballot races for the state legislature were likely to be the kind of elections where a moderation-crossover strategy would work because (1) state legislative districts are typically uncompetitive; and (2) this lack of competition leads to situations where minority party voters usually cast a wasted vote in their own primary and the general election; and (3) partisanship can be muddied because the charged symbolic issues that mobilize partisanship and ideology simultaneously are less common.

Three questions were asked to determine how many voters would respond to appeals by a moderate of the other party. The first question simulated the *opportunities* of the blanket primary. It provided no information other than the party and political orientation of the candidates. This "No Cue" question was designed to generate a baseline estimate of the equilibrium level of crossover voting that could occur in a blanket primary when voters where left to choose between the parties in approximately the same way they do in a general election. That question read as follows:

> As I said earlier, all the primary candidates for an office—Democrat, Republican, Peace and Freedom, and others—will be on the ballot together. Under this new system, you can vote for a candidate even if you are not registered with that candidate's party. Which of the following candidates would you vote for in the primary for the State Assembly: a liberal Democrat, a moderate Democrat, a moderate Republican, or a conservative Republican?

The results of that question were then compared to answers to a second "Cue" question that stimulated awareness of the competitiveness of the district in the general election and primed the ideological differences between the candidates seeking the nomination of the district's majority party. The second question varied depending upon the party preference of the voter. A respondent registered as a Democrat was asked:

> If you lived in a State Assembly district that always elected Republicans no matter who the parties nominated, who would you vote for if the primary election had the following candidates: a conservative Republican, a moderate Republican, or a Democrat who has no opposition for the Democrat nomination?

Republican registrants were asked:

> If you lived in a State Assembly district that always elected Democrats no matter who the parties nominated, who would you vote for if the primary election had the following candidates: a liberal Democrat, a moderate Democrat, or a Republican who has no opposition for the Republican nomination?

The Cue question was designed to simulate an appeal that a moderate candidate could make to create crossover voting.[23] It apprised the voters of the politics of "their" district in a way which sensitized them to two facts: (1) the certainty that the candidate of their party would be nominated and (2) the very low probability that the candidate of their party could win the general election. It implicitly presented them with a third fact. Mentioning, as the Cue question did, that the respondent could support a moderate or his ideological opposite also sensitized them (albeit more weakly) to their ability to cast a more effective vote against the candidate who stood for policies and programs they were especially likely to reject. In brief, the cue questions attempted to simulate a campaign that primed the party preference and general ideological orientation of the respondents in a way calculated to encourage crossover voting.[24]

Candidate Strategy and Voter Response

The Cue question induced a very high rate of crossover voting. As table 14.3 shows, about 10 percent crossed over to vote in the other party's primary in the No Cue situation, a rate that was virtually identical to the crossover rates that have been reported in open presidential primaries and for the recent blanket Senatorial primary in Washington state. Democratic crossovers split equally between a moderate and conservative Republican; Republican crossovers were more uniformly supportive of the moderate Democrat. But the differences between Democratic and Republican registrants are too small to be statistically significant.

However, crossover voting surged dramatically—to 44 percent for the Democrats and 39 percent for Republicans—when the Cue question sensitized respondents to the availability of a moderate candidate in the primary election and made them aware of the certain loss of their party's candidate in the general election. As expected, the ideological moderate was the overwhelming choice of those who crossed over. Overall, 71 percent of the crossover voters supported the moderate: 74 percent of all GOP crossovers (29 of 39 percent) chose the Democratic moderate, and 68 percent of the Democratic crossovers (30 of 43 percent) preferred the Republican moderate.

Only a small minority contradicted expectations and supported the other party's ideological candidate. They are of two types. The first (6 percent of all voters) were crossover voters who voted for the other party's ideological candidate (e.g., Democrats who crossed over and voted for a conservative Republican). These individuals—liberal Republicans and conservative Democrats—hold ideological positions that are at variance with their party preference, and their vote choices seem to reflect their ideological self-identification. Liberal Republicans and conservative Democrats appeared to be engaging in odd primary voting because, in the stylized world of the moderate-crossover strategy, crossover voters are expected to be ideological moderates attracted to the moderate candidate. In the real world of imperfect consistency between issue preferences and partisanship, some Democrats will be conservative, and some Republicans will be liberal—and the ideological candidate will be more attractive for at least some of these individuals.

TABLE 14.3   Crossover Voting as a Function of Ideological Cues

	Blanket Primary	
	With No Cues	With Cues
Registered Democrats (N = 300)		
Voted for a Democrat	90%	56%
Crossover to moderate Republican	5	30
Crossover to conservative Republican	5	14
TOTAL	100	100
Registered Republicans (N = 147)		
Voted for a Republican	91	61
Crossover to moderate Democrat	8	29
Crossover to liberal Democrat	1	10
TOTAL	100	100

NOTE: The question with no cues allowed the respondent to vote for a liberal or conservative Democrat. That result is collapsed in the table. The question with cues presumed a single candidate of the respondent's party and did not ask about an ideological distinction. See the question wording in the text.

A second group—also about 6 percent of all voters—registered a vote intention that is idiosyncratic and impossible to characterize with these data. These were conservative Republicans who voted for the liberal Democrat when they crossed over into the Democratic primary, and liberal Democrats who voted for the conservative Republican when they crossed over into the GOP primary. There is no obvious explanation for these choices. Respondent idiosyncrasies and random error behavior seems to be what is going on here.

The small fraction that cannot be characterized is trivial compared to the essential feature of table 14.3: many primary voters crossed over to support the moderate candidate in response to cues that prime (1) the uncompetitiveness of the district in the general election and (2) the presence of an ideologically tolerable candidate in the other party's primary. Crossovers are a trivial 10 percent without the priming, but over 40 percent with it. Not all of these crossovers support the moderate, but the 71 percent who did may be large enough to elect a moderate candidate in the dominant party's primary (depending, of course, on the distribution of Democrats, Republicans, independents—and liberals, conservatives, and moderates—among voters in the district).

A moderate is not guaranteed success with a strategy of soliciting crossover votes, but this "experiment" suggests that both Democratic and Republican rank-and-file voters, when they are the minority in an uncompetitive district, will respond to a candidate who solicits crossover support on the basis that she is a preferable moderate alternative to the

TABLE 14.4   Demographic Contours of Moderate Crossover Voting

	Percentage Crossing Over to Vote for:		
	Any Candidate	Moderate Candidate	Number of Cases
White	37%	31%	207
Hispanic	47	28	150
Black	52	31	52
Asian	36	20	25
Others[a]	45	45	11
Male	42	29	118
Female	42	31	229
Less than high school	46	19	74
High school degree	46	30	151
Junior College	45	36	69
BA	35	31	86
MA/LLB/Ph.D./etc.	36	33	67
$20,000 or less	47	22	90
$20,000–$40,000	47	30	118
$40,000–$70,000	42	29	102
More than $70,000	40	34	110
Married	43	30	246
Religiously observant	39	27	162
Fundamentalist	45	31	200
18–24 years of age	58	44	52
25–35 years of age	44	28	124
36–55 years of age	41	28	183
Over 55 years of age	33	26	82
Democrat	44	30	300
Republican	39	29	147
Stronger identifier	36	26	151
Weak identifier	43	27	222
Leaner/Independent	51	42	151

[a]Others are those who provide a multiracial identity; they describe themselves as having black and white parents, and so on.

ideological candidate who will otherwise win the primary and general elections.

WHO CROSSES OVER?

Crossover rates varied little with demographic characteristics, and in ways that do not indicate anything systematic (see table 14.4). Blacks and Hispanics, those with lower income, the less educated, and the youngest were the most likely to cross over. However, these small differences do not show up as any particular responsiveness to a crossover solicitation by a moderate candidate. As the data show, a moderate's strategy to solicit support does not receive a response that is differentiated by race, gender, social class, or most other social statuses. The only numerically visible differences in responsiveness to the appeal of moderates are found among young voters and higher income voters, but the differences are not statistically significant.

Democratic and Republican identifiers are equally likely (at 30 and 29 percent respectively) to support moderates who solicit their support. Avowed partisans are less likely to cross over (only about 26 percent did so) than leaners and independents (42 percent crossed over).[25] Neither difference is especially large, and only strength of party preference is statistically significant. There is also no correlation between a willingness to cross over (in general or on behalf of moderates) and generalized support for parties and the party system in the abstract. Those most committed to the notion that parties serve important functions and most likely to believe that party affiliation is a critical criterion for choosing a candidate are no less likely to cross over than those who find parties dispensable.[26]

The only consistent predictor of willingness to cross over on behalf of a political moderate is the intensity of the ideological commitment of the individual (see figure 14.1). Crossover voting averaged over 40 percent for the most ideologically moderate, with Republican moderates particularly likely to cross over. The willingness to cross over declined more or less consistently to about 21 percent among the most ideologically committed. Generally, as figure 14.1 shows, the effect of ideological commitment was equally strong for Democratic and Republican identifiers.

PROGRAMMATIC EFFECTS OF THE BLANKET PRIMARY: A SPECULATION

In an open primary, especially in a blanket primary, the ability of voters to cross over makes the primary electorate approximate the general election electorate. Therein lies the party-weakening effect of crossover voting in a blanket primary. A blanket Democratic primary might attract enough Republicans so that the median voter could be substantially to the right of the median voter in a closed Democratic primary; while the median voter in a GOP blanket primary could be substantially to the left (see table 14.1).

The blanket primary can increase ideological diversity *within* the parties and reduce programmatic differences *between* them because it greatly facilitates a moderate candidate strategy that can increase the number of moderate political elites within both parties. Legislative districts are never homogeneous in political and policy orientation, but most Democratic

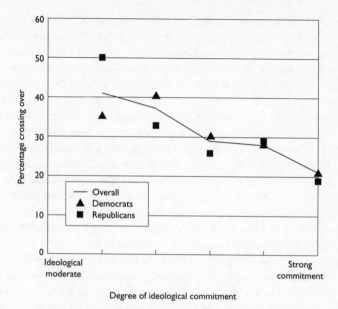

Figure 14.1. Crossovers to moderate challengers as a function of ideological commitment.

officeholders have a constituency that endorses their essentially liberal orientation, likewise most Republican incumbents have a constituency that supports their conservativeness. However, many districts are ideologically diverse, even when one party's electoral majority is secure. Still other districts have a reputation for being more liberal or conservative than the party of the incumbent. Incumbents manage to "fit" themselves to such districts by adopting a degree of programmatic moderation, and both parties have incumbents with a deserved reputation for being more moderate than their caucus. In the extreme, this produces a fractured party of the sort created by the southern conservative wing of the Democratic majority in Congress from the 1940s through the 1980s. A more modest contemporary manifestation, staying with examples provided by the Democrats, are the moderate factions associated with the Democratic Leadership Council and, more recently, the "Bluedog" Democrats. But whether a moderate or a conservative faction creates the divergence, the essential fact is the existence of officeholders that create intraparty programmatic diversity and conflict as by-products of their attempt to satisfy the preferences of their electoral majority.

The blanket primary can increase their numbers because it creates a structure within which candidates can employ a strategy that creates a more moderate nominating electorate than would be found in a purely partisan primary. The moderation strategy outlined above will not be universally effective. It is, for example, particularly unlikely to bring success when the partisanship of the district is too lopsided to permit an effective appeal for crossover voting. But where such an appeal is feasible, the moderate appeal seems to be a dominating strategy in both parties (as table 14.3 shows).

The ideological effect of the moderation-crossover strategy on the parties emerges from (1) its potential attractiveness as a campaign strategy and (2) the ease with which it can be employed. An incumbent who won with a crossover strategy has a strong incentive to behave moderately in office in order to avoid defeat by another candidate adopting the strategy in the future. The moderation strategy also becomes a model for the election of more moderates.[27] Over time, therefore, there are more opportunities for the number of moderates to increase than there are forces causing them to decline, *ceteris paribus;* and the proportion of moderates within both parties might be expected to increase (although the numbers will have a limit), just as the advocates of California's blanket primary hoped. As the number of moderates increases, the programmatic effect on the parties (hinted at in Haeberle's data) might become large as Democrats and Republicans elected in more secure districts are joined by those who won by appealing to crossovers and must maintain that posture to ensure their reelection.[28] The electoral pressures toward this outcome are clear in the following data.

The Meaning of Moderation

The programmatic threat raised by this tendency of candidates to adapt to the expectations of their primary constituency occurs because the policy preferences of moderates vary by party: Democratic moderates are measurably more liberal than Republican moderates; GOP moderates are measurably more conservative than Democratic moderates.[29] Consider the data in table 14.5, which presents the mean preferences of moderate Democrats and Republicans in four issue areas, stratified by the strength of their ideological commitments.

Measures.   Ideological commitment is measured by the "strength" of the individual's preferences on two political issues (health care and the proper role of the government in addressing problems in the society) and the intensity with which they identify as liberal or conservative.[30] This formulation allows respondents to share preferences on policy questions, but vary in the strength or intensity of that preference; and it is the strength of the preference that distinguishes a moderate.[31] Those who express a strong preference on both issues and also describe themselves as "strongly" liberal or conservative are categorized as having a strong ideological commitment.

TABLE 14.5   Political Preferences of Moderates

Ideological Commitment	Moderate		Weak		Strong	
	Rep.	Dem.	Rep.	Dem.	Rep.	Dem.
Social spending	.32	.19	.26	.19	.29	.15
Policies aiding minorities	.55	.40	.57	.36	.57	.32
Active government	.66	.39	.64	.35	.66	.29
National health care	.63	.44	.71	.40	.55	.31
AVERAGE	.54	.36	.55	.33	.52	.27

NOTE: Table entries are issue-opinion scores. The most liberal score is 0; the most conservative score is 1.0.

A person who did not express a strong preference on either issue and did not identify strongly as a conservative or liberal is regarded as a moderate. All other response patterns are characterized as a weak ideological commitment.

The social spending measure is a summary index which measures the respondent's general preference to have the government spend more money on education, child care, the environment, poor people, and African-Americans. The index of policies to aid minorities is an additive measure based on support for affirmative action, a general feeling about the government's responsibility to assure equal opportunity to minorities, English-language requirements, and bilingualism in general. These indices were evaluated with a factor analysis, and their suitability for a single index was evaluated by Cronbach's alpha. The "active government" measure is a single item that asked the respondent's feeling about how active the government should be in dealing with problems. The national health care measure is a single question that asked whether the respondent felt that the government should be more active in ensuring adequate health care for all.

Results.   The consistent result in the table is that differences *between* partisans of different parties far exceed issue preference differences *among* partisans. Republicans are more conservative than Democrats at every level of ideological commitment. The interparty differences increase with the strength of ideological commitment, but the change is small. The substantive opinions of Democratic moderates are almost as liberal as those of strongly committed Democrats; self-described Republican moderates have issue positions that are virtually indistinguishable from those of ideologically committed Republicans.[32]

Table 14.6 displays this fact by calculating the average pairwise difference in two ways. The first column reports the average issue difference

TABLE 14.6   The Partisan Meaning of Moderation

| | Average Issue Distance | |
	Between Party Identifiers	Within Party Identifiers
Social spending	.11	.03
Policies aiding minorities	.20	.03
Active government	.31	.04
National health care	.25	.10

NOTE: The between-party differences are significant at or above the .05 level by a one-tailed test that expects Republicans to be more conservative than Democrats.

between Democratic and Republican identifiers for any given level of ideological commitment. The number in the cell is the average difference, for each issue, of the issue scores of moderate Democrats compared to moderate Republicans, weakly committed Democrats compared to weakly committed Republicans, and strongly committed Democrats compared to strongly committed Republicans. The second column reports the average difference *among* partisans of the same party for any given intensity of ideological commitment. It reports, for each issue and among those who identify with the same party, the average issue-score difference between moderates, those weakly committed, and those with a strong commitment.

All of the differences *within* party identifiers hover just above zero. The *between*-party differences are noticeably larger. On average, for any given level of ideological commitment, Republicans are 11 points more conservative than Democrats on the social spending index, 20 points more conservative on the minority policy index, 31 points more conservative in their attitudes toward the appropriate role of the government, and 25 points more conservative on the question of the government's role in ensuring health care.

The consequences of this pattern are illustrated in figure 14.2. Because they are "moderate" in the intensity of their beliefs, they seem able to support a "moderate" candidate in the other party. But the "moderation" that makes a crossover vote easy for them brings to the winner's coalition a more programmatically heterogeneous constituency than would exist for a candidate selected within a closed primary. Crossover voters who find a moderate candidate more programmatically acceptable will create an incumbent with a nomination and reelection constituency that is significantly less liberal (if the incumbent is Democrat) or conservative (if Republican) than the constituency of a candidate elected in a closed primary. Figure 14.2 indicates what that might look like. Four positions are plotted. Each point is the average of the four issue positions discussed above.[33] The arrows in the bottom half point to the observed averages for Democratic and Repub-

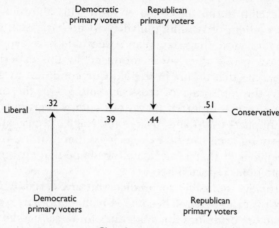

Figure 14.2. Projected issue positions of electorates in closed and blanket primaries.

lican identifiers. Presumably these scores would represent the issue constituency of a Democrat and Republican, respectively, in a closed primary. The top half of the figure calculates an issue score for a nomination constituency that is one-third partisans of the other party. For example, the nomination constituency of a "moderate strategy" Democrat in a blanket primary is approximately one-third Republican, and the issue preferences of this electorate reflect the size of the GOP vote and the issue positions characteristic of Republican identifiers.

It is pure speculation to assert that candidates elected under a blanket primary would shift as far to the center as the preferences of their voter's shift when a blanket primary produces crossover voting. However, as Adams's (1996) data demonstrates, a system that reduces a need to consider the preferences of opposition voters does create a more programmatically cohesive legislative delegation, and the blanket primary does the opposite. If the policy averages did move as much as the data in figure 14.2, it is easy to understand why crossover-elected legislators might cause policy cohesion within the parties to decline and issue conflict within the parties to increase.

CONCLUSION

In this survey "experiment," upwards of 30 percent of the moderates in both parties were successfully solicited to cross over on behalf of the moderate candidate in a blanket primary. Whether this result could be reproduced in an actual election is unknown. Several election cycles would have been required for California voters to become accustomed to the blanket primary and develop norms for crossover voting. If California voters had followed the precedent of Washington voters (who have been voting in a blanket primary for more than sixty years), we would have expected lower rates of crossover voting than those produced by this experiment, but higher than the rate that occurs in the No Cue condition in this experiment. However, the high rates of crossover voting—on the order of 40 percent in some races—reported by various county registrars ("Election Officials Study Impact" 1998) and Alvarez and Nagler (1997) are evidence that crossover voting itself can be extremely common in low-competition elections. It seems likely that a candidate can shape that crossover vote to produce the outcomes reported here.

It is also virtually impossible to predict with any certainty how much more moderate officeholders will become. A blanket primary system seems to offer strategic opportunities for moderates to defeat candidates with a reputation for strong liberal or conservative commitments. When these strongly committed candidates run in districts that are lopsidedly partisan, the kind of targeting and coalition strategy outlined in this chapter will not usually be successful. But when the party registration of the minority party is within 20 to 25 points of that of the dominant party, the blanket primary creates an opportunity for ambitious moderates to defeat their committed liberal or conservative colleagues with the help of crossover voters from the other side. When California's voters established the blanket primary in 1996, there were enough uncompetitive districts with a sufficient minority-party vote to make a moderation-crossover strategy an attractive option for an insurgent. A vigorous partisan redistricting (generally expected with the election of a Democratic governor in 1998) might have made more districts vulnerable to such a strategy, especially among the Democrats, since a larger number of Democratic districts could be achieved only by creating smaller Democratic majorities in more districts. It might also have produced the intraparty conflicts suggested by figure 14.2. The Supreme Court eliminated this hypothetical future. But the dynamics studied with this "experiment" were not undone by the Court. Blanket primaries can facilitate an antiparty insurgent strategy that in turn erodes party cohesion. It is an institution to avoid if we value programmatic cohesion in our parties.

NOTES

1. The literature is voluminous; see, for example, Hall (1923); Harris (1951); APSA (1950); Ranney (1951); and Key (1952). Various standard texts also summarize this material well. See, for example, Beck (1997); Keefe (1998); and Jewell and Olson (1982).

2. A blanket primary permits voting in more than one party primary, regardless of the party with which the voter is formally registered. In a blanket primary the voter can vote for any candidate, regardless of the candidate's party, seeking nomination for the office. This structure would allow a person to, for example, support a candidate seeking the Democratic nomination for governor, then vote for a Republican in the U.S. Senate primary, a Democrat seeking a congressional nomination, a Republican vying for the nomination for the State Assembly, and so forth. A more conventional "open" primary permits voting in any party's primary, but only one. In the latter, therefore, a decision to support a person seeking the Republican presidential nomination would require the voter to cast the remainder of his primary ballot for those seeking the Republican nomination.

3. As described in the introduction, this chapter uses a strict definition of crossover voting. A crossover voter is a partisan of a different party than the one in which he votes in the primary. This strict definition seems more conceptually faithful to the notion of "crossing over." Independents, by this definition, do not cast a crossover vote. See Wekkin's (1988) discussion of this also.

4. The study did not attempt to test any aspect of raiding. The inclusion of raiding and crossover experiments in this one survey was likely to be confounding without half-sampling each experiment, and the sample size was too small to create half-samples of sizes that would support the analysis.

5. The current popular and academic emphasis on "party decline" substantially overstates the drop in party voting during the last fifty years. During the 1950s, slightly more than 80 percent of the vote for president or members of Congress was a party vote. That is, 80 percent were either Democratic identifiers voting for the Democrat or Republicans voting for the GOP candidate. About 10 percent of the vote was contributed by independents, and another 10 percent was marked by defection. The rate of party voting for these same offices during the 1990s was in the mid- to low 70s. Put differently, party voting has declined only about 5 to 8 percentage points. Presumably, party voting was an even larger fraction of the total vote during the Golden Age when primaries were introduced, although we have no exact estimates of its magnitude.

6. Of course incumbents are rarely defeated today, and the reelection rates for most legislatures frequently exceed 90 percent.

7. In their original design, primaries attacked the control over nominations exercised by party leaders at caucuses and conventions. It expected voters to vote only within the primary of the party with which they identified by requiring a formal declaration of support through legal registration as a Democrat or Republican. Open primaries extend the logic of popular control over nominations by allowing voters to vote in either primary without a prior declaration of support.

8. In the nonpartisan nominating primaries that are common in local elections in California and other states, a majority of the total primary vote eliminates the general election. In these situations the public official can be selected by as little as 10 percent of the eligible electorate.

9. This point is corroborated by easily observed examples of wide disparities between the positions of public officials and those of their electoral base. For example, Republican officeholders of all stripes have been uniformly more opposed to abortion than Republican voters; Democrats have been consistently supportive

of affirmative action programs that are opposed by majorities of Democratic voters. This discrepancy probably reflects the structure of candidate recruitment, and the predominance of purposively (and ideologically) motivated activists in the pool of potential candidates.

10. The author has had personal experience with this belief in the extremity of activists. On virtually every occasion when he presented data on the representativeness of primary electorates to party figures, the data were rejected. The moderates always insisted that activists pulled the party to the extremes of a position. They were largely unpersuaded by the data showing small, erratic, and often trivial differences between rank-and-file voters and primary voters.

11. The table uses the 1980 National Election Study survey because the 1980 election study attempted to validate each respondent's report of participation in the primaries, and the nomination was contested in both parties. Both features are important. Since a sense of citizen duty leads many to report voting when they did not, any distinctiveness among primary voters compared to nonvoters is at least reduced when nonvoters are allowed to claim inaccurately to be voters. The validation of primary turnout minimizes the suppressing effect of misreporting on the distinctivness of primary voters. There may be some inaccuracies in these validation data, but they are less flawed than self-reports. The existence of a competitive presidential primary in both parties in 1980 offers a chance to confirm the effect.

12. Reality is less neat. Courts and legislatures have consistently eroded the partisan seal of closed primaries. In the past, many states had laws that made it difficult for uncommitted voters to vote in a primary. A person who wanted to change party registration was sometimes required to sit out one primary election cycle before voting in the primary of his or her "new" party affiliation. Others required a change of registration six months or a year before the primary election date. Today, it is possible in many places to change one's formal party registration as few as thirty days before the party primary. While there is no estimate of large numbers of crossovers in such primaries, there can be no question that crossovers can occur more easily now (in general, but not everywhere) than they could in past closed primaries.

13. These data come from a proprietary study done on behalf of one of the candidates for the U.S. Senate nomination in Washington in 1998. The numbers that are cited do not refer to the actual election, but to the reported intention of respondents some months prior to the primary.

14. I want to thank Christopher Blunt for calling this event to my attention.

15. These data are from the CNN Election 2000 web site.

16. However, crossovers were 17 percent of the Michigan GOP primary vote, and some observers believe that mischievous Democratic politicians and voters could not resist a chance to vote against Bush and the state's GOP Governor.

17. These conclusions are based on an analysis of the exit polls published on the CNN Election 2000 web site.

18. The blanket primary found a positive response in such an opinion climate, although the issue was not at all salient. In December of 1995, three months before the March 1996 election in which voters approved of the blanket primary in California, 85 percent of a sample interviewed by the Field Institute were unaware of the initiative. Seventy-eight percent were still unaware less than a month from the election date. Fifty-eight percent did not know about the initiative within a week of

the polls opening. Yet, at each survey date, overwhelming majorities supported it when a summary of the ballot proposition was read to them. In the December 1995 survey, attitudes toward the proposition were 65 percent positive and only 24 percent negative. The margin did not change over the next three months. It was 65 percent positive and 22 percent negative in the late February poll, and 65 percent positive and 28 percent negative in the mid-March survey (Field Institute polls, December 21, 1995; March 1, 1996; March 23, 1996).

19. On the other hand, a study of crossover voting by the San Bernardino registrar of voters did not find vote choices among the crossovers that were consistent with the moderation-crossover strategy outlined here. However, none of these studies had any evidence that candidates were pursuing the strategy, and that is what is at issue in this chapter. The focus in studies done thus far has been twofold: (1) How large was the crossover vote? (2) Did the crossovers help to decide nominations in 1998? The Alvarez and Nagler (1997) study and county registrar studies found relatively large crossover votes to the primary of the dominant party in competitive districts, consistent with previous findings.

20. The example is only that; it does not report any election. It only illustrates how a campaign might construct a winning coalition vote target of crossovers and independents. However, in searching for a district with characteristics that I thought exemplified vulnerability to the strategy examined here, I selected the Thirty-First Congressional District. At the time, the district was represented by Matthew Martinez. He was defeated in the 2000 primary, although not along the lines discussed here.

21. The 57 percent assumes that the liberal Democrat would win the 25 percent (the 24 percent who voted for the liberal and the 1 percent who voted for someone else) of the 44 percent who are Democrats.

22. The Los Angeles County Social Survey involved a representative sample of 694 adults in Los Angeles County. The study was focused on intergroup relationships, media use, and crime perceptions, and the general state of things in and around Los Angeles. The normal set of demographic characteristics was collected. A limited amount of political and party attitudes were collected in connection with the blanket primary portion of the study. The sample was generated by an in-house sampling system created by Genesys Sampling Systems. Genesys's In-Home Sampling System was used to draw a list-assisted telephone sample from the Los Angeles County population. Since coverage bias is a disadvantage of the list-assisted telephone sampling method (Black et al. 1995), it was decided to increase coverage by not using options to purge numbers and set the criteria for eligible banks of telephone numbers to an absolute minimum. Thus, Genesys's additional options to purge business and nonworking telephone numbers were not used. Furthermore, a bank of telephone numbers (a group of numbers denoting the first two digits of a four-digit suffix) was considered a working bank and, therefore, was included in the sample if it contained just one residential listing. No oversampling methods were used for this survey.

23. It is the kind of appeal that could be made directly to voters or the various institutions and organizations that might recommend a candidate on the grounds that she was a "moderate" who could work with and act on behalf of a wide segment of the district. How this appeal would be implemented is beyond the scope of this

chapter. However, direct mail messages, public position-taking, and planned inter-actions with appropriate formal groups can easily be used to create a reputation of acceptability to moderate voters in the minority party.

24. Democrats were overwhelmingly liberal or moderate in their self-identification; Republicans were equally moderate and conservative.

25. Some self-described Independents, according to the index of party identi-fication, are registered as Democrats or Republicans. As a result, some of them are included as crossover voters in the data because the defining legal characteristic for being a crossover voter in a blanket primary is voting in the primary of a party other than the one in which the individual is registered. The only way to "clean" these data would be to delete respondents whose party identification was at variance with their registration. That option was not selected. Registration, which is what matters in the real election, was chosen to define crossover status.

26. This conclusion is based on comparing crossover rates with an index of party support, which summed the number of times that a respondent made a pro-party response to the questions reported in table 14.1. The index ranges from zero to five. It had a mean of slightly less than 2.5.

27. Candidates are usually aware of the electorate's limited awareness of the policy orientation of the candidates among whom they must choose. Competing candidates fill in this blank space with campaigns.

28. They are likely to be secure because the partisanship of the district is too lopsided to permit an effective appeal for crossover voting.

29. This feature of "moderates" was pointed out to me several years ago by Dwaine Marvick, who studied party activists more intensively and over a longer pe-riod of time than almost any other student of these "middlemen" of politics.

30. These questions were approximately the same as the standard NES ques-tions. The exact wording is available upon request.

31. The model underlying this formulation parallels the "directional" issue the-ory of Rabinowitz and McDonald (1989).

32. Opinion intensity obviously does not correlate with substantive opinion. The exact dynamic that allows moderates to cross over may share some of the ori-enting qualities of "positive" and "negative" partisanship (Maggiotto and Piereson 1977). Voters with strong commitments have the behavior characteristic of the classic ideologue. Voters with moderately held preferences find it possible to vote against alternatives. In this case, the difference is expressed by a moderately con-servative Republican choosing a moderately liberal Democrat to minimize the pros-pects of a liberal Democrat. An otherwise similar, strongly conservative Republican would be so committed to his views that a moderate Democrat would be as unac-ceptable as a liberal Democrat on the grounds that "both support the Democratic agenda."

33. Lines for each issue for each group would have made the graph more difficult to read, and it would not show any material difference from what is pre-sented.

REFERENCES

Abramowitz, Alan; John McClennon; and Ronald Rapoport. 1981. "A Note on Strategic Voting in a Primary Election." *Journal of Politics* 43: 899–904.

Adamany, David. 1976. "Crossover Voting and the Democratic Party's Reform Rules." *American Political Science Review* 70: 536–41.

Adams, Greg D. 1996. "Legislative Effects of Single-Member vs. Multi-Member Districts." *American Journal of Political Science* 40: 129–44.

Alvarez, R. Michael, and Jonathan Nagler. 1997. "Analysis of Crossover and Strategic Voting." Expert testimony in *California Democratic Party et al. v. Jones.*

American Political Science Association. 1950. *Toward a More Responsible Two-Party System: A Report of the Committee on Political Parties, American Political Science Association.* New York: Rinehart.

Beck, Paul Allen. 1997. *Party Politics in America.* New York: Longman.

Black, Michael J.; J. Waksberg; D. Kulp; and A. Starer. 1995. "Bias in List-Assisted Telephone Samples." *Public Opinion Quarterly* 59: 218–35.

Cain, Bruce E. 1997. "Report on Blanket and Open Primaries." Expert testimony in *California Democratic Party et al. v. Jones.*

California Secretary of State. 1996. "Argument in Favor of Proposition 198." Ballot Pamphlet. Sacramento.

Cohen, Jonathan M., and John M. Sides. 1998. "The Incidence and Importance of Crossover Voting in a Blanket Primary: Washington State Senate Elections, 1986–1996." Paper presented at the Annual Meeting of the Western Political Science Association, Los Angeles, CA, March 19–22.

Costantini, Edmond. 1963. "Intraparty Attitude Conflict: Democratic Party Leadership in California." *Western Political Quarterly* 16: 956–72.

Downs, Anthony. 1957. *An Economic Theory of Democracy.* New York: Harper & Row.

"Election Officials Study Impact of Blanket Primary." 1998. *Seiler Report: A Newsletter of California Elections,* July 5, 6.

Fenno, Richard F. 1978. *Home Style: House Members in Their Districts.* Boston: Little, Brown.

Field Institute. 1983. "Electoral Process and the Party System." *California Opinion Index.* Vol. 8 (November).

———. 1995. "Voters Know Little about Four Controversial March Primary Initiatives." The Field Poll, December 21. San Francisco: The Field Institute.

———. 1996a. "Initial Voter Feeling in Favor of Open Primary Initiative and Divided on Mountain Line Measure." The Field Poll, March 1, 1996. San Francisco: The Field Institute.

———. 1996b. "Final Pre-Election Measure of Voter Awareness and Preferences on Seven Primary Election Ballot Provisions." The Field Poll, March 23, 1996. San Francisco: The Field Institute.

Froman, Lewis A. 1963. *Congressmen and Their Constituencies.* Chicago: Rand McNally.

Geer, John G. 1986. "Rules Governing Presidential Primaries." *Journal of Politics* 48: 1006–1025.

———. 1988. "Assessing the Representativeness of Electorates in Presidential Primaries." *American Journal of Political Science* 32: 929–45.

Haeberle, Steven H. 1985. "Closed Primaries and Party Support in Congress." *American Politics Quarterly* 13: 341–52.

Hall, Arnold B. 1923. "The Direct Primary and Party Responsibility in Wisconsin." *Annals of the American Academy of Political and Social Science* 71: 40–54.

Harris, Joseph P. 1951. *A Model Direct Primary Election System: Report of the Committee on the Direct Primary.* New York: National Municipal League.

Hedlund, Ronald D. 1977–78. "Crossover Voting in a 1976 Open Presidential Primary." *Public Opinion Quarterly* 41: 498–514.

Hedlund, Ronald D., and Meredith W. Watts. 1986. "The Wisconsin Open Primary, 1968 to 1984." *American Politics Quarterly* 14: 55–73.

Hedlund, Ronald D.; Meredith W. Watts; and David M. Hedge. 1982. "Voting in an Open Primary." *American Politics Quarterly* 10: 197–218.

Jewell, Malcolm E., and David M. Olson. 1982. *American State Political Parties and Elections.* Homewood, IL: Dorsey Press.

Keefe, William J. 1998. *Parties, Politics, and Public Policy in America.* Washington, D.C.: Congressional Quarterly Press.

Key, V. O. 1952. *Politics, Parties, and Pressure Groups.* New York: Crowell.

Kousser, Morgan J. 1996. "Estimating the Partisan Consequences of Redistricting Plans—Simply." *Legislative Studies Quarterly* 21, no. 4: 521–41.

Lengle, James I. 1981. *Representation and Presidential Primaries: The Democratic Party in the Post Reform Era.* Westport, CT: Greenwood Press.

Los Angeles Times. 1996. "Prop 198, for the Sake of Political Moderation." Editorial. March 18, B4.

Maggiotto, Michael A., and James E. Piereson. 1977. "Partisan Identification and Electoral Choice: The Hostility Hypothesis." *American Journal of Political Science* 21: 745–67.

Mayhew, David R. 1974. *Congress: The Electoral Connection.* New Haven, CT: Yale University Press.

———. 1991. *Divided We Govern: Party Control, Lawmaking, and Investigations, 1946–1990.* New Haven, CT: Yale University Press.

Merriam, C. Edward. 1908. *Primary Elections: A Study of History and Tendencies of Primary Election Legislation.* Chicago: University of Chicago Press.

Nie, Norman; Sidney Verba; and John R. Petrocik. 1979. *The Changing American Voter.* Enlarged ed. Cambridge, MA: Harvard University Press.

Petrocik, John R. 1979. "Levels of Issue Voting: The Effect of Candidate-Pairs in Presidential Elections." *American Politics Quarterly* 7: 303–27.

Petrocik, John R., and Joseph Doherty. 1996. "The Road to Divided Government: Paved Without Intention." In Peter F. Galderisi, Roberta Q. Hertzberg, and Peter McNamara, eds., *Divided Government: Change, Uncertainty, and the Constitutional Order.* New York: Rowman and Littlefield.

Quinn, Tony. 1998. "Report on Assembly Primary Election Crossover Voting." Presented at California's "Blanket/Open" Primary Conference: A Natural Experiment in Election Dynamics, Institute of Governmental Studies, University of California, Berkeley, CA, June 26.

Rabinowitz, George, and Stuart Elaine McDonald. 1989. "A Directional Theory of Issue Voting." *American Political Science Review* 83: 93–121.

Ranney, Austin. 1951. "Toward a More Responsible Two-Party System: A Commentary." *American Political Science Review* 45: 488–99.

———. 1972. "Turnout and Representation in Presidential Primary Elections." *American Political Science Review* 66: 21–37.

Sorauf, Frank J. 1963. *Party and Representation: Legislative Politics in Pennsylvania.* New York: Atherton Press.

Southwell, Patricia L. 1988. "Open versus Closed Primaries and Candidate Fortunes, 1972–1984." *American Politics Quarterly* 16: 280–95.

———. 1989. "Strategic Voting in the 1984 Democratic Presidential Primaries." *Social Science Journal* 26: 445–53.

———. 1991. "Open vs. Closed Primaries: The Effect on Strategic Voting and Candidate Fortunes." *Social Science Quarterly* 72: 789–96.

Wekkin, Gary D. 1988. "The Conceptualization and Measurement of Crossover Voting." *Western Political Quarterly* 41: 105–14.

Wisckol, Richard. 2000. "Analysis Proves Point for Open-Primary Foes." *Orange County Register,* April 11, morning edition, B4.

Wright, Gerald C., and Michael B. Berkman. 1986. "Candidates and Policy in United States Senate Elections." *American Political Science Review* 80: 565–88.

Zaller, John. 1998. "Know-Nothing Voters in U.S. Presidential Elections, 1948–1996." Paper presented at the Annual Meeting of the American Political Science Association, Boston, MA, September 3–6.

PART FOUR

Conclusions and Implications

CHAPTER FIFTEEN

The Blanket Primary in the Courts
The Precedent and Implications of
California Democratic Party v. Jones

Nathaniel Persily

In addition to the lessons it has taught political scientists about voting behavior, partisanship, and the effect of electoral rules, California's experiment with the blanket primary provided the courts with an opportunity to
define the constitutional character of political parties and primary elections. In the case of *California Democratic Party v. Jones,* 120 S. Ct. 2402
(2000), California's political parties successfully challenged the blanket
primary as unconstitutional under the First Amendment. Overruling the
District Court and Court of Appeals that had upheld the initiative as a
reasonable exercise of the state's power to increase participation and enhance the representativeness of elected officials, the Supreme Court of the
United States, in a 7–2 decision, found Proposition 198 to be a "severe and
unnecessary" (and therefore unconstitutional) burden on the political parties' protected freedom of association.

Both because of what they reveal about how judges and lawyers characterize political parties in the process of constitutional litigation and because
of the questions they leave unanswered, the courts' decisions in the blanket
primary case provide a rare colloquy on the proper role of the judiciary in
the regulation of elections and political parties. The "legal" story of the
blanket primary is, after all, one pitting the ultrademocracy of California's
initiative process against the ultimate antidemocracy of the unelected federal judiciary, with the political parties (at times exhibiting both oligarchic
and democratic tendencies) caught somewhere in between. The task thus
confronting the courts became how to reconcile political party autonomy—
which all agree is indispensable, at some level, to American democracy—
with the democratic mandate announced by the majority of California's
voters to rein in that autonomy at the critical stage of candidate nomination. As it had so frequently done in the past, the Supreme Court sided

with the right of the parties to determine the content of their message and the identity of their standard bearer.

THE CONSTITUTIONAL STATUS OF POLITICAL PARTIES AND PRIMARY ELECTIONS BEFORE *JONES*

The blanket primary case was hardly the first opportunity for the Supreme Court to draw a line between the state's authority to organize the selection processes leading up to a general election and the parties' autonomy to decide the character of their membership and nomination procedures. Indeed, for those who have watched closely the Court's jurisprudence in this area, the *Jones* decision was the natural consequence of a series of "pro-party" decisions emanating from the Court over the last half-century.

At the time *Jones* came before the U.S. District Court for the Eastern District of California in 1997, a few issues regarding the legal regulation of party nomination methods had become settled. First, in *Nader v. Schaffer*, 417 F. Supp. 837 (D. Conn.), *summarily aff'd*, 429 U.S. 989 (1976), the Supreme Court summarily affirmed a lower court ruling rejecting voters' claims that closed primaries violated their First and Fourteenth Amendment rights. Because Connecticut required party membership as a precondition for participating in a party's primary, Ralph Nader and the other plaintiffs argued that the state "coerced" voters into becoming party members in order to vote for their preferred candidate. The Constitution, they maintained, both prohibits such compelled associations and guarantees each voter's right to participate in any state-sponsored elections that can have the effect of selecting government officials. The Court rejected this novel claim by emphasizing the importance of the party's associational right to exclude nonmembers from its primary and the minimal intrusion that party registration imposes on would-be primary voters.

The case is an interesting one, even if rarely cited and not too difficult to resolve, because it highlights the constitutionally relevant actors in cases challenging rules governing a primary. Three actors exist in every party regulation case: a party organization, a voter, and the state. In most of these cases, either a party or an individual argues that the state law violates its First Amendment right of expressive association. When an individual makes such a claim, as in *Nader*, he alleges that by depriving him of the opportunity to express his candidate preference in the primary, the state prevents him from "associating" with others who support a given candidate. When a party challenges an identical state law, as in *Tashjian v. Connecticut*, discussed below, it makes a somewhat different claim on associational freedom. The party argues that state regulation of its primary undermines the ability of the party association to define itself and select its membership, leaders, and message. The same state law establishing primary voter qualifications, as we will see, might be vulnerable to a party's, but immune from an individual's, associational rights claim. Moreover, the associational rights claims of individuals (i.e., to associate with a given candidate and his supporters) naturally run up against a party's right to define its association as including some people but not others.

The seeds for the *Tashjian* decision were sown with the Court's decision in *Democratic Party of the United States v. Wisconsin ex rel. LaFollette*, 450 U.S. 107 (1981). The *LaFollette* Court adjudicated a challenge brought by the state of Wisconsin to the rules governing the seating of delegates at the 1980 Democratic National Convention. Those rules, in effect, prohibited the seating of delegates selected through primary systems that allowed the participation of non–party members. Wisconsin employed an open primary, meaning that any voter, regardless of party affiliation, could vote in the state's presidential preference primary. Because state law bound Wisconsin's delegates to vote in conformity with the results of the open primary, the delegates were not qualified to sit at the Democratic Convention.[1] In this conflict between national party rules and state law, the Court sided once again with the party, holding that the party had a First Amendment right to specify the credentials necessary for participation in the national convention.

Much of the language of the *LaFollette* opinion has become standard for party autonomy cases. Although the case itself had a federalism spin—that is, it presented a unique conflict between an individual state law and national party rules—the Court exploited the opportunity to shore up a party's robust First Amendment right of association, which included the right to exclude outsiders from participating in its nomination processes. "The freedom to associate for the 'common advancement of political beliefs,'" the Court held, "necessarily presupposes the freedom to identify the people who constitute the association, and to limit the association to those people only" (*LaFollette*, 450 U.S. at 122, quoting *Kusper v. Pontikes*, 414 U.S. 51, 56 (1973)). "The inclusion of persons unaffiliated with a political party may seriously distort its collective decisions—thus impairing the party's essential functions—and . . . political parties may accordingly protect themselves 'from intrusion by those with adverse political principles'" (id., quoting *Ray v. Blair*, 343 U.S. 214, 221–22 (1952)). After *LaFollette* it appeared that a national party convention enjoyed a degree of First Amendment protection from state regulation similar to that accorded to other meetings of private groups and associations. However, at the quadrennial national convention, a party takes on a momentary, even if heightened, associational form. Like a large Rotary Club, members assemble together to meet and discuss issues of collective concern; they craft the party's platform, choose its leaders, and stage a media event to broadcast the party's message to a larger audience. Whether the heightened associational protection for the convention would apply to a run-of-the-mill primary remained for the Court to decide in *Tashjian v. Republican Party of Connecticut,* 479 U.S. 208 (1996).

The law at issue in *Tashjian* was the same closed primary law upheld in *Nader.* This time, however, Connecticut's Republican Party, rather than an individual voter, brought a First Amendment challenge. Because the Republicans wanted to open their primary to independent voters and the Democratic legislature refused to change the law to allow them to do so, the party argued that the "state" violated its freedom to define the contours of its association. The state articulated interests typical for election laws: "administrability of the primary system, preventing raiding, avoiding voter confusion, and protecting the responsibility of party government" (id. at 217). As weighty and determinative as these concerns often are in the context of electoral regulation, the Court found them to be paternalistic in this particular context, a subterfuge for the state, which was dominated by one party (the Democrats), determining what was best for the party out of power (the Republicans). For, as Justice Thurgood Marshall's majority opinion explained,

> Under these circumstances, the views of the State, which to some extent represent the views of the one political party transiently enjoying majority power, as to the optimum methods for preserving party integrity lose much of their force. The State argues that its statute is well designed to save the Republican Party from undertaking a course of conduct destructive of its own interests. But on this point "even if the State were correct, a State, or a court, may not constitutionally substitute its own judgment for that of the Party." The Party's determination of the boundaries of its own association, and of the structure which best allows it to pursue its political goals, is protected by the Constitution. (Id. at 224)

Thus, after *Tashjian,* it was clear that the state could not force a party to restrict participation in its primary to party members. The precise question in *Jones,* however—whether a state could force a party to *expand* participation in its primary—remained unanswered.

The Supreme Court's final pre-*Jones* confrontation with state laws regulating party primaries came in *Eu v. San Francisco County Democratic Central Committee,* 489 U.S. 214 (1989). Unlike these other cases that challenged state qualifications for voter participation in primary elections, *Eu* involved a law that barred political parties from endorsing candidates in primary elections and regulated parties' internal organizational structure. The Court considered the ban on endorsements as a clear violation of the party's freedom of expression: it regulated what the organization could say and print. The laws regulating party organizational structure—limiting the term of office to two years for state central committee chairs and requiring that the chair rotate between residents of northern and southern California—also infringed the party's First Amendment rights, in this case (as in *Tashjian* and *LaFollette*), the party's freedom of expressive association. "By regulating the identity of the parties' leaders," the Court held, "the challenged statutes may also color the parties' message and interfere with the parties' decisions as to the best means to promote that message" (id. at 231 n. 21).

Given the law's clear restriction on the party organization's speech and core associational decisions, *Eu* did not appear to be a difficult case in the abstract. What made the case interesting was the state's allegation that the parties had consented to the law by urging its earlier passage in the legislature. Thus, the Court was confronted with the question: Who speaks for and constitutes the party? Is it the party-in-the-electorate, whose main act of affiliation is voting in primary elections (Key 1964, 163–65)? Is it the party-in-the-legislature, which, under favorable conditions of majority control or acquiescence, can enact its internal regulations into state law? Or is it the professional party organizations and governing bodies, which, although frequently defined and regulated by state electoral law, most closely resemble the leaders of a private association? Indeed, as the very existence of the named plaintiff, San Francisco County Democratic Central Committee, suggested, even these traditional categories needed to be disaggregated to account for the different, geographically specific components of the party organization, for example. In a rare opinion that paid attention to this multidimensionality of political parties, Justice Marshall detached incumbent party legislators from local party organizations and average members. "We have never held that a political party's consent will cure a statute that otherwise violates the First Amendment." He wrote for the Court, "Simply because a legislator belongs to a political party does not make her at all times a representative of party interest. In supporting the endorsement ban, an individual legislator may be acting on her understanding of the public good or her interest in reelection" (489 U.S. at 226). Even bipartisan legislative consent to an election law, it appeared after *Eu*, could intrude on the "party's" rights—meaning that party members and officials outside of government would be forced to operate under a rule they did not choose. Even a subdivision of the party organization could now seek court protection from a law passed with the party's consent.

Of course, the Court does not side with party organizations in every case. When a party organization seeks to discriminate on the basis of race, the Court has been especially vigilant in protecting voters' rights at the expense of party autonomy. Moreover, when a minor party asserts its First Amendment rights, the Court has given greater weight to the state's interests in avoiding ballot confusion and preserving the integrity of elections.

The "race" cases begin with the so-called *White Primary Cases,* in which the Court scrutinized the electoral laws of Southern states, the rules of the state Democratic Party, and even the practices of informal subdivisions of the party under the Equal Protection Clause of the Fourteenth Amendment and the Fifteenth Amendment's guarantee that voting rights not be abridged on account of race. Alongside poll taxes, grandfather clauses, literacy tests, and other more coercive tactics of disenfranchisement, white primaries were used by Southern states and state parties to prevent blacks from voting in what turned out to be the critical and determinative election in those one-party states.[2] Between 1927 and 1953, the Court overruled its previous precedents and struck down a state statute that forbade the participation of blacks in the Democratic primary (*Nixon v. Herndon*, 273 U.S. 536 (1927)) and a statute that delegated to the party executive committee the power to determine qualifications to vote in a party primary, which it then exercised to ban blacks from primary voting (*Nixon v. Condon*, 286 U.S. 73 (1932)). Moreover, drawing on its decision in *United States v. Classic*, 313 U.S. 299 (1941), a case that upheld the prosecution under federal law of those stuffing primary ballot boxes because the primary was "an integral part of the election machinery," the Court struck down the Democratic Party's practice (apart from state law) of excluding blacks from primaries (*Smith v. Allwright*, 321 U.S. 649 (1944)). The Court held that "the recognition of the place of the primary in the electoral scheme makes clear that state delegation to a party of the power to fix the qualifications of primary elections is delegation of a state function that may make the party's action the action of the State" (id. at 660). Considering the primary in this way, the Court interpreted the Fifteenth Amendment as preventing a state "from casting its electoral process in a form which permits a private organization to practice racial discrimination in an election" (id. at 664). Then, in a highly fractured decision in the last of the *White Primary Cases, Terry v. Adams*, 345 U.S. 461 (1953), the Court extended this reasoning even to the conduct of an unofficial subdivision (or alter ego) of the party, whose candidate selection mechanism effectively determined the Democratic nominee that appeared on the ballot.

There are at least two ways to view the *White Primary Cases*. The first is to dismiss them as *sui generis* holdings limited to the unique party monopolistic conditions of the South and the fundamental importance of race to the post–Civil War amendments. After all, the Democratic primary in various Southern states constituted, for all practical purposes, the general election. The incumbent officeholders, party functionaries in the cloak of state law, or individuals with power equal to that of official state actors used the primaries to disenfranchise the voters whom the Fourteenth and Fifteenth Amendments were enacted to protect.

A second way to view the *White Primary Cases*, however, is to consider them definitive interpretations of the constitutional status of party primaries. Much of the language in those cases suggests that when the primary forms an integral part of the electoral machinery used to select governing officials, constitutional restrictions applicable to general elections would similarly apply. A short step away from that rule is a corollary maintaining that state or federal laws seeking to preserve those constitutional rights are also valid, meaning that the party (viewed more as a state actor than as a private association) cannot assert its First Amendment rights as a barrier to the enforcement of such a law. For example, when the Virginia Republican Party required the payment of a registration fee as a precondition to participation in the convention used to nominate the party's candidate for United States Senator, the Court held that the Voting Rights Act of 1964 applied (*Morse v. Republican Party of Virginia,* 517 U.S. 186 (1996)).[3] One of the questions confronting the Court in *Jones* was whether the blanket primary law—to the degree that it, like the Voting Rights Act, was expanding the franchise and enriching the constitutional protection of the right to vote—was similarly immune to the party's associational rights claims.

In the second class of "anti-party" opinions, the Court upholds state laws against First Amendment and Equal Protection challenges brought by minor parties. In such cases the Court has applied a balancing test, weighing the severity of the rights deprivation against the importance of the state interests and then determining whether the law is properly tailored toward the achievement of those interests. Such a test applies not only to minor-party cases, but also to most widely applied electoral rules, such as signature requirements for candidate petitions for ballot access. In the most recent case on point, the Court rejected a claim brought by the Minnesota New Party challenging the state's ban on "fusion" candidacies, which prohibited a candidate from appearing on the ballot as the candidate of more than one party (*Timmons v. Twin Cities Area New Party,* 520 U.S. 351 (1997)). The New Party wanted to nominate the same candidate whom the Democrats had nominated. Although it reemphasized its holdings in *Eu* and *Tashjian* that the party has the right to choose its own "standard bearer," the Court did not consider the fusion ban a severe burden on the party's rights. Although the law prevented the party's preferred candidate from appearing alongside the party's name on the general election ballot, the party's members still had an opportunity to vote for that candidate on another party's line. Thus, the Court found that the state's interests in the fusion ban—preserving the integrity of the ballot and stabilizing the two-party system—justified this minor intrusion on the party's rights.

THE DISTRICT COURT DECISION IN *JONES*

The U.S. District Court that initially heard the challenge to California's blanket primary law relied heavily on *Timmons.* Performing the balancing test familiar to election law cases, Judge David Levi found that the blanket primary imposed "a significant but not severe burden on the [parties'] associational rights," and that the state's interest in "enhanc[ing] the democratic nature of the election process and the representativeness of elected officials" was "substantial, indeed compelling" (*California Democratic Party v. Jones*, 984 F. Supp. 1288, 1300–1301, 1303 (E.D. Cal. 1997)). On the constitutional scales, as Judge Levi viewed them, the balance appeared to tip just slightly in favor of the state, and thus the blanket primary was constitutional.

The District Court opinion in *Jones* is revealing both because, on the one hand, it appears to be the most honest attempt yet to perform the balancing test typical of election law cases, and, on the other, it shows why such "balancing" inevitably masks a threshold determination on the importance of party autonomy under the First Amendment. After pointing out that neither *Tashjian* nor *LaFollette* dealt with the precise question at issue and that the Alaska and Washington Supreme Courts had already upheld the blanket primaries against these precise constitutional challenges (see *O'Callaghan v. Alaska*, 914 P. 2d 1250 (Alaska 1996); *Heavey v. Chapman*, 93 Wash.2d 700 (1980)), the District Court proceeded to state the *Timmons* balancing test:

> When deciding whether a state election law violated First and Fourteenth Amendment associational rights, we weigh the "character and magnitude" of the burden the State's rule imposes on those rights against the interests the State contends justify that burden, and consider the extent to which the State's concerns make the burden necessary. Regulations imposing severe burdens on plaintiffs' rights must be narrowly tailored and advance a compelling state interest. Lesser burdens, however, trigger less-exacting review, and a State's "important regulatory interests" will usually be enough to justify "reasonable nondiscriminatory restrictions." (*Jones*, 984 F. Supp. at 1294, quoting *Timmons*, 520 U.S. at 358)

En route to characterizing the rights deprivation at issue, the Court then spent several pages distinguishing parties' associational rights from those of other private clubs and associations. Emphasizing the distinctive tripartite nature of the party (government-electorate-organization),[4] the Court pointed out that states have substantial regulatory authority over parties that they could not exercise over other private associations: they define the qualifications for membership (i.e., you need only be a registered voter) and can specify the form of the selection process (i.e., mandate primary elections). And the majority of states have laws that allow non–party members to choose any party's ballot on primary election day. Thus, parties' associational rights are neither absolute nor of the same character as "true," out-of-government, private associations.

While not absolute, the rights at issue were not to be dismissed out of hand by the Court. Judge Levi therefore engaged in a detailed factual inquiry—of both the probable consequences of the blanket primary for California and the experience of Washington and Alaska—to determine the severity of the burden on the parties' First Amendment rights. He found concerted party raiding to be unlikely and "benevolent cross-over voting" to hover on average at around 15 percent and rarely to change the outcome of an election. While admitting that the purpose of the blanket primary was to "wrest control" from the party and its members and thus impose a "significant" burden on their First Amendment rights, the Court found that the evidence from strong parties in Washington and the open primary states suggested that inclusion of nonmembers in the primary "will not diminish the efficacy or strength of the political parties in California by any substantial degree" (Jones, 984 F. Supp. at 1300).

Placing on one side of the scales this "significant," though "not severe," burden, Judge Levi then turned toward weighing the state's interest to discover whether it was sufficiently "important." He viewed the blanket primary as akin to other Progressive Era reforms (e.g., direct election of senators, the innovation of the primary itself, and the referendum and initiative) that sought to open up the electoral process and restore popular accountability to a system plagued by party bosses and machines. The blanket primary "enfranchised" independent voters and members of minority parties in safe districts by allowing them, without affiliating with a particular party, to participate in the critical election that determined the identity of the officeholder. An intended side-benefit of this enfranchisement would be the election of more moderate candidates who would be more representative of their districts and less beholden to party members and activists. Thus, as in Timmons and various ballot access cases, the state articulated an interest deeply rooted in the American constitutional tradition: the prevention of factionalism. Like those measures that enhanced the stabilizing forces of America's two-party system (e.g., heightened ballot access requirements for third parties and independent candidates, prohibitions on "sore loser" and fusion candidacies), so too the blanket primary sought to mute the divisive forces of even the two-party system—organizing the electorate in such a way as to produce the candidate most likely to be representative of the median voter in a given constituency. These interests in expanding participation and enhancing representation, combined with the significant and unique fact that a majority of the members of both political parties (i.e., the parties in the electorate) supported Proposition 198, were sufficiently "important," "substantial," and even "compelling" that parties could not use the First Amendment as a veto to strike down the popular will.

THE SUPREME COURT DECISION IN *JONES*

Observers may look at the lopsided (7–2) Supreme Court decision in *Jones* as somehow suggesting that this was an easy case. But not only did Judge Levi sustain the blanket primary, as did the three-judge appellate panel that adopted his opinion as their own, but four justices on Alaska's Supreme Court and nine on Washington's had also found the blanket primary constitutional within the previous five years.[5] Moreover, an eclectic group of *amici curiae* filed briefs on both sides in the case.[6] Given the Supreme Court precedents in *Tashjian, LaFollette,* and *Eu,* though, the trend in the law seemed pretty clear, and Justice Scalia's opinion for the seven-member majority treated it as such.

The Supreme Court's decision was striking for a number of reasons, however. First, its author, Justice Scalia, along with Justice O'Connor and Chief Justice Rehnquist, dissented in *Tashjian;* that is, they believed that a state had the right to close off its primary even when a party demanded the right to open it up to independents. Second, the mode of inquiry differs substantially from the obsessive balancing and hand-wringing engaged in by Judge Levi. The *Timmons* balancing test barely presents itself, reduced to a blurb that says, "[R]egulations imposing severe burdens . . . must be narrowly tailored and advance a compelling state interest" (*Jones,* 120 S. Ct. at 2412), and implying that no interest could justify the type of intrusion on party rights portended by the blanket primary.

The Supreme Court considered the same evidence of the threat to party autonomy as did the District Court; it just came to a different conclusion. Whereas the District Court focused on the primary as a highly regulated activity, the Supreme Court viewed the "candidate-selection process" as the "'basic function of a political party'" that was "adulterated" "by opening it up to persons wholly unaffiliated with the party." Whereas the District Court saw the blanket primary as causing the infrequent scenario of non–party members casting decisive primary votes, the Supreme Court viewed the blanket primary as having the intended effect of "changing the parties' message," "hijack[ing] the party," and presenting a "clear and present danger" of "having a party's nominee determined by adherents of an opposing party." The Court "could think of no heavier burden on a political party's associational freedom." "There is simply no substitute for a party's selecting its own candidates," the Court concluded (id. at 2412).

The Supreme Court found the state's interests in the blanket primary insufficiently compelling to justify the law's intrusion on the parties' associational freedoms. Those interests included: (1) producing elected officials who better represent the electorate; (2) expanding candidate debate beyond the scope of partisan concerns; (3) enfranchising independents and voters in "safe" districts; (4) promoting fairness by allowing any voter, regardless of party affiliation, the equal choice at the ballot box; (5) expanding choices by allowing any voter to vote from an array of candidates; (6) increasing voter participation; and (7) protecting their privacy by not forcing them to reveal their party affiliation. All of these interests depended on a characterization of the primary election as a public, government-sponsored, first-stage general election, a characterization the Court rejected at the outset. After all, how could increasing debate, representation, choice, or participation be a *state* interest when that increase would occur wholly within a selection process the Court (and therefore the Constitution) considers a "private" decision? Indeed, not only was there no state interest in changing the character of a primary election to produce a particular result, but it was that very feature of the blanket primary that made the law unconstitutional.

The real nail in the coffin of the blanket primary, though, came when the Court considered whether the means used by the state were appropriately tailored to achieve the ends the state listed. Given the rigor of its analysis in executing the balancing test, one cannot help but be mystified by the District Court's suggestion that "the fundamental goal of enhancing representativeness by providing all voters with a choice that is not predetermined by party members alone can only be advanced by the blanket primary" (*Jones,* 984 F. Supp at 1303). Justice Scalia prepared the appropriate response: a nonpartisan primary could achieve all of the alleged state interests without the concomitant hijacking of the party's candidate-selection process. Such a primary allows voters to choose from the entire field of candidates and winnow them down for the general election, but not "force the political parties to associate with those who do not share their political beliefs" (*Jones,* 120 S. Ct. at 2414). For the Supreme Court majority, then, the blanket primary cut out the heart of the party where the First Amendment was supposed to be its shield. Or, as Justice O'Connor put it at oral argument, the primary is "precisely the point at which the associational interest of the party is at its zenith. . . . What's left [of any associational rights], if this can stand?" (*California Democratic Party v. Jones,* No. 99–401, 2000 WL 486738 at *26; oral argument transcript).

Justice Stevens's dissent, joined by Justice Ginsburg, relied on a wholly different interpretation of the constitutional character of a party primary. Drawing on the *White Primary Cases,* the dissent considered California's primary, funded as it is by public money and conducted by state officials, the "quintessential [form] of state action" and "an election, unlike a convention or a caucus, . . . a public affair" (*Jones,* 120 S. Ct. at 2418, Stevens, J., dissenting). Party associational rights thus take on a completely different character in this context, as opposed to a case, such as *Eu,* where the parties' core First Amendment right to expression was at stake.

Moreover, for the dissent, the motivation behind the law—to encourage electoral participation—distinguished this case from *Tashjian,* where the law sought to restrict participation. "When a State acts not to limit democratic participation but to expand the ability of individuals to participate in the democratic process," the dissent argued, "it is acting not as a foe of the First Amendment but as a friend and ally" (id.). First Amendment interests fell on both scales of the constitutional balance, according to the dissent. Although it may have limited the power of party activists to control primary outcomes, the blanket primary expanded expression by allowing all voters the opportunity to pledge their support to the candidate of their choice. That same pro-participation justification underlies virtually every state's decision to intrude on party autonomy by mandating the primary as the form of nomination method or allowing some nonmembers to choose the ballot of the party of their choice on election day. Justice Stevens therefore warned, "The Court's reliance on a political party's 'right not to associate' as a basis for limiting a State's power to conduct primary elections will inevitably require it either to draw unprincipled distinctions among various primary configurations or to alter voting practices throughout the Nation in fundamental ways" (id. at 2420).

THE AFTERMATH OF *JONES*

The Supreme Court's decision in *Jones* was, in one sense, unsurprising, as it did follow a long string of decisions, such as *LaFollette, Tashjian,* and *Eu,* bolstering party associational rights. So long as the issue is neither race nor a third party's assertion of rights that might destabilize the two-party system or confuse the ballot, the Court will generally side with the political party against either a state law trying to rein it in or an individual claiming the party rules, as in *Nader,* violate his First or Fourteenth Amendment rights. But *Jones* represents the most emphatic defense yet of a robust First Amendment right of party autonomy, and in the coming years state governments may reconfigure their electoral laws to comply with it.

The Implications for Other Types of Primaries

The first question states will ask is the one Justice Stevens announced in his dissent: What about open primaries? While stating quite specifically that *Jones* "does not require us to determine the constitutionality of open primaries," Justice Scalia tried to distinguish them from blanket primaries by saying that at least under the open primary voters "affiliate" with a party— that is, confine themselves to a single party's primary ballot for the time they spend in the voting booth. That distinction may have been necessary to avoid calling into question the primary systems in most states, but when

juxtaposed alongside the broad declarations of the party's First Amendment right not to associate with those who share different beliefs, it loses
much of its force.

This line-drawing problem is both familiar to constitutional law (particularly in the election law context) and was probably unavoidable irrespec-
tive of the holding in *Jones*. Although *Jones* took one issue off the table by
affirming the right of states to mandate primaries as the format for selecting
party nominees,[7] every type of state-mandated primary still burdens a
party's associational rights to some degree. Even a closed primary, which
requires voters to declare their affiliation some time in advance of the
primary in order to vote in it, forces parties to accept voters with whom
they might not want to affiliate. For example, a law that allows voters to
change parties up until a week before the primary election infringes on the
party's right to require more than an ephemeral, one-election commitment
for membership. A judicial foray into the esoterica of the amount of time
the Constitution allows states to require for a demonstration of "authentic"
membership may be unlikely, but courts will soon need to decide whether
laws that force parties to include independents and / or non–party members in their primaries are constitutional.

The only real difference between an open primary and a blanket primary, after all, is that under a blanket primary, voters can change their
"party affiliation" as they go down the ballot, whereas the open primary
forces voters to commit to one party's entire ballot. Given the variety of
open primary systems, however, characterizing a voter's commitment to a
party's primary ballot as an "act of affiliation" presents some difficulties.
Some open primary states allow voters to change their party affiliation up
until election day; others just don't ask (or even keep records of) voters'
party affiliation and allow voters to choose whichever ballot they wish; still
others give voters all parties' ballots when they enter the voting booth and
allow them to privately cast votes on the party's ballot of their choosing.

The current stopping point—allowing a state to require open primaries,
but not blanket ones—may be arbitrary but easier to specify than others.
In addition to the Court's contention that open primaries require at least
a day's worth of affiliation, one possible rationale for choosing this stopping
point could be an empirical argument that blanket primaries make crossover voting much more likely.[8] Therefore, according to the Court's logic,
blanket primaries present a more "clear and present danger" of "having a
party's nominee determined by adherents of an opposing party" (*Jones*, S.
Ct. 120 at 2410). A stronger case might even be made for those states that
allow only independents to "cross over" on election day: One could argue
that such a system is the best marriage between the state's interest in increasing participation (i.e., allowing everyone to cast a ballot on primary

day) with the party's interests in preventing as few "outsiders" as possible from casting what might be decisive votes. Nevertheless, the language of *Jones* will be nearly impossible to get around:

> A "nonmember's desire to participate in the party's affairs is overborne by the countervailing and legitimate right of the party to determine its own membership qualifications." . . . The voter's desire to participate does not become more weighty simply because the State supports it. . . . The voter who feels himself disenfranchised should simply join the party. (Id. at 2413, quoting *Tashjian,* 479 U.S. at 215–16 n. 6)

These same arguments will apply with equal force to open primaries.

Party Consent and Initiative versus Legislative Lawmaking

Because California's voters passed the blanket primary law by popular initiative, *Jones* presented a unique opportunity for the Court to address fundamental questions regarding the relevance of the source of a party regulation and the proper entity that enjoys a party's rights. By treating this case like the state-legislated restrictions on party autonomy in *Tashjian, LaFollette,* and *Eu,* the Court chose not to take advantage of this opportunity.

The alignment of the litigants in *Jones* was perhaps as interesting as the result. All political parties (both major and minor) joined together to sue the state, with the citizen group that proposed Proposition 198, "Californians for an Open Primary," intervening on the state's behalf. Thus, the facts were quite different than in *Tashjian,* for example, where the "state" meant the party controlling the legislature and preventing the party out-of-power from organizing itself in the way it preferred. Here, the party organizations litigating the case appeared at odds with their membership, the majority of whom voted in favor of the restriction on party autonomy. The "state" meant the parties' membership, and the party organizations sought vindication of their own right of expressive association at the expense of the preference already expressed by the parties-in-the-electorate. Unlike the dissent or the District Court, the Supreme Court majority found it unimportant that a majority of voters in each party supported the blanket primary initiative. Unfortunately for the state, so did its attorney, who admitted at oral argument that "it should not make any constitutional difference whether this was passed by initiative or by the legislature" (oral argument transcript at *35).

The Court has never drawn a constitutional distinction based on the source (i.e., popular or legislative) of a restriction on First Amendment or other rights,[9] nor has it adopted a rigorous definition of what exactly the "party" is whose associational rights rise to First Amendment protection. The opinion in *Eu,* discussed above, came the closest. It, combined with

Jones, appears to stand for the proposition that the party organization, representing that aspect of the party most like a "pure" First Amendment association, is the entity that "speaks" (and therefore litigates) on behalf of the party. Unanimous support for a law, either in the legislature or at the ballot, can still be constitutionally suspect if the party organization objects.

These questions of "who" can vindicate the party's associational rights and how to know when the party has given its consent may become important in the litigation spawned by *Jones.* The shadow that *Jones* cast over the open primary systems in most states may be somewhat illusory because, like the Republican Party in *Tashjian,* many state parties actually want to open up their primaries to outsiders in order to elect more competitive candidates, and they have enacted bylaws and internal rules to that effect. The Democratic and Republican Parties rarely need judicial protection to implement their preferred nomination method. Only when its opponents or a segment of the party itself use state power to impose an undesired nomination method does a political party go to court.

State Interests in Expanding Participation and Enhancing Representation

"Political participation" is a tricky and elastic concept. For the state, the District Court, and the dissent in *Jones,* the blanket primary, quite obviously, expanded participation; that is, it maximized the opportunity for influence of every voter. After all, blanket primary voters, regardless of party affiliation, can cast two ballots to express their candidate preferences: one for their top choice among all candidates in the primary and another for their preferred candidate in the general election. But there are many different ways to define as well as increase participation. Had the Court taken the invitation of the state and found such an interest compelling, there is no reason to believe that it could only justify elements of the Progressive program such as the blanket primary.[10]

The Progressive argument overlooks the fundamental, indeed irreplaceable, role that strong parties have played as the principal institutions fostering participation not only in American democracy, but throughout the world. In particular, when parties are more easily identified with other social groupings—what political scientists call "party-group linkages" (Powell 1982)—voter turnout tends to be higher. When party differences are blurred, parties less relevant as electoral institutions, and voters less connected to parties—in other words, the intended effects of the blanket primary—participation both at the polls and in other aspects of the democracy tends to decline. The same counterintuitive effects are found in other aspects of the Progressive program, such as direct democracy. The longer the ballot, the more propositions and offices placed to a popular vote, the less likely that a given voter will actually complete the entire ballot. Indeed, the mere existence of primary elections has contributed, some argue, to lower voter turnout at the general election (Boyd 1989).

These contentions about the role of parties in fostering turnout are not uncontroversial. But neither are the Progressive arguments about the seemingly obvious pro-participation consequences of certain institutional reforms. In the constitutional balance, then, the state interest in "expanding participation" could be offered in support of all types of primary systems.

Similar arguments can be made with regard to representation. Why is a system that channels elections toward the choice of the median voter in each district necessarily more representative than one that represents the diversity and extremes of opinion throughout the state? Are "Tweedle-dee" and "Tweedle-dum" parties—that is, those that straddle the ideological middle ground instead of seeking some differentiation—more representative than ones catering to more divergent interests? Political theorists could advance good arguments for both sides. Had the Court deemed "fostering representativeness" a compelling state interest, however, a law seeking party differentiation, such as that at issue in *Tashjian,* could just as easily have latched onto that justification.

Minor and Major Parties

One of the traditionally unspoken secrets in the cases adjudicating party associational rights is that major and minor parties have a different constitutional character. Quoting Justice Powell's dissent in *LaFollette,* the District Court in *Jones* explained, "The major political parties lack the unity of purpose and cohesive membership characteristic of most private organizations. The major political parties 'have been characterized by a fluidity and overlap of philosophy and membership.' It can hardly be denied that [the parties] generally [have] been composed of various elements reflecting most of the American political spectrum" (*Jones,* 984 F. Supp. at 1296, quoting *LaFollette,* 450 U.S. at 133 (Powell, J., dissenting)). Although they recognize the differences between major and minor parties, courts have not yet assigned to them different constitutional values[11]—admitted that one is less a state actor than the other or that one has a greater or lesser claim to First or Fourteenth Amendment protection.

Along the constitutional continuum between state actors and private associations, most would agree that minor parties, clinging as they do to more narrow ideologies or group affiliations, would be closer to the association pole than would the Democrats and Republicans (although the Democrats and Republicans of today would appear more ideologically cohesive than the major parties of thirty years ago (Rohde 1991)). Historically, minor parties' role in American democracy has been to elevate issues on the national agenda that the major parties later co-opt (Rosenstone,

Behr, and Lazarus 1996, 8–9). They are, in a sense, pure First Amendment creations, existing less to gain elective office than to "express" a particular point of view, sometimes only on a single or limited number of issues. And as Christian Collet's earlier chapter (chapter 11) in this volume demonstrated, to the degree that crossover voting constitutes a threat to a party's First Amendment associational rights, that threat was orders of magnitude greater for California's minor parties, whose primaries sometimes gained twenty times more voters than under the previous closed system.

Although the Court has failed to develop a more textured constitutional analysis that accounts for the differences between major and minor parties, the cases the *Jones* opinions used in their respective arguments helped point in some directions. First, the majority opinion in *Jones,* by virtually ignoring *Timmons* and the other cases where minor parties sought ballot access or other rights, suggests quite strongly that the familiar election law balancing test rarely applies when major-party associational rights are involved. Stated a bit differently, if a court concludes that a law constitutes a "severe" intrusion on a major party's freedom of association—and after *Jones,* a severe intrusion exists whenever the law allows outsiders to "adulterate" the party's message—the inquiry ends, the law is unconstitutional. Had only the Libertarian and Peace and Freedom Parties—that is, truly ideological and "expressive" parties—challenged the blanket primary, we can only wonder whether the same result would have followed. Second, because *Timmons* reaffirms that preserving a stable two-party system is a "strong" and probably "compelling" state interest, interesting questions might arise in situations where only minor parties consider their associational rights in jeopardy. That concern should not be overblown, however. Several of the minor-party-friendly ballot access cases probably provide a ceiling on how far the state can go in intruding uniquely on minor-party rights; see, for example, *Anderson v. Celebrezze,* 460 U.S. 780, 793–94 (1983): "A burden that falls unequally on new or small political parties or on independent candidates impinges, by its very nature, on associational choices protected by the First Amendment. It discriminates against those candidates and—of particular importance—against those voters whose political preferences lie outside the existing political parties" (citing *Clements v. Fashion,* 457 U.S. 957, 963–64 (1982); plurality opinion).

CONCLUSION

This chapter has attempted to highlight the constitutional causes and consequences of the Supreme Court's decision to strike down California's blanket primary. Elsewhere one editor of this book and I have set forth the schools of thought underlying the judicial opinions in cases involving political parties more generally, and the normative concerns we think judges ought to take into account in their decisions assessing the constitutionality of laws that intrude on party autonomy specifically (Persily and Cain 2000). The U.S. Constitution, properly described by some scholars as "a constitution against parties" (Hofstadter 1969, chap. 5), is not terribly helpful when it comes to adjudicating party autonomy cases such as *California Democratic Party v. Jones.* Given their unique position and role among America's democratic institutions, the political parties do not fall neatly into the analytical boxes developed for other constitutional controversies regarding state action, equal protection, or the freedoms of expression and association. The Supreme Court's decision in *Jones,* while representing an "interpretation" of the First Amendment, also stands as the latest chapter in the chronicle of judicial development of the concept of party autonomy. Like those that preceded it, this newest one may create more questions than it answers. In upcoming decisions, we will learn whether the primary systems currently governing the majority of states are also constitutionally suspect.

NOTES

1. This description overlooks many nuances of both the state and national Democratic party rules and the Wisconsin electoral law, such as the fact that Wisconsin employed both an open presidential preference primary plus a separate caucus limited to Democratic party members. Because the delegates selected by the caucus were bound by Wisconsin law to vote according to the presidential preference primary, the Court still viewed the state law as in conflict with the rules of the Democratic National Convention. The case was thus somewhat similar to an earlier case, *Cousins v. Wigoda,* 418 U.S. 477 (1975), in which the Supreme Court held that Illinois state courts did not have the power to force the seating of delegates elected through state party procedures that violated the national party's rules.

2. For a more extensive discussion of the *White Primary Cases* that space considerations prevent here, see Issacharoff, Karlan, and Pildes (1998, 79–95).

3. Of course, *Morse* falls squarely under the first view of the *White Primary Cases* as well. After all, the whole purpose of the Voting Rights Act of 1965 was to prevent states from using "standards, practices, and procedures" with respect to voting that they had used to disenfranchise racial minorities.

4. "Unlike other private associations, at least in one of their avatars—the party in the government—the political parties are very much like the government itself. And the parties perform functions that are fairly characterized as governmental in nature, such as the nomination of candidates" (*Jones,* 984 F. Supp. at 1296).

5. If you count the lower court opinions in the Washington and Alaska cases, you get a total of twenty judges and justices who have voted to sustain blanket primary laws, and nine (seven U.S. Supreme Court Justices, plus one dissenting Alaska Supreme Court Justice and one Alaska Superior Court Judge) who have voted to strike them down.

6. The groups filing briefs on behalf of the Petitioners, the political parties challenging the initiative, included "The Northern California Committee for Party Re-

newal" (a collection of political scientists and law professors); the Republican and Democratic National Committees; the Eagle Forum Education and Legal Defense Fund (a conservative public interest organization apparently run by Phyllis Schlafly); and several Alaskan political parties. On behalf of the Respondent, the State of California, the following filed briefs supporting the blanket primary: Senators John McCain and William Brock, various political scientists and law professors, the Hispanic Republican Caucus, "Alaskan Voters for an Open Primary," California Governor Gray Davis, and the states of Washington and Alaska. The Brennan Center for Justice at the New York University School of Law (with which this author is affiliated) filed a brief on behalf of neither party, arguing that the blanket primary was constitutional as applied to the Democrats and Republicans but unconstitutional as applied to the minor political parties.

7. "We have considered it 'too plain for argument,' for example, that a State may require parties to use the primary format for selecting their nominees, in order to assure that intraparty competition is resolved in a democratic fashion" (*Jones*, 120 S. Ct. at 2407, quoting *American Party of Tex. v. White*, 415 U.S. 767, 781 (1974)).

8. Though the Court found this empirical argument persuasive, it seems to me that an equally strong argument could be made that open primaries can actually cause greater mischief-making and dilution of the parties' message. For example, in those open primary states where Democrats chose to vote in the 2000 Republican primary in order to cast a presidential ballot for John McCain, the down-ballot races were polluted by outsiders who would rather have returned to their party's ballot under a blanket primary.

9. However, Justice Stevens's dissent made a very interesting point, not raised by any of the parties or lower courts in the *Jones* litigation and thus not before the Court, distinguishing initiatives from legislation in this particular context. According to the Elections Clause of the U.S Constitution, Article I, section 4, clause 1, "The Times, Places and Manner of holding Elections for Senators and Representatives, shall be prescribed in each State by the Legislature thereof." Justice Stevens posited that a popular initiative regulating the manner of those federal elections might violate the Elections Clause (*Jones*, 120 S. Ct. at 2422–23).

10. Of course, the Progressive program of institutional reform contained several internal contradictions. Most of the reforms I describe as Progressive here were part of the Populist subset of Progressive reforms that sought to bring "power back to the people" and remove it from the corporate trusts and party machines (Persily 1997).

11. An exception to this general rule can be found in campaign finance disclosure cases where the Court has recognized unique dangers faced by minor parties if they were forced to disclose lists of their contributors. Thus, in *Buckley v. Valeo*, 424 U.S. 1, 70–75 (1976), and *Brown v. Socialist Workers '74 Campaign Comm.*, 459 U.S. 87, 95–102 (1982), the Court recognized that a fear of retribution against supporters of fringe parties justified a double standard between major and minor parties when it came to compelled disclosure of contributor lists.

REFERENCES

Boyd, Richard. 1989. "The Effects of Primaries and Statewide Races on Voter Turnout." *Journal of Politics* 51: 730–39.

California Democratic Party v. Jones, No. 99–401, 2000 WL 486738 at *26 (oral argument transcript).

Hofstadter, Richard. 1969. *The Idea of a Party System: The Rise of Legitimate Opposition in the United States, 1780–1840.* Berkeley: University of California Press.

Issacharoff, Samuel; Pamela S. Karlan; and Richard H. Pildes. 1998. *The Law of Democracy: Legal Structure of the Political Process.* New York: Foundation Press.

Key, V. O., Jr. 1964. *Politics, Parties, and Pressure Groups.* New York: Thomas Y. Crowell.

Persily, Nathaniel. 1997. "The Peculiar Geography of Direct Democracy: Why the Initiative, Referendum, and Recall Developed in the American West." *Michigan Law and Policy Review* 2: 11–41.

Persily, Nathaniel, and Bruce E. Cain. 2000. "The Legal Status of Political Parties: A Reassessment of Competing Paradigms." *Columbia Law Review* 100: 775–812.

Powell, G. Bingham, Jr. 1982. *Contemporary Democracies: Participation, Stability, and Violence.* Cambridge, MA: Harvard University Press.

Rohde, David W. 1991. *Parties and Leaders in the Postreform House.* Chicago: University of Chicago Press.

Rosenstone, Steven J.; Roy L. Behr; and Edward H. Lazarus. 1996. *Third Parties in America: Citizen Response to Major Party Failure.* Princeton, NJ: Princeton University Press.

CASES CITED

American Party of Texas v. White, 415 U.S. 767, 781 (1974).

Anderson v. Celebrezze, 460 U.S. 780 (1983).

Bullock v. Carter, 405 U.S. 134 (1972).

California Democratic Party v. Jones, 984 F. Supp. 1288 (E.D. Cal. 1997), *aff'd* 169 F. 3d 646 (9th Cir. 1999), *rev'd* 120 S. Ct. 2402 (2000).

Clements v. Fashion, 457 U.S. 957 (1982).

Cousins v. Wigoda, 418 U.S. 477 (1975).

Democratic Party of the United States v. Wisconsin ex rel. LaFollette, 450 U.S. 107 (1981).

Duke v. Massey, 87 F. 3d 1226 (11th Cir. 1996).

Eu v. San Francisco County Democratic Central Committee, 489 U.S. 214 (1989).

Heavey v. Chapman, 93 Wash. 2d 700 (1980).

Kusper v. Pontikes, 414 U.S. 51 (1973).

Morse v. Republican Party of Virginia, 517 U.S. 186 (1996).

Nader v. Schaffer, 417 F. Supp. 837 (D. Conn.), *summarily aff'd,* 429 U.S. 989 (1976).

Nixon v. Condon, 286 U.S. 73 (1932).

Nixon v. Herndon, 273 U.S. 536 (1927).

O'Callaghan v. Alaska, 914 P. 2d 1250 (Alaska 1996).

Ray v. Blair, 343 U.S. 214 (1952).

Smith v. Allwright, 321 U.S. 649 (1944).

Tashjian v. Republican Party of Connecticut, 479 U.S. 208 (1996).

Terry v. Adams, 345 U.S. 461 (1953).

Timmons v. Twin Cities Area New Party, 520 U.S. 351 (1997).

United States v. Classic, 313 U.S. 299 (1941).

CHAPTER SIXTEEN

Strategies and Rules

Lessons from the 2000 Presidential Primary

Bruce E. Cain and Megan Mullin

In this chapter, we consider some similarities between California's blanket primary debate and the controversies caused by Senator John McCain's open primary strategy for winning the 2000 Republican presidential nomination. As we have indicated throughout this book, nomination rules dictate who gets to decide a party's nominee, and by inference, the candidate's ideological appeal. Allowing independents and members of other parties to cross over and vote in a primary election changes the strategic incentives and opportunities that candidates face. In the end, the question of who gets to choose a party's nominee critically determines the types of candidates who prevail and even the definition of what a party is.

Though few, if any, could have predicted it, the 2000 Republican presidential nomination turned out to be more competitive than the Democratic race. Throughout the fall of 1999, Republican leaders were working feverishly to ensure that Texas Governor George W. Bush would win early and decisively behind a united party, while Democrats seemed to be headed toward yet another divided primary featuring a serious challenge by former Senator Bill Bradley to Vice President Al Gore. But the slated anointment of Bush got seriously derailed in New Hampshire by the unlikely and unconventional candidacy of Senator John McCain. McCain's unexpected insurgency took off in New Hampshire, faltered in South Carolina, and then miraculously revived itself in Michigan despite—or perhaps because of—the efforts of Governor Engler to assist Bush. The Bush-McCain contest finally came to an abrupt halt with Bush's decisive victory on Super Tuesday, March 7.

Various personal and political factors help to explain the McCain challenge in retrospect. McCain is a charismatic war hero with a compelling story of imprisonment and torture. Bush's inexperience as a national candidate and his overconfidence following his caucus victory in Iowa led him to be unprepared for New Hampshire. McCain skillfully parlayed the campaign finance reform issue to create an image of moderation and independence, allowing him to appeal to crossover voters and to benefit from the growing schisms within the Republican ranks between moderates and conservatives over social policy and reform issues. Add to all of this McCain's courting of reporters on the Straight Talk Express, and one has a fairly complete explanation.

This story needs only to be tweaked slightly to account for McCain's ultimate demise. In addition to his strengths, McCain had some liabilities as a candidate that became more apparent as the campaign wore on (e.g., his temper and tendency to say politically incorrect and offensive things in the company of reporters). And while he made some smart strategic choices early on, he also made some bad tactical choices after Michigan (e.g., taking on Pat Robertson and comparing Bush to President Clinton). Although this account is quite persuasive by itself, the abruptness of the change in McCain's fortunes on Super Tuesday is hard to explain without also considering the structural parameters of the 2000 primary: that is, the way in which primary rules structured the opportunities for McCain's candidacy after the Iowa caucuses and then closed them off following the Michigan primary.

Simply put, McCain benefited in the early races from the prevalence of open primary rules, and also, in several instances, from the absence of a Democratic party primary on the same day. These factors allowed McCain to be a credible candidate even though Bush was preferred by self-identified Republican voters in every primary after New Hampshire (except in McCain's home state of Arizona). By Super Tuesday, the primary rules became less favorable. The two largest states on Super Tuesday, California and New York, restricted participation to registered Republicans, creating an impossible strategic dilemma for McCain. In California, McCain's fate was sealed by the California legislature's decision to yield to pressure from the national parties and create an exception to the state's blanket primary rules for the presidential race. As a consequence, the California presidential primary proved to be a natural experiment on the differences between closed and blanket primary rules, illustrating that different rules can potentially yield different outcomes.

OPEN PRIMARIES AND THE McCAIN CANDIDACY

It would be claiming too much to say that the McCain candidacy was created by favorable nomination rules in some of the early contests, but it is not an exaggeration to say that the rules boosted his prospects considerably. To put the argument in the language of this study, McCain's candidacy was assisted by nomination rules that lowered the opportunity costs for independents and Democrats to participate in the Republican nomination process. As was discussed earlier, we can think of the rules as lying on a continuum with respect to the ease with which crossover voting can occur. As the opportunity costs increase, the level of crossover voting should diminish, and vice versa.

At the restrictive end of the continuum are the states that held closed primaries in 2000, such as New York, Connecticut, California, and Florida. In order to cast a ballot for John McCain, a Democrat or independent in these states would have had to change his or her registration before the state's deadline prior to the election (e.g., twenty-nine days in California). In addition, Democrats voting for McCain would in most closed primary states lose the opportunity to vote for Democratic candidates running for other offices down the ballot. California was a notable exception in 2000 since it retained the blanket primary rules for all races except the presidential one. Hence, a California Democrat could re-register as a Republican in order to vote for John McCain and still preserve the right to vote for any candidate for U.S. Senate, Congressional, and state offices. Perhaps for that reason (i.e., it did not preclude voters' down-ballot freedom), the McCain forces were fairly successful in getting independents and Democrats to re-register as Republicans just prior to Super Tuesday. According to registration reports prepared by the California Secretary of State, the Republican ranks in the state increased by nearly 24,000 in the month before the registration deadline for the primary election. During the same period, the overall number of registered voters in California declined by more than 44,000, due to ongoing efforts to eliminate duplicate and erroneous registrations from the voter rolls.

Next in the continuum are states that allowed the participation of independents and registered party members only—the so-called semi-open systems. These rules lowered the opportunity costs for independents but not for Democrats, thereby limiting the number of crossover Democrats. Examples of this type of system exist in Rhode Island, Utah, and Maryland.[1] Because this type of primary voting system retained a fairly substantial barrier against potential Democratic crossovers, there was generally less concern about the possible "hijacking" of the Republican presidential nomination in the states using these rules.

The last category, occupying the farthest point toward the end of the continuum, are the open primaries, in which any voter could participate in any party's primary on election day. As we can see from table 16.1, the number of open primaries on the Republican side has gradually increased from thirteen in 1980 to seventeen in 2000. On the Democratic side, it has increased from ten to thirteen in the same time period. The number of semi-open primaries has almost doubled for both Democrats and Repub-

TABLE 16.1   Voting Systems over Time
(Number of Presidential Nominating Events)

Type of Nominating Event	1980		1992		2000	
	Dem.	Rep.	Dem.	Rep.	Dem.	Rep.
Open primary	10	13	13[a]	14	13[a]	17[b]
Semi-open primary	5	5	6	8	9	10
Closed primary	15	16	16	14	14	14
Caucus or convention	20	16	16	14	15	10

SOURCE: Austin Ranney, ed., *The American Elections of 1984* (Durham, NC: Duke University Press, 1985), 330–32; Rhodes Cook, *The Race for the Presidency: Winning the 1992 Election* (Washington, DC: Congressional Quarterly Press, 1991), 3; Rhodes Cook, *The Race for the Presidency: Winning the 2000 Election* (Washington, DC: Congressional Quarterly Press, 2000), viii–ix.

[a]Texas Democrats are double-counted because they selected delegates based on an open primary and a caucus.

[b]Washington Republicans are double-counted because they selected delegates based on an open primary and a caucus.

licans over this time. In short, the trend in recent years has been for the parties to adopt more open rules to allow the participation of the growing numbers of independents and weak partisans throughout the country.

In addition to this general categorization from closed to open, there are three additional distinctions that might have affected the opportunity costs facing potential crossover voters: whether there was a Democratic primary on the same day, whether voters were required to take a pledge to participate in the Republican primary only, and the timing of the state's registration deadline. In the first case, asymmetric opportunity situations arose where state parties chose different dates for their primary elections. In the states with an open Republican primary and no concurrent Democratic primary, such as South Carolina and Michigan, the absence of a Democratic primary lowered the opportunity costs for Democrats who wanted to vote in the Republican primary. Table 16.2 breaks down the distribution of states with concurrent and nonconcurrent Democratic contests. It shows clearly the accidental vulnerability of the Republicans to this problem in 2000. Five Republican primary states had the potentially lethal combination of open primaries that were not concurrent with Democratic contests. Delegates selected under these circumstances totaled more than 9 percent of the total delegates to the Republican convention. Four of these states, with nearly 8 percent of the national Republican delegate total, held their primaries during February, creating the possibility that a candidate with limited support from party members could lead the field going into Super Tuesday.

The asymmetric opportunities faced by the parties in the 2000 presi-

TABLE 16.2   Correspondence of 2000 Republican and Democratic Presidential Nominating Events

Type of Republican Nominating Event	Democratic Nominating Event Held on Different Day		Democratic Nominating Event Held on Same Day	
	Events	Delegates	Events	Delegates
Open primary	5[a]	191 9.2%	12	598 29.0%
Semi-open primary	0	0 0.0%	10	316 15.3%
Closed primary	2	42 2.0%	12	640 31.0%
Caucus	4	90 4.4%	6	147 7.1%
TOTALS[b]	11	323 15.6%	40	1,701 82.4%

SOURCE: Rhodes Cook, *The Race for the Presidency: Winning the 2000 Election* (Washington, DC: Congressional Quarterly Press, 2000), viii–ix.

NOTE: Table reports number of Republican nominating events and number and percentage of delegates selected.

[a]Virginia Republicans required voters to sign a pledge not to participate in another party's nominating process.

[b]Washington Republicans are double-counted because they selected delegates based on an open primary and a caucus. Nominating events in the District of Columbia and the U.S. territories are not included here.

dential primary are strikingly similar to the asymmetric competition issue in the blanket primary. In both cases, the lack of a contest in one party creates an incentive for some voters to cross over and participate in the other party's primary. In the blanket primary case, there might formally be an election in the Democratic primary, but if in fact there is no real contest (i.e., one candidate is a sure winner), the race can amount to a non-election, and Democrats have a reason to vote in the Republican contest. In the 2000 presidential primary, both types of asymmetry could be found: a general lack of competition in all Democratic primaries after New Hampshire due to the early collapse of the Bradley challenge, and also, in some states, the non-concurrence of the Democratic and Republican contests. The dual lack of a formal nominating event and of real competition between Bradley and Gore increased Democratic crossover voting into Republican primaries up until the Republican nomination race was finally decided on Super Tuesday.

The second potentially important distinction is whether voters were required to promise to participate in the Republican primary only. A pledge system raised the opportunity costs for would-be crossover Democrats and independents who might have wanted to influence both parties' nomination processes. Since participation in non-concurrent, privately run primaries cannot easily be monitored to prevent an individual voter from taking part in both parties' contests, Virginia's Republican party used a pledge to close its primary to potential Democratic voters. Virginia voters attempting to vote in the Republican contest had to sign a statement affirming, "I, the undersigned, state that I do not intend to participate in the nominating process of any other party than the Republican Party." Going into the Virginia election, the media reported that McCain forces were expressing concern that the Republican pledge would "discourage the kind of voters—independents and Democrats—who have been voting for John McCain,"[2] but it is hard to tell from the results how much of an impact the pledge might have had. The percentages of independents and Democrats participating in the Virginia Republican primary were 29 percent and 8 percent, respectively. This was comparable to the participation of these groups in South Carolina (30 percent independent and 9 percent Democratic), but considerably less than in Michigan (35 percent independent and 17 percent Democratic). Like Virginia, both of these states had open primaries with no Democratic contests on the same day. Thus, without good polling data, we cannot estimate the impact of the Virginia pledge. The most we can say is that the pledge might have prevented a high Democratic crossover scenario in Virginia such as occurred in Michigan, but it is also quite possible that Virginia crossover voting would have occurred at a lower rate anyway, as it did in South Carolina.

Finally, variation across states in the closing date for registering to vote before the primary may have affected the degree of crossover voting and hence had an impact on McCain's candidacy. Most states have a deadline for registering to vote and changing party affiliation that falls twenty to thirty days before the primary.[3] In some states, however, the deadline is later—in Connecticut, for example, the cutoff date is one day before the election. Thus, while Connecticut has a closed primary, the opportunity costs for crossing over are considerably lower than in states with closed primaries and earlier registration deadlines. While voters can participate in only one party's primary, they can wait until the day before the election to decide which primary they prefer. In contrast with California or New York, Connecticut Democrats and independents who were inspired by McCain's Michigan victory were able to change their party registration in order to participate in their state's closed Republican contest. While changes in party affiliation are not tracked at the state level, reports indicate that thousands of voters crossed over to the Republican party in the final days before the primary (Keating and Daly 2000). And exit polls suggest that it might have made the difference for McCain: in his three-point victory over Bush, 26 percent of those who voted identified themselves as independents, and they overwhelmingly supported McCain (69 percent to 25 percent).

THE FORTUITY OF THE SCHEDULE

The full story of the structural factors behind McCain's strong challenge requires an appreciation of the sequencing of the primaries as well. In the period from January 24 (the date of the Alaska and Iowa caucuses) to March 7, 2000 (the date of Super Tuesday), there were twenty-four Republican presidential nominating events in the states. As we can see in table 16.3, almost half the delegates to the Republican national convention were selected during this period. By comparison, there were only eighteen Democratic state events including Super Tuesday, and only two (New Hampshire and Iowa) in the critical early period from January 24 to February 29. In a year when presidential primary elections were more front-loaded than ever, the Republicans were more front-loaded than the Democrats. That meant that they were more vulnerable to early strategic biases.

Also, since there were only two Democratic events in this early period, all but two of the Republican primaries and caucuses during this time were non-concurrent with a Democratic event. Of the seven Republican primaries held in the pre–Super Tuesday period, the only two with closed rules were Delaware and McCain's home state of Arizona, a state he was sure to win as the favorite son. All the other primaries used semi-open (i.e., New Hampshire) or open rules. This was ideally designed for McCain's crossover appeal. The better-organized candidate with support from the party establishment was likely to do better in the caucus states, but the candidate with crossover appeal was given a fortuitous break in the sense that four of the five Republican open primaries without concurrent Democratic events took place before Super Tuesday. The redeeming grace for George Bush in the first period was that there were four state caucuses as well.

However, with respect to the rules, John McCain was not so fortunate in the Super Tuesday events. First, all of the primaries featured formal contests for both party nominations. Hence, there was an election on the Democratic side that could potentially keep the Democrats home. In reality, of course, the Bradley campaign was all but finished at that point, and one might say that those contests therefore were informally asymmetric—in other words, they were formally contested on the Democratic side but not informally competitive. Secondly, three of the contests, including the two largest (California with 162 delegates and New York with 101), were closed. We will consider California in some detail later, but clearly the legislature's decision to switch from blanket to closed rules for the presidential primary made an enormous strategic difference for the McCain campaign. Had the state retained the blanket rules for the presidential primary, McCain could

TABLE 16.3 2000 Republican Nominating Season

Type of Republican Nominating Event	Iowa to Michigan (January 24 to February 22)		Post-Michigan and Super Tuesday (February 29 to March 7)		Post-Super Tuesday (March 9 to June 6)		Totals	
	Events	Delegates	Events	Delegates	Events	Delegates	Events	Delegates
Open primary	2	95 / 4.6%	6	238 / 11.5%	9	456 / 22.1%	17	789 / 38.2%
Semi-open primary	1	17 / 0.8%	4	96 / 4.6%	5	203 / 9.8%	10	316 / 15.3%
Closed primary	2	42 / 2.0%	3	288 / 13.9%	9	352 / 17.0%	14	682 / 33.0%
Caucus	3	62 / 3.0%	3	78 / 3.8%	4	97 / 4.7%	10	237 / 11.5%
TOTALS[a]	8	216 / 10.5%	16	700 / 33.9%	27	1,108 / 53.7%	51	2,024 / 98.0%

SOURCE: Rhodes Cook, The Race for the Presidency: Winning the 2000 Election (Washington, DC: Congressional Quarterly Press, 2000), viii–ix.

NOTE: Table reports number of nominating events and number and percentage of delegates selected.

[a]Washington Republicans are double-counted because they selected delegates based on an open primary and a caucus. Nominating events in the District of Columbia and the U.S. territories are not included here.

have concentrated on attracting Democrats and independent crossover votes, as he had done in the earlier primaries. But as we shall see shortly, the necessities of the rules dictated that McCain win registered Republicans if he wanted to stay in the hunt for the nomination. This presented him with a difficult and ultimately insoluble strategic dilemma. To appeal to the more moderate crossovers in the early primaries, he needed to continue to talk about campaign finance reform and to hedge his position on abortion. To win over the registered Republicans in the closed primaries that occurred later, he needed to put his conservative credentials forward.

Hence the combination of Bush's advantage among Republican registered voters and party identifiers and the shifting bias of the rules after the early primaries meant that McCain's "open arms" appeal was doomed. As table 16.4 indicates, McCain could not clearly win a majority of self-identified Republicans in any pre–Super Tuesday primary outside his home state of Arizona (taking the GOP voters 56 percent to 41 percent despite the opposition of the state's Republican Governor). The New Hampshire result varies somewhat by poll, but none of the other states are even close. Bush took the GOP vote in Delaware, Michigan, Virginia, and South Carolina by margins of over forty points. By contrast, McCain took a majority of independents in all five states and of Democrats in the three where it was permitted. Going into Super Tuesday, the conservative columnist Bob Novak exclaimed, "I have never seen a front-runner [McCain] who starts off getting murdered in his own party two-to-one nationally in state after state. And usually you start off with your own support, and then you build the others. He has the other people's support."[4]

The same pattern held in the Super Tuesday states. Bush won a majority of the GOP vote in every state, with the possible exception of Massachusetts, where exit polls indicate that Republicans were divided between Bush (49 percent) and McCain (48 percent). Even in Connecticut, where McCain won the closed primary, self-identified Republicans preferred Bush to McCain 56 percent to 39 percent. McCain won the majority of Democrats in the four states (Georgia, Missouri, Ohio, and Vermont) where the primary was open, and only in Georgia did he lose among self-identified independents.

In the pre–Super Tuesday contests, self-identified Democratic crossovers varied from a high of 17 percent in Michigan to 2 percent in Arizona and Delaware. The effect of the rules on Democratic crossovers is quite clear. In the closed states, a negligible 2 percent of voters identified themselves as Democrats, and in New Hampshire, with its dual contest, semi-open primary, the crossover vote was 4 percent. But in the open primary states that held only one contest, between 8 percent and 17 percent of primary voters crossed over from the Democratic party. On Super Tuesday, Democratic crossovers in the four open states, all of which held dual primaries,

TABLE 16.4 Early and Mid-Season Republican Primary Vote Choice, by Party Self-Identification

Republican Primary	Primary Type	Republicans			Independents			Democrats		
		Percentage of Voters	Bush	McCain	Percentage of Voters	Bush	McCain	Percentage of Voters	Bush	McCain
New Hampshire (*January 24*)	Semi-open	53%	42%	37%	41%	19%	61%	4%	10%	80%
Delaware (*February 8*)	Closed	80	56	20	18	28	42	2	—	—
South Carolina (*February 19*)	Open	61	69	26	30	34	60	9	18	79
Arizona (*February 22*)	Closed	80	41	56	18	20	72	2	—	—
Michigan (*February 22*)	Open	48	66	29	35	26	67	17	10	82
Virginia (*February 29*)	Open	63	69	28	29	31	64	8	11	87
California (*March 7*)	Closed	82	63	32	16	41	50	—	—	—
Connecticut (*March 7*)	Closed	72	56	39	26	25	69	—	—	—
Georgia (*March 7*)	Open	63	77	18	29	53	40	8	45	54
Maine (*March 7*)	Semi-open	66	56	39	31	33	62	—	—	—
Maryland (*March 7*)	Semi-open	69	66	27	28	33	59	—	—	—
Massachusetts (*March 7*)	Semi-open	38	49	48	62	21	76	—	—	—
Missouri (*March 7*)	Open	61	72	21	29	43	49	10	21	76
New York (*March 7*)	Closed	74	57	38	23	33	58	—	—	—
Ohio (*March 7*)	Open	69	68	28	24	36	56	7	28	68
Rhode Island (*March 7*)	Semi-open	38	55	42	62	24	73	—	—	—
Vermont (*March 7*)	Open	50	51	44	42	23	74	8	19	81

SOURCE: Exit polls conducted for various media, compiled by *Hotline* (March 1 and 9, 2000).

ranged between 7 percent and 10 percent. In several states during the early and mid-season, registered, self-identified Republican voters did not make up a majority of the Republican primary electorate. In Michigan, Massachusetts, and Rhode Island, independents and Democrats turned out in greater numbers than Republicans did, and in Vermont the electorate was evenly split between GOP and non-GOP voters.

No doubt many of the crossover voters were sincere (as defined in earlier chapters), while others, as we shall see shortly, may have been hedgers or raiders. However, the important point for the moment is not so much the distinction among the types of crossover voters as it is the following: in some states, the rules made it possible for a candidate to win the delegates of that state even though the candidate did not have the support of self-identified party supporters. McCain supporters argued that this was a good thing, demonstrating that favorable rules allowed the selection of a candidate who could appeal to non–party members and win in November. By contrast, Bush loyalists and party regulars saw this a "hijacking" of the Republican nomination by non-party voters.

Clearly, this controversy is strongly related to the issues raised by the blanket primary case in California. Under blanket rules, it was theoretically possible, and empirically inevitable, that at some point non–party members would swamp the primary of the other side and make the selection for that party. Whether this is a good or bad thing depends upon how one views and defines a party (Cain and Persily 2000). If a party is a private association of like-minded individuals, then opening the selection to any and all is a violation of the party members' rights, and leads to the unsatisfactory possibility of the party being saddled with a candidate who is not majority-preferred by party affiliates. On the other hand, if one views parties as state-funded vehicles for election purposes, then there is no violation of party member rights. It is simply a question of producing viable candidates on both sides who can run a competitive election in November.

MICHIGAN: THE CASE OF THE HIJACKED ELECTION?

The normative issues surrounding nomination rules and the definition of a political party are most dramatically illustrated by the 2000 Michigan primary contest. Even if all the allegations surrounding this remarkable contest were untrue, the fact that these suspicions arose at all raises important questions about the perceived legitimacy of rules that are vulnerable to strategic voting behavior. American constitutional law maintains a distinction between corruption and the appearance of corruption, and recognizes that states can have a compelling interest to prevent both. Perhaps there is a parallel distinction between the actual manipulability of an electoral system and its perceived vulnerability to manipulation that plays a role in determining the legitimacy of a party's nominee. The key question is, Perceived by whom: by party regulars or by the electorate as a whole? The answer to this question depends on one's view of the party. If it is a private association, its membership of party regulars should be able to have strong confidence that the party's nomination process is protected from manipulation by nonmembers. If the party is an instrument of the state, then the goal should be maximizing participation, even if the resulting process might be perceived as vulnerable to manipulation. The Michigan primary provides a good example of an electoral outcome that is widely perceived as illegitimate by party regulars yet accepted by the wider public, in reflection of their conflicting interpretations of the role of a political party.

The 2000 Michigan GOP primary fell three days following the bitter South Carolina primary held on February 19. Having lost in New Hampshire, Bush pulled out the stops and won an acrimonious battle with McCain 53 percent to 42 percent. McCain gave what was widely regarded as a bitter concession speech, angered by Bush's negative advertising and irritated by Bush's claim to be a reformer with a record. Said McCain, "If he's a reformer, I'm an astronaut" (Christoff and Montemurri 2000, 1A). One of the keys to Bush's success in South Carolina had been his strong support from the religious right, which, rightly or wrongly, was attributed in part to Bush's visit to Bob Jones University. For Bush, the visit had been intended to reassure the right that he stood with them on abortion and other social issues. But as the press uncovered more information about the university, it became apparent that being identified with a university that was associated with prohibitions on interracial dating and with anti-Semitic and anti-Catholic statements would be a liability. The implication of this for the Michigan primary was that Bush might have won South Carolina, but he simultaneously weakened his prospects in Michigan among the state's blue-collar, white ethnic voters. Crossovers from this group had formed the so-called Reagan Democrats in the eighties. Bush, when criticized for his visit to Bob Jones, responded, "Tell the people that are nervous about me to think about Ronald Reagan. He went to Bob Jones University, and he picked up huge ethnic Catholic votes, and I'm going to as well."[5] However, Bush's ties with Bob Jones and the Christian right so bothered Representative Peter King of New York that less than twenty-four hours after the South Carolina primary, he announced that he was switching his allegiance from Bush to McCain (Archibold 2000).

Michigan was supposed to be a "firewall" for Bush that would contain the McCain insurrection. Governor John Engler, a strong Bush supporter, had supported making the primary open and early, thinking that the moderate crossover voters would protect Bush from challenges by more conservative candidates such as Gary Bauer, Alan Keyes, Steve Forbes, Orrin Hatch, and Dan Quayle. Illustrating the law of unintended consequences,

Engler did not foresee that Bush would be outflanked by McCain on the left, and that the very conditions that he thought would favor Bush would in the end hurt him. A curious and distinctive aspect of the Michigan contest was that Engler himself had become a factor in at least some of the Democratic voters' minds. It was reported that ministers in Detroit's African-American churches were urging their congregations to vote for McCain as an act of "political revenge" against Engler (Dixon and Montemurri 2000). Geoffrey Fieger, the 1998 Democratic gubernatorial nominee and former attorney for assisted-suicide advocate Jack Kevorkian, ran a radio ad urging Democrats to "come out and vote against" Engler (Mayes 2000). And the Detroit chapter of the NAACP and state Representative LaMar Lemmons III helped to set up an unofficial campaign for McCain called "Detroiters Out to Get Even with Governor Engler." Said Lemmons, "In doing so, we can deliver the Governor a political spanking for the mischief he has wrought," such as the takeover of the Detroit schools (Martinez 2000, A1). McCain himself did not encourage this: "If someone is voting for me because of any personal vendetta and for any other reason than they think I'm going to be the best President, . . . I do not want their votes," he asserted (Dixon and Montemurri 2000, A1). These activities by Detroit-area Democrats amounted to an attempt to localize the presidential race and turn it into a referendum on the state's Governor.

Some of the voters may have responded to this effort. "I would drop my pants in the middle of Times Square if I thought it would hurt Engler," declared a Detroit private investigator and self-professed "old liberal" who said he voted for McCain (Flesher 2000a, n.p.). A retired teacher who planned to vote Democratic in the fall, even though he voted for McCain in the primary, said, "Number 1, I don't want to see George W. run away with it. Number 2, I don't like the fact that our Governor has been such a cheerleader for George W." (Martinez 2000, A1). In all, about 15 percent of voters said that Engler had a great deal of influence on their vote, and of those, 70 percent supported McCain (Flesher 2000a).

At the same time, other Democratic voters were clearly sincere McCain supporters. In the words of one unionist, "I'm a UAW. They tell us to vote for the Democrats. . . . But I like McCain. . . . I like how he fights in Congress and he doesn't back down . . . and I don't like the way things are going in politics" (Martinez 2000, A1). Asked to characterize the motives of the Democratic crossovers, Bill Ballenger, publisher of the *Inside Michigan Politics* newsletter, stated, "I don't think that they're a monolithic group. There was a diversity of motives, sometimes overlapping" (Flesher 2000b, n.p.).

The strategies of the Democratic groups gave rise to the counterstrategies of the Bush campaign. Turning attack to advantage, Bush and his supporters prominently played up the possibility of a hostile takeover of the party, hoping that this would rally the troops on election day. Two days before the election, Governor Engler stated on national TV, "McCain has absolutely courted, fraternized with some of the worst people, politically speaking—they are sworn foes; he had tried to bring them in to influence the result."[6] In a letter to Republicans, Engler wrote, "Your help is urgently needed because some of Al Gore's leading supporters here in Michigan . . . plan to interfere with our February 22 primary" (Hoffman 2000, n.p.). Ironically, the man who initially intended the open primary as a firewall for his friend George Bush told CNN that the key to the primary was "getting the Republican support that's so overwhelming for George Bush to the polls to make sure that nothing untoward happens on election day by the intervention of non-Republicans who cast votes in this open primary."[7] Even for Democrats, the strategy of promoting Democratic crossovers for McCain was problematic. As several leaders pointed out, McCain could actually have been the harder candidate to defeat in a November election, so promoting his candidacy in order to stop Bush could have been risky in the long run.

As it turned out, exit polls suggested that about 17 percent of the vote in the GOP primary came from self-identified Democrats, and that McCain got over 80 percent of their votes. After the dust settled, the question of whether the large crossover vote was a good thing for the Republican party was much discussed. Bush himself had to tread a fine line in post-election interviews since he had lost the election due to the Democratic and independent voters but planned to campaign for their votes in the fall: "I think when I am the nominee, you are going to find I attract a lot of new faces . . . a lot of Democrats. There's a difference between attracting people who are going to stay with you throughout the entire race and people who come into our primary to make a statement and then intend to support Al Gore in the general election."[8] But Bush and Engler aside, there were many observers who felt that party nominations should be made by party members, not outsiders, and should be less vulnerable to potential hijackings. In the words of a *Detroit News* editorial, "This ought to spell the end of the good-government idea that primaries should be open to all." Arguing that mischief was not the primary problem, the paper criticized the concept of open primaries: "While they demonstrate a candidate's ability to reach across party lines, they also dilute the meaning and value of political parties. Parties exist to organize voters around an identifiable philosophy, thus offering voters real choices in the general election. Open primaries weaken this important process" ("The Non-Primary Primary" 2000, A14).

The Michigan experience very much parallels the debate that Californians had in 1996 when Proposition 198, the blanket primary law, was placed on the ballot, and in 1997, when the blanket primary was challenged in court. Engler and the Republican-controlled legislature had changed the rules from closed to open in 1995, hoping that it would paint the GOP as the party of inclusion (Hornbeck and Cain 2000). Similarly, as we have seen, Tom Campbell and his supporters saw the blanket primary as the technical solution to the California Republican party's problem of nominating extremist candidates. The trouble in each instance is that one cannot always and accurately foresee who will benefit from rule changes, and vulnerability to mischief, even when it does not concern most voters, tends to undermine confidence in the party's choices. The Democrats added to Engler's troubles by deciding to hold a caucus on another date instead of a simultaneous primary, and by encouraging strategic behavior of various forms. In this way, the Michigan Republicans got more than they had bargained for when they changed the rules. On the other hand, Michigan had an election that was highly competitive and brought out many new voters. Said Ballenger, "I would argue that it's the most exciting primary we've seen in a long time in Michigan" (Hoffman 2000, n.p.). Once Bush was assured of the Republican nomination, even Engler expressed satisfaction with the large turnout in the Michigan primary and predicted that it would help the GOP in the fall (Weeks 2000a).

Again, the question we return to is whether the primary exists for the party or for the state. McCain embraced the open primary goals of inclusion and high turnout, urging "independents, Democrats, libertarians, vegetarians" all to exercise their opportunity to vote in open Republican primaries. In a campaign flyer, he reminded Michigan Democrats that they would still be able to participate in their party's caucuses even after voting in the Republican primary (Weeks 2000b). Many non-Republicans enjoyed the opportunity to participate in the tight race, and felt it was their right to cast a meaningful vote in this stage of the presidential selection process. Ironically, it was Engler who best expressed the weakness of the open primary. In accusing McCain of "renting Democrats" for the primary and "party-borrowing," not party-building (Weeks 2000c, A15), he pointed out the vulnerability of the system to manipulation by non–party members. In Michigan, the result was a primary outcome that was perceived as illegitimate by an individual who had been one of the system's strongest supporters.

CALIFORNIA IN 2000: A NEW EXPERIMENT

California added a new twist to the blanket primary story in 2000. With the passage of Proposition 198, the state found itself in violation of the national Democratic and Republican party rules that prohibited the seating of delegates chosen under the blanket primary system. Needing an exception to the state's blanket primary requirement, Governor Pete Wilson and the state legislature placed Proposition 3 on the November 1998 ballot, proposing that the presidential primary vote in California be conducted under the old, closed-primary rules. The Republican state party, in particular, made it clear in its public statements that it would have no choice if Proposition 3 failed but to adopt a caucus or convention system to select convention delegates (Purdum 1998). Despite the near absence of formal opposition to the initiative, little or no money or effort was spent that year to help Proposition 3, and it failed 46 percent to 54 percent.

This put the legislature back in the quandary it had tried to avoid. Two proposals emerged. One, favored by the Secretary of State Bill Jones, would code the ballots so that voters could still choose any candidate they wanted, but only the votes of party registrants would count toward the selection of delegates. In effect, there would be two counts: a blanket beauty contest and a closed delegate vote. The other proposal, put forward by Senate President Pro Tem John Burton, would have created two separate ballots, one closed and the other a blanket. The legislature voted out the Burton bill (on a 37–0 vote in the Senate and a 66–5 vote in the Assembly), but Democratic Governor Gray Davis subsequently vetoed the bill, arguing that it invited a lawsuit that he "did not want to defend" ("Legislation on Primary" 1999, A21). The Senate came back with the Jones proposal, and the Governor signed that (Gunnison 1999, A22).

Returning the presidential race to closed rules had several implications. First, as suggested earlier, it altered the incentives for those running in the California primary. No longer did it make sense to court independent and crossover voters, since their votes would only be for show and not count toward the actual delegate choice. Second, the fact that there would be two counts raised the specter of two different outcomes: a winner under the closed rules might not necessarily be a winner under the blanket rules. In particular, if McCain won the blanket beauty contest and Bush the delegates, then it was possible that this might lead to a huge credentials fight at the Republican convention.

Early polling in February indicated that a split decision was possible. Virtually every poll had Bush leading McCain by wide, double-digit margins among the registered Republicans, but the two were in a very competitive race for the blanket beauty vote. For instance, a Zogby/Reuters/MSNBC poll conducted between February 29 and March 2 had Bush leading McCain 48 percent to 30 percent in the closed poll, but only 26 percent to 24 percent in the blanket beauty vote. Even a week later, after McCain had changed strategies and moved to the right, Zogby/Reuters/MSNBC still had Bush leading among registered GOP voters 54 percent to 26 percent and the blanket race at 26 percent to 20 percent.

Faced with the reality that the closed primary changed his prospects drastically, McCain altered his strategy after Michigan. Although his supporters undertook a hurried registration effort to convince Democrats and independents to re-register as Republicans in order to have their votes count, it was destined to be futile. In a state with over 14 million registered voters, their goal of 30,000 switches could only be a drop in the bucket. The McCain campaign fell short of its goal, but the 20,000-plus new voters it did recruit added to the ranks of Republicans measurably and strengthened McCain's case that the Republican party could fortify its position by reaching out to non-party voters. As Assembly Republican leader Scott Baugh explained, the GOP in the 1990s picked up only 10 percent of newly registered voters, but in the month before California registration closed for the 2000 primary, the party captured 43 percent (Bunis 2000). If California had allowed voter registrations in the month before the March primary, as Connecticut did, then perhaps this strategy would have been more rewarding for McCain.

In addition to re-registering Democrats and independents, the other possibility for McCain was to try to win over registered Republicans by emphasizing his conservative credentials. Evidence from the Field Poll indicates why this was important. According to a poll taken between February 22 and 27, 40 percent of California Republicans called themselves strongly conservative, and they preferred Bush 64 percent to 16 percent. Another 23 percent regarded themselves as moderately conservative, and they favored Bush 44 percent to 33 percent. Only the middle-of-the-roaders (37 percent of the registered Republicans) went for McCain (36 percent to 33 percent). Clearly, he could only win the Republican primary by convincing conservatives that he was one of them, but how could he do this after fighting with the Christian right in South Carolina and Virginia, raising questions about his commitment to abortion in interviews, and differing from the tax-cut line that fiscal conservatives in Congress were espousing? Add to this the fact that members of the Christian right adamantly believed that campaign finance reform would hurt their political influence, and it was clear that winning back the right would be no easy task for John McCain.

Nonetheless, McCain did try. A day after the Michigan primary, which he won with heavy support from independents and Democrats, McCain declared in a speech to the Seattle Rotary Club, "I am a Reagan Republican. . . . Have no doubt about that" (Connelly 2000, A1). Unfortunately, the polls indicated that the right did have doubts. McCain did not help matters a few days later when he told California reporters on his bus that Pat Robertson and Jerry Falwell were "agents of intolerance" and "forces of evil." Among other things, the effect was to step on the message that he was a conservative. In addition, polling data revealed that McCain had better chances in New York than California, because of the presence of large numbers of ethnic white Catholics who were still angry at Bush for the Bob Jones University visit. This caused the McCain campaign to rethink its previous intention to spend a lot of time campaigning in California, almost to the point of canceling out on the one scheduled debate in Los Angeles. What time he did spend in the state was confined largely to the Central Valley and Southern California, trolling for conservative Republicans rather than for moderates in the Bay Area and coastal regions.

In other words, the shift in primary rules and opportunities caused a shift in strategies. No longer able to rely on crossover Democrats and independents, McCain was forced to try to prove his conservative credentials to registered Republicans. This caused him to adopt a politically schizophrenic approach, displaying his moderate reformist side in some moments and his conservative side in others. In the end, Bush won the beauty contest 53 percent to 43 percent and the closed race 60 percent to 35 percent. McCain received 15 percent of the Democratic partisan vote as compared to 7 percent for Bush, and 28 percent of the independents as compared to 21 percent for Bush. In a *Los Angeles Times* exit poll, when asked whether everyone's vote should count in the blanket primary or only the votes of registered members, respondents favored the former 70 percent to 30 percent.[9] As it turned out, had the public received its wish and nothing else changed, the blanket primary rule would have changed the margin but not the outcome. What we cannot know, however, is the likelihood of the counterfactual possibility that had the blanket vote been for real, there could have been enough crossover voting to alter the final vote as well.

CONCLUSION

The themes pursued in this book were echoed in the controversies of the 2000 presidential primary. As more states opened their primaries to non–party members, they discovered the mixed blessings such innovations can bring. The party that takes in large numbers of crossover voters can increase interest in its nominee and fashion appeals that might work in November. At the same time, there is the danger that a party can be swamped by crossover voters with very different preferences than the party regulars. To the Court, this is a constitutional question: should the party be required to give its party label to nominees who are not majority-preferred by party members? Writing for the majority in *California Democratic Party v. Jones,* Justice Scalia argued that this amounted to forced association. To the political scientist, vulnerability to strategic behavior is an important institutional design problem. The best system would be one that faithfully reflects the sincere preferences of voters. Systems that increase incentives to be insincere are problematic. While data from the blanket primary experience in California suggests that "raiders" (i.e., those who vote for the weakest candidate on the other side in order to improve the general election chances for their own party) make up less than 5 percent of the total electorate, the 2000 Michigan primary reminds us that we cannot always distinguish between raiding and hedging (i.e., crossing over to vote for one's favorite candidate in the opposing primary even while preferring a candidate in one's own party), and that both behaviors, if publicized, can undermine an election's legitimacy. Finally, California's experience with the two-count system in the March 7 primary demonstrates that different rules can yield very different results—if not changing the winner, then at least changing the margin of victory. If nothing else, California's experiment proves that rules do matter.

NOTES

1. This was the type of system the Supreme Court considered in *Tashjian v. Republican Party of Connecticut.*

2. Bill Plante on *The Early Show*, CBS, February 29, 2000, quoted in *Hotline*, February 29, 2000.

3. States that do not have party registration and allow voters to participate in either party's nominating process are considered here to have an open primary system, and states that allow independents to register as members of a party at the polling place are considered to have a semi-open system.

4. Bob Novak on *The Capital Gang*, CNN, February 26, 2000, quoted in *Hotline*, February 28, 2000.

5. George W. Bush on *Late Edition*, CNN, February 20, 2000, quoted in *Hotline*, February 21, 2000.

6. John Engler on *Face the Nation*, CBS, February 20, 2000, quoted in *Hotline*, February 20, 2000.

7. John Engler on CNN, February 19, 2000, quoted in *Hotline*, February 21, 2000.

8. George W. Bush on *Today*, NBC, February 23, 2000, quoted in *Hotline*, February 23, 2000.

9. See exit poll results at http://www.latimes.com/news/timespoll/pdf/439grph2.pdf.

REFERENCES

Archibold, Randal C. 2000. "New York Lawmaker Switches to McCain." *New York Times*, February 21, A12.

Bunis, Dena. 2000. "Bradley, McCain Vie for O. C. Vote." *Orange County Register*, February 29, A1.

Christoff, Chris, and Patricia Montemurri. 2000. "GOP Takes Brawl to Michigan Streets." *Detroit Free Press*, February 21, 1A.

Connelly, Joel. 2000. "State Gives McCain Big Smile." *Seattle Post-Intelligencer*, February 24, A1.

Dixon, Jennifer, and Patricia Montemurri. 2000. "Preacher Calls for Spiteful Turnout." *Detroit Free Press*, February 21, A1.

Flesher, John. 2000a. "Heavy Democratic, Independent Turnout Boosts McCain." Associated Press wire, February 22, AM cycle.

———. 2000b. "Multiple Motives for Democrats, Independents Who Backed McCain." Associated Press wire, February 23, BC (both cycles).

Gunnison, Robert B. 1999. "Davis Signs Bill to Permit Delegate Voting in Primary." *San Francisco Chronicle*, May 5, A22.

Hoffman, Kathy Barks. 2000. "Michigan Primary a Vital Contest for GOP Candidates." Associated Press wire, February 19, AM cycle.

Hornbeck, Mark, and Charlie Cain. 2000. "History: GOP Let Dems Crash Primary." *Detroit News*, February 24, A4.

Keating, Christopher, and Matthew Daly. 2000. "McCain Overcomes Bush, and the Odds, in State." *Hartford Courant*, March 8, A1.

"Legislation on Primary Has Defect, Davis Says." 1999. *San Francisco Chronicle*, April 9, A21.

Martinez, Gebe. 2000. "Blacks Use Vote to Go After Engler." *Detroit News*, February 18, A1.

Mayes, Kris. 2000. "Candidates Sling Mud in Michigan." *Arizona Republic*, February 21, A1.

"The Non-Primary Primary." 2000. *Detroit News*, February 24, A14.

Persily, Nathaniel, and Bruce E. Cain. 2000. "The Legal Status of Political Parties: A Reassessment of Competing Paradigms." *Columbia Law Review* 100, no. 3: 775–812.

Purdum, Todd S. 1998. "Quest for Presidential Primary Clout May Hinge on Passage of Obscure Ballot Measure." *New York Times*, November 24, A12.

Weeks, George. 2000a. "In Hindsight, Primary Pleases Engler." *Detroit News*, March 12, 10.

———. 2000b. "Intensity Is Building for Michigan's Primary." *Detroit News*, February 20, B1.

———. 2000c. "Now McCain Camp Must Beware Mischief." *Detroit News*, February 24, A15.

CHAPTER SEVENTEEN

Conclusion

Bruce E. Cain and Elisabeth R. Gerber

This volume has several purposes. One is to explain the background and motivation for the passage of the blanket primary reform in California. A second is to assess the impact of this election system change on numerous aspects of the electoral process, including voter participation and behavior, campaign strategy, election costs, the ideological makeup of the legislature, and the viability of women, minority, and minor-party candidates. However, there are important caveats to any generalizations we might derive from this exercise. To begin with, the authors do not agree on every point. But also, it is important to remember that the full impact of this experiment may not have been realized in California since candidates, strategists, and voters had only two primary elections (and one complete election cycle) of experience with the blanket system. Nevertheless, it is illuminating to identify the areas of scholarly consensus that emerged from the studies in this volume and to ponder the meaning of these findings.

IMPACT OF THE BLANKET PRIMARY

Did the imposition of the blanket primary accomplish what experts and advocates predicted that it would? The results are mixed. In several respects, such as the level of participation and the cost of running campaigns, California's first blanket primary had modest or nonexistent effects. But in two other important respects, namely the level of crossover voting and the moderation of candidate ideology, the effects were more significant. To start with the small or nonexistent impacts, the blanket primary did not dramatically increase turnout in the 1998 California primary. Cho and Gaines (chapter 9) claim that there was roughly a 2.4 percent surge in primary turnout over the decade average of 27.4 percent. The 1998 blanket primary turnout was lower than the 1996 closed primary turnout of 31.1 percent, but higher than the 1994 midterm election closed primary turnout of 26.2 percent. Further, it appears that among nonpartisans—the group that was presumably the biggest beneficiary of the rule change—turnout was roughly the same as among partisans (turnout among both groups is estimated at approximately 27 percent). Nor did the marginal increase in primary participation carry over into November, as the 1998 general election turnout was also average by the standards of the decade.

In retrospect, this finding is not too surprising, since political science research has already uncovered many other factors to explain turnout, such as registration rules (e.g., same-day versus thirty-day close), the demographic makeup of the electorate, the quality of the candidates, and the like (see Wolfinger and Rosenstone 1980). The blanket primary opened up new opportunities for independent voters, but it did not guarantee that they would be more motivated to take advantage of those choices. Given that the large number of initiatives and nonpartisan races on California's closed primary ballots has always provided a reason for nonpartisans to vote, the chance to participate in presidential nominations and other primary races may not have added much to the existing incentive for them to participate. This is not to imply that the new opportunities made no difference at all to independent voters. Those who turned out had more races to participate in. But judging from the data, the new system did not stimulate large numbers of previously nonvoting independents into voting.

Had the Supreme Court allowed California to continue using the blanket rules, Cho and Gaines suggest that there might have been an increase in nonpartisan voter registration, since the value of being a registered partisan was lessened by the new blanket rules. However, the possibility of an increase between 1998 and 2000 in the number of independents was probably undercut by the way in which the California state legislature handled the presidential primary question. In 1998, California voters rejected Proposition 3, a measure that would have created an exception to the blanket primary rules for presidential races. Subsequently, the California legislature passed an exemption to the blanket primary law that only counted the votes of registered partisans for the selection of official delegates to the national presidential nomination conventions. Since this in effect deprived independents and minor-party registrants of an opportunity to cast a meaningful vote for the most salient race, we cannot rule out the possibility that it discouraged voters from choosing nonpartisan status.

Cho and Gaines also find very modest changes in the level of electoral competitiveness and campaign spending before and after the introduction of the blanket primary. Asking whether the 1998 returns were more or less competitive than California's district normal votes (see chapter 9), they conclude that there was a small increase in competitiveness in California's congressional districts as measured by the normal vote. This small increase was offset by increases in incumbency and experience factors that tend to suppress competitiveness between incumbents and challengers. This conforms to findings in chapter 7 (Salvanto and Wattenberg) that show strong incumbency advantages under the blanket primary. In chapter 2, Gaines and Cho remind us that incumbency was also strong under the cross-filing system that California adopted several decades earlier, a system which allowed candidates to run under more than one party label simultaneously. The two systems are similar, except that in cross-filing, candidates can choose to cross party lines, whereas in the blanket system the voters do so. Several of the studies in this volume point out that many of the sincere and hedging voters were attracted to popular incumbents under the blanket system, just as voters were several decades ago under the cross-filing system.

While it appears that the blanket primary strengthened incumbents by giving them access to supporters in all parties, one should bear in mind Baldassare's important point (chapter 4) that the 1998 election was fought at a time when voters were relatively content with conditions in California. The economy had recovered from the difficulties of the mid-nineties, and voters were not looking to shake things up by voting for unproven outsiders. Experienced candidates and familiar faces did well up and down the ballot. Therefore, it is difficult to parse out how much of this apparent incumbency advantage was the result of the new rules per se, and how much was also a reflection of the tenor of the times.

Cho and Gaines (chapter 9) also find that the blanket primary did not dramatically increase campaign costs, as many opponents had predicted. The opponents argued that since candidates had to appeal to a larger electorate—essentially the same voters they would face in November, rather than strictly voters registered in their own parties—campaign costs would increase considerably. Using a model that pools Congressional spending data from 1992–1998, they conclude that the change to the blanket primary did not significantly alter the proportion of individual contributions that were earmarked for or spent during the primary election.

Another change that some experts predicted was that the blanket primary would open up new opportunities for women, minority, and minorparty candidates. Caul and Tate suggest in chapter 12 that, at least for women, the blanket primary created few new opportunities. Indeed, they predicted that if anything, movement away from stronger party control might actually set the progress of female candidates back, not forward. Looking at the evidence, however, they conclude that there was no change in terms of the absolute numbers of women running in statewide races under the blanket and closed primary systems. At the same time, they did find that the women who ran under the blanket rules tended to be better qualified; that is, they had substantial personal political resources such as wealth, experience as political officeholders, or name recognition due to family ties. They found no similar differences among male candidates and speculated that this may have to do with the interaction between gender differences and organizational structure. In other words, since women rely more heavily on organizational resources rather than personal political resources, the absence of strong party control under the blanket primary required women to compensate with better qualifications.

Segura and Woods (chapter 13) are more positive about the effects of the blanket primary on Latinos, but in a very particular sense. They find that moderate Latino Republican candidates were more viable under the blanket primary. Because the blanket primary encourages crossover voting from independents and moderate Democrats, it increases the chances of moderate Republicans being elected. Also, it allows Latino voters in districts with uncontested Democratic primaries to support Republican Latino candidates. Interestingly, they found no such effects on the Democratic side, suggesting the peculiarity of the California Republican Party and its "Latino problem." Further, by empowering moderate Latino candidates, the blanket primary also presumably undercuts the incentive of the Republican Party to undertake confrontational politics. We will return to the general point about moderation shortly.

Collet (chapter 11) similarly sees that minor parties benefited marginally from the new rules, although it is important to note that they "benefited" only if one thinks of minor parties as electoral rather than as expressive parties. By an electoral party, we mean one that is trying to win the election (or swing election outcomes) and therefore adapts to voter demands. By comparison, an expressive party cares less about trying to win (recognizing that this is usually not an option anyway) and gives voice to ideas that would otherwise be ignored by the major parties. Collet finds evidence that the vote for almost all minor parties increased dramatically in the 1998 election. This, he claims, offers the hope of broadening the otherwise narrow base of these parties and moderating their politics. This, as Collet acknowledges, can be defined as a benefit if the goal of minor parties is to become more electorally competitive, but not if their goal is to act as a voice of conscience, principle, and innovation. This illustrates an important point about electoral rules: namely, that the effects sometimes can be both subtle and profound. Changing the rules in this case may actually change the role that minor parties play from one of conscience to one of electoral competitor, something that was not predicted or discussed in the Prop 198 campaign.

The more dramatic effects caused by the introduction of the blanket primary center on two points: first, the incentives for voters to cross back and forth across party lines, and second, the effects this may have on candidate positioning. With regard to the first point, a number of the chapters in this volume have examined the rate of crossover voting using a variety of data and estimation strategies. Some looked at survey data (Sides, Cohen, and Citrin, chapter 5; Alvarez and Nagler, chapter 6), others at aggregate data (Kousser, chapter 8), and still others at actual ballot image information (Salvanto and Wattenberg, chapter 7). While they do not agree in all of their conclusions, there are some points of consensus.

First, it is clear that voters did use the opportunity to cross party lines. For instance, looking at absentee ballots in Los Angeles County, Salvanto and Wattenberg claim that only 45 percent of registered Democrats voted for Democrats only (i.e., a straight ticket), 40 percent of registered Republicans voted for Republicans only, and only 5 percent of minor-party registrants voted for minor-party candidates only. To put it another way, a majority of voters in Los Angeles County took the opportunity to split their ballots between parties. If doing something indicates liking it, clearly a majority of voters seem to like the new system. This might explain why Proposition 3, which sought to exempt the presidential primary from the blanket rules, failed in 1998.

Salvanto and Wattenberg also argue that voters behaved in the blanket primary very much as they do in general elections. So one conclusion we can draw is that the blanket primary allowed voters two rounds of essentially general election behavior. However, as Kousser shows, this does not mean that voters will make the same choices twice, even when they have the opportunity to do so. A significant number of voters who cross over to vote for a particular candidate in the primary return to their own party in the general election, for reasons we will discuss shortly. Kousser reports that what he calls the "stickiness factor" (i.e., the likelihood that a crossover voter will support the same candidate in the general election) varies greatly depending on the electoral circumstances. When voters leave their own contested primary to vote in another race that is less competitive, the stickiness factor is very high, varying from 90 percent for Republicans to 82 percent for Democrats. But when voters leave their own uncontested primary to participate in a more competitive one, the stickiness factor is more like 44 percent. Because of this, Kousser takes some issue with Salvanto and Wattenberg in that he finds similar patterns but higher rates of crossover voting in the primary than the general election.

The second point of consensus is that the propensity for crossover voting varies according to the electoral circumstances of a race—for example, which race is competitive in the primary, and who is likely to win in the general. Controlling for different strategic situations, Alvarez and Nagler (chapter 6) find that the level of crossover voting in five 1998 Assembly district races varied from a little over 1 percent of Democrats in a heavily minority Democratic seat, Assembly District 49, to 85.9 percent of Republicans in the same seat. Presumably, Republicans in that seat understood that the "action" was in the Democratic primary in the sense that the winner of the Democratic primary was virtually assured election in November. In the other seats, the partisan crossover vote varied from 5 percent to 41 percent. Salvanto and Wattenberg find that Republican crossover into Democratic races varied from a high of approximately 27 percent in the Governor's and Controller's races to a low of 6 percent in the Secretary of State race. For Republican statewide candidates, the crossover appeal to Democratic registrants was less, ranging from a high of approximately 18 percent in the Secretary of State and Insurance Commissioner races to a low of 5 percent in the Controller's race. A similar point about the strategic context of crossover voting can be found in chapter 5, which uses Field Poll data at various points in the primary. It shows that by May 1998, 23 percent of Republican party identifiers intended to cross over into the highly contested Democratic gubernatorial race, but only 5 percent of Democrats were inclined to vote in the predetermined Republican gubernatorial contest. In the U.S. Senate race, where the action was on the Republican side, only 8.6 percent of Republican identifiers intended to cross over to vote in the Democratic race versus 15.8 percent of Democrats who planned to participate in the Republican primary.

This leads us to perhaps the greatest areas of scholarly disagreement in this volume—why did voters cross over, and why does the rate of crossover voting vary so much from race to race? One answer that each chapter rules out is widespread raiding. Only a small fraction of voters seems to be crossing over to vote for the weakest candidate in the other party in order to improve the chances of their preferred candidate. This can be inferred from the moderate ideology and partisanship of the cross-over voters (chapter 5), their pro-incumbency bias (chapter 7), the rank orderings that voters assigned to candidates (chapter 6), and the relatively high number of those who vote the same way in November and in the primary (chapter 8).

If mischief is not the primary reason, then what else motivates crossover voting? One answer seems to be the attraction of popular incumbents, as we mentioned earlier. But the deeper question, which is far more controversial and divides our authors, is the proportion of voters who are acting sincerely as compared to those who act strategically. Sincere voters are supporting their most preferred candidate, while strategic voters are choosing a candidate who is not their most preferred for various reasons. Since we have ruled out sabotage in most cases, the more common strategic motive is hedging or impact voting: voting for a second-choice candidate with a higher probability of winning, or picking the best of the candidates in the other party's primary so that if the preferred candidate does not win, the voter gets her second-best candidate. However, it is very hard to infer exactly how many voters fit into the sincere or hedging categories since they both tend to reside in the same part of the ideological spectrum (i.e., the middle), and it is difficult to get voters to state their honest motives in a survey. Since, according to Kousser's calculations (chapter 8), a significant number of voters who supported the other party's candidate in the primary returned to their own party in November, we can infer that many of them must have voted strategically in the primary.[1]

Does it matter whether voters act strategically in the primary? In terms of the effects on candidate strategies, the answer is that it requires some adjustments of expectations. Candidates need to discount their expectations of how much of the crossover vote they can expect to retain in November according to the strategic circumstances they find themselves in. But this, by itself, poses no vital threat to democracy. It does illustrate a point of principle about political parties, however. If enough voters are strategic, it means that races can be determined by fortuitous factors such as whether the other party has a contested primary or not. An important question that is as yet unanswered is whether this promotes perverse elite behavior, such as parties trying to prevent competitive races in order to keep the other party's supporters from interfering in their nominations. Systems that promote manipulative elite behavior tend to have a short life in American politics, as the U.S. experience with cumulative and limited voting suggests.

The other important effect of the blanket primary is on candidate ideology. It is clear from the official ballot pamphlet arguments and the known preferences of Proposition 198's backers that this was the main motivation behind the blanket primary reform. Representative Tom Campbell and other moderate Republicans believed that the closed primary system kept the California Republican party captive of the right wing. As both the Gerber and Petrocik essays explain (chapters 10 and 14), Campbell's fears in this regard comport with the logic and evidence of political science. Since registered partisans are both more motivated to vote in primary elections and more ideologically polarized than the general electorate, candidates are forced to play to the ends of the ideological spectrum in order to win in a closed primary and then trim to the middle to be competitive in the November contest. Campbell's hope was that this structurally induced schizophrenia could be lessened with the help of nonpartisans and moderate members of other parties.

Gerber finds that the moderating effect on candidate ideology was minimal in the top-of-the-ticket races, but substantial in the state legislative races. Her statistical model for predicting the probability of nominating a moderate candidate for the State Assembly in 1996 and 1998 suggests that the odds were significantly higher in 1998, even after controlling for other factors such as district ideology, the presence of an extreme challenger, race type, and party. The fact that the Republicans did not nominate moderates in the high-visibility U.S. Senate and Governor's races might have been the result of many years of closed primaries in the sense that there are not many prominent moderates who could have run for either seat. Presumably, the cumulative effect of several election cycles under the blanket primary might have created a deeper bench of moderates in the future. It is also fair to say that there was some confusion about the definition of a moderate Republican candidate. The 1998 Republican nominee for the U.S. Senate, Matt Fong, for instance, tried very hard to portray himself as a centrist candidate in his November race with Barbara Boxer and did receive a greater share of the crossover vote than his primary opponent (see chapters 6 and 7). In the end, however, Boxer was able to portray him as a noncentrist and minimized the November crossovers (see Baldassare's chapter 4).

Petrocik agrees with Gerber that the new blanket rules were designed to moderate the parties, but argues that the result will instead be greater programmatic heterogeneity and hence less party cohesion. Using a specially designed survey that gave information about the strategic circumstances of a hypothetical race to some respondents but not to others, Petrocik concludes that the perceived hopelessness of a seat (e.g., by a Republican voter in a safe Democratic seat) greatly increased the odds of crossover voting. He then produces evidence that the types of moderate voters who will cross over tend to have more diverse policy attitudes, which causes him to speculate that this could ultimately lead to less party cohesion.

MOTIVES AND THE ADOPTION OF THE BLANKET PRIMARY

Given what we know about the impact of the blanket primary, we can return to the question of whether it achieved its intended purposes. Bowler and Donovan in chapter 3 examine various hypotheses about which voters supported the blanket primary and why. They find that weak partisans and minor-party voters, the voters who were most likely to exercise the crossover voting options the blanket primary offered, were also the most likely to have voted for it. They conclude that many voters engaged in instrumental voting on Prop 198. Voters who were most likely to take advantage of the opportunities to cross over were also most likely to support Prop 198, and those least likely to cross over were most likely to oppose the reform.

It should come as no surprise to students of politics that people support changes in the political rules of the game when they expect to benefit from them, and oppose rules changes when they do not. It is unlikely that many of California's voters could have accurately and in any detail explained the operation of a blanket system in 1996, but they sensed that it offered them more freedom of choice and opportunities to split their ballot. Those who wanted to split their ballot sensed that they should vote yes, and those who normally voted a straight ticket opposed the measure on the grounds that they did not need the option. Since most opinion surveys in California suggest that a majority of voters are in the middle of the ideological spectrum, and since voters in the middle of the ideological spectrum are the most likely to split their ballots, it is easy to see in retrospect why Prop 198 passed in 1996 and Prop 3 failed in 1998. Indeed, as the Los Angeles County ballot image data analyzed in chapter 7 show, over half the voters in the state's most populous county did make use of the freedom of choice the blanket primary gave them.

Prop 198 was not a reform intended to make everyone better off. The intended winners were ballot splitters and the more moderate candidates they supported, and the intended losers were straight ticket partisans and their preferred, ideologically polar candidates. Unless the number of straight ticket partisans had come to exceed the number of centrist ballot splitters, it was unlikely Prop 198 would have been reversed by the voters. In the court case, *California Democratic Party v. Jones,* the political parties argued that they, not the state by legislation or initiative, had the right to determine the rules of nomination. As Persily explains in chapter 15, while the federal District court and Circuit Court of Appeals ruled otherwise, the Supreme Court was more sympathetic to this issue and reversed Prop 198. Based on public attitudes toward the blanket primary, the Court ended up doing what the voters refused to do.

In the meantime, stepping back from the questions of who won and who lost, we can ask what has been gained and what has been lost in more abstract terms. On the plus side, the blanket primary clearly gave voters more choices than they had before. They were essentially free to participate in the selection of candidates for all parties if they so desired. Their only constraint was that they could only participate in one party's primary per race. In the sense that the blanket primary's flexibility prevented votes from being pigeonholed into one party or another, this can be seen as an advantage.

Another gain, one could argue, was that the blanket primary gave more voters the chance to cast an effective vote, meaning a vote that might determine the election outcome. For voters trapped in seats dominated by a party other than the one they were registered with, this meant that they could abandon the primary in which their votes did not matter and vote in the primary in which they did. In theory, casting a vote that matters should enhance the incentive to participate and even encourage general feelings of voter efficacy. In reality, it produced no dramatic changes in California's voter participation rates. But even if it did not result in more electoral enthusiasm and participation, voters in noncompetitive seats might have gained some expressive value in acquiring the chance to cast a vote that mattered.

Against these gains are some problems. First, as a blanket primary system succeeds in moving candidates toward more centrist positions, it could lessen the distinctiveness of the choices voters are given in the November elections. In the extreme, the centrist logic pushes candidates to virtually identical positions at or near the middle of the ideological spectrum. This may lead to the perception that there are no real choices being offered by competing candidates.

Second, there is the problem of an enhanced incumbency effect. Several studies in this volume suggest that incumbents were quite successful in drawing votes from the ranks of nonpartisans and other party identifiers. At a time when the incumbency advantage is already considerable and over 90 percent of state legislative and Congressional incumbents win reelection, the added boost incumbents receive from the blanket rules may have been an unwelcome development and a setback for the cause of more competitive elections.

And finally, there is the question of where voices at the ends of the ideological spectrum will find expression. If the electoral incentives are strongly centrist, this will dampen the chances of more ideological voters to be represented. Is this a good development? Some will think not. In particular, there are some who think that the problem with American politics is the lack of choice rather than the extremity of the candidates who are nominated. For them, the added incentive for sameness only exacerbates an already bad problem.

So in the end, California's experiment with the blanket primary yielded a few empirical surprises, but demonstrated nonetheless that changing the rules does seem to change the incentives of voters and candidates. Given the parties' opposition to the blanket primary, it is not surprising to find that such changes do matter—political actors usually do not waste resources unless something is at stake. The other point to bear in mind is that different primary systems present different trade-offs in term of advantages and disadvantages. This frames the normative debate in relativistic terms. Moving from a closed to a blanket or an open system is not necessarily an improvement or a step backward. Rather, it changes the winners and losers, confers some improvements and some losses, and raises fundamentally political issues. This guarantees that although California's recent blanket experiment is over, there will be other experiments in the future.

NOTES

1. An alternative possibility, which is not systematically considered in any of the chapters in this volume, is that voters received new information between the primary and the general election and switched to their new, sincere first preference.

REFERENCES

Wolfinger, Raymond E., and Steven J. Rosenstone. 1980. *Who Votes?* New Haven, CT: Yale University Press.

CONTRIBUTORS

R. MICHAEL ALVAREZ is Associate Professor of Political Science at the California Institute of Technology. Most of his research and teaching focus on the study of electoral politics in the United States. He is the author of *Information and Elections* (University of Michigan Press, 1997) and numerous articles in scholarly journals. His current research projects consider American public opinion about divisive social and political issues; voting behavior in primary elections; and the causes of gender differences in opinions about economic issues. He was an expert witness for the State of California in *California Democratic Party v. Jones* and was an outside consultant for Knight Ridder on its 2000 Hispanic Voter Poll.

MARK BALDASSARE is a Senior Fellow and Program Director in Governance at the Public Policy Institute of California in San Francisco, where he holds the Arjay and Frances Miller Chair in Public Policy. He currently directs the PPIC Statewide Survey, a large-scale public-opinion project aimed at developing an in-depth profile of the social, economic, and political forces that are at work in California elections and that shape the state's public policies. Baldassare previously held the Roger and Janice W. Johnson Chair in Civic Governance and Professional Management at the University of California at Irvine. His most recent book is *California in the New Millennium: The Changing Social and Political Landscape* (University of California Press, 2000).

SHAUN BOWLER is Professor of Political Science at the University of California, Riverside. His major research interests concern comparative voting behavior. His work examines the interaction between institutional arrangements and voter choice in a variety of settings, ranging from the Republic of Ireland to California's direct democracy elections. Additional interests of his include assessing the effects of campaigns on voter choices (he co-edited *Electoral Strategies and Political Marketing*) and the European Parliament. He is coauthor of *Demanding Choices: Opinion Voting and Direct Democracy* (University of Michigan Press, 1998) and coeditor of *Citizens as Legislators: Direct Democracy in the United States* (Ohio State University Press, 1998).

BRUCE E. CAIN is Robson Professor of Political Science and Director of the Institute of Governmental Studies at the University of California, Berkeley. In addition to his numerous journal and law review articles, he is the author of *The Reapportionment Puzzle* (1984), coauthor of *The Personal Vote* (1987) and *Congressional Redistricting* (1991), and coeditor of *Developments in American Politics,* vols. I (1992), II (1994), and III (1998). He has served as a polling consultant to Fairbank, Canapary, and Maulin (1985–86) and as a redistricting consultant to the Los Angeles City Council (1986), the San Diego City Council (2001), and the Attorney General of the State of Massachusetts (1987–88). He has been a consultant to the *Los Angeles Times* (1986–89) and is a political analyst for numerous radio and television stations in the Bay Area. Professor Cain was elected to the Academy of Arts and Sciences in March 2000 and received Stanford University's Zale Award for Distinction in Scholarship and Public Service in May 2000. He was an expert witness for the parties in *California Democratic Party v. Jones.*

MIKI CAUL is Assistant Professor of Political Science at SUNY Binghamton. Her research interests focus on political parties, participation, and women in politics in advanced industrial democracies. She has published articles in *Comparative Political Studies* and *Party Politics* and is completing research on women's integration into political parties in Western Europe.

WENDY K. TAM CHO is Associate Professor at the University of Illinois at Urbana-Champaign, where she holds appointments in Political Science and Statistics. She received her Ph.D. from the University of California at Berkeley. She has published articles in scholarly journals on the topics of racial and ethnic politics, statistical methods, and elections. An avid triathlete, she recently interrupted her competition schedule to produce Matthew Cho in collaboration with her husband, Lawrence.

JACK CITRIN is Professor of Political Science at the University of California, Berkeley. He is author of *Tax Revolt: Something for Nothing in California* (Harvard University Press, 1985), *The Politics of Disaffection among British and American Youth* (University of California Press, 1976), and the forthcoming *The Politics of Multiculturalism and the Crisis of American Identity.* His research interests are trust in government, nationalism and immigration, ethnic politics, and California politics and elections.

JONATHAN COHEN is a Ph.D. candidate in Political Science at the University of California, Berkeley, and recently served as Survey Analyst at the Public Policy Institute of California. His fields of interest include California politics, fiscal policy, and organizational behavior. Jon's dissertation about the politics and political implications of state tax policy is currently on hold while he works as Director of Product Marketing for Mobileum, a wireless software platform provider.

CHRISTIAN COLLET received his Ph.D. from the University of California, Irvine, where he is currently a postdoctoral researcher in the Department of Political Science, completing a book on the rise of minor-party politics. His research focuses on the interaction between mass and elite behavior in the contexts of partisan and ethnic politics. He also serves as president of Pacific Opinions, an independent company that conducts polls and opinion research for local governments, media, and nonprofit organizations.

TODD DONOVAN is Professor of Political Science at Western Washington University and defending champion of the Bellingham Pub Run. His research focuses on voting behavior, the politics of state taxation, direct democracy, electoral systems and representation, and the political economy of local development. His is coauthor of *Demanding Choices: Opinion and Voting in Direct Democracy* (University of Michigan Press, 1998) and coeditor of *Citizens as Legislators: Direct Democracy in the United States* (Ohio State University Press, 1998). His research on democracy and representation has appeared in the *American Journal of Political Science,* the *Journal of Politics, Political Research Quarterly, Electoral Studies,* and several other journals.

BRIAN J. GAINES is Associate Professor of Political Science and an affiliate of the Institute of Government and Public Affairs at the University of Illinois at Urbana-Champaign. He has been a visiting scholar at the Department of Applied Economics at the Catholic University at Leuven. He earned his Ph.D. from Stanford University, where he was also (playing) president of the ice hockey club. His research is focused on elections, electoral law, voting behaviour, and mass and elite attitudes in modern democracies, and he has contributed to ten journals. As his spelling suggests, he remains a Canadian citizen.

ELISABETH R. GERBER is Professor of Public Policy and Director of the State and Local Policy Center in the Gerald R. Ford School of Public Policy at the University of Michigan. Gerber's research is concerned with the policy consequences of electoral laws and other political institutions. She has written on the use of initiatives and referendums in California and other states and recently completed two books on the subject: *The Populist Paradox* (Princeton University Press, 1999) and *Stealing the Initiatives* (Prentice Hall,

2000). She is involved in a study of electoral laws in the American states and their effects on election outcomes and representation, and on the politics of land use and the dynamics of local ballot initiatives. She was an expert witness for the State of California in *California Democratic Party v. Jones.*

THAD KOUSSER is a Ph.D. candidate in American Politics at the University of California, Berkeley, and a researcher at the Institute of Governmental Studies. His focus is on the links among electoral law, institutional design, legislative elections, and legislative behavior. His dissertation will explore how professionalization and deprofessionalization through term limits have changed the form and function of American state legislatures.

MEGAN MULLIN is a doctoral student in the Department of Political Science and a research assistant at the Institute of Governmental Studies at the University of California, Berkeley. She is interested in state and local politics, political participation, and the intersection of democracy and technology.

JONATHAN NAGLER is Associate Professor of Politics at New York University. He has previously taught at Harvard University and Caltech. Professor Nagler's primary areas of research are the relative impact on elections of economic conditions and issues; strategic voting; turnout; and political methodology. Articles on these subjects by Professor Nagler have appeared in the *American Political Science Review, British Journal of Politics, American Journal of Political Science,* and other scholarly journals. He was an expert witness for the State of California in *California Democratic Party v. Jones.*

NATHANIEL PERSILY is an Assistant Professor at the University of Pennsylvania Law School. Before joining the law school, Professor Persily was Associate Counsel at the Brennan Center for Justice at New York University School of Law, where he specialized in voting rights and election law. In addition to filing Supreme Court amicus briefs in *Bush v. Gore* and *California Democratic Party v. Jones,* Professor Persily was one of the lawyers representing Senator John McCain in his successful challenge to the 2000 New York Republican presidential primary ballot access laws. His research, publications, and congressional testimony have focused on topics of election law, the census, redistricting, voting rights, and political parties. An expanded version of his chapter here can be found in "Toward a Functional Defense of Political Party Autonomy," *New York University Law Review* 76, June 2001, pp. 750–824. Professor Persily is a graduate of Yale College (B.A. and M.A. 1992) and Stanford Law School (1998), where he was President of Volume 50 of the *Stanford Law Review.* Currently completing his dissertation on political parties and the courts, he is a Ph.D. candidate in political science at U.C. Berkeley.

JOHN R. PETROCIK is Professor of Political Science and Chair of the Political Science Department at the University of Missouri-Columbia. He has authored or coauthored numerous books and research articles on mass attitudes and behavior, political parties, elections and campaigns, and survey research and analysis. One of these books, *The Changing American Voter* (Harvard University Press, 1976; rev. ed. 1979), received the Woodrow Wilson Award in 1977. Currently, he is working on a book that analyzes the role of candidates in setting the issue criteria with which voters choose among candidates.

ANTHONY M. SALVANTO's work focuses on American elections and voting behavior, with emphasis on initiative voting, ballot design, and electoral systems. He has recently served on the Carter-Ford National Commission on Electoral Reform's task force on voting systems and ballot access. Prior to that, Dr. Salvanto led the analysis of the 2000 Presidential election for the *Miami Herald/USA Today* examination of overvotes and also documented problems with mispunched ballots in Miami-Dade County. He is currently at work on a book about voter behavior on complex ballots, the 2000 election, and what it can teach us about electoral reform. He earned his Ph.D. from the University of California, Irvine (2000), and subsequently was the 2000–2001 Faculty Fellow in the Department of Political Science.

GARY M. SEGURA is Associate Professor in the Department of Political Science at the University of Iowa. His research focus is on political representation, with particular emphasis on the representation of Latinos and other minority groups. He has published articles in the *Journal of Politics,* the *Political Research Quarterly,* the *Journal of Conflict Resolution,* and *Legislative Studies Quarterly.*

JOHN SIDES is a Ph.D. candidate in the Department of Political Science at the University of California, Berkeley. His dissertation research centers on the interaction of public opinion and elite action in political campaigns.

KATHERINE TATE is Professor of Political Science at the University of California, Irvine. She is the author of *From Protest to Politics: The New Black Voters in American Elections* (Harvard University Press, 1993) and coauthor of *African Americans and the American Political System,* 4th ed. (Prentice Hall, 1998). She is the principal investigator of the 1996 National Black Election Studies, which was funded by the National Science Foundation. She reports on these data in her forthcoming book, *Black Faces in the Mirror: Black Constituents and Their Representatives in the U.S. Congress* (Princeton University Press, 2002).

MARTIN P. WATTENBERG is Professor of Political Science at the University of California, Irvine. He is interested in elections and political parties, both in the United States and around the world. He is the author of *The Decline of American Political Parties* (1998) and *The Rise of Candidate-Centered Politics* (1991), both published by Harvard University Press. Most recently, he coedited *Parties without Partisans* (2000) and *Mixed-Member Electoral Systems* (2001), both published by Oxford University Press. He testified as an expert witness on behalf of the parties in *California Democratic Party v. Jones*, the court case that challenged Proposition 198.

NATHAN D. WOODS is a doctoral candidate in the School of Politics and Economics at the Claremont Graduate University. He received his M.A. in American Politics from Claremont Graduate University in 1999. His research interests lie broadly in political behavior, campaigns and elections, representation, and minority politics.

INDEX

Page numbers in italics indicate tables and figures.

AB 118 (1959), 17

Abramowitz, Alan, 156

absentee ballots (1998 L.A. County primary), 124–25, 126, 127, 139, *140*

ACA 3 (1908), 14

Adams, Greg D., 272

Adams, Terry v., 308

ADA scores, 211*nn*7,10,12

affiliation pledges, 15

age variable, 46, 47, *48*, 55*n*7, 90, 91

AIP (American Independent party), 217, 219

AKIP (Alaska Independence party), 230–31

Alaska, O'Callaghan et al. v., 4

Alaska primaries, 4, 230–31, 240, 245–46*n*3, 312, 320*n*5

alienation model of voters, 41–42, 55*n*3

Allen, Doris, 261

Alvarez, R. Michael, 5–6, 7, 134, 146, 156, 157, 158, 168*n*3, 280, 295*n*19, 348–49

Amador, Donald, 203

American Independent party (AIP), 217, 219

Anderson, Joel, 261

Anderson v. Celebrezze, 319

anti-party populism: California's history of, 14–18; of cross-filing system, 12–13, 32–33*n*1, 33*n*2; of institutional reform initiatives, 53–54; of Proposition 198 proponents, 12, 43–44

Asian financial crisis, 60–61

Assembly District 9 (Sacramento), 109, 111, *114*, 117–19, 121*n*2

Assembly District 33 (Santa Maria, San Luis Obispo, Pismo Beach), 259–60

Assembly District 49 (East Los Angeles and Monterey Park), 109, 111–12, 113, *114*, 116, *117*, 121*nn*1,2,5, 348–49

Assembly District 53 (South Bay, LAX), 109, 111, 112–13, *114*, 116, *117*, 121*n*2

Assembly District 60 (West Covina, Whittier, La Habra Heights, Walnut), 260

Assembly District 61 (Pomona and Montclair), 109, 111, *115*, 116, *118*, *120*, 121*n*2, 122*n*10

Assembly District 75 (East San Diego County), 109, 111, 112, *115*, 116, *118*, 121*n*2, 260–61, 267*n*11, 268*n*12

Assembly district crossovers: calculating stickiness of, 146–49, 151–53, 155, 157–58, *158*, 168*n*4, 169*n*12; competitiveness factor in, 148–49, 168*n*7; by Latinos, for legitimate candidate, 259–61; Latinos' motivation for, 252–53, 256, 258–59, 264–65, 267*nn*8–9; by party identification, 110; predictive model for, 119, *120*, 122*nn*8–10; reasons to examine, 107; results of, by district, 111–13, *112*, *114–15*, 121*n*5; by type of district, 108–9, 121*n*1; voter motivations for, 113, 116–19, *117–18*

Assembly primaries (1996), 206, *207, 208,* 212*n*17, 350

Assembly primaries (1998): compared to 1996 primaries, 206, *207, 208,* 350; Latino GOP candidates in, 253–54, *255, 256,* 267*nn*4–5; moderation effects in, 204, *205,* 209, 212*n*15, 212*nn*17–19

associational rights of parties: in closed primaries, 315; Court's affirmation of, 3, 303–7, 312–14, 320*n*1; Court's anti-party opinions on, 307–9, 320*n*3; of minor parties, 215–17, 232*n*2, 309, 318–19, 321*n*11; *Nader's* challenge to, 304; in open vs. blanket primaries, 315–16, 321*n*8; source of restrictions on, 316–17, 321*n*9; *Timmons* balancing test for, 309–11, 320*n*4

Baldassare, Mark, 10, 346

Ball, Charles, 203

Ballenger, Bill, 336, 338

Ballot Access News, 216

ballot pamphlets, 30, 31, 189*n*1; as information source, 42–43; Proposition 198 debate in, 172–74

Bauer, Gary, 335

Baugh, Scott, 261, 340

benign strategic voting. *See* hedging

Benoit, Kenneth, 169*n*12

Blake, Gordon, 203

blanket primaries: arguments for/against, 43–45, 172–74, 215–17, 222, 352–53; California's experiment with, 3–4, 10–11, 29–31; campaign financing of, 10, 181–82, 187–89, 235, 346; candidate opinion survey on, 227, *228,* 229, 233*n*11; candidates' crossover strategies in, 271, 279–81, 293*n*4, 295*nn*19–21; competitiveness of, in safe districts, 182, 190*n*8; cross-filing's ties to, 20–22, 33–34*n*9; crossover voter motivations in, 5–7; experimental simulation of, 281–85, *284,* 295*nn*22–24; female candidates in, 240–44, *242, 244–45,* 245*nn*2–3, 246*n*4, 346–47; and minor parties, 215–17, 224–27, 231–32, 232*n*2, 233*nn*8–9, 292; moderation effects of, 9–10, 124, 192, 194, 211*n*3, 252, 275, 286–88, *287,* 296*nn*26–27; open primaries vs., 314–16, 321*n*8; as plurality system, 236; rules of, 5; speculative nomination constituency of, 290–91, *291;* ticket-splitting

freedom of, 43–44, 55*nn*5–6, 127–28, *128,* 348, 351–52; turnout and registration for, 7–8, 174–76, *175,* 188, 344–45; with two-count system, 31–32, 339, 341, 345; universe of voters in, 8, 78, 102*n*4; and weakened party role, 235, 237, 238–39, 270–71, 286–88, *287,* 293*n*2, 351. *See also* 1998 primaries; Proposition 198 (1996)

Blanket Primary Initiative. *See* Proposition 198 (1996)

Bob Jones University, 335

Bock, Audie, 214, 226, 232*n*1

Bohman, Charmayne, 204

Bono, Mary, 202

Bordonaro, Tom, 202, 259

Bowler, Shaun, 7, 9, 351

Boxer, Barbara, 59, 71, 81, 88, 198, 234, 239, 351; ideological positioning of, 200, 212*n*12

Bradley, Bill, 278, 324, 328, 330

Brady, Henry E., 238

Bravo, Rick, 259, 260

Brock, William, 320–21*n*6

Brown, Edmund G. (Pat), 17

Brunell, Thomas L., 211*n*7

Buchanan, Pat, 233*n*9

Burger, C. R., 20–21

Burrell, Barbara, 236

Burton, John, 339

Bush, George, 250, 266–67*n*1, 278

Bush, George W., 249, 278, 324, 325, 332; in 2000 presidential primaries, 335–38, 339, 340, 341

Bustamante, Cruz, 249

Cain, Bruce E., 11, 102*n*1

California: closed presidential primary in (2000), 325, 326, 330, 332, 338–41; economy of, 60, *61;* female representation in, 234; policy issues in, 62–64, *63;* re-registration period in, 193, 339–40; two-count system in (2000), 31–32, 339, 341, 345

California Democratic Party et al. v. Jones, 4; briefs filed for/against, 320–21*n*6; defendant's response in, 216–17; litigants in, 316; plaintiffs' arguments in, 215–16, 217, 222; U.S. District Court's ruling on, 309–11, 313; U.S. Supreme Court's ruling on, 303–4, 312–16, 319, 321*n*7, 352. *See also* Proposition 198 (1996)

California Journal, 260, 261

California residents. *See* voters

California Target Book (Hoffenblum), 212*nn*14–15

Calvert, Ken, 204

campaign finance: blanket primary's impact on, 8, 10, 188–89, 346; competitiveness factor of, 181–82, 187–88, 190*n*8; by female candidates, 235–36, 238–39; of gubernatorial races (1998), 239; incumbency advantage in, 133, 138; individual contributions to candidates (1992–98), 184–85, *186,* 187–88, 190*n*9; PAC component of, 183–84, *184;* of U.S. House races (1992–98), 183–88, *183;* of U.S. Senate races (1998), 67

Campbell, Tom, 30, 338, 350

candidates: affiliation pledges of, 15; attracted to minor parties, 227, 233*n*9; blanket primary finance strategies of, 8, 10, 181–82, 188–89; candidate-labeling rules for, 26; cross-filing by, 12–13, 15, 32–33*n*1, 33*nn*2–3; "effective" number of, 33*n*7, 177, 190*n*5; moderation hypothesis on, 9–10, 194, 211*n*3; of open vs. closed primaries, 270; preferred qualifications for, 70–71, *71,* 73*n*4; retirement decisions of, 212*n*13; as spoilers, 20–21. *See also* crossover-seeker candidates; female candidates; Latino GOP candidates

Capps, Lois, 202, 259

Carter, Chuck, 258

Casso, James, 202

Caul, Miki, 10, 346–47

CBS News/*New York Times* exit polls, 266–67*n*1

Celebrezze, Anderson v., 319

Center for the Study of Society and Politics of the Institute for Social Science Research (UCLA), 281

Central Valley residents, 60

Chapman, Heavey et al. v., 4

Chavez, Phil, 258

Checchi, Al, 59, 71, 80, 81, 129; campaign spending by, 67; centrist positioning by, 129–30, 197–98; general election crossovers for, 99, *99;* primary election crossovers for, 86, *87;* vote share of, 239

Cho, Wendy K. Tam, 8, 158, 344–46

Chryson, Mark, 230

Citrin, Jack, 5–6, 7, 134, 277

Clark, Janet, 237, 238

Classic, United States v., 308

Clinton, Bill, 69, 325

closed primaries: associational rights in, 315; criticism of, 9; cross-filing mechanism for, 15–16; crossovers in, 193, 294*n*12; general election viability factor of, 275–76; legislation to enact, 14–15; of minor parties, as competitive, 218; *Nader's* litigation over, 304; nomination constituency of, 290–91, *291;* rules of, 5, 8, 78, 102*n*2, 193; use of, in 2000 presidential race, 325, 326, 330, 332, 339–41

Cohen, Jonathan, 5–6, 7, 102*n*1, 134, 156, 157, 168*n*3, 277

Collet, Christian, 319, 347

commercials, 67

competitiveness: after-the-fact evaluation of, 176–77, 189–90*n*3; Assembly district study of, 109, 111, 112–13, 116; and campaign finance, 181–82, 187–88, 190*n*8; and cross-filing incumbency, 27–28, 34*n*10; and crossover voting, 29, 95–96, 125–26, 138, 148–49, *149,* 168*n*7, 348–49; of gubernatorial race, 80–81, 96, 129–30; incumbency advantage vs., 133–34, *134;* and Latino crossover voting, 252–53; of presidential primaries, 327–28, *328;* of safe district primaries, 182, 190*n*8; and stickiness factor, 151–53, *152–54,* 155, 348; U.S. House race analysis of (1992–98), 177, *178,* 179–81, *179,* 190*nn*6–7, 345–46; of U.S. Senate races, 81, 86, 96. *See also* contested-challenger primaries; contested-incumbent primaries; contested minor-party primaries

Condit, Tom, 223, 224, 225

Condon, Nixon v., 308

Congressional Quarterly Weekly, 241

Connecticut primaries, 304, 329–30

Connell, Kathleen, 130

Conservative party (New York), 13, 32–33*n*1

consistent crossover voting, 96–97, *97*

contested-challenger primaries: for Assembly seats, 204, 206, *208,* 209, 212*nn*17–19; Latino participation in, 253–54, 256, 267*n*8; for U.S. House seats, 200, *201,* 203–4

contested-incumbent primaries, 135, *135,* 200, *201,* 204

contested minor-party primaries: from 1960–66, 232n3; from 1968–98, 217–18, *218*, 232n4; number of votes in (1968–96 vs. 1998), 219, *220*

Controller's race (1998), 130, 131

Cortese, Dom, 232n1

Cousins v. Wigoda, 320n1

Cox, Dave, 262

CQ Weekly Report, 172

crime issue, 63, *63*

cross-filing: for Assembly seats (1914), 15, 33n3; in California and New York, 12–13, 32–33n1, 33n2; with crossover voting, 20–22, *21, 23;* and incumbency status (1910–64), 18, 26–29, *28*, 346; legislation for/against, 16–17, 33n4; partisan views of, 17–18, 33n5; for State Senate seats (1910–64), 18, *19;* for U.S. House seats (1910–64), 18, *19*, 33n8

crossover-seeker candidates: ideological effects on, 271, *272*, 273–74, 293–94n9, 294n10; moderation strategy of, 279–81, *281*, 293n4, 295nn19–21

crossover voters: attitudinal trends of, *61*, *62*, *65*, *68*, 69, 72n1; crossover motivations of, 6–7, 349–50; defined, 77–79, 102n2, 293n3; demographics of, 89–90, 103n16, 285–86, *285*, 296nn25–26; policy issues of, *63*, 64; preferences of, between and within parties, 271, 288–91, *289, 290, 291*, 296nn29–32; strategy to attract, 282–85, *284*, 295–96n23, 296n24. *See also* Democratic crossovers; Republican crossovers; voter motivation

crossover voting: in asymmetric nominating events, 327–28; average district rates of (1910–64), 24, *25*, 26; candidates' moderation strategy for, 279–81, *281*, 293n4, 295nn19–21; in closed primaries, 193, 294n12; competitiveness factor of, 125–26, 133–34, *134*, 138, 148–49, 168n7, 348–49; consistency in, 96–97, *97;* cross-filing's ties to, 20–22, *21, 23*, 27–29, *28;* definitional issues of, 77–79, 102nn2–3; in down-ballot races, 102n1; ecological inference model of, 146–49, 151, 156–59, 169nn12,14,15; experimental simulation of, 282–85, *284*, 295nn22–24; incumbency advantage of, 26–27, 121, 125, 132–33, 138, 353; Latinos' motiva-

tion for, 252–53, 256, 264–66, 267nn8–9, 347; logic of, 194–96, *195*, 211nn4–5; low opportunity cost of, 5–6; for minor-party candidates, 137–38, *137*, 190n4, 292; moderation effects of, 9–10, 124, 192, 194, 211n3, 252; in 1984–96 general elections, 79–80; in 1998 Assembly races, 111–13, *112*, *114–15*, 116–19, *117–18*, 121nn4–5; in 1998 general elections, 148, *160–63*; in 1998 primaries, 86–88, *87*, 147–51, *160–63*; in partisan districts, 131, *131;* partisan votes matched with, 136–37, *136*, *140;* by party identification, for Governor, 79–81, *82–83*, 349; by party identification, for U.S. Senator, 79, 81, *84–85*, 86, 103nn13–14, 349; by party registration, for Governor, 79, 86, *87*, 103n8, 129–30; by party registration, for U.S. Senator, 79, 87–88, *87*, 103n8; polarization hypothesis on, 194; from primary to general election, 97–101, *99*, 105n28, 152–53, *153, 154*, 155, 277; registration deadline's impact on, 329–30, 339–40; in 2000 presidential primaries, 278, 294nn16–17, 326–30, 334; in 2000 primary and general elections, 159, *164–66. See also* crossover voters; voter motivation

Darcy, R., 237, 238

Davis, Gray, 31, 59, 71, 320–21n6; campaign spending by, 67; centrist positioning by, 197–98; general election crossovers for, 80–81, 98, *99*, 129–30, 145; on Jones proposal, 339; primary election crossovers for, 86, *87;* recall bias for, 98, 104–5n27; vote share of, 239

DeMallie, Bob, 119, *120*, 122n9

Democratic crossovers: for Assembly races, 111, 112–13, *112*, 116, 118–19; as consistent/inconsistent, 96–97, *97;* in general elections (1984–96), 79–80, 103n9; in general elections (1998), 148; for Governor, 80, 81, 86, *92*, 93, 129–30, *130;* for McCain, 336–37; multivariate analysis of, 89–90, *92*, 93, *94*, 95; in partisan Republican district, 131, *131;* in primary races (1998), *129*, 147–48; for statewide offices, 129–30, *130;* stickiness factor of, 151–53, *153, 154*, 155; ticket splitting by, 127, *128;* for U.S. Senator, 88, *94,* 95

Democratic party: on blanket primary, 30, 229; on cross-filing, 17, 33*n*5; Latino attachment to, 248, 250; Latino crossover from, 252–53, 256, 258–61, 347; Latino crossover to, 262–63; open primaries of (1980–2000), 326–27, *327;* presidential primaries of (2000), 327–29, *328;* white Southern state primaries of, 307–9

Democratic Party of the United States v. Wisconsin ex rel. LaFollette, 305, 318, 320*n*1

Democratic voters: instrumental voting probability for, on Prop 198, *48,* 49, *50;* political apathy of, 64; recall bias of, 104–5*n*27; registered voter advantage of, 168–69*n*10; as turnout share (1998), 158, 169*n*13; voting patterns of, by party registration, 127, *128,* 349. *See also* Democratic crossovers

Detroit News, 337

direct primaries: forms of, 5, 11*n*1; legislation to amend, 16; opportunity cost of, 5–6; political intention of, 272–73, 293*nn*5–7. *See also* blanket primaries; closed primaries; open primaries

district normal vote, 179–81, 190*n*6

Dole, Bob, 250

Donovan, Todd, 7, 9, 41, 351

Dornan, Robert, 202, 251, 265

double-filing, 13

Downs, Anthony, 276

Dukakis, Michael, 278

Dunn, Sandy, 202

Duverger's law, 188

ecological inference model, 146, 156–59, 169*nn*12,14,15

economic issues, 60–61, *61*

education: as crossover voting variable, 90, 91, 93, *94,* 95; and instrumental voting probability, 46, *48,* 50–52, *51,* 55*n*8; as policy issue, 62–63, *63*

"effective" number index, 33*n*7, 177, 190*n*5

election law decisions: as anti-party, 307–9; favoring party autonomy, 303–7; using *Timmons* balancing test, 309–11

Engler, John, 335–36, 337, 338

Equal Protection Clause of the Fourteenth Amendment, 308

Escobar, Irma, 258, 267*n*10

ethnicity. *See* race/ethnicity variable

Eu v. San Francisco County Democratic Central Committee, 306–7, 313, 316–17

EzI program, 157–59, 169*n*12

Fair Political Practices Commission, 43

Falwell, Jerry, 340

Farris, Michael, 224, 225

Feinland, Marsha, 219, 223

Feinstein, Dianne, 234

female candidates, 9–10; in blanket vs. partisan primaries, 240–44, *242,* *244–45,* 245*nn*2–3, 246*n*4, 346–47; campaign finance resources of, 235–36, 238–39; in PR vs. plurality systems, 236–37, 245*n*1; rates of officeholding by, 234; term limits' impact on, 243; in U.S. House races, 235–36

Fieger, Geoffrey, 336

Field Institute polls, 102–3*n*6, 103*n*9, 104*n*20; on California Republicans, 340; party identification measures in, 102*n*5; pre- and post-primary, 77, 102*n*1; recall bias in, 98, 104*nn*25,27; on support for Prop 198, 294–95*n*18

Fifteenth Amendment, 308

Firestone, Brooks, 259

First Amendment, 304. *See also* associational rights of parties

fixed-effects panel data model, 179–81, 190*nn*6–7

Fong, Matt, 59, 71, 81, 240; crossover/nonpartisan votes for, 136, *136;* general election crossovers for, 98, 99, *99,* 145; ideological positioning of, 199–200, 351; primary vote for, by party registration, 87–88, *87;* and race/ethnicity variable, 90; recall bias for, 98, 104*n*25

Forbes, Steve, 335

Ford, Gerald, 266–67*n*1

Fourteenth Amendment, 304, 308

fund-raising. *See* campaign finance

Gaines, Brian J., 8, 190*n*7, 344–46

Gelman, Joe, 203

gender: as crossover voting variable, 89–90, 91, *92,* 93, *94,* 95, 103*n*16, 104*n*23, 220–21; disproportionate representation of, 234–35; qualifications/participation by, 241–44, *242,* 246*n*4; quotas on

gender *(continued)*
  candidates by, 238–39. *See also* female
  candidates
general elections: competitiveness-crossover
  factor in, 148–49, *149*, 153, 168*n*7; competitiveness trends in (1992–98), 179–
  81, *179;* crossover voting in (1984–96),
  79–80; incumbency advantage in, 133;
  multivariate models of stickiness in
  (1998), 151–53, *152–54*, 155, 168*n*4;
  primary voter motivation and, 97–101,
  99, 105*n*28, 143–44, 155, 156, 168*nn*1,3;
  registration and crossover factor in, 149,
  150, 152–53; registration and turnout
  for (1994–98), 174–75, *175;* and strategic voting, 80, 103*n*10, 129; viability factor of, 275–76; voter composition in
  (1984–96), 103*n*11. *See also specific
  general elections by year*
Genesys Sampling Systems, 295*n*22
Gerber, Elisabeth R., 8, 196, 350–51
Ginsburg, Ruth Bader, 313
Golding, Susan, 239
Goldsmith, Jan, 268*n*12
Gonzales, Henry, 258
Gonzales, Paul, 261–62
Gore, Al, 278, 324, 328
Green party: abstention rate for (1994),
  233*n*5; on blanket primary, 229, 232*n*2,
  233*n*11; contested primaries of, 217,
  232*n*3; primary vote share for (1994 vs.
  1998), 219, *220;* State Legislative victory
  for, 214
Grofman, Bernard, 211*n*7
gubernatorial primaries (1998): campaign
  financing of, 67, 239; candidates in, 59,
  197, 211*n*9; competitiveness factor of,
  129–30, 197–98; crossover intentions in,
  by party identification, 79, 80–81, *82–
  83*, 103*n*8, 349; crossover voting in, and
  general election, 97–101, *99*, 145; crossover voting in, by party registration, 86,
  87; ideological positioning in, 197–98,
  211*n*10, 350–51; mood of voters during,
  59–66, *61, 63, 65,* 72*n*1; multivariate
  analysis of, 91, *92*, 93, 104*nn*20–22; strategic voting behavior in, 148

Haeberle, Steven H., 270
Hahn, Janice, 202
Hall, Arnold Bennet, 157
Hall, Gus, 223

Harman, Jane, 59, 71, 80, 86, 241; ADA
  score of, 211*n*10; campaign spending by,
  67; in competitive primary, 129–30, 197–
  98; general election crossovers for, 99,
  99; vote share of, 239
Harris, Elihu, 214
Hatch, Orrin, 335
Heavey et al. v. Chapman, 4
hedging: Assembly district study of, 109,
  110–11, 113, 121*n*6, 156; candidates'
  strategic use of, 279–80; definition of
  and reasons for, 6, 88, 107–8, 125–26,
  144, 168*n*3; estimating prevalence of,
  95, 97–100, 105*nn*29–30, 349–50,
  354*n*1; and general elections, 80,
  103*n*10; impact form of, 108; little evi-
  dence of, 88–89; as minimax behavior,
  276; moderation effects of, 194, 196–97
Hedlund, Ronald, 102*n*5
Hennefer, Jim, 202
Herndon, Nixon v., 308
Herschensohn, Bruce, 31, 44
Hewlett, William, 30
Hibbing, John, 38
Hichborn, Franklin, 16
Hickel, Walter, 230
Hoch, Ed, 230
Hoffenblum, Allan, 212*nn*14–15
Hoffman, Randy, 203
Huffington, Michael, 183

ideological variable: in crossover voting, 89,
  92, 93, *94*, 95, 104*nn*22–23; measurement of, 91; role of, in primaries, 273–
  74, 293–94*n*9, 294*n*10. *See also* moderation effect
immigration policy, 63–64, *63*
impact voting behavior, 108, 109, 110–11,
  113, 121*n*6. *See also* hedging
income variable, 90, 91, *92*, 93
incumbency: crossover voting for/against
  (1910–64), 24, 25, 26–27; drawing
  power of, 121, 125, 132–34, *133, 134,*
  138, 346, 353; fixed-effects panel data
  model of, 179–81, 190*n*7; fund-raising
  advantage of, 133, 138; and raiding behavior analysis, 134–35, *135;* with/with-
  out cross-filing, 18, 27–29, *28*, 236
independent voters: crossover estimates
  with, 79, 103*n*8; definitional issues for,
  78, 102*nn*3,5, 103*n*8, 296*n*25; for Fong
  vs. Issa, 136, *136;* instrumental voting

probability for, on Prop 198, 47, *48;*
party voting patterns of, 127–28, *128,*
130–31, *130;* party voting patterns of, in
partisan districts, 131, *131;* registration
and turnout of, in blanket primary, 175–
76, 345; ticket splitting by, 43–44
initiative process, 36–37. *See also* institutional reform initiatives
Inside Michigan Politics (newsletter), 336
institutional reform initiatives: categories/
passage of (1912–98), 38, *39,* 40, 55*nn*1–
2; and legitimacy issues, 37–38, 53–54,
341–42; participation consequences of,
317–18, 321*n*10; pre-/post-1980, *40;*
voter motivation for, 41–42, 53, 55*n*3
Issa, Darell, 59, 67, 71, 81, 87–88, 99, 136,
199, 239–40

Jackson, Jesse, 278
Johnson, A. B., 20
Johnson, Hiram, 15–16
Jones, Bill, 130, 216, 339
Jones case. See *California Democratic Party et
al. v. Jones*

Katz, Richard, 168*n*1
KCAL-TV News survey (1994), 60, 62
Kevorkian, Jack, 336
Key, V. O., 78, 237–38
Keyes, Alan, 335
Khoury, Joe, 204
Killea, Lucy, 30, 43, 232*n*1
Kim, Jay, 204
King, Gary, 146, 197; ecological inference
model of, 156–59, 169*nn*14–15; EzI pro-
gram of, 169*n*12
King, Peter, 335
Kopp, Quentin, 232*n*1
Kousser, J. Morgan, 168*n*8
Kousser, Thad, 7, 102*n*1, 156, 168*n*3, 348,
350
Kuchel, Thomas, 18
Kuykendall, Steve, 202

Laakso-Taagepera index (1979), 33*n*7
LaFollette case. See *Democratic Party of the
United States v. Wisconsin ex rel. LaFollette*
Landrieu, Mary, 241
Lane, Dick, 203
La Riva, Gloria, 219, 224
Latino GOP candidates: for Assembly seats,
253–54, 255, 256, 267*nn*4–5; blanket

primary's impact on, 252, 263–65, 347;
characteristics of districts with, 256, 257,
258; in contested vs. uncontested races,
256, 257, 264, 267*n*8; general elections
lost by, 261–62; legitimate winner type
of, 259–61; representing white districts,
265; "sacrificial lamb" type of, 258–59
Latino voters: anti-Republican sentiment of,
248–51, 266*n*1, 267*nn*2–3; crossover by,
from GOP, 262–63; crossover by, for legitimate candidates, 259–61; crossover
motivations of, 252–53, 256, 264–66,
267*nn*8–9, 347; ethnically driven voting
by, 264–66; GOP primary turnout of
(1998), 253–54, 255, 256, 267*nn*6–7;
statewide electoral power of, 249
League of Women Voters, 17
LeBoutillier, John, 32–33*n*1
Lee, Barbara, 202
Lee, Eugene, 43
legitimacy issues, 37–38, 53–54, 341–42
Lemmons, LaMar, III, 336
Leonard, Bill, 144, 168*n*1
Levi, David, 309–11
Levitt, Steven D., 190*n*7
liberalism variable, 91, *92,* 93, *94,* 95
Liberal party (New York), 13, 32–33*n*1
Libertarian party (LP): abstention rate for
(1994), 233*n*5; in Alaska, 230; in Assembly District 75 race (1998), 267*n*11; on
blanket primary, 227, 229; competitive
primaries of, 217, 219; ideological purity
of, 231; right-to-association argument of,
215–17; vote share of (1994 and 1998),
219, 220
Los Angeles County Social Survey, 281,
295*n*22
Los Angeles metro-area residents, 60, 62–63
Los Angeles Times polls: on blanket vs. closed
primaries, 341; on policy-driven crossover, 103*n*15; pre-primary (1996), 46–
47, *48,* 49–52, *51;* primary election exit
poll (1998), 77, 86, 98, 169*n*13; stickiness findings from, 145; on strategic voting behavior, 89
Louisiana primaries, 240
LP. *See* Libertarian party (LP)
Lungren, Dan, 59, 71, 73*n*4, 80, 86, 89;
campaign spending by, 67; Latino vote
for, 251; in noncompetitive primary,
130, 197, 211*n*8; and Proposition 227,
104*n*19

Magleby, David, 41
Maldonado, Abel, 259–60
Manton, Tom, 32–33*n*1
Marshall, Thurgood, 306, 307
Martinez, Matthew, 295*n*20
Marvick, Dwaine, 296*n*29
Mather, F. D., 20–21
Matthews, Donald, 237, 238
McCain, John, 11, 102*n*4, 278, 320–21*n*6;
    in California primary (2000), 339–41; in
    Michigan primary (2000), 335–38; pri-
    mary rules' impact on, 325–27, 330,
    331, 332, *333*, 334; registration dead-
    line's impact on, 329–30, 339–40;
    strengths/liabilities of, 324–25
McCampbell, Bill, 203
McDonald, Stuart Elaine, 296*n*31
McGlennon, John, 156
McLeod, Gloria, 119, *120*, 122*n*9
Measure BB (school bond initiative), 249
Michigan primary (2000), 335–38
Miller, Gary, 204
Minnesota New Party, 309
minority candidates, 9–10. *See also* Latino
    GOP candidates
minority voters, 46. *See also* Latino voters
minor parties: in Alaska, 230–31; associa-
    tional rights of, 215–17, 232*n*2, 309, 318–
    19, 321*n*11; blanket primary's impact
    on, 10, 215–17, 224–27, 231–32,
    233*nn*8–9, 292, 347; California successes
    of, 214, 232*n*1; candidates attracted to,
    227, 233*n*9; candidate survey of, on
    blanket primary, 223*n*11, 227, *228*, 229,
    233*n*10; contested primaries of, 217–19,
    218, 220, 232*nn*3–4; crossover voting for
    (1998), 137–38, *137*, 190*n*4, 220–21,
    221; as electoral vs. expressive, 231–32,
    347; multifiling by, 13, 32–33*n*1; pri-
    mary vs. general votes for (1998), 221–
    22, *222*; primary vote share for (1994
    and 1998), 219, *220*; in Washington
    State, 229–30
minor-party voters: growth of (1990–98),
    214; instrumental voting probability for,
    on Prop 198, 46, 47, *48*, 49; low turnout
    of, 218, 233*n*5; ticket splitting by, 43–44,
    55*nn*5–6, 351–52; voting patterns of, by
    party registration, 128, *128*
moderate voters: crossover-seekers' solicita-
    tion of, 271, 279–81, 293*n*4, 295*nn*19–
    21; predictive crossover by, 286, *287;*

preferences of, between and within par-
    ties, 271, 288–91, *289*, *290*, *291*,
    296*nn*29–32; ticket splitting by, 43–44,
    351–52
moderation-crossover strategy: candidates'
    use of, 271, 279–81, 293*n*4, 295*nn*19–21;
    experimental simulation of, 281–85,
    284, 295*n*23, 296*n*24; impact of, on po-
    litical parties, 286–88, 292, 296*nn*27–28,
    351; voters attracted by, 285–86, *285*,
    296*nn*25–26
moderation effect: of blanket primary sys-
    tem, 9–10, 173, 192, 194, 252, 275; on
    crossover-seeker candidates, 211*nn*1,3,
    271, 272, 295*n*19; and Latino vote, 248,
    252, 259–60, 261, 266, 347; on minor
    parties, 225–26, 347; in 1996 Assembly
    primaries, 206, *207*, 350; in 1998 Assem-
    bly primaries, 204, *205*, 206, *208*, 209,
    212*nn*17–19, 350; in 1998 gubernatorial
    primaries, 197–98, 211*nn*8–10, 351; in
    1998 U.S. House primaries, 200, *201*,
    202–4, 212*n*14; in 1998 U.S. Senate pri-
    maries, 198–200, 211*nn*11–12, 351; po-
    larization vs., 196–97, 204, 206;
    predictive probabilities for, 209, *210*,
    286, *287;* of semi-closed systems, 196;
    source material for assessing, 212*nn*14–
    15. *See also* moderate voters; moderation-
    crossover strategy
moderation hypothesis, defined, 194, 211*n*3
Monnot, Michael, 232*n*2
Morgan, Becky, 30, 43
Morse v. Republican Party of Virginia, 309,
    320*n*3
Morton, Rebecca B., 196
Mullin, Megan, 11
multiple filing. *See* cross-filing
Murdoch, Rupert, 30
Murray, Patty, 277

Nader, Ralph, 304
Nader v. Schaffer, 304
Nagler, Jonathan, 6, 7, 134, 146, 156, 157,
    158, 168*n*3, 280, 295*n*19, 348–49
Napolitano, Grace Flores, 202
National Election Studies, 68, 294*n*11
Natural Law party, 217, 267*n*11
newspaper readership, 66, *67*
New York State primaries, 12–13, 32–33*n*1,
    193
New York Times, 17, 266–67*n*1

1994 general election, 128–29, *129*
1994 primaries, 175, 176, 219, *220*, 267*n*6
1996 general election, 249–50
1996 primaries, 185, 267*n*6; for Assembly seats, 206, *207, 208,* 212*n*17, 350
1996 Primary Voters' Handbook, 30, 31
1998 general election: campaign financing for, 183–84, *183, 184;* crossover rates in primary vs., *160–63;* crossover stickiness in, 146–49, *150,* 151–53, *152, 153, 154, 155,* 157–59, *158;* Latino GOP Assembly losers in, 261–62; Latino GOP Assembly winners in, 259–61; 1994 voting patterns vs., 128–29, *129*
1998 primaries: absentee votes in, 124–25, 126–27, 139, *140;* candidate qualification preferences in, 70, *71;* consumer confidence during, 60–62, *61;* crossover voting in, and general election, 97–101, *99,* 105*n*28, 152–53, *153, 154,* 155, 277; crossover voting in, by party identification, 79–81, *82–85,* 103*nn*8,12; crossover voting in, by party registration, 79–80, 86–88, *87,* 103*n*8, 127–31, *128–31;* ecologically inferred crossover rates in, 147–51, *160–63;* individual campaign contributions to, *186,* 187–88; with Latino GOP candidates, 253–54, *255,* 256, 267*nn*4–5; news sources for, 66–67, *67;* policy concerns during, 62–64, *63;* strategic crossovers in, 148–49, *149;* voter apathy/distrust during, 64–66, *68;* voter turnout for, 175–76, *175,* 344–45. *See also specific primaries by office*
Nixon, Richard, 26–27, 33*n*8
Nixon v. Condon, 308
Nixon v. Herndon, 308
nominating process: constituency of, in closed primary, 290–91, *291;* constitutional status of, before *Jones,* 304–6; crossover voting's impact on, 136–37, *136;* in direct party system, 272–73, 293*nn*6–7; hijacking controversy of (2000), 334; for minor-party candidates in blanket system, 215–17, 226; parties' asymmetric timing of, 327–28; parties' weak control over, 235, 237, 238–39, 241, 243, 270–71, 293*n*2; raiding of PFP's, 222–24; state's authority to mandate, 315, 321*n*7; *Timmons* balancing test for, 309–11, 320*n*4
nonpartisan primaries, defined, 211*n*2

nonpartisan voters. *See* independent voters
normal district vote, 179–81, 190*n*6
Novak, Bob, 332
Nuñez, Albert, 258

O'Bannon, Mary, 230
O'Callaghan et al. v. Alaska, 4
O'Connor, Sandra Day, 312, 313
open primaries: benefiting McCain, 325; vs. blanket primaries, 314–16, 321*n*8; defined, 211*n*2, 293*n*2, 342*n*3; *Detroit News* on, 337; increase of, from 1980–2000, 326–27, *327;* in Michigan's 2000 presidential race, 335–38; moderating effects of, 196; specialization incentives of, 197. *See also* blanket primaries
open-seat primaries, 200, *201,* 202, 206, *208,* 209
Ose, Doug, 202

PAC funding, 183–84, *184,* 188–89
Pacheco, Robert, 259, 260
Pacheco, Rod, 253–54, 256, 259, 266
Packard, David, 30
Paredes, Sam, 262
partisan voters: crossover by, for incumbent, 132–33, *133;* crossover by, to competitive race, 133–34, *134,* 138, 148–49, *150,* 252–53; with education variable, 52; instrumental voting probabilities for, on Prop 198, 45–47, *48,* 49–53, *50–52;* inter-/intraparty differences of, 289–91, *290, 291,* 296*n*32; minor-party votes by, *137,* 137–38; party vs. crossover votes of, 134–37, *135, 136, 140;* ticket-splitting immunity of, 44
party identification: in Assembly district study, 110; and consistent crossover voting, 96–97, *97;* crossover voting by, for Governor, 79–81, *82–83,* 349; crossover voting by, for U.S. Senator, 79, 81, *84–85,* 86, 103*nn*13–14, 349; as crossover voting variable, 89, 91, *92,* 93, 103*n*15; defined, 78; of independents, 78; party registration's ties to, 78–79, 102*n*5, 103*n*8, 296*n*25; scale used for, 80, 91, 103*n*12, 104*n*18
party registration: crossover voting by, for Governor, 79, 86, *87,* 103*n*8, 129–30; crossover voting by, for U.S. Senator, 79, 87–88, *87,* 103*n*8; crossover voting by, in 1998 primaries, 79–80, 127–31, *128–31;*

party registration *(continued)*
defined, 78; of independents, 78,
102*nn*3,5; moderation-crossover testing
by, 281–85, *284,* 286, 296*n*24; party
identification's ties to, 78–79, 102*n*5,
103*n*8, 296*n*25; and re-registration period, 193, 329–30, 339–40. *See also* partisan voters
Patterson, Kelly, 41
Peace and Freedom party (PFP): abstention
rate for (1994), 233*n*5; blanket primary
experience of, 222–24, 225, 233*n*7; candidate survey of, on blanket primary,
198, 229, 231, 233*n*11; contested primaries of, 217, 219, 223; primary vote
share for (1994 vs. 1998), 219, *220;*
right-to-association argument of,
215–17
Perez, Ed, 202
Perot, Ross, 227
Persily, Nate, 4, 352
Petrocik, John R., 8, 351
Pew Research Center Surveys, 64, 65, 68
PFP. *See* Peace and Freedom party (PFP)
pledge systems, 15, 328–29
plurality systems, 236, 237
polarization effect: in Assembly primaries,
204, *205,* 206, *207, 208,* 209; defined,
194; in gubernatorial primaries, 197–98;
little evidence for, 210; in U.S. House
primaries, 200, *201,* 202–4; in U.S. Senate primaries, 198–200
policy issues: of Californians, 62–64, *63;* as
crossover voting variable, 89, 103*n*15; initiatives on, 36–37
political information sources, 42–43, 66–67,
67, 172
political parties: associational rights of, 303–
7, 312–14, 320*n*1; constitutional status
of, before *Jones,* 304–9; definitional issues for, 307, 316–17, 321*n*9, 334–35,
341; in direct primary system, 272–73,
293*n*7; electorate's weak support of, 279,
293*n*5, 294–95*n*18; female candidates'
reliance on, 237, 238–39, 346–47; inter-/
intraparty differences of, 289–91, *290,*
291, 296*n*32; major vs. minor, 318–19,
321*n*11; moderation-crossover strategy's
impact on, 286–88, *287,* 296*nn*27–28,
351; in open primary system, 334–35,
338; participation/representation roles
of, 317–18; race case rulings on, 307–8;

strategic voting concerns of, 143–44,
350; weakened nominating role of, 235,
237, 238–39, 241, 243, 270–71, 293*n*2
political reform initiatives. *See* institutional
reform initiatives
populism. *See* anti-party populism
Powell, Lewis F., 318
PPIC (Public Policy Institute of California)
Statewide Surveys, 59, 62, 64, 66, 69, 70
presidential primaries. *See* 2000 presidential
primaries
Price, Mark, 261
primaries: characteristics of voters in,
103*n*11, 273–75, *274,* 293–94*n*9,
294*nn*10–11; crossover voting in (1910–
64), 22, *23,* 24, 25, 26–28, *28,* 33–34*n*9;
forms of, 193, 211*n*2; individual campaign donations to (1992–98), 184–85,
186, 187–88, 190*n*9; judicial rulings on,
before *Jones,* 304–7; origins/history of,
14–18, 33*nn*3–4; seven regimes of (1910–
2000), 20, *21;* voter turnout in, 174–76,
175, 273, 293*n*8; and weakened party
role, 241, 243, 270–71; white Southern,
307–9; women's success in, 236. *See also*
blanket primaries; closed primaries;
direct primaries; 1998 primaries; open
primaries
Progressive programs, 15, 317–18, 321*n*10
proportional representation (PR) systems,
53, 236–37
Proposition 3 (1998), 29–30, 31, 34*n*13,
338–39, 345, 348
Proposition 4 (1979), 37
Proposition 7 (1952), 17
Proposition 13 (1952), 16–17
Proposition 13 (1978), 12, 37
Proposition 187 (1994), 62, 250, 267*nn*2–3
Proposition 198 (1996): ballot arguments
for/against, 43–45, 172–73; California's
passage of, 3, 8–9, 12, 30, 171; dollars
spent on, 30, 42; electorate's unaware-
ness of, 294–95*n*18; lawsuit against, 4,
215–17; minor parties on, 215, 227,
228, 229, 232*n*2, 233*n*11; negation of,
for presidential primaries, 31–32, 34*n*13,
338–39; probabilities for instrumental
voting on, 41, 47, *48,* 49–53, *50–52;*
U.S. Supreme Court's ruling on, 3, 30,
303–4, 312–16, 319, 321*n*7, 352
Proposition 209 (1996), 249, 250,
267*nn*2–3

Proposition 226 (1996), 91, *92*, 93, *94*, 95, 96, *97*, 158
Proposition 227 (1998), 91, *92*, 93, 104*n*19, 250, 251, 267*n*2
PR (proportional representation) systems, 53, 236–37
Public Policy Institute of California State-wide Surveys. *See* PPIC (Public Policy Institute of California) Statewide Surveys
public schools issue, 62–63

quasi-open-seat primaries, 200, 202. *See also* open-seat primaries
Quayle, Dan, 335

Rabinowitz, George, 296*n*31
race/ethnicity variable, 90, 91, 109, 220–21, 253, 264–65
Radlovic, Mike, 260
raiding: Assembly district study of, 110–11, 113, 116–17, *117–18*, 119, 121, 121*n*4; in contested-incumbency races, 134–35, *135;* definition and impact of, 6–7, 88, 108, 126, 192, 341–42; and general elections, 80, 129; little evidence of, 88–89, 119, 121, 126, 135, 138, 271, 277–78, 293*n*4, 349; mirroring minimax behavior, 276; reasons for, 144, 194; as sophisticated behavior, 193–94
Rangel, Charlie, 33*n*2
Rapoport, Ronald, 156
Reagan, Ronald, 250, 266–67*n*1
Reform party, 217, 224–25, 227, 229, 232*n*1
registration. *See* party registration
Rehnquist, William, 312
religiosity variable, 90, 91, *92*, 93, 250
Republican crossovers: for Assembly races, 111–13, *112*, 116, 118–19, 121*n*5; 122*n*8; as consistent/inconsistent, 96–97, *97;* in general elections (1984–96), 80, 103*n*9; in general elections (1998), 148; for Governor, 80–81, 86, 91, *92*, 93; multivariate analysis of, 89–90, 91, *92*, 93, *94*, 95; in partisan Democratic district, 131, *131*, 149, *150;* in primary races (1998), *129*, 147–48; for statewide offices, 129–30, *130;* stickiness factor of, 151–53, *152*, *154*, 155; for U.S. Senator, 87–88, 93, *94*, 95
Republican party: Alaska primary system of, 240; on blanket primary, 30, 229; on

cross-filing, 17–18, 33*n*5; and identity politics, 265, 266; Latino Assembly candidates of (1998), 253–54, *255*, 256, 267*nn*4–5; Latino crossovers from, 262–63; Latino crossovers to, 252–53, 256, 258–61, 264–65; Latinos' distance from, 248–51, 266–67*n*1, 267*nn*2–3; McCain voters' re-registration in, 329–30, 339–40; open primaries of (1980–2000), 326–27, *327;* presidential primary rules of (2000), 327–29, 330, *331*, 332, *333*, 334; primary pledge requirement of, 328–29
Republican Party of Connecticut, Tashjian v., 304, 306, 312, 314, 316, 342*n*1
Republican Party of Virginia, Morse v., 309, 320*n*3
Republican voters: instrumental voting probability for, on Prop 198, *48*, 49, *50;* party voting patterns of, by party registration, 127, *128*, 349; political apathy of, 64; recall bias of, 104–5*n*27; registered voter disadvantage of, 168–69*n*10; as turnout share (1998), 158, 169*n*13. *See also* Republican crossovers
Riggs, Frank, 103*n*13, 104*n*25
right to association. *See* associational rights of parties
Rivers, Douglas, 190*n*7
Robertson, Pat, 325, 340
Rocha, Felix, 261
Rohrbacker, Dana, 204
Rolph, James, Jr., 16
Rule, Wilma, 236

safe districts, 151, 168*n*8, 182, 187–88, 190*n*8
Salvanto, Anthony M., 6, 7, 348
Sanchez, Bob, 258, 267*n*10
Sanchez, Loretta, 202, 251, 265
San Francisco Bay–area residents, 60, 62–63
San Francisco County Democratic Central Committee, Eu v., 306–7, 313, 316–17
SB 100 (1999), 30, 31
SB 1505 (1998), 31
Scalia, Antonin, 312, 313, 314, 341
Schaffer, Nader v., 304
Schlozman, Kay Lehman, 235, 238
Scott, Jack, 31
Secretary of State's race (1998), 130
Segura, Gary M., 10, 347

semi-closed/semi-open primaries, 196, 211n2, 326–27, 327, 342nn1,3

Sides, John, 5–6, 7, 102n1, 134, 156, 157, 168n3, 277

sincere voting behavior: Assembly district study of, 110–11, 113, 116, 117–18, 119, 121; defined, 6, 88, 97–98, 107; estimating prevalence of, 349–50, 354n1; in gubernatorial race, 98–100, 99, 105nn28–29; incumbency preference of, 121, 125, 132; as maximizing behavior, 276; moderating effects of, 194, 196–97; stickiness measurement of, 146–49, 151, 154, 155; in U.S. Senate race, 98, 99, 99, 100, 105n28

single-member district systems, 236, 237

Skropos, Gus, 119, 120, 122n9

Snipp, Joseph, 41

Sorauf, Frank J., 270

Soto, Nell, 109, 119, 122n9

South Carolina primary (2000), 335

special-interest money, 183–84, 184, 188–89

state authority: judicial rulings against, 303–7, 312–15, 320n1, 321n7; judicial rulings favoring, 307–9; Timmons balancing test of, 309–11, 320n4

State Senate districts: competitiveness variable in, 27–29, 34n10; cross-filing in (1910–64), 18, 19, 27–29; crossover stickiness in (1998), 157–58, 158; primary crossover voting in (1910–64), 22, 23, 24, 25, 26–28, 28, 33–34n9

Steinberg, Darrel, 117–18, 122n7

Stevens, John Paul, 313, 314, 321n9

stickiness factor: defined, 147; as ecologically inferred, 146–49, 149, 150, 151, 160–63, 168n4; EzI's computation of, 156–59, 168n8, 169nn12,14,15; multivariate models of, 147, 151–53, 152, 153, 168n4, 168n10; shift in, by type of election, 153, 154, 155, 348

strategic voting: Assembly district study of, 116–18, 117–18, 121n6; and general elections, 80, 103n10, 129; and legitimacy issues, 341–42; little evidence of, 88–89, 119, 121, 126; in 1998 primaries, 148–49, 149; parties' concerns over, 143–44, 350; primary and general election indicators of, 147, 151, 154, 155, 156; reasons for, 144, 194; as sophisticated behavior, 193–94; types of, 6–7. See also hedging; raiding

Tam, Wendy K. See Cho, Wendy K. Tam

Tashjian v. Republican Party of Connecticut, 304, 306, 312, 314, 316, 342n1

Tate, Katherine, 10, 346–47

television news/commercials, 66–67, 67

Telford, Paul, 229

term limits, 41, 53, 243

Terry v. Adams, 308

Thalman, James, 120, 122n9

Theiss-Morse, Elizabeth, 38

Thompson, Mike, 202

Thompson, Tommy, 278

ticket splitting: by minor-party voters, 43–44, 55nn5–6, 351–52; by party registration, 127–28, 128, 348

Timmons v. Twin Cities Area New Party, 309, 310, 311, 319

tort reform initiatives, 42, 55n4

TRPI (Tomás Rivera Policy Institute) study, 250, 267n3

Tucker, Jan B., 223–24, 225

Twin Cities Area New Party, Timmons v., 309, 310, 311, 319

two-count system, 31–32, 339, 341, 345

2000 general election, 159, 164–67

2000 presidential primaries: asymmetric competition issues in, 327–28, 328; California's closed system of, 325, 326, 330, 332, 339–41; California's two-count system of, 31–32, 339, 341, 345; crossover voting in, 278, 294nn16–17; in Michigan, 335–38; non-party nomination controversy of, 334; Republican rules of, 328–29, 330, 331, 332, 333, 334

2000 primaries, 159, 164–67

Uhlaner, Carole Jean, 235

union membership variable, 90, 91, 93, 104n17

United States v. Classic, 308

Unruh, Jesse, 44

U.S. House districts: campaign financing trends in, 183–84, 183, 184; candidate's ideological positioning in, 196, 202, 203, 204, 211n7, 212n14; competitiveness trends in (1992–98), 177, 178, 179–81, 179, 190nn6–7, 345–46; competitiveness variable in (1910–64), 27–29, 34n10; contested-challenger races in, 201, 203–4; contested-incumbent races in, 201, 204; cross-filing in (1910–64), 18, 19, 27–29, 33n8; crossover voting in (1910–64), 22,

23, 24, 25, 26–28, *28*, 33–34*n*9; Latino
GOP candidates of, 265; open-seat races
in, 200, *201*, 202; partisanship of, and
crossover voting, 131, *131*, 190*nn*6–7
U.S. Senate primaries (1998): candidates in,
198, 211*n*11; crossover intentions in, by
party identification, 79, 81, *84–85*, 86,
103*nn*13–14, 349; crossover voting in,
and general election, 98–99, *99*, 100–1,
145; crossover voting in, by party registration, 87–88, *87*; ideological positioning in, 196, 198–99, 212*n*12, 350–51;
mood of voters during, 59–66, *61*, *63*,
65; multivariate analysis of, 93, *94*, 95,
104*n*23; partisan vs. crossover analysis of,
136, *136*; Republican campaign financing of, 239–40; strategic voting behavior
in, 148; in Washington State, 277–78,
294*n*13
U.S. Supreme Court: anti-party opinions of,
307–9; on party's association rights, 305–
7, 320*n*1; ruling of, on California blanket primary, 3, 30, 303–4, 312–16, 319,
321*n*7, 352

Van de Kamp, John, 44
Vargas-Widmar, Linda, 262
Verba, Sidney, 238
Villaraigosa, Antonio, 249
Virginia pledge, 329
Voorhis, Jerry, 27
voter motivation: alienation model of, 41–
42, 55*n*3; Assembly district study of, 108–
11, 113, 116–19, *117–18*, 121*nn*4,6; demographic contours of, 89–90, 103*n*16,
285–86, *285*, 296*nn*25–26; electoral-
individual confluence in, 95–97; general
election's revelation of, 143–44, 155, *156*;
as hedging, 6, 88, 103*n*10, 107–8, 125–
26, 276, 349–50; ideologically based
model of, 41, 89; instrumental model of,
on Prop 198, 46–47, *48*, 49–53, *50–52*;
logic of, 195–96, *195*, 211*nn*4–5; as policy driven, 64, 89, 103*n*15; as raiding, 6–
7, 80, 88, 108, 126, 276; self-interest
model of, 40–41, 45; as sincere, 6, 88,
107, 125, 276, 349–50; variables of, in
gubernatorial race, 91, *92*, 93, 104*nn*20–
22; variables of, in U.S. Senate race, 93,
94, 95, 104*n*23. *See also* hedging; raiding;
sincere voting behavior
Voter Research and Surveys (VRS), 249

voters: on candidate qualifications, 70–71,
71, 73*n*4; characteristics of, in primaries,
103*n*11, 273–75, *274*, 293–94*n*9,
294*nn*10–11; consumer confidence of,
60–62, *61*; as distrustful of government,
67–70, *68*, 73*n*3; instrumental voting
probabilities for, on Prop 198, 41, 45–
47, *48*, 49–53, *50–52*; on party institutions, 279, 294–95*n*18; policy concerns
of, 62–64, *63*; political apathy of, 64–66,
65, 73*n*2; political news sources of, 42–
43, 66–67, *67*, 172; ticket splitting by, 43–
44, 55*nn*5–6, 127–28, *128*, 348, 351–52;
turnout issues for, 7–8; universe of, in
blanket system, 8, 78, 102*n*4. *See also*
crossover voters; minor-party voters;
partisan voters; voter motivation; voter
turnout
voters' handbook. *See* ballot pamphlets
voter turnout, 7–8, 188, 273, 293*n*8; in California primary (1998), 73*n*2, 175–76,
344–45; by minor-party voters, 218,
233*n*5; by party, in 1998 primary, 158,
169*n*13; in primary and general
elections (1944–98), 174–76, *175*; role
of parties in, 317–18
Voting Rights Act (1964), 309, 320*n*3
VRS (Voter Research and Surveys), 249

Washington State primaries, 4, 147–48, 229–
30, 240, 277–78, 294*n*13, 312, 320*n*5
Wattenberg, Martin P., 6, 7, 348
Watts, Meredith, 102*n*5
Wekkin, Gary D., 102*n*5, 156
Welch, Susan, 237, 238
Westmiller, William, 203
White Primary Cases, 307–9, 313, 320*n*3
Wickman, Michael, *120*, 122*n*9
Wigoda, Cousins v., 320*n*1
Wilson, Pete, 29, 59, 69, 250, 338–39
Winger, Richard, 216
Wisconsin primaries, 157, 305, 320*n*1
Wolff, Lester, 32–33*n*1
Wolfram, Catherine D., 190*n*7
Wong, Ben, 260
Woods, Nathan D., 10, 347
write-in votes, 20, 22

Young, Cecil, 33*n*8

Zager, Jonelle, 262
Zettel, Charlene Gonzales, 259, 260–61
Zetterberg, Stephen, 26

Text: 10/12 Baskerville
Display: Baskerville
Compositor: Binghamton Valley Composition
Printer and Binder: Maple-Vail Book Manufacturing Group